D1578893

ONE WEEK LOAN

1 3 FEB 200⁵

FINANCIAL TIMES

MASTERING INFORMATION MANAGEMENT

Academic Editors
Donald A. Marchand   **Thomas H. Davenport**

FT Prentice Hall
FINANCIAL TIMES

London • New York • San Francisco • Toronto • Sydney • Tokyo
Singapore • Hong Kong • Cape Town • Madrid • Paris • Milan
Munich • Amsterdam

Executive editor	Tim Dickson
Subeditor	Neville Hawcock
Website editor	James Pickford
FT Mastering co-ordinator	Laura Scanga
Graphics	Graham Parrish
Cover design	Newell and Sorrell

PEARSON EDUCATION LIMITED

Head Office
Edinburgh Gate
Harlow CM20 2JE
Tel: +44 (0)1279 623623
Fax: +44 (0)1279 431059

London Office
128 Long Acre
London WC2E 9AN
Tel: +44 (0)20 7447 2000
Fax: +44 (0)20 7447 2170
Website: www.business-minds.com

First published in Great Britain in 2000

Compilation © Donald A. Marchand and Thomas H. Davenport 2000
Contributions © individual authors 2000

pbk ISBN 0 273 64352 5
hbk ISBN 0 273 64355 X

British Library Cataloguing in Publication Data
A CIP catalogue record for this book can be obtained from the British Library

10 9

Typeset by Land and Unwin (Data Sciences) Limited, Bugbrooke
Printed and bound in Great Britain by Ashford Colour Press, Hampshire

The Publishers' policy is to use paper manufactured from sustainable forests.

About the academic editors

Donald A. Marchand

Donald A. Marchand is Professor of Information Management and Strategy at the International Institute for Management Development (IMD) in Lausanne, Switzerland – one of the leading executive development institutes and business schools in Europe and globally.

Professor Marchand is currently Director for the IMD/Andersen Consulting Partnership Research Project entitled Navigating Business Success. This two-year study examines the perspectives of senior executives on the management of information, people, and information technology in achieving superior business performance. The study includes surveys of over 1300 senior managers, representing 103 international companies in 22 countries and 25 industries, as well as over 25 case studies.

Professor Marchand is an advisor to senior executives of leading service and manufacturing companies in Europe, North America and Asia Pacific.

He is the author/co-author of six books and over 140 articles, book chapters, cases and reports. He is the editor of *Competing With Information*, the first volume of the IMD Executive Development Series published by John Wiley & Sons (2000). He is also the co-author of *Information Orientation: The Link to Business Performance*, a forthcoming book published by Oxford University Press (2000).

From July 1987 to June 1994, Professor Marchand was Dean and Professor of Information Management at the School of Information Studies at Syracuse University.

He received his PhD and MA at UCLA and his BA at the University of California at Berkeley. He has also served as Vice President of Worldwide Chapter and Alliance Development for the Society for Information Management – SIM International.

Thomas H. Davenport

Thomas H. Davenport is Director of the Andersen Consulting Institute for Strategic Change, a Professor in the Management Information Systems Department at the Boston University Graduate School of Management and is currently Distinguished Scholar in Residence at Babson College.

He is a widely published author and acclaimed speaker on the topics of information and knowledge management, re-engineering, enterprise systems and the use of information technology in business. He has a PhD from Harvard University in organizational behavior and has taught at the Harvard Business School, the University of Chicago, and the University of Texas at Austin Graduate School of Business. He has also directed research at Ernst & Young, McKinsey & Company, and CSC Index.

Dr Davenport wrote the first article on re-engineering and the first book, *Process Innovation: Reengineering Work through Information Technology* (Harvard Business School Press, 1993). His most recent work focuses on new approaches to information and knowledge management. He has recently published two well-received books on this topic, *Information Ecology: Mastering the Information and Knowledge Environment* (Oxford University Press, May 1997) and *Working Knowledge: Managing What Your Organization Knows* (Harvard Business School Press, November 1997). His next book on enterprise systems, *Mission Critical*, is scheduled for publication by Harvard Business School Press in January 2000.

His articles have appeared in *Harvard Business Review, Sloan Management Review, California Management Review* and many other publications. Tom also writes a monthly column created expressly for him by *CIO Magazine* called "Think Tank". He is one of the founding editors of *Knowledge, Inc*, and has been a board member for a variety of organizations.

Contents

Introduction

The *Financial Times Mastering* series is the product of a unique collaboration between the *FT* and some of the world's leading international business schools. *Mastering Information Management*, drawn from a weekly series that appeared in the newspaper, is the sixth book to emerge from this partnership. As with its predecessors, we believe it combines some of the important basic principles of managing in this area with fresh ideas for 21st century students and practitioners.

Why *Mastering Information Management*? Few topics are more pressing at present – or more relevant to a company's short-term profitability and long-term survival prospects – yet executives remain confused by much of the advice they receive and disappointed by the payback on many of their investments. One reason may be companies' growing obsession with technology and their tendency to neglect the actual information which is stored, accessed, retrieved and distributed by that technology, the quality of the information, and the needs of users.

Note that the title of this book is not *Mastering IT* – that would imply more concentration on what goes on inside the boxes on your desk and on how networks actually function. The purpose of *Mastering Information Management*, as clearly explained in the opening article, is to put the "I" squarely back in IT.

There are 11 modules: Improving Company Performance; Competing with Knowledge; Managing IT in the Business; The Smarter Supply Chain; New Organizational Forms; Knowledge Management; Electronic Commerce; The Human Factor; Strategic Uses of IT; Innovation and the Learning Organization; and Guru and Practitioner Perspectives.

Readers will find analysis of, and solutions to, a wide range of problems – everything from data-

mining and building trust in cyberspace to collaborative product development and the role of chief knowledge officers.

There is a strong emphasis on the human dimension, notably on how people react to technology-led change; there are articles on virtual offices and networks, and there are case studies on the information challenges in traditional manufacturing companies and internet start-ups alike.

Brief introductions to each module outline the main themes, and the summaries accompanying each article are designed to help readers quickly identify particular areas of interest. Lists of further reading should be helpful for those who want to delve deeper or look up references.

As with other *FT Mastering* books there are individuals to thank. Appropriately e-mail greatly facilitated the planning and construction of this series, but as this book constantly stresses technology is merely the enabler. My co-editors Tom Davenport and Donald Marchand provided enormous support throughout while others (notably Ahmet Aykac, general director of Theseus International Management Institute) also contributed valuable insights and advice.

The real heroes are the professors, other business school faculty and management experts who generously gave of their time to write the 50 or so articles in this book. They came from the following academic institutions and businesses: Accenture; Babcock Graduate School of Management, Wake Forest University; The Boston Consulting Group; Boston University School of Management; University of California, San Diego; University of California, Los Angeles; Claremont Graduate University; Cranfield School of Management; Darla Moore School of Business, University of South Carolina; Gartner

Group Pacific; Harvard Business School; IBM Institute for Knowledge Management; IMD; INSEAD; Intel; London Business School; Marseille Graduate School of Business; Melbourne Business School; University of Miami, Florida; University of Missouri; MIT Center for Co-ordination Science; MIT Sloan School of Management; Nationwide Building Society; Peter F. Drucker Graduate School of Management, Claremont Graduate University; Rotterdam School of Management; Sprint Business;

Templeton College, Oxford University; University of Texas at Austin; Theseus International Management Institute; Ukerna; University of Toronto; Wharton School of the University of Pennsylvania.

Finally, if you enjoy this book you will be glad to know that there are more Mastering books on the way. The next topic in the series will be *Mastering Strategy*.

Tim Dickson

IMPROVING COMPANY PERFORMANCE

Contributors

Thomas H. Davenport is professor of management information systems at Boston University's School of Management and Director of the Accenture Institute for Strategic Change.

Michael J. Earl is professor of information management at London Business School.

Donald A. Marchand is professor of information management and strategy at IMD, Switzerland.

David Feeny is vice-president of Templeton College, Oxford University, and director of the Oxford Institute of Information Management.

William J. Kettinger is director of the Center for Information Management and Technology Research at the Darla Moore School of Business, University of South Carolina.

Robert Plant is associate professor of computer information systems at the University of Miami, Florida.

John D. Rollins is a managing partner at Accenture, London.

Geneviève Feraud is professor of information management at Theseus International Management Institute, Sophia Antipolis, France.

Contents

Introduction

Mastering Information Management is fundamentally about how to capture, store, access, distribute and exploit information inside organizations and throughout the networks of suppliers, customers and other partners which increasingly make up modern business. Such activities, of course, can only be justified if they underpin and improve business performance. All the articles in this introductory module therefore address that issue in some way. Included is a framework for implementing an information management program; a description of how information is driving the strategies of all companies (pharmaceutical and consumer goods groups as much as content providers and IT giants); and a case study showing how good information management spurred the development of Land Rover's Freelander project. For those wanting a longer perspective, there is a review of the main developments since the birth of "office Taylorism" a century or so ago.

Putting the I in IT

by Thomas H. Davenport

Imagine a world obsessed with plumbing. In this bizarre place, hundreds of magazines and books, and even a few television channels, cover the plumbing industry, celebrating the latest advances in valves, fixtures and pipes. Cocktail party conversation is dominated by the issue of whether one brand of sink drains faster than another. Plumbing equipment magnates are on the cover of business and even general interest publications, and become the world's richest citizens. Companies pay millions, billions, trillions to connect all their plumbing devices and to ensure that pipes reach every desktop, every home office, even every car.

Only one plumbing-related issue is overlooked in this strange world – water. Is it clean and fresh? Is water even what consumers want to drink? Are they thirsty?

Oddly enough, a similar situation prevails in our own world. We need only substitute computers for plumbing fixtures and networks for pipes. Just as plumbing technology overshadows water in our imaginary environment, information technology (IT) outshines information itself in the real world. But although good water can easily be obtained from a clear mountain stream, good information is rarely synonymous with advanced IT. It is time that we focused on the "I" rather than the "T" in the world of business IT.

The signs of our obsession with technology are everywhere. Companies and consumers spend over one trillion dollars a year on IT. About half of business capital expenditures in the US go to IT. "Information Systems" departments in corporations focus almost exclusively on procuring, connecting and maintaining computers, software and communications networks; so-called "chief information officers" are actually chiefs of technology management. A philosophy of "If we build IT, they will come" prevails, regardless of whether the technology really meets business needs or delivers better information.

What are the fruits of this obsession? The harvest is depressingly sparse. Even the most rigorous economists have difficulty finding correlations between IT spending and productivity, profits, growth, revenues or any other measure of financial benefit. Surveys of managers suggest that they feel the information they get today is no better than it ever was.

While at the moment there seems to be a relationship between the societies that spend most on IT (notably the US) and the health of those societies' economies, it is doubtful that the correlation would hold up if the US was dropped from the analysis, and it certainly has not held up over time. Paul Strassmann, the US academic and writer who is perhaps the world's leading authority on the relationship between IT and business economics, is also one of the most passionate believers in our over-spending.

Since companies have so much technology, they tend to gravitate towards the form of information that is most easily addressed with it – that is, highly-structured transaction data. We could, in fact, more accurately describe the past 40 years as the "data age" rather than the "information age". Companies can now gather automated data on almost every aspect of their operations; new enterprise systems are particularly effective at processing and gathering transaction data.

My research suggests that this data is rarely transformed into information and knowledge. Enterprise systems are rarely used to manage the business any differently; point-of-sale data is seldom used to do highly segmented marketing. The transformation of data into something more useful requires considerable human attention and intelligence but most organizations view the issue only in technological terms. Having a data warehouse or a data mining system is, like all information technologies, necessary but not sufficient for good information and knowledge.

Why does technology dominate?

Perhaps trying to understand our society's focus on technology over information will be useful. First of all, the idea that technology will solve all our problems – "technological utopianism" – is not restricted to IT. Industrialized societies have long believed in the transformative power of technologies, from railroads to electricity to cars to television.

In the specific realm of IT, our hopes may have been particularly stimulated by the undeniably rapid progress in computing, communications and (to a much lesser degree) software. We have been distracted by the speed of technological change from asking ourselves the real question – what to do with all that computing and communicative power?

Another reason for the heavy emphasis on technology in our society is the power of IT vendors. Hardware, communications and software companies have an interest in our belief that buying more technology will solve our information problems. Of course, there are also information vendors, but they are small and disaggregated compared to IT vendors. As IT consumers, we go along with the fiction of buying information effectiveness. Just as it is easier to go to the hardware store and buy power tools than to build an extension to one's home, it is easier to buy IT hardware than to build a good information environment.

If technology is not the key to good information, what is? You may guess that it is people. But most managers have little understanding of how people relate to information. What kind of information do the various people within an organization need and want? How do we get different workers to agree on what a piece of information means? What motivates individuals to share – or to hoard – information?

Even those managers who do understand the human side of information do not necessarily act upon their knowledge. As US consultant and author Tom Peters once noted, success in managing information is 5 per cent technology and 95 per cent psychology – but most companies do not even spend 1 per cent of their information management time and expense budgets on psychological or human issues.

Perhaps another reason why organizations do not really manage information is that they lack an awareness of what life would be like if they did. Managers do not know what approaches to take or what benefits would result. They have simply never seen an example of focusing on information rather than technology. Given a choice, however, they might well choose the information-centered route.

The progress being made in this regard is coming largely through the advent of "knowledge management". In practice, many companies have both knowledge and information in their knowledge management initiatives and find it difficult to distinguish between them. The good news is that most knowledge managers

6

recognize the importance of the human factor in knowledge, even when their organizations are otherwise technically focused.

Good practices

I now turn to the various components of an information management programme, with examples of companies that have adopted each component. While I have found only a few companies that may be said to be fully information-focused, there are many examples of returning at least part of the "I" to "IT".

From models to maps

One of the simplest information management tools is an "information map", which tells members of an organization where to find particular types of information. The paucity of such maps, which are a simple, inexpensive, seemingly obvious approach, is a testimonial to how rarely information management is practised. Instead of maps, companies usually produce elaborate information models that specify where computer-based information will reside when (and, more importantly, if) they ever install that new relational database and get all their information rationalized. The problem is that they never *do* get everything rationalized, so they never have any guide as to where information is at any particular moment.

Most maps specify the location of only a portion of an organization's information assets, since a complete mapping effort would be very ambitious. IBM, for example, created a map for its marketing information in the context of an effort to improve marketing processes. American Express created a map that focused on the major repositories of computerized information. Several governmental bodies (particularly in Canada) have created full maps of their information environments. While the mapping of information can be labour-intensive, the seeking of unmapped information by all employees is usually even more so.

New views of information staff

In a technology-focused world, most "information staff" are actually programmers, network managers and technical support analysts. But if such technically-orientated workers represent the bulk of your information workers, it is a fair guess that your information is not very good. Fortunately there are several other categories of information worker that can be drawn upon to create a more effective information environment.

Chief among these are librarians (or, as some prefer, "information scientists", though their best work is not very scientific). Librarians, with their skills in categorization, search and retrieval, and understanding information needs, offer great potential to any organization embarking on information management. However, for several reasons, they are in danger of being left behind at a time when their potential value to organizations is at its height.

One problem is that many librarians, and the institutions that train them, are rushing headlong towards computerization. Librarians certainly need computer skills, because more and more information is computer-based, but they do not need to know the intricacies of client/server networks; there are already people who do. Another problem is that many librarians still think of themselves as custodians of physical documents in a physical library. However, the information action is not restricted to any particular place; instead it involves working with other employees to help meet their information needs.

Finally, librarians have long been plagued by the stereotype of passivity. While this may still apply in some cases, it is becoming decreasingly legitimate. At Owens-Corning, for example, librarians shed their traditional functions through an outsourcing arrangement and became a "Knowledge Resource Center", focused on meeting employees' information and knowledge needs regardless of the medium or location.

Librarians and other information-orientated staff (from IT, market research, communications, technical writing and even management accounting) need to co-ordinate their responses to information needs. In some cases it may make sense to join together as a single organization so that those who need information can have "one-stop shopping". Monsanto, for example, has combined its corporate library and information systems group.

Info-journalism

The most successful example of information transmission and use in Western societies is undoubtedly television, the consumption of which far exceeds any other medium. A key lesson from television is that people prefer information to be in the form of a story or narrative. Therefore information providers in companies should strive to find ways in which they can present important information in story form. In the US at least, corporate storytelling at gatherings of employees is becoming popular.

Television news is also an effective way to convey information. A news item is relatively short, with a clear beginning and ending. It is current and heavily edited for arresting content and easy comprehension. The best newspaper journalism has the same approach.

Companies might benefit from using similar approaches in disseminating corporate information. An example of such practices in action is provided by Verifone, a high-technology manufacturing company acquired by Hewlett-Packard in 1997. Every day its chief information officer produces a "flash report" on important news, sales figures, new product introductions and so on and sends it via e-mail to employees around the world. In a one-page summary employees can find out what they need to know about the company and its business. Perhaps not coincidentally, the executive who prepares the report is a former journalist.

Another lesson from television is that technology rarely gets in the way. For the most part, one plugs in a cable or two and turns on the power and the picture appears. Information is thus relatively easy to acquire and thus more likely to be acquired and retained. (Whether this will still be the case with digital television is at present unclear.)

The anthropology of information

In the technically orientated information environment we tend to use technical means to determine what information people need. We may analyze web page transaction patterns and search and retrieval records, or put out some prototype pages to see how many people click on them.

An alternative, more human, approach is simply to watch a few consumers and observe what information they use and need. This may be called "shadowing" or, in anthropological terms, "information ethnography".

Research suggests that most managers and workers are poorly attuned to their own information needs, so observation by an astute analyst can be extremely helpful. Hoffmann-La Roche, for example, used this type of ethnography to determine what information was needed by pharmaceutical researchers in order to decrease the cycle time for new drug development.

Common information

Many companies today want to increase the level of common information across the organization. Thus they want terms such as "customer" and "product number" to mean the same everywhere. Technical approaches to this goal have involved carrying out substantial data-modelling or trying to mandate commonality by getting the whole organization to adopt a particular computer system. But technical mandates will not necessarily stop organizational renegades from building their own unique desktop or departmental systems, thereby eroding commonality.

So how can companies ensure information commonality? Again, a more human approach is the answer. Key stakeholders in a given piece of information should have the opportunity to debate how broad a meaning certain terms should have and how widely those meanings should be used in the company. The behavioral changes needed to make information common should be identified and any necessary interventions planned. It is all too easy for individual workers to create their own autonomous databases these days; given this potential, companies will have to address motivational factors to bring about common information.

Conclusion

We can focus on plumbing or we can think about water and its use. We can continue to try to manage information by throwing vast amounts of technology at the problem or we can address the human side of information. After all, it is humans who add the context, meaning and value that transforms data into information, and it is these same humans who are supposed to benefit from the information.

IT can help in the middle stages of the information life cycle – storage, summary and transmission – but it is not particularly helpful in its creation or use. Technology's power is such that it seemed to promise to master information all by itself, but that has not happened. In the end, mastering information management is an essentially human task.

Summary

We spend over one trillion dollars a year on information technology. Yet economists have found little correlation between companies' IT expenditures and financial performance, while managers complain that the information they receive is little better than before. The reason for this, says **Thomas Davenport**, is that most IT programmes neglect the human side of the information equation – that is, they take little account of what information people want or need and how they use it. To redress this balance, there are several steps that companies can take. These include mapping where information resides in the organization; giving librarians a more prominent role than technicians; adopting journalistic or narrative techniques for corporate communication; and observing how workers actually use information. We have the technology; the challenge now is to manage information.

Company performance and IM: the view from the top

by Donald A. Marchand, William J. Kettinger and John D. Rollins

Many senior executives have a decidedly negative opinion of the relationship between IT and business performance. They are dissatisfied with the investments and practices related to IT and information use in their companies. Ironically, this stream of dissatisfaction runs alongside widely held expectations that IT has the potential to transform economies, industries and business.

Over the past five years, many surveys in Western Europe and North America have shown that the main concern of chief information officers – the senior managers responsible for IT in their companies – has been to align IT investments with corporate strategies. At the same time, senior executives have been concerned with getting business results from their investments in IT. Neither group seems to have found what it is looking for. Economists attempt to explain this gap as the "IT productivity paradox" – companies spend billions on IT worldwide with no clear link to improved macroeconomic productivity or business performance.

Where do we go from here?

Picture the following scene. A CEO and a CIO are in a corporate meeting room. The CEO wants business results from his investments in IT and the CIO really wants to deliver these results. Generally, the CIO speaks about using IT to gain competitive advantage and presents his plans to deliver IT in the business. The CEO talks about using information and knowledge to improve product innovation, speed up operations and improve customer service. The CEO focuses on the use of information and the CIO confirms his plans for new IT solutions and services.

If the CEO and CIO agree on the role of IT in the business, and the IT function really delivers IT to the business, then why is it still so hard to find a direct link between IT practices and improved business performance?

In our research into senior managers' perceptions and expectations of the role of IT and information use in over 100 international companies, we have uncovered three different views of how IT and information use may be linked to business performance.

Good IT practices will increase business performance

Paradoxically, the most widely held view is that IT practices will increase business performance if IT priorities are properly aligned with the business and if the IT function works effectively with the business to deliver IT applications and infrastructure. Senior managers expect IT today to improve business performance in four key ways.

First, IT should improve the efficiency of business operations. Most manufacturing companies are busily upgrading their software and systems in finance, manufacturing and distribution; this is being done not only for the sake of Y2K and euro compliance but also to increase operational control, speed, and flexibility with customers.

Second, IT should improve communications in support of smoothly functioning business processes. Many companies such as ABB and General Electric are using collaborative software such as Lotus Notes and intranets to improve networking and information sharing among employees in diverse locations. They are also using electronic data interchange (EDI) and extranets to link their business processes with suppliers, distributors and customers.

Third, IT should facilitate managerial decision making by providing appropriate information for market forecasting, managing business risks, spotting new customer trends or simply helping people to locate and share knowledge. While the history of executive information systems and decision support systems has been mixed, many senior managers continue to feel that using IT in support of these applications will improve decision making and business results.

Finally, IT should support innovation in new product and service development and facilitate growth and new initiatives. Many companies are investing in computer-aided design systems, which they are linking to databases of knowledge and expertise in the business. Some are going a step further by using the internet to link with external business partners and key customers.

Senior managers subscribing to this view perceive that if the business could only "manage IT right", then improvements in business performance would follow.

Better information practices will increase business performance

Senior managers who subscribe to this view contend that good IT practices are necessary but not sufficient to improve business performance. They hold that careful attention to the ways in which information is sensed, collected, organized, processed and maintained is also essential to improving both IT and business performance. According to this view, how people turn data into information that can be used to improve customer relations, product innovation, sales, marketing, operations and financial controls is critical to improved performance. If this view is correct, then managers need to examine more carefully their business information practices.

For example, is our company good at sensing competitors' innovations and anticipating market shifts or evolving customer demand? Can we identify problems with customers or suppliers before they become serious and address them rapidly? Are our employees trained and rewarded for collecting key customer or services information and entering this information daily into our systems? How effective is our company at linking databases about customers or products? Do we index or classify information to ensure the reuse of our company's knowledge and experience? Does our company use the data collected in databases to derive information and knowledge? Are employees trained and rewarded for using information effectively to solve problems, improve their team's performance and share project experiences with others?

Finally, how good is our company at reusing information to avoid collecting it twice? Do we update customer and operational databases to make sure that they are current? Is the information used for executive decisions continuously refreshed to ensure that our managers are using the best available?

At the center of this view is the perception that a company's information practices are critical for turning data into information and knowledge to improve performance. Many managers who are interested in "knowledge management" are supporting efforts to accelerate the use of information, knowledge and expertise in their companies to obtain better business results.

Better information behaviors and values will increase business performance

If the first view is IT-centred and the second is information-centred, then the third is decidedly people-centred. Executives in this camp believe that the main reasons why IT has not lived up to its many promises or why information and knowledge are not shared come down to the way employees behave and to the company's cultural values.

If the company is becoming more dependent on sharing and using information and knowledge, then senior managers should pay careful attention to the cultural values and behaviors associated with information and IT use in their company. For example, do our people actively seek out information to respond quickly to customers and partners? Do they trust one another to share information about process or product failures?

Does our company encourage openness in using information or do people frequently keep information to themselves? Do employees believe that sharing their knowledge and information improves the company's overall performance or do they keep it to themselves because it defines their value added to the company? Do our people share information within teams, or across functions or with customers and suppliers, as appropriate?

Is information on company and business unit performance presented to employees continuously to improve their effectiveness or is performance information tightly controlled by managers and made available only on a "need to know" basis? Do our people trust the databases and formal sources of information or do they make use of informal information because the quality and integrity of our systems and databases are suspect?

For senior managers, the third view is often linked to their commitment and ability to lead and motivate people. They perceive the information and knowledge used by their departments as critical to the company's success. These leaders focus on the ways their people use new computer systems and IT tools. At the heart of the IT and business performance challenge are the ways people are motivated, rewarded and encouraged to use information and knowledge to achieve business results.

A difference of opinion?

Let us return to our CEO and CIO for a moment. How will they react to each view? If the CEO expects IT to improve business performance and the CIO delivers good IT practices, there seems to be no problem. The CIO has a dream job since IT meets or exceeds what the business expects. The problem is that, given the IT productivity paradox, we know that good IT practices alone do not lead to increased business performance.

If the CEO holds the second view – and therefore expects better information to be available in the organization – and the CIO delivers only good IT practices, then there is a perceptual gap between the CEO and the CIO. In this case, because of differing expectations, the CEO will tend to be disappointed in the CIO.

If the CEO expects improved information behavior and values, as well as better information practices, and the CIO delivers only good IT practices, then the gap between expectations and delivery in the business widens further still.

So with information practices, behaviors and values often beyond the CIO's direct control, it is no surprise that the position of the CIO in many companies today is short-lived, stressful and disappointing for CIOs and senior managers alike.

Information orientation

We believe that a new mindset is emerging among senior managers. It is likely to provide a way to resolve the IT productivity paradox, as well as to reconcile the conflicting expectations of CIOs and senior managers.

Over the past 40 years, the growth of IT in business and the huge changes in the IT industry have tended to overshadow the role of information practices, behaviors and values in contributing to business success. However, our research suggests that what differentiates today's high-performing companies are the capabilities and behaviors associated with effective information use. We call these the "information orientation" of the company and its leaders.

Information orientation embraces IT practices, information practices, and information behaviors and values. Heightened information orientation among senior managers could lead to new and important views of how information, people and IT are leveraged to increase business performance.

An important aspect of information orientation is the fact that optimizing one dimension at the expense of the others will not lead to greater business performance. However, in recent years, many senior managers have focused most of their attention on IT practices, which they have seen as the key to improving their company's information orientation.

As Figure 1 illustrates, the link between business performance and information orientation can help managers to understand the positioning of their company or business unit.

"Blind and confused" companies are poor performers and see no reason for significant improvements in their information orientation. Senior managers in these companies perceive IT as a cost to be cut and view information management in traditional bureaucratic and hierarchical terms.

"Information-orientated laggards" are companies that understand what they

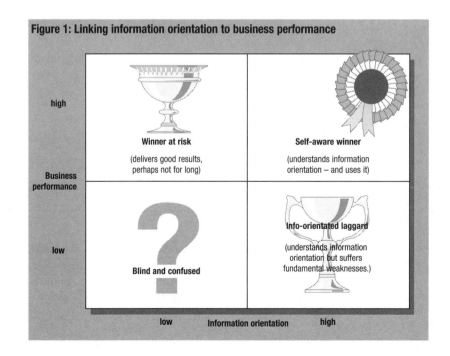

Figure 1: Linking information orientation to business performance

13 Oct 1998

INSIDE TRACK

Managers need to put technological progress in perspective, Carl Shapiro and Hal Varian tell Louise Kehoe

Financial Times

by Louise Kehoe

"As the century closed, the world became smaller. The public rapidly gained access to new and dramatically faster communications technologies. Entrepreneurs . . . built vast empires. The government demanded these powerful new monopolists be held accountable under antitrust law."* That could be a description of today's information technology industry, the emergence of the global internet and the antitrust charges facing Microsoft and Intel. But Carl Shapiro and Hal Varian, professors at the University of California, Berkeley, are referring to the emergence of telephone networks 100 years ago.

"People get carried away with breathless talk of a new economy," says Prof Shapiro. Executives charged with rolling out cutting-edge software products or online versions of their magazines are tempted to abandon the classic lessons of economics, he suggests. "We think a dose of historic reality is called for."

The economic impact of the internet and corporate computer networks is similar to that of earlier "networks" such as the railways, telephones and bank machines, the Berkeley economists maintain.

The common characteristic is that the value of a network is enhanced by the number of people who use it. Telephones, for example, became useful only when many people had them installed. Similarly, electronic mail and the worldwide web derive their value from their reach.

Rapid growth of the internet has demonstrated the self-reinforcing "positive feedback" loop of network economics, for which Prof Shapiro (with Michael Katz, also of Berkeley) coined the term "network effects" in 1985. Big networks – whether real ones such as the internet, or virtual networks comprising the users of a particular software product – tend to grow bigger, while smaller networks shrink. Eventually, the winner takes all.

Microsoft and Intel's domination of world markets

for software and semiconductor chips respectively, demonstrates this. Whereas the industrial economy was driven by economies of scale that tended to create oligopolies, the information economy is driven by the economics of networks, which tend to create monopolies, say Profs Shapiro and Varian. (These monopolies have not been bad for consumers, according to Prof Shapiro. A consultant to Intel, he maintains the chip company's rapid development of ever-faster microprocessors has benefited computer users.)

For producers of IT products, the effects of positive feedback can be either a boon or a threat. The Berkeley economists warn: "If consumers expect your product to become popular, a bandwagon will form . . . but if consumers expect your product to flop . . . the vicious cycle will take over." So, in this winner-takes-all world, what hope is there for smaller, regional suppliers? According to Prof Shapiro: "The threat is to the small player who does not get a partner, not to companies in any particular part of the world."

The key for companies trying to build markets, or government entities establishing policies, is to "look at the industry and gauge the extent to which there are network effects and the extent of switching costs, and build your strategy around this", Prof Varian advises.

Old economic rules may still apply, but the "network economy" is driven by "information goods" – ranging from computer software to stock data. Moreover, the internet has become part of the infra-structure of industry. But the professors are quick to cut through the internet hype. "The web is not that impressive as an information resource," says Prof Varian. It contains about two terabytes of information, roughly equivalent to a million books, he estimates. "The US Berkeley Library has 8m volumes, and the average quality of the Berkeley library content is much higher. "People are always talking about information overload, and the quantity of information

Continued

on the internet, but the real change is that the cost of accessing information has fallen dramatically."

Information technology has vastly increased our ability to store, retrieve, sort, filter and distribute information, adds Prof Shapiro. He offers the example of a distribution company which uses on-board computers to access information, updated in real time, on the cheapest source of fuel within 100 miles of its lorries.

Varian points to the use of IT by supermarkets which analyse consumers' buying habits and then offer them price discounts on an individual basis, via direct mail or with coupons on the back of their receipts. "They are saving hundreds of thousands of dollars per store on broadcast newspaper adverts."

The publishing industry, similarly, is moving toward customised or even "personalised" products. Although the internet is often seen as a threat to magazine and newspaper publishers, "content

providers should not be afraid of this. They should look at it as a way to distribute their content to many more people at low cost." They can create different product versions and pricing schemes to specialise their offerings.

Amid the hype, the professors urge business people to keep a sense of perspective: "Many of today's managers are so focused on the trees of technological change they fail to see the forest: the underlying economic forces that determine success and failure."

Information Rules: A Strategic Guide to the Network Economy, Carl Shapiro and Hal R. Varian, Harvard Business School Press. Publication date November 10 1998.

Carl Shapiro is Transamerica Professor of Business Strategy, Haas School of Business and Department of Economics, UC Berkeley. Hal R. Varian is Class of 1944 Professor and the Dean of the School of Information Management and Systems, UC Berkeley.

must do with respect to information orientation but cannot implement changes effectively. They may suffer other fundamental weaknesses such as declining demand for their products or extreme business cycles in their industry.

"Winners at risk" have achieved significant business success but have not paid enough attention to improving their information orientation. While successful today, these companies may slip if they do not improve their information orientation in the future.

Finally, "self-aware winners" have already systematically improved their information orientation to achieve superior performance, but are concerned about keeping their leading position through their information orientation in the future.

Emphasis on information orientation implies a change in the performance metrics that senior managers and CIOs use. In most companies the classic performance measure of the CIO and the IT function has been whether managers are satisfied with IT delivery. Most CIOs have been pleased to receive positive scores on this measure, even as senior executives have been grumbling in the boardroom about the poor performance payoffs from IT investments.

The IT satisfaction metric may no longer suffice today. Information-orientated senior managers will evaluate performance in terms of information practices and behaviors in addition to IT practices and delivery. In the future, senior executives will expect performance measures that evaluate not IT usage alone, but how people actually use information and IT to achieve business results.

Was information orientation there all along?

There is a well-known story about a man who loses his keys one night after a visit to the pub. As he drunkenly searches for them near a street light, a passer-by asks what he is doing. The man explains that he is looking for his keys. The passer-by asks if he lost them near the street light. "No," replies the man, "but it's easier to look for them where it's light."

Perhaps senior executives today are like the man looking for his keys. The spotlight on IT in recent years has been so intense that many managers have perhaps lost sight of the role that information practices, behaviors and values can play in improving business performance. While IT itself will continue to be a strong force for change in companies and industries, we conclude that the highest-performing companies will be those whose senior managers see information orientation as critical to success. People who use IT to manipulate information and knowledge effectively will become "the difference that makes a difference" in tomorrow's most successful companies.

Summary

Senior managers' views on the relation between information and corporate performance fall into three main categories. First, there are those who believe that improved IT alone will boost performance. Then there are those who believe that improved information practices – for example, policies for capturing customer information – are what matters. Finally, some senior managers believe that behavioral factors, such as whether people trust one another enough to share information, are critical. According to **Donald Marchand**, **William Kettinger** and **John Rollins** this explains why so many senior executives are disappointed by their chief information officers' performance – their views on this issue fall into different categories. However, the authors' research indicates that such discrepancies will soon be a thing of the past in the highest-performing companies, as senior managers move towards a more inclusive perspective. This emerging "information orientation" mindset should ultimately close the – currently yawning – gap between corporate performance and the expectations that senior executives have on the basis of their IT investments.

Every business is an information business

by Michael J. Earl

Whether they call it "the post-industrial society", "the third wave" or "the knowledge era", most policy makers, academics and business leaders would agree that we have recently entered a new era. Undoubtedly, some of the defining characteristics of this era – which I shall refer to here as "the information age" – have still to emerge and develop; after all, the industrial era evolved over two centuries or more. However, we now recognize that the information age differs markedly from the industrial age in several important respects. These differences are summarized in Figure 1.

Over the past 40 years or so, many commentators have tried to determine what

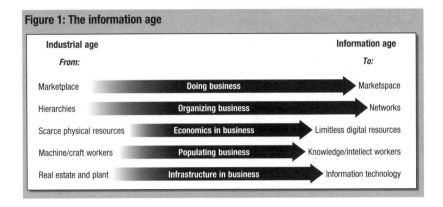

Figure 1: The information age

Industrial age		Information age
From:		*To:*
Marketplace	Doing business	Marketspace
Hierarchies	Organizing business	Networks
Scarce physical resources	Economics in business	Limitless digital resources
Machine/craft workers	Populating business	Knowledge/intellect workers
Real estate and plant	Infrastructure in business	Information technology

has been driving these changes. The consensus has shifted over time. At first it was thought to be the automating power of computers and computation. Then it was the ability to collapse time and space through telecommunications. More recently it has been seen as the value-creating power of information, a resource which can be reused, shared, distributed or exchanged without any inevitable loss of value; indeed, value is sometimes multiplied. And today's fascination with competing on invisible assets means that people now see knowledge and its relationship with intellectual capital as the critical resource, because it underpins innovation and renewal.

Information and strategy

All these claims are valid in some ways and therefore there are diminishing returns to arguing which is the critical motive force. But we can recognize that today every business is an information business.

First, let us take the perspective of industry structure. We see battles in the marketplace all the time as "content" companies try to acquire related content businesses, not only because of their thirst for information but also because of the opportunities for synergy created by repackaging, reuse and navigation.

More significantly, perhaps, content companies acquire or build alliances with communication companies, and vice versa. Both sides recognize that to command the airwaves is to command the distribution channels of the information age, and that the high value-added opportunities are likely to lie in selling content and repackaging and reusing it in manifold ways. The film of the book of the television programme is an established example of such repackaging opportunities.

Disney's marriage with ABC is a case in point. Even Sky's bid for Manchester United can be analyzed from this perspective. We also see regulators on the sidelines of these information wars stepping in to control market power. If they are steeped in industrial-age competitive logic, they may actually try to constrain the growth of corporations that could help build the information highways of our dreams.

But it is not just the obviously information-intensive companies that are playing out these new strategies. More "traditional" companies see some of the same logic. So when SmithKline Beecham acquired Diversified Pharmaceutical Services in 1994, the purchase was as much about buying the data embedded in prescriptions and healthcare administration processes – which could than guide research and

17

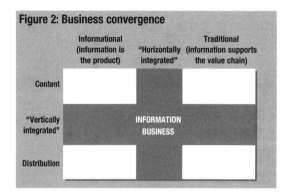

Figure 2: Business convergence

development programmes and sales management – as about more conventional synergies.

Likewise, when Johnson & Johnson acquired a diagnostics business previously owned by both Kodak and Amersham International, the sale soon turned out to have a similar information thread. So we need to rewrite, or at least re-examine, the industrial economics rules of vertical integration and diversification. When Ralph Larsen, chairman of Johnson & Johnson, announces that "We are not in the product business; we are in the knowledge business" we start to see different logics at work.

Indeed, it becomes difficult in the world of intangible assets and electronic distribution channels to be clear to define vertical or horizontal integration. Microsoft takes stakes in software, communications and information-providing businesses. And America Online acquires Netscape. Are these "horizontal" or "vertical" maneuvers?

In other words, if you choose to take an information perspective, businesses are converging on the middle of Figure 2, partly because of digital convergence. In some cases this is happening because the product is information-based, as in the case of Disney and ABC. In other cases it is because processes are information-based, such as in our pharmaceuticals examples. In still other cases it is simply because market understanding or decision-making is information-based. So retailers, financial services organizations and airlines will stitch together alliances because of the information (and sales) potential of customer cards.

The virtual value chain

One way of understanding the strategic opportunities and threats of information as digital technologies converge, is to think not just of the physical value chains of business popularized by Michael Porter but to consider the "virtual value chain" devised by Harvard academics Jeffrey Rayport and John Sviokla (see Figure 3).

Information can be captured at all stages of the physical value chain. Such information can be used to improve performance at each stage of the physical value chain and to co-ordinate across it. However, it can also be analyzed and repackaged to build content-based products or to create new lines of business. Thus insurance companies, for example, are becoming adept at analyzing customer and claims information and then teleselling both financial and physical products. A company can also use its information to reach out to other companies' customers or operations, thereby rearranging the value system of an industry; if you like, sectors become "value jigsaws" which can be rearranged so that traditional sector

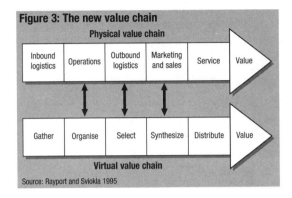

Figure 3: The new value chain

Physical value chain

| Inbound logistics | Operations | Outbound logistics | Marketing and sales | Service | Value |

| Gather | Organise | Select | Synthesize | Distribute | Value |

Virtual value chain

Source: Rayport and Sviokla 1995

boundaries disappear. This is why analysts coin expressions such as "infotainment".

Ralph Larsen sees Johnson & Johnson as a knowledge business. Similarly, Toshifumi Suzuki, former president of retail chain Seven-Eleven Japan, saw his business as "not in the retail business but in the information business". He used information technology to address convenience, quality, service and customer needs by ensuring that shelves were replenished several times a day in response to orders from individual store managers. He also established a large field counsellor organization to train store operators not only how to capture customer and sales information but how to use it. For Suzuki, systems, processes, information and people were an integrated set of key resources. According to this view, then, a business is an information business when it is systems-dependent and requires its personnel to be smart information workers.

James Robinson, former chairman of American Express, saw his company in the same light some 20 years ago: "All the financial analysts keep saying we're in the financial services business. They're wrong. American Express is in the information business." We see this perspective in sector after sector today. Managers and staff have to be adept at information processing. Operations come to a halt when the systems break down. You actually seem to see more PCs and terminals than people.

However, even if we were still in the industrial age, some theorists would still suggest that every business is an information business. One reason for this is the way in which we design our organizations, often based on an information-processing goal.

We decentralize to allow managers to get their hands on the specialized information of specific environments and tasks and to reduce the information load of centralized organizations. We centralize again when we want to gain control or improve co-ordination by bringing information flows back to the center. We deploy IT in federal organizations to distribute information to those empowered in local units, who then send back information for central planners and co-ordinators to process too. Or we use IT to enable networked or virtual organizations to work.

Likewise, some theorists will see the work of managers themselves as information processors, not only in the execution of daily tasks but also in the way they plan, co-ordinate, control and make decisions. Today managers are also expected to be competent users of PCs, e-mail, decision support systems and executive information systems.

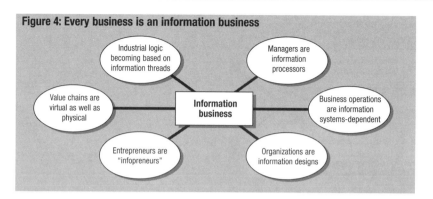

Figure 4: Every business is an information business

And while entrepreneurs are often adept at collecting and processing information about threats and opportunities – by networking, observing and getting about – many now look to information and IT as their source of new products and services. The entrepreneurs of the future are "infopreneurs".

From IT to IR

Figure 4 summarizes the discussion so far. From at least six perspectives, every business is an information business.

One consequence of this is that either no business strategy is complete without an information strategy or that business strategy and information strategy need to be integrated. IT, information systems and information as a resource no longer just support business strategy; they also help to determine it. But what does an information strategy look like?

I developed a conceptual framework over 10 years ago that has had considerable influence on practice. It sought to distinguish information systems (IS) strategy from IT strategy. IT, which was about the "how" – the technology infrastructure or platform – often seemed to distract attention from IS, which was the "what" – the identification and prioritization of systems or applications for development.

Then I added information management strategy, which was about the "who" – the all-important question of roles and responsibilities in the delivery, support and strategic development of IS and IT. All of these were influenced by – and influenced – the business or organizational strategy (the "why"), which was concerned with strategic intent and organizational architecture. In a perfect world, corporations strove for a good fit between these four domains.

Now we can see that a fifth domain was missing – one we still find difficult to formalize but in which companies increasingly have objectives, principles and policies. This is the domain of information as a resource, or of information resource (IR) strategy. It is perhaps the "where" question: where are we going? Much value creation can come from information but it is not always clear what the end result will look like. The five-point framework is summarized in Figure 5.

In British Petroleum, where chief executive John Browne is trying to build a learning organization based on knowledge, the principle of information-sharing has driven many IT and IS strategy decisions. In Safeway, the supermarket retailer, there is a policy of never throwing any data away. Electronic point-of-sale data and customer loyalty card data – often shared with suppliers – drive much of what it does and help it monitor and evaluate many of its strategic experiments.

In more traditional content companies, such as advertising agencies, broadcasters

Figure 5: Information strategy framework

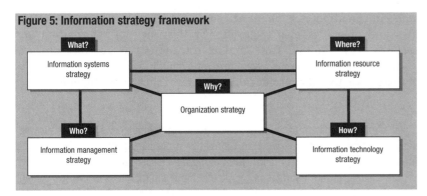

and movie companies, you will find policies about not giving away or even releasing content that others could reuse. Disney is a past master at this. And in financial services companies you will find executives scratching their heads and saying "Why did we never collect critical data such as date of birth when our customers joined us?" and "Why do information resellers make money out of our transaction data?"

One aspect of IR strategy is an increasing interest in the distinction between data, information and knowledge. Some chief information officers and chief knowledge officers – whom we examine later in the series – believe that such classifications are unhelpful, and some academics have certainly put their careers back by agonising over such questions. Others, however, feel that conceptualizations such as that in Figure 6 offer at least three lessons:

1. To some degree, information is derived from data, and knowledge from information, and thus we are reminded that data has enormous potential – far beyond just being representative of a transaction.
2. Information has characteristics, particularly of human interpretation, above and beyond data. Knowledge has something more than information, perhaps learning. A logical test of the value of an additional piece of knowledge could be whether it provides new understanding.
3. Articulating and seeking to classify these intangible resources at least alerts people to their value and, more particularly, to the different sorts of investments they require. Technology is suited to data processing. Knowledge processing is much more of a human activity.

What is clear is that such frameworks and the past work of philosophers, economists, political scientists, computer scientists, psychologists and management scholars on the nature of information, as a commodity or a process, has relevance

Figure 6: From data to knowledge

	Data	Information	Knowledge
Content	Events	Trends	Expertise
Form	Transactions	Patterns	Learnings
Information task	Representation	Manipulation	Codification
Human element	Observation	Judgment	Experience
Organizational intent	Automation	Decision-making	Action
Value test	Building block	Uncertainty reduction	New understanding

and value for the information age. There are some old lessons to be re-learnt but some new rules and ideas are also required. For the world of information and intangible assets is very different from that of the industrial age and physical assets. That overworked and in some ways abused term "paradigm shift" seems to be just right for once; we are all experiencing one in our information businesses.

Summary

There is nothing new about information-based businesses. Even in the industrial age, some theorists argue, organizational structure was a consequence of information-processing goals. And the tasks that managers perform – planning, co-ordination and decision-making – essentially involve manipulating information. What has changed in the "information age" is that more and more businesses are defining their strategies in terms of information or knowledge. As **Michael Earl** points out, this is true not just of "content" companies such as publishers or film studios but of companies in sectors such as pharmaceuticals or consumer goods. The result is a blurring of traditional industrial boundaries, a breakdown in the standard distinction between "horizontal" and "vertical" integration, and a new analysis of the value chain in terms of opportunities for capturing information.

Suggested further reading

Rayport, J.F. and Sviokla, J.J. (1998) "Exploiting the virtual value chain", *Harvard Business Review* (Nov.–Dec.). (The source for Figure 3.)

IT: a vehicle for project success

by David Feeny and Robert Plant

Managers confronted with the rhetoric of the "information age" may experience a variety of emotions, ranging from excitement to suspicion or even outright skepticism.

On the one hand the evidence is all around us that information technologies now available represent remarkable new capabilities. Many pundits have forecast how these will be harnessed to transform our business and personal lives. On the other hand, have we not heard such prophecies before, through four decades of rapid IT development, and yet experienced disappointment at least as often as delight from our IT investments?

Are there lessons we can learn from successes with existing technologies? And if so, how much of that learning will remain valid for managers seeking to exploit newer technologies over the next decade? To address these questions, let us look at a recent case study – set in a real and familiar business rather than an internet start-up which we might suspect to be here today and gone tomorrow.

Land Rover has been making four-wheel drive vehicles (and nothing else) for 50 years. Its initial design is still in production as the Land Rover Defender. In the company's first 46 years it introduced only two other models – the Range Rover in

1970 and the Discovery in 1989. Over the next few years, with funding from its new parent BMW, Land Rover launched three new models: the (already planned) new version of the Range Rover; the Land Rover Freelander; and, most recently, a new version of the Discovery. The development of the all-new Freelander provides particular insights into successful information management.

The Freelander project

For Land Rover the Freelander represented a revolutionary, not an evolutionary, project. The challenge was to develop a class-leading entrant for the emerging market segment of compact "sports utility" vehicles. The marketing brief, according to Land Rover managing director Ian Robertson, was to uphold the established values of the Land Rover brand while interpreting them for a younger group of owners with lower budgets.

Considerable technological innovation was required, with, for example, hill descent control providing a driver-friendly alternative to the traditional second gear box. This was to be the first Land Rover with a monocoque construction in place of the familiar chassis. And time was of the essence: the market niche had been pioneered by others during a period in which Land Rover had been starved of investment.

Responding to the challenge, the project team delivered an acclaimed vehicle within 30 months of project launch while simultaneously achieving excellent performance in parameters key to profitability and customer acceptance. Successful information management was integral to each dimension of that achievement.

To enable rapid creation of a high-quality design, Land Rover made an unequivocal commitment to computer-aided engineering. The vehicle was divided into 10 sections, each of which was allocated a team of design and production engineers. To ensure the integrity of the vehicle as a whole, each team had immediate access to the work of its peers using Computervision's concurrent assembly mock-up system.

Each team also had access to an electronic library of blueprinted concepts. If working on a component invisible to the customer – for example, an electric window mechanism – a designer could draw on a Rover-wide blueprint. Components visible to the customer used blueprints specific to Land Rover, to reinforce the look and feel associated with the brand.

The most obvious benefits of such use of blueprints are the time saved by "not reinventing the wheel" and the tapping of available purchasing scale economies across model ranges. But there are also more fundamental economic issues involved. According to Robertson: "70 per cent of product cost is driven by design-time decisions on components. Any issuance of a new part number has implications all along the supply chain – for bill of materials, suppliers, quality, packaging, pallets, accounting systems, dealers and right through to parts distribution for aftersales service."

An electronic design environment was also provided for the planning of the Freelander assembly line. A three-dimensional electronic model of the target assembly building was created, complete with accurate representations of internal stanchions and the main conveyor system. The model was then furnished with planned facilities for a number of critical assembly stations, where, for reasons of layout, cycle time or operator ergonomics, the production engineering task was complex in nature and difficult to evaluate.

Using advanced virtual reality (VR) equipment, planners were able to simulate the experience of operating the processes in real time. Assembly workers, process specialists, suppliers who would be directly feeding the line, and health and safety professionals were all drawn into the manufacturing design process through the VR model. Once the electronic process was complete, the facility was built, equipped and put into operation in 28 weeks – half the time required by previous practice.

Another challenge was to devise a supply chain and production process that could effectively manufacture a "lot size of one". A customer anywhere in Europe had to be able to specify his or her preferred vehicle – five- or three-door, soft or hard top, gasoline or diesel, color (out of 10), optional extras (out of 16) and interior trim design – and obtain it within two weeks. Allowing a week for shipment, this meant that any of several thousand possible variants had to be capable of completion within seven working days of the customer's order.

To achieve this goal, Land Rover used a "funnel" concept to design the supply chain. The long thin neck of the funnel, stretching back to the beginning of the supply chain, represents completely standard production: where necessary, redundancy was designed into affected components to keep all vehicle options open until the later stages. Variations are achieved within the broadening mouth of the funnel, which represents the last seven days of the supply chain.

All activity during the final period must be capable of rapid response to the customer's specification. Suppliers to this end of the chain have online electronic links to Land Rover. Microelectronics control the robotic paint guns in the paint shop so that they can clear and change color within three seconds. In an integrated information management system, Land Rover dealers enter the customer's order online and identify from the system's internal model of the production plan the first unallocated vehicle in the pipeline; the system then orchestrates that vehicle's completion as required.

Not so long ago the delivery of this degree of customization would have added further increments of complexity, inventory and cost to the already high levels of inventory held in case of assembly line outages. The final gauge of Land Rover's achievement is that the Freelander line operates with inventory levels equivalent to less than a day and a half's production. Close partnership and sophisticated electronic links with suppliers – many of whom were involved throughout the product design – have been instrumental in delivering a world-class "lean production" system.

CHANGING STANDARDS IN THE AUTOMOTIVE INDUSTRY

	Industry norms early 1990s	Land Rover Freelander 1997/8
"Concept to customer" time (new vehicles)	~60 months	30 months
Build and commission production line	~60 weeks	28 weeks
Deliver to customer order	~4/6 weeks	2 weeks
Inventory levels	~20 days	1.5 days

Lessons from Land Rover

We have described the Freelander project as a success story, which is what we believe it to be. However, it is not unique, either with respect to the automotive sector or beyond. What has happened at Land Rover illustrates a wider phenomenon: the way in which IT – even in mature industry sectors – has enabled radically different ways of working that deliver new standards of performance.

Behind the hype, and the skepticism, successes have been achieved. In sector after sector – in oil, construction, pharmaceuticals and consumer packaged goods, as well as airlines and financial services – IT has become part of the solution rather than part of the problem. Thus the first lesson from Land Rover is that the information age is already very much with us.

The second lesson is that while IT is now part of the solution, it is only one part of it. IT investments alone do not deliver business advantage. Land Rover's ability to complete the Freelander project in 30 months was dependent on three things: the use of multidisciplinary teams; the fact that those teams worked in parallel, in an iterative and learning-orientated development process; and the provision of an information infrastructure that integrated all project activity and provided a common language for contributions. While details may vary by business context, these three elements are found in all examples of reducing time to market.

Equally, Land Rover's ability to deliver quickly to customer specification without high levels of complexity and cost depends on redesign of the supply chain to support the funnel concept, and reduction of the supplier base to achieve closer partnerships, as well as the integrated enterprise-wide information network. We saw the same elements in the production process developed by Sony's TV factory at Bridgend, Wales, in the early 1990s; we see them now at Dell Computer. Successful information management is consistently one integral part of the implementation of a superior business idea.

The third lesson from Land Rover is that the involvement and leadership of senior managers is essential to successful information management. Absence of such leadership can be very costly: one of the larger carmakers discovered in the early 1990s that it was actually spending more than twice as much on IT as a key rival, yet that rival strongly outperformed it on exactly those business performance measures at which Land Rover excelled. This company was failing to focus its expenditure on the most critical business issues.

The basic problem is that information technologies are developed without predetermined application purposes: application is defined at the point of use rather than of manufacture. A case in point at present is internet technology. This can be applied in many different ways by any business – and well-meaning professionals and middle managers will be inclined to propose that it is.

Land Rover provides a contrasting model. First, the focus of senior management interest – development of the Freelander – was clear. IT investment which supported that aim was welcome; other proposals were not.

Second, stretch targets were set – a class-leading vehicle, a 30-month schedule, lot-size-of-one capability and so on – and Robertson made it clear that there could be no slippage: the 30 months had to end with the launch of the Freelander at the Frankfurt Motor Show in September 1997.

Third, by contrast, the "solution" was not closely defined; all that was clear at the outset was that the project demanded radically new approaches. "Sacred cows have no place in the Freelander project," declared Robertson.

The technology of virtual reality

The technology of virtual reality is often associated with computer games or the entertainment industry. In fact it has for several years now found application in industry, in the evaluation of proposed factories, supermarkets, oil rigs and the like. The essence of VR is that the user can interact with a computerized model to experience what it will be like to fly the proposed airplane, say, or shop in the planned supermarket.

The display changes in real time to reflect the consequences of the user's decisions and actions. In the newer "immersive" VR technology, which was used by Land Rover, the user dons a helmet, a head-mounted display that increases the sensation of immersion in the model; the display changes in accordance with the actions and movements of the wearer. Thus Land Rover workers were able to look down and see "components" on the "floor" of the planned assembly facility, pick them up and manipulate them. The company expects that the classic industrial ills of back strain and repetitive strain injury will be greatly reduced through this approach to planning the workplace.

All this created an environment in which the team was hungry for uses of IT that would enable radical change; it had no interest in uses peripheral to the business focus. It was the sort of environment for information management that Sir John Browne has created at BP Amoco; it is the context for information management's success.

Finally, are these simply lessons from history or are they lessons for the future, relevant to the exploitation of tomorrow's technologies?, We think the latter. Senior managers need to see IT as an agent of business transformation, and to focus its use on radical improvement of the business activities that matter most.

As technology continues to develop, ideas familiar in one business context become viable in new contexts. For example, we have a colleague who is now building his dream house; the virtual team of owner, architect, builder and interior designer are all based in different cities but a shared website with electronic modelling and visualization software underpins their own version of a Freelander-type project. As possibilities multiply, the importance of – and potential reward from – successful information management increases.

Summary

Leading-edge information management is not confined to internet start-ups with astronomic market capitalizations. Companies in more traditional sectors too are showing the way. Here **David Feeny** and **Robert Plant** describe how focused use of IT enabled Land Rover to make a success of its innovative Freelander project.

Suggested further reading

Feeny, D., Plant, R. and Mughal, H., "Land Rover Vehicles: the CB40 Project", case study, Templeton College.

Feeny, D. (1997) "Lasting ideas within turbulent technology", introduction to *Managing IT as a Strategic Resource* (eds Willcocks, L., Feeny, D. and Islei, G.), McGraw-Hill; reprinted in Leer, A. (ed.) (1997) *Masters of the Wired World*, London: Financial Times Pitman.

A century of information management

by Geneviève Feraud

A fashionable concept in information management is "data-mining", or extracting specific data from huge fields of information. This metaphor reminds us of the beginnings of the industrial revolution in Europe. Economic growth was rooted in coal mines, where people toiled to extract the energy that would sustain society's development.

As the industrial economy expanded and companies increased in complexity, one of their first problems was to record and transmit ever-larger amounts of information. Given the simplicity of the technology available, solutions tended to be labor-intensive.

In banks, for example, managers organized the work of young, unqualified people whose main responsibility was to identify signatures on cheques and draft amounts on ledger cards. In other companies, the big problem was despatching bills without too much delay. Managers thus had to supervise the storage of information and ensure that it was communicated to the right person at the right time.

Companies and other administrative bodies looked for ways to process information in an organized way, just as they processed raw materials to produce goods. The focus was on mass treatment and mass production, both of tangible and intangible products.

Office Taylorism

The advent of "scientific management", championed by US engineer Frederick Taylor in the early 20th century, did not affect only factory production lines. As there were obvious parallels between screwing thousands of identical bolts into thousands of identical plates, and copying thousands of figures and adding them into thousands of "result" columns, it was natural for managers to seek ways of "rationalising" office work.

Armies of clerks, whose white collars and literacy did not entirely hide the essentially unskilled nature of their work, implemented these tightly orchestrated, minutely timed information management systems. People were employed whose sole task was to add columns of figures. The adding machines and sorting devices that these clerks used were among the ancestors of modern office systems.

The holy PC (punch card)

An early icon of of bureaucracy and information processing was the punch card. Punch cards were first used in the early 19th century in automated looms and in the calculating machines built by computer pioneer Charles Babbage. Later the idea was taken up by Herman Hollerith, who worked for the US Census Office. His patenting of a "Census Machine" in 1884 marks the beginning of the punch card's almost 100-year reign.

Like most innovations, Hollerith's was by no means the obvious way forward at the time. His new technique was only one among many and it seemed difficult to prove its profitability. But the government decided to use it for the 1890 census, and was able to announce the result (62,622,250) on December 12 after six weeks of counting; the 1880 census had taken seven years to count. This saved the government some $5m and, because of the way the data were stored, further analysis could be carried out relatively easily.

After his census success, Hollerith established the Tabulating Machine Company to manufacture the equipment needed to read punch cards. After a series of mergers this became the International Business Machine Company – IBM.

The first computers

Major advances in computer technology were made in the 1940s. A number of machines from this period have some claim to be the first electronic computer, but the term is largely one of definition. Perhaps the best-known candidate is the Electronic Numerical Integrator and Calculator built by John Mauchly and J. Presper Eckert at the University of Pennsylvania in 1943–46.

Like other computing machines of this time, Eniac was hardly a laptop: it weighed 30 tons and had 70,000 resistors and 18,000 vacuum tubes. Philadelphia's lighting flickered when it was turned on. But unlike earlier machines, Eniac was designed to be programmed for a variety of purposes. Its creators went on to develop the first commercial computer, Univac, in 1951.

These developments are generally considered to be the beginning of the modern information era. The basic anatomy of present-day computers evolved during these years. Operating systems and programming languages were developed. And all the factors that make IT management necessary moved into place: an electronic machine, some specialists to run it, and other people to use it.

The age of the mainframe

Mainframe computers reigned unchallenged at the beginning of modern information management. However, numbers were small – in 1961, there were only around 6,000 computers worldwide. Most mainframes used punch cards as inputs and stored information on magnetic tape. Terminals were usually installed in a separate area, apart from the rest of the company. The organizational model was centralized and hierarchical.

Applications developed in the 1950s and 1960s focused on reducing inputs of labour, usually by automating already existing procedures. No creativity was involved; established structures were simply copied. Computerized applications did the same as "manual" applications but much more quickly and in much larger volumes.

These first applications focused on quite narrow areas, such as very specific optimization calculations. Oil companies, for example, developed programs to improve yield and inventory control. Other companies used computers mainly for accounting. Because it was completely formalized, accounting was the ideal business process to automate. It was a simple matter to express an accounting formula as a piece of program code.

Computers did not process information with the same degree of sophistication that they can now; they did not project, model or simulate. They were essentially giant calculators that just took in data and performed arithmetic. The structure of these early applications was quite simple, essentially mimicking the balance sheet.

The IT department tended to be an enclave of initiates who preferred to communicate only with one another. They tended to ignore other employees' requirements and spent all their days and nights running The Machine – which often broke down at the exact moment it was most needed. (Even today, disillusioned users may feel little has changed.)

The internet had its earliest beginnings in this period, as a reaction to such systems centralization. It was an initiative of the US Department of Defense, which wanted to create a communication system that would be able to withstand a nuclear attack. The idea was that a decentralized network would be less vulnerable than a system with a single "nerve center".

The distributed era

In the 1970s, the appearance of microprocessors led to smaller (departmental) computers and at the beginning of the 1980s terminals linked to mainframes were quickly replaced by personal computers. Processing power was increasing rapidly; between 1982 and 1986, for example, the world total increased by a factor of four.

Information systems developed at this time had sufficient processing power to support large, complex applications and were reasonably reliable. Applications began to broaden their focus from accountancy. Manufacturing support systems helped floor managers to monitor production. Then came decision-making systems, which could be applied at a high level of the company to obtain a full picture of its current situation. Finance, human resource management and marketing in turn were targetted by the programmers.

It was not easy to evaluate the costs and benefits of the new technology, especially as the best applications enabled users to perform tasks that would have been impossible without a computer. But the consensus was that the benefits outweighed the costs and that abandoning computer technology would be a step backwards.

This period was the golden age of "application development methodologies". These had two goals: to provide analysts with an objective view of a company's processes, so that those processes could be automated; and to establish a common language for IT specialists and users – in practice, this often meant that users had to learn a simplified version of the specialists' language. Barriers between users and specialists weakened but never really disappeared. Companies began to see greater and greater returns on their IT investments, especially when they backed them up with "quality implementation" initiatives.

The ubiquitous era

At the end of the 1980s and beginning of the 1990s, the personal computer market grew with extraordinary speed. So too did processing power, as price came down: based on the US Department of Commerce Computer Price Deflator, computing power was approximately three and a half times cheaper in 1990 than in 1980 (and 20 times cheaper than in 1970; and 125 times cheaper than in 1960).

Information systems were now sophisticated enough to deal with large volumes of data while allowing customization by individual users. This flexibility, combined with declining costs and the fact that the expertise needed to set up and run PCs was widely available, encouraged companies to use them to solve an ever-wider range of business problems. Companies became more and more dependent on their computers. Better information systems were one of the drivers of globalization.

The power relationship between IT professionals and users changed dramatically. As more and more people gained first-hand experience of computing – and, thanks in particular to spreadsheet software, became able to customise their own applications – the dominance of the mainframe and its attendant technicians

The "cascade" model

McKenney shows that one way to think of the evolution of information management is as a "cascade" phenomenon. That is, companies' adoption of IT consists of a series of jumps.

First, a company faces an information-processing crisis and adopts an IT solution. This happened to airlines when jet engines made trips so short that there was no longer enough time to process reservations manually.

Second, the company tries to build its IT competence, often through trial and error.

The third jump consists in expanding the scope of IT – by allowing it to become a necessary part of the production process, for example.

The final jump leads the company to a position where it uses IT to drive strategy, thus maximizing IT's potential to confer competitive advantage.

waned. Users gained the ascendancy. But it soon became clear that the complexity generated by user customization needed careful management, which could best be provided by IT professionals. A new equilibrium of competencies, responsibilities and powers arose.

Computers were now everywhere, preparing the way for the next – but surely not final – stage in this evolution: the arrival of the networked society.

New challenges

Where are we today?

Information has never been so important for our economy. The worldwide value of goods traded over the internet – both business-to-business and business-to-consumer – is around $15,000m; some forecasters predict that by 2000 this will have risen to around $42,000m, with exponential growth thereafter.

Companies' business models are undergoing a profound change, with increasing emphasis being given to innovation and the concept of service-provision. The idea that the company is essentially an information processor is becoming more widespread. More and more companies and governmental agencies are defining themselves as a collection of processes supported by software packages, as indicated by increased use of "enterprise planning systems". Information management is thus attaining an unprecedented importance in companies.

The changing concerns of chief executives reflect these shifts.

Strategic exploitation of the full potential of information systems is seen as a matter of survival. A critical challenge for companies is to move beyond automation to innovation. Automation simply means using computers to perform clerical tasks that used to be carried out by people – the punch card paradigm. This may increase profits, but leads to only modest improvements in the company's efficiency. Innovation, however, means using IT to tap the potential of people's creativity. Making innovation possible may require considerable modification of the company's infrastructure but the gains in profits and efficiency are likely to be considerable.

Where are we going?

Prediction is always difficult but where IT is concerned, it seems almost impossible. For the sake of argument I shall make a linear projection here but it is essential to remember that discontinuities are always possible (or even likely).

Networked microprocessor-based systems, organized in a "client–server architecture", will supplant mainframes and supercomputers for most applications.

Advances in optical fiber technology will increase the capacity of transmission lines, and the diversity and versatility of transmission technologies will enable users anywhere in the world to link to networks.

The distribution of information will become faster, integrating graphics, video, sound and text in a single flow of information. Increasingly sophisticated and quality-conscious consumers will demand more from the information and communication systems in their working and private lives.

Personal computers and networks now offer all the conditions for the development of "network-centric" communities, where society, work and personal life will be organized around the opposed concepts of "the Net and the Self". Developed by University of California sociologist Manuel Castells, this is the idea that each person will live in a perpetual balance between integration in a worldwide stream of electronically mediated thought and activity, and focus on his or her own psychological and cultural identity.

The global networks of economic wealth, political power and media will depend more and more on knowledge generation. Society will become more and more symbolic – that is, the capacity to produce and distribute goods and services will become increasingly dependent on the ability to create and manipulate electronic symbols. This is already obvious in the development of e-commerce, where producers and buyers exchange electronic money in a virtual marketplace. According to Castells, "for the first time in history, the human mind is a direct productive force, not just a decisive element of the production system".

Companies will have to adapt to this new environment, although the process will not be easy. Managing knowledge is a potentially Sisyphean task, as the amount of information available in any field is always growing. Novel organizational structures will be needed to cope. Companies will have to conceive of themselves as located within a shifting network of suppliers, competitors and consumers; their boundaries will accordingly be highly fluid. Permanent flexibility will be the key to survival in the new economy.

Summary

As enterprises grow in size and complexity, information management increases in importance. And as **Geneviève Feraud** shows here, the way information is managed depends upon the technology available. For much of the 20th century, relatively cumbersome technology – punch cards and mainframes – necessitated a centralized, hierarchical approach. But now the advent of the networked PC has shifted the focus to innovation.

Suggested further reading

Castells, M. (1996) *The Rise of the Network Society*, Oxford: Blackwell.

Cortada, J.W. (1996) *Information Technology as Business History: Issues in the History and Management of Computers*, Westport, CT: Greenwood.

Kobrin, S.J. (1998) "Back to the future: neomedievalism and the postmodern digital world economy", *Journal of International Affairs* 51.

McKenney, J.L., Copeland, D.C., Mason, R.O. (1995) *Waves of Change: Business Evolution through Information Technology*, Boston, MA: Harvard Business School Press.

COMPETING WITH KNOWLEDGE

2

Contributors

 **Philip Evans** is senior vice-president of The Boston Consulting Group.

 **Yury Boshyk** is professor of political economy and strategy at Theseus International Management Institute, France.

 **Jeffrey F. Rayport** is an associate professor at Harvard Business School.

 **Eric K. Clemons** is professor of information strategy, systems and economics at the Wharton School, University of Pennsylvania.

 **Thomas H. Davenport** is professor of information management at Boston University's School of Management and director of the Accenture Institute for Strategic Change.

Contents

Introduction

This module addresses strategic issues about what it means to compete in a world freely flowing with information, as well as highlighting some specifics (e.g. customer targeting techniques like data-mining). What is the future of companies founded on fast-eroding information asymmetries? Is there still a tradeoff between the richness of an information exchange and the number of people involved with it? How do you get "eyeballs" to visit your website or – more frustratingly perhaps – your corporate intranet? How can managers deal with information overload and what are the best ways for information providers to grab their attention? These and many other questions are answered. Knowledge management receives more detailed treatment in Module 6 but the basic terminology and several mini case studies are introduced here.

Strategy and the new economics of information

by Philip Evans

Information used to be a functional discipline but now it is becoming the fulcrum of strategy. This is true for all businesses, not just so-called "information" businesses. Information is shifting the vector of economic forces that defines competitive advantage and many companies need therefore to rethink – almost from first principles – their strategic focus.

A new economics of information is emerging. Universal connectivity and standards are eroding established asymmetries of knowledge, loosening choke-holds on the flow of information and reducing towards zero the costs of searching, switching and transacting. But it is upon precisely these asymmetries, choke-holds and costs that many business structures and competitive advantages are based.

The value chains that define a business, the supply chains that define an industry, the customer relationships and brands that define a franchise, and the organization charts that define hierarchy, power and the boundaries of the corporation are all premised on the "glue" of information. That glue is melting. Markets are interpenetrating where organization had previously prevailed. Information flows are separating from physical ones. Businesses are therefore being redefined. So is the scope of the corporation. So is the universe of possible suppliers, customers and competitors.

Richness versus reach

The new economics of information attacks a pervasive and fundamental aspect of the old economics: the tradeoff between richness and reach. Consider, for example, the alternative information channels through which sellers persuade buyers. Newspaper advertisements reach a wide range of possible customers but have a limited, static content. Direct mail or telemarketing are a bit richer in customization and interactivity but are much more expensive, and therefore have to be targeted. Relative to advertisers, direct marketers give up reach in order to add richness. A salesman giving his pitch offers the highest level of customization, dialogue and empathy but with only one customer at a time. The marketing mix is thus the apportionment of information resources across a tradeoff between richness and reach.

Buyers live with, and adapt to, the same tradeoff. It forces them to search hierarchically and navigate their way from high reach/low richness sources of information (such as the phone book) towards high richness/low reach sources (the salesman). Brand knowledge, from the customer's point of view, is simply a high richness/low reach information channel that short-circuits the laborious task of hierarchical search.

Supply chains exhibit the same tradeoff: Citibank obtains euros and pounds from hundreds of institutions precisely because the informational richness needed to support currency trading amounts to just a few numbers. Toyota or Wal-Mart, in contrast, have built rich and expensive systems for EDI with their suppliers but have narrowed their supply base – and thus sacrificed reach – in order to do so. The hierarchical structure of industrial supply chains, in which each participant deals with its immediate suppliers and its immediate customers only, reflects the richness/reach tradeoff.

Organizations support richer information exchange among a small number of insiders, whereas markets trade thin information in a wider universe. The boundary of the corporation is thus a point on the tradeoff. Within the organization, hierarchy is shaped by span of control, which reflects a tradeoff between richness and reach in how people collaborate. "Relationships", among and within corporations, as well as with retail customers, "loyalty" to a product or an employer, and "trust" of a person or a brand, are all the products of rich exchanges of information among people who by doing so have narrowed the reach of their options.

The marketing mix, searching and switching behavior, branding, retail franchises, supply chain relationships, organizations and even the boundaries of the corporation are all built on this pervasive, universal and obvious tradeoff between richness and reach. However, the tradeoff is ceasing to be obvious. In critical ways it is rapidly becoming obsolete. Over the next decade the signal impact of advances in information technology will be the displacement – and in some cases obliteration – of precisely this tradeoff.

Two forces are driving this displacement: the explosion of connectivity and the adoption of standards. The connectivity point is now well known. By 2005 (according to an estimate by International Data Corporation) one billion people worldwide will have direct access to the internet. Even as recently as four years ago, none of the computer industry's moguls anticipated such growth.

The standards point is more subtle. Proprietary e-mail is being supplanted by the protocols of the internet. Proprietary EDI is being supplanted by industry-wide extranets, such as ANX in the automotive industry. Proprietary online services are transforming themselves into internet access providers. Within the corporation, functional information "silos" are being supplanted by intranets. But the internet, extranets and intranets are all variants on exactly the same thing. Lowest common denominator technology is simply good enough for the benefits of universality to outweigh those of dedication and customization. And universality of information standards is what destroys the tradeoff between richness and reach.

Over just the past three or four years, this lowest common denominator technology has swept the board for static, textual information where security and speed are not critical. Over the next 10 years, many other types of information will succumb to the same open, universal standards: high-volume, mission-critical applications, logic-intensive processing, confidential data, even full-screen, high-definition video entertainment. There are no fundamental technical barriers because bandwidth, memory and processing power continue to be driven by the inexorable force of Moore's Law (which states that the number of transistors that can fit on a silicon chip – and hence the power of computers – will double every 18 months). By about 2015, a $200 chip will be a thousand times faster than it is today and thus able to store the entire current contents of the British Library. For some applications, there is legitimate argument over when. There can be no argument over whether.

If universal and open standards were restricted to the transportation layer, this would be dramatic enough, comparable to the adoption of uniform rail widths in the late 19th century or of a universal interconnection standard for telephone companies – dial tone – around the turn of the 20th. Both were standards that enabled a new communication infrastructure to blow up previous tradeoffs between richness and reach.

However, in the digital world (unlike railways and telephones) there is no qualitative difference between transportation standards and content standards and there is therefore a natural evolution from one into the other. TCP/IP defines the rules for switching messages; HTML defines how a web page is presented; SET defines how it can be encrypted; PICS defines how a web page describes itself; XML defines how databases describe themselves; OFX defines how personal financial information is presented; KONA defines how patients' medical records can be kept. As new standards are developed and reach "critical mass" they permit rich interpretation of information across a domain limited only by their universe of adoption. And by a logic that has become familiar from the computer industry, the more people adopt a standard, the more compelling it becomes. Each standard blows up a richness/ reach tradeoff and in turn enables the development of higher-order standards.

Describing the Edvac computer project in 1945, the mathematician John von Neumann showed how a digital computer could store and retrieve instructions in exactly the same way that it stored and retrieved data. Instructions could therefore serve as the raw material for other instructions, programs could read and write programs, and hardwired functions would therefore be the starting point, not the end point, of a machine's capabilities. Von Neumann was the first to recognize how this unique characteristic of the stored-program computer would enable a degree of sophistication and adaptability that had previously been inconceivable. In the world of cyberspace the ability of content standards to evolve out of transportation standards and out of each other is a manifestation of exactly the same logic. This logic is playing out not by design but through self-organization, and not within a machine but across a global network of people and institutions.

Connectivity and standards together massively displace the tradeoff between richness and reach. They allow advising, alerting, authenticating, bidding, collaborating, comparing, informing, searching, specifying and switching with a richness that is constrained only by the underlying standards and a reach that is constrained only by the number of players connected. For example, OFX, as it evolves into a comprehensive standard for personal financial information, will allow an individual to specify a financial need, request, receive and compare bids, incorporate data or advice from any source, apply systematic selection criteria, execute transactions, automate routine tasks and integrate financial statements, all while dealing with an essentially unlimited number of institutions.

Ordinary individuals can exercise the purchasing sophistication of professionals. The comprehensive financial planning previously available only to private banking clients becomes available to all. The seamless integration previously achieved only by putting all one's business with a single institution is now available across multiple accounts. The customer enjoys both richness and reach.

Deconstruction

The displacement of the richness/reach tradeoff "deconstructs" the competitive architecture of businesses. It melts the informational glue that ties elements of the value chain together, and it allows information and physical flows to separate,

39

causing components of the business to coalesce into radically different business definitions.

To continue the financial services example. In the presence of the prevailing richness/reach tradeoffs, financial services businesses today are largely defined by three sets of forces that bundle product offerings together and lock in customer relationships: the economics of common physical delivery, cross-selling on the basis of superior knowledge of the customer, and the customer's preference for one-stop shopping and established relationships (because of the high cost of searching, switching and complexity). In short, these businesses are defined by "department store" economics.

But all three forces are significantly weakened when the richness/reach tradeoff is blown up. Physical delivery becomes largely irrelevant in a world of home electronic banking. (What remains, such as cash dispensing, is more economically done by grocery shops.) As the cost of gathering, packaging and reselling information goes to zero, the most advantaged owner of information about the individual is the individual. That is, the customer can assemble more valuable information about him- or herself than any third party, and can profit accordingly. And the costs of searching, switching and complexity are massively reduced – for higher value products, they are effectively eliminated. As the informational glue melts, competitive advantage in delivering the bundle comes to matter less than advantage in each of the constituent products and services. Advantage tilts towards the focused player. Navigators, advisors and mono-line product providers are the winners: category killers, not department stores.

Obviously this is not yet the case and it will not happen overnight. But there is a certain logic that guarantees that when deconstruction does hit, it will be where the bundled business is most vulnerable. Only 13 per cent of households in the US use financial software to manage their affairs today but because they have dispro-portionate income and assets they account for over 80 per cent of the profitability of the retail banking system. Similarly, big-ticket, discrete products such as loans and investments are more likely to be shopped around for than basic transactional services. But it is on big-ticket items that most profits are currently earned: basic transactional services are operated at break-even, for the sake of the "relationship".

Many customers are not so rigorous. There will always be some (perhaps the majority) for whom time is more important than money, and relationships more important than cost or choice. Many investors want financial advice and reassurance from a person, not a database. But where this is true the abiding strength of the informational glue at this nexus in the value chain serves merely to deepen the fissures elsewhere. Those selfsame financial advisors find that their own costs of searching and switching among suppliers of products and information plummet. They find that they can exploit the vast product reach and rich analytical capabilities that their customers prefer not to touch. And by so doing they can offer their customers a broader array of better products at lower cost. Freed from the obligation to push their employers' current securities inventory, they can gain competitive advantage by behaving less like salesmen and more like advisors. This shift in affiliation by intermediaries presents as big a threat to institutions as the onset of hard-nosed customer rationality. The impact of deconstruction simply moves up the value chain.

Deconstruction can occur wherever information economics hold a physical bundle together and wherever the informational activities themselves can evolve into separate businesses. Deconstruction will occur when breaking up the business releases economic value – when activities cross-subsidize one another or when the economics of one activity are compromised for the sake of another.

Such logic, with varying speed and intensity, will apply to wide swathes of the economy. It can operate on the consumer relationship but also on corporate supply chains. Within a business it can undermine the rationale for vertical integration and enable the business's informational and physical components to separate. It can loosen the bonds between a corporation and its own employees. It undermines hierarchy in all its forms, including that of the organization chart.

Implications for strategy

People tend to overestimate the immediacy but underestimate the profundity of underlying economic shifts. The digital revolution is no exception. The world in five or even ten years will probably look much the same as it does today and deconstruction may not have an impact on some businesses until the economics of information are a thousand times more compelling. That will take 15 years. And when deconstruction occurs it may attack only a small sliver of value added: the sliver that accounts for the preponderance of competitive advantage and profitability.

Prediction, especially of timing, is very difficult. But a "wait and see" strategy is usually wrong. It is better to fail five times over through trying too early than it is to fail once by being too late.

Deconstruction can put the incumbent at a huge disadvantage because of legacy systems, legacy thinking and the real dilemmas of cannibalizing an established business. Advantage shifts to the insurgent, who has no such inhibitions. But by breaking down the barriers between businesses and industries, deconstruction enables every incumbent to play insurgent on someone else's turf.

Conventional strategic thinking assumes a value chain. It assumes an industry. It assumes a finite, known and similar set of competitors. It often assumes a customer base. This no longer works. Precisely which value chain defines the business, and which competitive set defines the context, are now part of the question, not premises of the answer. It is necessary to deconstruct one's own business mentally, rethinking how the pieces fit together from first principles. It is necessary then to deconstruct it economically, refocusing the value chain around a competitively defensible core.

If not, someone, at some point, will deconstruct the business for you.

Summary

Many business and industrial structures are based on the inefficient flow of information. But the increasing power of information technology will eliminate many of the traditional bottlenecks and asymmetries in information. In particular, says **Philip Evans**, the traditional tradeoff between "richness" and "reach" – between the richness of information exchanges and the number of people with whom those exchanges can take place – will disappear. This change is being driven by massive growth in the number of people with direct access to the internet and by the fact that more and more applications are developing universal standards, not only for transmission but for the way information is stored and accessed. Large numbers of individuals will be able to obtain, manipulate and evaluate information – about personal finance, say – with the ease of professionals. As a result, there will be less incentive for them to accept the conveniently bundled offerings of traditional businesses, which may have to redefine themselves in order to survive. Over the next two decades, such shifts will transform not only traditional relationships with consumers but also corporate supply chains and even organizational hierarchies.

This article draws on ideas described at greater length in Blown to Bits: *How the New Economics of Information Transforms Strategy* by Philip Evans and Thomas Wurster, Harvard Business School Press, 2000.

Information resources: don't attract, addict

by Jeffrey F. Rayport

It's everyone's business nightmare. You build the best mousetrap, you let all your customers or constituents know, and the world does not beat a path to your door. There is no better recipe for professional aggravation and despair in the knowledge management field.

Yet that's exactly what every information officer I know has experienced at one point or another in building knowledge resources for a company or its clients. It's not enough to build a better intranet or extranet or website and let people know about it. Even if they initially arrive in droves to pay homage to the new offering, it's retention that counts. As anyone who does business on the internet knows, getting traffic is easy but making it stick is hard.

The lifeblood of business?

Those information professionals who have built loyal followings (either internal or external to the organization) for their information resources all have one strategy in common. They don't aim merely to attract users to their offerings; their goal is to addict. If knowledge is mission-critical in business, they reason, then users should seek it out with a sense of raw and visceral desire. If deep, rich information is the lifeblood of business, then users should develop a thirst for it at the source. This is tantamount to addiction – and, for information officers building information resources, that has to be the goal.

Consider, for example, a chief technology officer at one of the major record labels in Hollywood. Two years ago, his job depended on selling into his organization the value of a new global intranet to support sales and marketing staff, artists and musicians, financial planners, and everyone else who had a role at the label, including the pop stars themselves. These were extremely talented people, but they did not exactly present the profile of early adopters of high-tech services. Yet they desperately needed a set of knowledge resources to do their jobs – from radio play by station and by minute in every major market throughout the US to takeaway menus for recommended Chinese restaurants in New York and Los Angeles.

Of course, like most large organizations, the label's operations were geographically far-flung and dispersed. Some staffers worked from the road and in their home offices, while others dwelt in leather- and marble-lined splendor in imposing offices located at a hotspot along Sunset Boulevard. So it was not obvious how the chief technologist might successfully convince his colleagues to dive into his intranet. And e-mail was not going to make the sale, since most of his colleagues did not use it – even though they had all been issued with laptops and PCs.

His only option was to apply some entertainment industry savvy to what was an information systems problem. He began tinkering with his product until he got the ratings, literally, that the job required.

It's the beauty of life in the digital age that every click of a mouse and every move on a screen leaves a digital trace: an electronic fingerprint. There are dark, Orwellian aspects to this fundamental truth but the bright side is that it's easier to determine what people want and give it to them – if you bother to pay attention.

At the record label, our technologist started to assemble his staff of programmers and editors at the beginning of every business day to review the data from his intranet's server, which indicated how much use each of its pages, features and functions received. TV executives, he reasoned, wake up to the Nielsen ratings every morning; they live and die according to those numbers. Why should knowledge management professionals have it any different?

Out of these meetings, the concept was born. The goal was not merely to attract, but to addict. Using server data, the information services staff could determine – without invading any individual's right to privacy – what the organization's population was using a lot, a little and not at all. They then "programmed" the intranet to respond to preferences and needs within the organization.

People began increasingly to depend on the intranet, just as the information and knowledge they most desired became increasingly focused and relevant. If the ultimate goal was to make the intranet mission-critical, then addiction was the way to get there. And addiction came (as it does in TV, music and movies) from the discovery or creation of a compelling need, followed by the fulfilment of that need in escalating doses.

Creating addiction

There are, of course, lots of ways to build addiction to knowledge and information. Paying attention to the feedback loops intrinsic to electronic networks is just one of them. Indeed, you might argue that not all organizations have the luxury of analyzing "ratings" to drive knowledge programming. In order to have ratings, you have to have users. And for you to have users, the world must first have beaten a path to your intranet, extranet or website. So what's the solution?

Companies I work with have developed a variety of approaches to their intranets. But there is a lot of common ground. Because the goal is addiction, the strategies they share have nothing to do with technology and everything to do with the psychology of human behavior in organizations and communities. To put this differently, the approaches that work have to do with people rather than high-tech engineering.

Along with the time-honored maxims (make the intranet easy to use, build an intuitive interface, ensure speed and reliability), several such strategies can be outlined.

Be viral

Several years ago, I wrote an article for a new US business magazine that dismayed many readers. It suggested that marketers could learn a lot by studying

43

that scourge of modern medicine, the virus. The logic was simple: marketers are constantly trying to "infect" markets with ideas about products, brands or concepts, in the belief that infection will breed conditions characterized by desired behaviors (talking about or buying a given product or brand). Given the notorious effectiveness of viruses as opposed to common-or-garden bacteria, this seemed a reasonable, albeit unappealing, notion.

Getting people to use information resources means building the need into the fabric of their business lives in a manner similar to that of a virus. In fact, viruses often triumph by co-opting existing, often social, behavior and using human contact to propagate themselves. Driving intranet use is not so different. Many companies start by using the technology platform to do lots of things that no-one in the organization has ever done before; this way, information systems people can show off the capabilities of new technology. But the real effect comes from showcasing new ways to support what everyone in the organization already does all the time. The more pressing the activity, the better a candidate it becomes – no matter how trivial or initially unproductive it may appear.

For example, if there is a propensity among staff to check the weather obsessively, to review sports scores or to follow the stock market, that's what should go on the intranet. If there is a race to order the best lunches delivered to the office every Friday at midday, that's what should go into the system. Once addiction is established, more substantive content may follow. Being viral is the power of harnessing pre-existing patterns of desire to shift usage into the new information resource.

Build word-of-mouth

No-one in organizations that are not already tech-savvy will read memos or e-mails and instantly rush to the intranet to see what the information department has done. Once pressing activities within the organization have been drawn into the web, the challenge becomes one of spreading social acceptance.

At Southwest Airlines, the highly successful discount carrier in the US, the litmus test for new pricing policies is that air fares should be low enough for people to talk about them at cocktail parties. If you're aiming for dramatic impact, this is a simple, and practical, criterion to apply. If you want intranet addiction, the intranet needs to achieve that word-of-mouth effect.

Reinforce the positive

This is the concept that our music industry professionals applied. If you are not interested in results, you won't know what works. And without paying scrupulous, attention to such information in real time, there is no reason to expect that users within the organization will want to use it in real time (or at all). Discovering what is building usage and reinforcing it is critical. Such responsiveness is so unusual among corporate information systems departments that it alone will be cause for comment. And comment will drive trial by others and subsequently addiction.

To be mission critical, act mission critical

Too often, I encounter knowledge managers who lament the lack of attention their activities have attracted. They declaim that information is the lifeblood of business, yet their colleagues eschew the riches these managers lay before them. In many cases they have a point, especially when the intranet they have created is well conceived and richly populated with information. But more often than not there is a reason why their offerings are not taking hold – and it has nothing to do with the often-deplored apathy of the masses. Rather, lack of adoption often has everything to do with a mission-critical application that does not act mission-critical. There are many ways of failing to act mission-critical. Among them are being rude to users, ignoring the cost of downtime, and failing to respond to requests or to update the content frequently.

No-one will come to depend on an intranet as the lifeblood of the business if it is slow, poorly designed, difficult to navigate, unresponsive to feedback or simply unreliable. Indeed, the worst of all possible worlds is to create an application that is mission-critical, convince an entire population of users of that truth, and then fail to deliver it in a robust form.

No-one will trust themselves to become addicted to knowledge resources unless they know that escalating doses, with bullet-proof reliability, are but a mouse-click away – and that when they're not, the information services staff will respond straight away. No-one should ever aspire to addiction to a drug that's in short or serendipitous supply, yet that's exactly what information on an unreliable intranet is like. It's no wonder addiction fails to take hold.

Promote lock-in

Ultimately, of course, the goal is to make an intranet indispensable to a company. That means finding a way to cement its role as central to the standards and protocols of how a company does business. One way to achieve this is to target the most essential activities performed in a business – submitting sales reports or preparing travel expense reimbursements – and to make of them things of digital beauty and elegance.

After all, the goal of every intranet should be to become the operating system of the organization; it should provide the platform upon which all other activities become the value-adding applications layer. This depends upon making the intranet the locus of a set of essential business or organizational activities, so it becomes the virtual glue for an otherwise physical enterprise. When a critical mass of such activities belong self-evidently to the intranet, then lock-in has occurred. And the potential for addiction begins.

It's not enough simply to build the information resource, because users won't come on their own. And making sure that they do has nearly everything to do with people and organizations, and much less to do with information and technology. Put differently, the intranet may be necessary but not sufficient for the task. What is sufficient is the social engineering. And addiction must be the goal.

Summary

As information officers know all too well, building an intranet is only half the battle. The other half consists in getting people in the organization actually to use it. The best strategy, says **Jeffrey Rayport**, is to make it central to users' working lives – in short, to addict them. Like viruses, intranets need to exploit existing behavior and thus must support activities (however trivial) that employees regularly perform. They need to do so well that employees will spread the word among themselves – the "cocktail gossip" test. The ultimate goal is to promote lock-in by making the intranet the medium of choice for essential business processes. Information officers should pay close attention to the "audience ratings" that different features generate, and ensure that their intranets are run as mission-critical applications.

Attention: the next information frontier

by Thomas H. Davenport

It is common to hear talk of the information economy today, and indeed information seems to be what economic actors often exchange. But economies are generally built on exchange of what is scarce, and scarcity is not a term you'd associate with the business information environment. The truly scarce resource, and thus the most likely currency of the new economy, is actually human attention.

Information is certainly not in short supply. Who has time to read all the books and magazines they'd like to, answer all the voicemails, letters and e-mails (192 messages in all media per employee per day, according to a recent study by the Institute for the Future) click on all the web pages they're tempted to – and still do some real work?

We have become very accomplished at providing access to information and we can even "push" information to those who need it – or at some point thought they needed it. The internet and associated technologies have made easily accessible a good portion of the world's digitized information. Information providers of various sorts both within and outside our companies earnestly work to produce more information content.

But while technology and information production have increased the amount and availability of information, they have done little or nothing for human attention. This remains constant and our ability to allocate it has not been affected by technology. In fact, some observers have speculated that businesspeople are increasingly contracting "attention deficit syndrome" because the overwhelming volume of information limits their ability to focus on any given piece. If organizations are to ensure that their most important information is actually seen and attended to, they must begin to face the issue of attention management – understanding where attention goes and helping employees to allocate it effectively.

Providers of information must also begin to think about attention. If the information you produce or distribute does not get attention, you might as well not bother. Perhaps the least attention-grabbing information in organizations comes from the IT group. Numbers printed in rows and columns do not attract much attention, whether they are on paper or a computer screen. Dry textual information is not much more appealing. Information providers would be wise to take lessons from the various "attention industries" – publishing, entertainment, advertising and the like – to understand how to attract and keep attention.

Attention is not a new subject; it was of great interest to the philosopher and psychologist William James in the 19th century, for example. However, with the exception of a few observers (such as Richard Lanham, professor of English at UCLA and author of *The Electronic Word*), little attention has been paid to the subject within the context of information and IT.

Thus far technology has been more the problem than the solution with regard to attention. It has produced substantially more information without giving us new tools to attend to it. In the future it is likely that multimedia business information will be as attention-getting as video games are today, and we may even have technology that monitors whether we are paying attention at any given time. Both carmakers and airplane manufacturers already have devices that can tell if the person at the controls is awake.

Technologists and everyone else have a lot to learn about managing attention, so let me suggest four non-technical themes that can serve as starting points for a dialogue about the issue. They are, in no particular order: medium, design, participation and content. If any of those words got your attention, read on.

Medium

Please excuse the hypocritical nature of my argument. I'm attempting to communicate the importance of attention but I'm using unadulterated text – perhaps the least engaging medium of the age – to do it. At least the text is printed in an attractive book format, which I presume is an attention-getting mechanism. But we have got to move beyond text and print as the preferred media for our information.

The alternative is as familiar as television: audio and video. There is probably something in our genes that predisposes us to attend to images, motion and noise; what once helped to ensure survival should now be exploited for effective attention management. Instead of writing this chapter I should be producing a video on attention – not a talking-head broadcast but rather a lifelike story, play or vignette that draws your attention to the topic of attention. We have all got to become video producers for the information that really matters.

When we do employ text, it should be framed in the context of a story. Human brains respond well to stories and have been doing so for thousands of years, as cognitive scientist Roger Schank has noted. Stories provide more context and meaning than stand-alone facts. Companies are increasingly likely to hire professional storytellers to make important information more attention-getting.

For evidence of the power of stories, one need only examine *The Goal*, a "business novel" by Elihu Goldratt and Jeff Cox about quality in manufacturing and supply chain processes. This book about a somewhat dry business issue has been a perennial best-seller. If we have got to read business books, they might as well be novels.

Design

Realistically, of course, not all information will be presented in video and audio format or in stories. For the remainder we need to get much better at information design – how information looks on the screen and page, and how it draws your attention to what is important.

Wisdom is particularly lacking in the design of online information. Online information providers in most companies know only the most primitive guidelines: do not use too many fonts, graphics are good, use big buttons for the activities most likely to be undertaken by users, leave some white space. External designers are available to upgrade a company's internal information offerings but most of them are largely focused on print media. And unfortunately, there are not many schools where one can study online information design – perhaps because there are few knowledgeable professors available to teach it.

The good news is that some experts have written books that, if properly attended to, can radically upgrade anyone's information design skills. Anything by Richard

47

Saul Wurman (general information design), Clement Mok (online design) and Edward Tufte (quantitative and graphical information) can be trusted.

Participation

I know of no good data on this, but I'm confident that the single most important factor in attention management is the level of participation by the receiver. Again, the format of this book is inconsistent with my message; you as the reader are the passive receiver of its information, and it is difficult to get your attention in that kind of role.

If I'm really interested in engaging you, I'll get you involved in the information as an active participant. In a business school case study, for example, you are asked to play the role of the protagonist and you are more likely to think about the issues. If I really want your attention for a particular topic, I'll ask you to present it yourself. Any teacher knows that the best way to learn a subject thoroughly is to offer a course in it.

The participation factor accounts for the growth in popularity of such "information experiences" as simulations, scenarios and "war games"; the next best thing to learning from an actual business situation is pretending to be there. In some cases the experience can be very lifelike. At the Lexus division of Toyota, when the chief engineer of the first Lexus car wanted designers to understand the Western concept of luxury, he chose not to give them reports and statistics about it. Instead, he sent several key designers to a California resort to live and play with the American rich for two weeks. Similarly, Nike sends market researchers out to urban playgrounds to find out what hip teenagers want to wear.

Even the career paths of employees can be structured to produce effective information experiences. For example, if a company believes that it is important for marketing people to know something about manufacturing, it can put them to work there for a while. This rotational approach to staffing is common in large Japanese companies.

Content

The nature of information content is an important factor in whether people pay attention. This should be obvious but judging from corporate practice it is not. Few organizations have put much effort into determining what kind of content managers and employees really want and need. Part of the difficulty is that employees cannot easily articulate their information needs. Discovering what these are therefore requires a high level of human effort by analysts who are familiar with not only IT but also the array of information available and the oddities of human behavior.

Peter Drucker has long discussed the information content problem, arguing that senior executives primarily need information on customers, competitors and markets, whereas IT groups furnish them with internally focused data instead. One academic study found that information consumers paid most attention to information about people – who is joining and who is leaving the organization, who is rising and who is falling, and why. Of course, this type of information is in relatively short supply in most companies (especially the leaving and falling parts). A more extensive study, carried out by US academics Sharon McKinnon and William Bruns, of what information managers actually use in manufacturing companies revealed that managers were typically more interested in operational data than financial data, simply because they felt that operations were more amenable to change than finances.

One implication of the importance of content in managing attention is that all information is not equal in its importance and the level of attention that should be devoted to it. Packaging information in an attention-getting way requires considerable resources and not all information deserves such preparation. The creation of information experiences, as described in the previous section, is particularly difficult and time-consuming for both producers and consumers.

Thus someone in an organization needs to decide which information is important for employees to consume. This will vary with regard to the organization's business environment and strategy. Therefore someone who is highly familiar with the company's markets, offerings and strategic direction should be responsible for determining what information should be emphasized. This will rarely be someone from the IT group; more often it will be a strategic planner or senior general manager. These executives can determine whether an organization needs to place primary emphasis on information about customers, finances, competitors, external regulation or some other business domain. Then the most important information can be effectively packaged to gather the attention it deserves. Otherwise the organization's attention will go to those who are best at "marketing" their information, regardless of its importance.

If you made it this far, I've succeeded in keeping your attention. Why not start thinking about how to get and keep it for the information you provide? Start by simply observing the customers of your information in order to get some idea of whether they are paying attention or not. Given all the information that is contending for attention today, your information could undoubtedly use some help.

Summary

The amount of information with which people are bombarded has grown enormously in recent years, yet the human capacity for attention has remained constant. Therefore the time has come, says **Thomas Davenport**, to pay attention to attention. Otherwise managers will find that the information that is most important to them and their employees will simply be swamped. The four most important aspects to consider are: the medium used to convey the information (an audio-visual narrative, for example, is far more attractive than a set of printed facts); the design of printed or online pages (many companies seem to grasp only the most rudimentary principles); the level of active participation by the people at whom the information is aimed (perhaps the most critical factor in attention management); and the content (is it what people really want and need?). As a first step, companies should at least see how much attention the information they currently put out receives.

Suggested further reading

Goldratt, E. and Jeff Cox, (1994) *The Goal: A Process of Ongoing Improvement*, North Barrington, MA: North River Press, 2nd edn.

Lanham, R. (1995) *The Electronic Word: Democracy, Technology, and the Arts*, Chicago: University of Chicago Press.

McKinnon, S. and Bruns, W. (1992) *The Information Mosaic*, Boston, MA: Harvard Business School Press.

Mok, C. (1996) *Designing Business: Multiple Media, Multiple Disciplines*, Basingstoke: Macmillan Computer Publishing.

Schank, R. (1990) *Tell Me A Story: A New Look at Real and Artificial Memory*, New York: Scribner's.

Tufte, E.R. (1992) *The Visual Display of Quantitative Information*, Graphics Press.

Wurman, R.S. (1989) *Information Anxiety*, New York: Doubleday.

15 Oct 1998

DIGITAL BUSINESS

Cathy Newman finds newspaper executives relying on their brands to fight off new online rivals for revenue

Financial Times

by Cathy Newman

Several newspapers can be found free of charge on the internet: a growing number of people have taken to reading their favourite papers online, at home or in the office, instead of venturing out to a newsagent and opening their wallets.

The implications are worrying for national newspaper owners such as the UK's Daily Mail and General Trust. Peter Williams, finance director, agrees the plethora of free news and information on the internet is a challenge for titles like the *Daily Mail*.

However, he says, DMGT has avoided cannibalising sales of its print newspaper by offering themed internet sites related to the *Daily Mail* rather than reproducing the title wholesale online.

One of DMGT's main consumer web sites is Soccernet, a football themed site. The group is also considering developing an internet version of the *Daily Mail*'s Femail women's section.

Although Mr Williams does not feel too threatened by free editorial online, he does have concerns about classified advertising on the internet. "That is the big area where we will be affected because the internet search engine is suited to someone finding the right sort of car and making the transaction," he says.

New media ventures like The Monster Board, the US-backed online recruitment company founded in 1994, are trespassing on the territory of traditional media groups. DMGT's regional newspaper group – Northcliffe Newspapers – is more threatened by digital business than its national titles, Mr Williams believes. Classified advertising represents between 30–40 per cent of Northcliffe's total revenues, compared with between 10–15 per cent of the national titles' turnover.

In response to this threat Northcliffe and other regional groups formed AdHunter, an online classified advertising database. The consortium has one big advantage over newer competitors – its well-known

local brands. "You go into AdHunter through your local newspaper," Mr Williams explains. "On the internet, the brands and quality of the product will win out."

David Landau, chairman and co-founder of *Loot*, a UK-based classified advertising publication, agrees. "There are now more than 1,000 small, new classified web sites in the US. They are not making it because they do not have brand recognition."

The company now feels confident enough about its appeal over other, less well established online rivals, to have started charging for its internet edition. For £1.30, you can browse 14 regional editions from 6am the day they are published.

If you bought them all in their print format, it would cost nearly £20. In the first two days after it started charging, 3,500 people paid to view *Loot* over the internet. The company sells 300,000 print editions each week.

Mr Landau is positive about the impact digital business has already had. It has helped *Loot* expand into different fields. The decision to introduce its own loans service to finance readers' purchases, for example, was partly inspired by the ease with which the new venture could be publicised over the internet. The company did not need to go to the expense of advertising Loot Loans with flyers or other printed matter.

DMGT, although it does not charge for access to its consumer web sites, also benefits from a fee for entry to parts of the site owned by Euromoney Publications, the financial publisher in which DMGT has a 71 per cent stake. People are prepared to pay for specialised, detailed information delivered in an easily searchable online format, Mr Williams says.

He also believes the internet has helped DMGT broaden into other areas. Soccernet has set up a shop selling football merchandise, and even though access to the site is free it breaks even because the group gets a commission on the sale of goods.

Continued

But as DMGT begins to enter new fields it has also left old ones. The group once printed all its newspapers on its own presses but it now uses 10 plants owned by other companies. The unpicking of that particular part of the value chain allowed DMGT to make cost savings. "We outsourced printing because it's extremely expensive to build print plants," Mr Williams says.

He maintains there are other ways in which digital business, far from undermining the group's traditional economic basis, may help it by driving newsprint prices down. "There have been

suggestions in the States there hasn't been the same increase in demand for newsprint because more classified advertising is going online," he says.

Mr Landau is perhaps more willing than Mr Williams to embrace digital business, because *Loot,* launched in 1985, has less of a heritage in print media. He is confident that, perhaps as soon as a decade hence, *Loot* will do most of its business online. "If we managed to sell all our copies via the internet we'd be immensely rich," he says. "We wouldn't have to pay commission to newsagents, wholesalers, distributors; and we wouldn't have to pay for paper."

Beyond knowledge management: how companies mobilize experience

by Yury Boshyk

Executives can be forgiven for being a little confused about the new terminology around what used to be called "knowhow" or, in the Japanese context, "business wisdom". We hear and read a lot about "the learning organization", "working knowledge", "knowledge networks", "business intelligence", "competitor intelligence" and especially "knowledge management". These terms and concepts may be popular but to many people – including academics studying these issues – they are confusing and sometimes imprecise.

Unfortunately, executives cannot afford imprecision on such matters. They must be very clear about these definitions, their strengths and weaknesses: the future of their company's performance depends on it. They must look at the fundamental requirements for using these tools but also recognize that they are more than tools and techniques – they are a way of life and the most important way to gain strategic advantage in the new competitive environment.

Without doubt, knowledge management (KM) is the most influential of all the above concepts. One reason for this is that new technological and software developments have allowed us to capture and share information throughout the organization, be it from the competitor intelligence unit in sales and marketing or the person in charge of intellectual capital in human resources. Just as importantly, we can now measure the results of this process. For example, there are several studies that purport to show that 20 to 30 per cent of company resources are wasted due to "reinventing the wheel" over and over again. As one Hewlett-Packard executive put it: "if HP knew what HP knows, we would be three times as profitable."

But attractive though it may be, KM is not easily accessible to everyone. A company's culture and values play a decisive role. It is no secret that the most valuable competitive intelligence and knowledge comes overwhelmingly from within one's own organization and from one's own people. One study, for example, found that two-thirds of managers get their information and knowledge from face-to-face meetings or phone conversations. But is there a supportive culture that encourages openness and sharing of knowledge? One strong clue that such a culture does not exist is when IT or IS people are put in charge of KM. They should only play a supportive role. The concepts of KM are essentially people-focused and technology-enabled, not technology-driven.

KM systems are expensive and the technology often takes longer to implement than originally planned. Software company SAP estimates that it costs at least $100,000–$200,000 to set up its system for a medium-sized company and that customization can add to this substantially. Another problem is that KM systems generate so much information and data that they can inhibit and even undermine clarity of perception, thought and executive decision-making. After all, these concepts and processes are only worthwhile when they are actionable.

KM and beyond

The concepts that cluster around KM have many things in common. They all refer to processes, methods and systems for generating, gathering, analyzing, organizing, disseminating and applying collective past, present (and sometimes future) experiences, information and understanding for the benefit of an organization or society.

Some of these concepts complement one another better than others. Take, for example, the concept and practice of "competitive intelligence" and "business intelligence". Competitive intelligence is mainly focused on competitors, whereas business intelligence is broader in scope, dealing with the company's general business environment as well; it therefore considers matters such as government regulation. These two in turn fit into the broader notion of KM, which has been defined – by Thomas Stewart in *Fortune* magazine – as "the management of . . . intellectual material that has been formalized, captured and leveraged to produce a higher-valued asset". Anne Stewart, in *CIO* magazine, has described it as "concerted efforts to capture, organize, and share what employees know".

Of all the concepts I mentioned at the beginning, it seems that the "learning organization" has the least support from executives. While they have little difficulty in understanding the concept, they do not clearly understand the processes and are skeptical about the practicality of some of its methods and philosophy.

In the end, however, the biggest issue for executives is linking KM to financial results. Many companies have not found a satisfactory way to correlate investments in KM with improvements in the bottom line. So it is natural to look for alternatives to KM.

One that has emerged recently is "mobilization of collective intelligence" (MCI). Its proponents – such as Bernhard Prestel of Geneva consultancy TC Team Consult AG – speak of it as being a step beyond, rather than a substitute for, KM. They argue that "mobilizing" is more dynamic than "managing" and therefore lends itself more to innovation. Furthermore, intelligence is more important to a company than

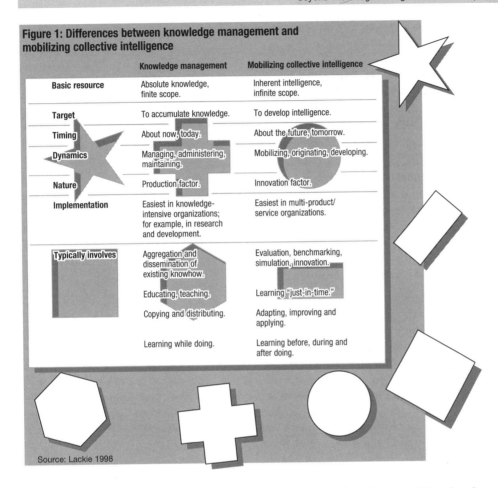

Figure 1: Differences between knowledge management and mobilizing collective intelligence

	Knowledge management	Mobilizing collective intelligence
Basic resource	Absolute knowledge, finite scope.	Inherent intelligence, infinite scope.
Target	To accumulate knowledge.	To develop intelligence.
Timing	About now, today.	About the future, tomorrow.
Dynamics	Managing, administering, maintaining.	Mobilizing, originating, developing.
Nature	Production factor.	Innovation factor.
Implementation	Easiest in knowledge-intensive organizations; for example, in research and development.	Easiest in multi-product/service organizations.
Typically involves	Aggregation and dissemination of existing knowhow.	Evaluation, benchmarking, simulation, innovation.
	Educating, teaching.	Learning "just-in-time."
	Copying and distributing.	Adapting, improving and applying.
	Learning while doing.	Learning before, during and after doing.

Source: Lackie 1998

knowledge – MCI advocates companies to consider whether they would rather have an intelligent or a knowledgeable team of executives.

According to Gordon Lackie, until recently head of corporate management training at Ballast Nedam NV, there are three main types of collective intelligence: "the intelligence of individual employees; intelligence relating to the organization (including values, systems, and procedures); intelligence in terms of markets, clients, partners, and suppliers (including product-market mixes, market share, and profitability)".

Figure 1 summarizes the differences between KM and MCI. However, there is plenty of common ground. Lackie, for example, argues that both "can only be developed and deployed on the basis of a strong learning organization, culture and attitude – a culture in which people work together to learn, and learn to work together".

Work on implementing MCI has already begun. Somfy, for example, a French multinational which manufactures automatic shutter controls, has reported positive results from its implementation programme. Several questions still remain, such as whether MCI comprises a particular set of methods, whether those methods work globally, and whether MCI can be used in large companies. Generally, its pioneers have tended to emphasize the more active, dynamic and co-operative nature of wealth creation through leveraging intelligence, knowledge and understanding. However, at this early stage perhaps we should keep in mind the

53

old CIA adage never to rely on just one source – and therefore not rely on just one concept or process.

Mobilizing collective experience

Whether we support KM or other concepts and approaches, it is worth remembering that many societies, countries and companies have managed to mobilize collective experience effectively – and have done so without getting overly involved with technology and processes or becoming too burdened with costs and self-inflicted complexity.

Postwar reconstruction

After the second world war both Japan and Germany had to rebuild themselves economically. They did this in a number of ways, including a systematic gathering of international experiences and benchmarking of best practices. Teams of engineers, managers and scientists travelled extensively to ensure that their efforts were in line with the best the world had to offer. Entire industries and leading companies were part of the process.

Closing the generation gap

Some companies preserve both the collective historical company experience and encourage innovation through the presence of "mentors" or "elder statesman", usually very senior executives or retired executives who are deeply aware of past accomplishments and issues. This is often the case in Nordic companies; one that comes to mind is Sweden's Skandia, which has undergone remarkable change – from the championing of "intellectual capital" to the development of "future centres" – while maintaining an excellent record of growth and profitability. The company has an in-house "eminence" who, although officially retired, acts as a "collective memory" and source of ideas.

The "Unilever way"

Yet another way of innovation through mobilizing experience is what has become known in some circles as the "Unilever way" – spreading innovation by moving people around. A classic example was Unilever's discovery of the need for smaller soap sizes in emerging economies after a local manufacturer made serious inroads into the company's market share in India. The executive in charge in the region rose to the challenge and created a new product in order to compete and soon profits were restored. The experience was then duplicated in Latin America, not through any formal process of sharing or dissemination of learning – this was before KM was widely discussed – but because that was where the executive was posted next.

Global mobilization

As the cold war came to an end about a decade ago, centrally planned economies fell like dominoes while previously introverted and highly protectionist societies became more open at a very rapid pace. This provided remarkable opportunities – and challenges – for business.

In time, and through a process of trial and error, major companies began to see common patterns in widely separated markets – in Latin America, southern Africa, central and eastern Europe, China and south-east Asia. By identifying patterns in a market of around 3 billion people, companies have been able to leverage their experience for global strategic advantage. Below are three examples of how multinationals have succeeded in mobilizing their collective experience in emerging markets.

Appraising the past

Recently a European cement company was interested in entering the Asian market. After some discussion, the executive team decided that it should first analyze the company's previous experiences in emerging markets to see if it possessed the necessary capabilities. Accordingly, the head of human resources and organizational development put teams of young "high potentials" on the project to see what the company had "learned and earned".

Over about six months the "youngsters" were assigned to country businesses and given free rein to look into what the company had done well (and badly) in the past, and to find what was needed to enter the markets under consideration. Their findings were discussed in a series of programme retreats by senior managers, whose comments on the reports and recommendations on how to share the lessons learned were subsequently discussed by the board. The company is now more confident that it has the managerial talent to enter most markets it chooses and that it has learned from this process of historical appraisal and reflection.

Reality checks

China can be a difficult market for some companies and this was indeed the case for General Electric of the US. Soon after the market opened up the company found that preferential treatment was being given to companies with a presence there. GE realized that it had to become an insider – to become local – by moving rapidly from just importing and licensing to assembly in the country and then to manufacturing, sourcing and developing engineering capacity there.

Then a second major lesson was learned – that China wanted GE to help it develop. The government insisted that the various GE divisions should offer a comprehensive and clear portfolio of goods and services that would help the country's national economic development. Did GE fit the national strategy of China and was it in China for the long term? GE quickly adjusted and came as a united group to do business with the Chinese government.

GE also learned two other crucial lessons: that being in China was a balancing act between short-term access and survival and long-term autonomous market penetration, and that such markets required tough decisions up-front.

Finally, the company learned that these four best practices – essentially "reality checks" – were also transferable to other major emerging markets, in particular Russia. It took GE several years and some bitter experiences to come to this conclusion but to its credit the transfer of learning was accomplished. It is a rare achievement for a large, decentralized organization such as GE to learn to change its tactics – and then to pass this learning on.

Learning at the top

Emerging markets are high-risk markets for most Western executives and companies. A thorough risk analysis by one's own staff is the usual starting point. However, when oil company Conoco was considering investing in northern Russia after the collapse of the Soviet Union, it went beyond this. It took the approach that all executive committee members, including the chief executive, were responsible for coming to an understanding of the market and society in question. Outside

15 Oct 1998

DIGITAL BUSINESS

Supermarkets take on the high street leviathans: Banking services have given stores the opportunity to exploit the strength of their brands, writes Christopher Brown-Humes

Financial Times

by Christopher Brown-Humes

"We are bringing more of the high street into the supermarket." This is how Stuart Sinclair, chief executive of Tesco Personal Finance, explains moves by supermarkets into banking.

TPF, a joint venture between Tesco and Royal Bank of Scotland, began operating last year, one of a new breed of supermarket banks to challenge the high street leviathans. It has accumulated 700,000 customers and more than £700 million in deposits in a year.

Mr Sinclair says it was logical for supermarkets to enter banking after their earlier forays into other areas outside their traditional domain, such as dry cleaning, wines and spirits, photo-processing and petrol. He suggests it was also natural for them to follow other new entrants, specifically phone-based providers such as Direct Line in insurance and First Direct, into the market. "Supermarket banking is an extension of the new paradigm – non branch-based banking. We are contributing to the unbundling of financial services," he says.

Banking has given supermarkets the chance to exploit the strength of their brands in an area where there is dissatisfaction with traditional providers. The supermarkets' biggest advantages are low costs and "warm" customer bases – shoppers who do not need to be solicited or cold-called. They do not operate branch networks; moreover they have low customer acquisition costs. Because they are pitching for business from their own shoppers, their advertising bill amounts to little more than the posters in their stores. "One of our great advantages is that we have so many millions of visits a week," says Mr Sinclair.

Low costs have enabled the supermarkets to offer competitive rates, with TPF's deposit rate of 6.75 per cent twice the level offered on many bank accounts.

The first profits from the business are forecast for next year. Neither Tesco, with its RBS link, nor J. Sainsbury, which has teamed up with Bank of Scotland, are going it alone in banking. Both retailers rely on their partners for fundamental expertise. Mr Sinclair says Tesco needs RBS's expertise in areas like risk pricing for loans and credit cards and servicing and processing. The bank also provides call centre and back office functions. Tesco brings ideas on merchandising, customer acquisition and product design.

So far the partnership has worked happily – although an earlier link between Tesco and National Westminster Bank foundered, apparently because of NatWest's concern about Tesco's banking ambitions. Some would not be surprised if the RBS link is also severed eventually as the overlap between the activities of TPF and RBS grows.

It is generally assumed that sophisticated digital or internet-based technologies are necessary for these ventures to succeed, but Mr Sinclair says the supermarket advantage is not primarily in technology. "Technology is not central to the business. What is essential is that we offer good value, transparent products very simply."

He also says TPF is not recruiting customers aggressively, with its services being bought, rather than sold. Hence, the retailer is not yet using the information gleaned from its Clubcard loyalty scheme to solicit banking customers from among its shoppers. Nor is it targeting non-Tesco shoppers, in the way that the Prudential, for example, is targeting non-Pru customers through its Egg direct banking venture. "Our first million or two customers will come entirely through self-selection," says Mr Sinclair.

Nor is TPF trying to build relationships with its bank customers. "We are not emphasising relation-

Continued

ships in the short term because we think a lot of customers simply want a good deal," says Mr Sinclair.

TPF is offering savings accounts, credit cards, loans, home insurance, travel insurance, and – through a link with Scottish Widows – pensions. Mr Sinclair says these are all products where customers seem willing to shop around.

Mortgages are not yet offered – given current tight pricing – but might be added to the product list. Only current accounts seem out of the question in the long term – partly because they involve high transaction costs and partly because customers seem loath to switch away from the big high street banks.

The latter are starting to react to the challenge posed by new entrants: borrowing costs on personal loans have fallen and deposit account rates are keener. Moreover, they have become more active in phone banking.

But the high street banks still regard the supermarkets more as a nuisance than a real threat. They continue to make large profits, based on customer inertia from accounts held over many years. The banks also believe that the supermarkets may do well in some simple products – such as deposits – but they will struggle to be successful with pensions, mortgages and credit cards. They could even end up alienating their shoppers if they refuse them loans or credit cards or evict them from their homes because of a mortgage default. The wider challenge for supermarket banks will be to offer attractive rates on products while making the sort of profits on the business shareholders expect.

experts were used sparingly (in a Delphi-like study) but it was the top team, under the guidance of a specially assigned and experienced person, that needed to build enough knowledge of the business environment to decide whether to go in.

The result was a deeper understanding of the risks and benefits. Because of this Conoco was able to gain the respect of its Russian partners and to make a profit on its investment. The ride on the rollercoaster of the emerging Russian market was smoother because executives were more able to anticipate problems and obstacles.

Business-driven action learning

As well as both requiring a strong culture of organizational learning, another common feature of KM and MCI is their unorthodox view of management development. This is bad news for many business schools. Companies that have embraced new thinking on mobilizing knowledge and intelligence – companies such as DuPont, Johnson & Johnson, Motorola and Siemens – are becoming more involved with business-driven action learning and less with traditional business schools. New types of learning and development are needed, such as "just-in time" information and analysis coaching, learning how to learn, continuous learning, personal development techniques that are tailored to individuals, and "real world", business-driven action learning projects – in which managers sharpen team-working and individual skills while tackling issues of immediate strategic concern.

Not all consulting firms are pleased with this development. Business issues that were previously given to them to study are now given to mobilized internal teams to analyze, advise on and sometimes act on. The knowledge and intelligence stays inside the company. If managed effectively, this approach helps solve business problems, develops new businesses, encourages real teamwork and hones leadership skills. According to the companies involved the results are very impressive.

Conclusion

The competitive environment is characterized by a concerted effort by corporations to harness the knowledge and intelligence of employees for sustainable and strategic advantage. Academics, practitioners and consulting and software companies advocate several concepts and processes. However, no simple process, concept or term, let alone software package, has yet been developed that can adequately integrate the various approaches. Executives should be cautious, even suspicious, of the technological and software solutions being offered, and skeptical that one approach or concept can do it all.

This is not surprising because we are dealing with knowledge, information and, above all, people. Add these together and we are, to paraphrase the physicist Freeman Dyson, "infinite in all directions". Nevertheless, companies are dauntlessly moving ahead with mobilizing the collective experience of their executives and managers. They understand that past experience has shown that a common purpose, culture and focus can mobilize people for profitable and personally rewarding creativity and achievement. The future competitive landscape demands no less.

Summary

Surveys indicate that most companies regard knowledge management as a critical part of their strategy. Yet the concept is problematic. The plethora of terms surrounding it is confusing, and implementation requires a learning culture already in place. It can be expensive. Perhaps worst of all, it is hard to correlate with financial performance. Hence it is not surprising that people are trying to devise refinements. An exciting one is "mobilising collective intelligence", which, according to its advocates, is more dynamic and adaptable than knowledge management. **Yury Boshyk**, however, counsels against reliance on only a single concept or process at this early stage. Using a number of examples, he describes how companies and even nations have managed to mobilize their collective experience without becoming bogged down in methodological or technological complexity.

Suggested further reading

Boshyk, Y. (ed.) (1999) *Business Driven Action Learning: Global Best Practices*, Basingstoke: Macmillan. (Contains over 20 company perspectives on the subject.)

Davenport, T.H. and Prusak, L. (1998) *Working Knowledge: How Organizations Manage What They Know*, Boston, MA: Harvard Business School Press, p. 12. (Cites the study into how managers gather information.)

Lackie, G.L. (1998) "The mobilization of collective intelligence: one step further than knowledge management", published in Dutch in *Tijdschrift voor Management Development* (September). (Includes the survey of KM in Dutch companies; I am grateful to the author for giving me the original English text of his article.)

Society for Competitive Intelligence Professionals – Cambridge (Massachusetts) Educational Programme, 16–17 November 1998. (A valuable source for some of the data used in this article.)

Tamotsu Nishizawa (1996) "Business studies and management education in Japan's economic development – an institutional perspective", in R.P. Amdam (ed.) *Management, Education and Competitiveness: Europe, Japan and the US*, London: Routledge, pp. 106–9. (On the rebuilding of Japan.)

In search of the ideal customer

by Eric K. Clemons

In the 1980s the main strategic driver for companies in a wide range of service industries was scale-based competition to reduce unit costs. In the 1990s it was loyalty-based retention programmes to reduce the acquisition costs associated with scale-based competition. Now the most successful service companies have moved to skill-based competition. Biggest is no longer necessarily seen as best; competition is less a matter of building scale than of locating, acquiring and retaining business under terms that make it profitable.

Due to pioneering work by Jim McCormick and Rick Spitler at the First Manhattan Consulting Group, it is now widely understood that there are extreme differences in customer profitability. In some segments of banking, such as credit cards, there may be a tenfold difference between the most profitable customers and average accounts. In general, it is estimated that the top two deciles of customer accounts generate more than 100 per cent of a bank's profits; the bottom two deciles actually generate losses for the bank that serves them.

This has profound strategic implications, especially for banks that are still engaging in scale-based competition. It is often more profitable to focus on attracting the best customers than to attempt to reduce costs; indeed, a recent First Manhattan study demonstrates that the most profitable banks are no longer the largest.

Significantly, understanding the importance of differences in customer profitability does not immediately translate into the ability to identify profitable customers or even profitable market segments. Companies therefore often resort to uniform pricing based on an average mark-up on their average costs. That is, if companies cannot distinguish between desirable and undesirable customers, they charge them all the same price; this is equivalent to overcharging the best customers and using the surplus generated to subsidize the remainder.

This subsidy represents a "money pump" that pipes money from some accounts to others and causes the best accounts to be overcharged; this in turn creates an opportunity for a new entrant to target the best customers, cut the pipe and rebate much of what would otherwise have been an overcharge, while still earning significant profits. Indeed, we have seen this phenomenon contribute to the rapid growth of some US credit card issuers, such as Capital One Financial.

Threats and opportunities

Information endowments may represent both competitive opportunities and competitive threats. Opportunities exist, of course, when a company can increase market share and margins, as the best new entrants have done in deregulating industries in the US and the UK. Threats arise when competitors know more than you do about the costs of serving individual customers – their claims frequency, future volumes of profitable business, or other measures of desirability – and use this information to target your best accounts:

- what if an insurance company's competitors could identify safe drivers more accurately and offer lower premiums to them and only to them?

- what if a mobile phone company's competitors could identify those customers who will use their mobiles at least 600 minutes a month and could offer lower rates to them and only to them?
- what if competitors of a hotel chain serving business travellers could identify those travellers who make extensive use of profitable additional hotel services, such as room service and hotel restaurants and bars, and could offer them better room rates, or superior service in some way?
- what if your competitors could identify customers who were easier to serve, or lower-risk, or made more extensive use of high-margin incremental fee-generating services, or who were more profitable than the norm for some other reason?

Extreme differences in customer profitability make these threats and opportunities greater. In the presence of such a steep customer profitability gradient, if one party can obtain information about the desirability of a potential account, you need to be able to do so too. Here we will explore ways in which entrants with an information advantage can adopt "cream-skimming" strategies that once-dominant competitors often cannot replicate.

Achieving information advantage

There are three principal mechanisms that companies use to increase their information endowment.

Data-mining

Data-mining entails looking for patterns in detailed customer data that may be correlated with customer profitability, or with changes in profitability. For example, credit card operations used to correlate profitability with seasonal workers (such as teachers) who owned their own homes (low risk), had held the same job for years (low risk) and were likely to travel over summer, carrying balances until the start of term and paying finance charges. And there is often a correlation between use of a credit card for cash advances and at fast food restaurants and a rapid decrease in the cardholder's creditworthiness.

The data for data-mining may come from the company's own transactional histories of current customers if it is exploring opportunities to cross- and up-sell. Alternatively, data may come from public sources or purchased proprietary data when a company tries to target potential applicants.

Signalling

Signalling actions are performed by potential customers to indicate their profitability or desirability. For example, a couple who have a small child and who want to rent a furnished home might volunteer to pay a double- or even triple-sized security deposit to signal their confidence that they are unlikely to damage the house or its contents.

Screening

Screening mechanisms are in many ways similar to signalling, except that they are designed by the seller; if the screening mechanism is properly designed then the buyer's selection of a particular option or package of options will correctly indicate his or her profitability to the seller, and will permit accurate pricing. A classic example of a screening mechanism is differential pricing of insurance coverage on the basis of policy exclusions and the size of deductibles; the idea is that a customer willing to accept a high deductible of £400 or more is signalling a sincere belief that he or she is unlikely to be involved in a traffic accident.

Screening provides an incentive for customers to reveal their desirability to the company accurately through their selection among product and service offerings; ideally, the bundle of offerings should be designed so that all customers would be profitable under the terms of the offerings they selected.

Each technique has pros and cons

Data-mining can yield powerful results but often does so without explanatory power. For example, having a poor credit history is often correlated with being a poor risk for car insurance but while numerous explanations can be created for this correlation, none has proved to be convincing. Other correlations purport to show that subscription to a given magazine or use of a credit card in a particular restaurant chain is related to the probability of credit card default and declaration of bankruptcy; again, no convincing explanation is available. A risk of data-mining, therefore, is that spurious relationships may show up as characteristics of the particular data set being studied; these relationships may not hold under future market conditions or for different sets of customers, and may lead to significant mistakes in pricing.

Signalling consists of actions on the part of customers or applicants to indicate their desirability. The classic, first published account of signalling was written in 1974 by Michael Spence, then dean of Harvard College, in an assessment of the economic value provided by obtaining a degree there. He concluded that the higher starting salaries of Harvard graduates could not be explained directly by the economic value of specific skills they had learned. Instead, he argued that by attending and graduating from Harvard, students were sending a credible signal to prospective employers about their general intelligence and skills.

We can readily see that the design of credible signalling mechanisms is in the best interest both of high-quality applicants (students who successfully graduate) and prospective employers who seek the best applicants (and are willing to reward them with better starting salaries). Unfortunately, it is difficult to calibrate signalling mechanisms because they are developed by individuals and are often unique to each individual. Generally, no single employer has enough experience with a given signal – a particular qualification from a particular institution, say – to interpret it with full certainty. The same goes for signals from customers.

Unlike signals, which are initiated by the customer and selected by the seller, screening mechanisms are designed and offered by the seller and selected by the customer. Let us continue with the example of attracting high-quality employees (in which we treat the applicant as the "customer" seeking a job and the employer as the "seller" of the job). Employers who wish to attract employees interested in their long-term career performance – people interested in working hard and doing accordingly well – could provide significant educational benefits. Employers who want their best and most-educated employees to remain with the company could also design a long-term compensation package, or provide educational loans that are forgiven over the course of several years, or demonstrate a history of promoting employees from within the company.

Screening mechanisms transfer information from the customer to the seller. The information transfer process begins when the company makes a binding commitment to a customer or applicant in order to obtain information; the process culminates when the customer makes his or her selection. For example, an

61

insurance company might seek to attract good drivers by offering a policy with an attractive premium and a very high deductible, as well as a more expensive policy with lower deductibles; similarly, a private medical insurance company might seek to attract healthy applicants by offering better rates but reducing coverage for illnesses that could be attributed to smoking, as well as offering a more expensive package with more complete medical coverage.

The difference in cost between the offerings in both cases reflects not only the different costs imposed by the different deductibles but also the difference in actuarial risk that results from the fact that each policy appeals to different drivers or different potential consumers of medical services. Each package represents a binding commitment from the insurer or seller to the applicant or buyer; this commitment implies a significant cost of errors should the company misdesign its set of offerings so that bad drivers are tempted to apply for the policy designed and priced for good drivers, or so that smokers are tempted to apply for the policy designed and priced for non-smokers.

Screening mechanisms can be designed with greater precision than signals because it is possible to model responses and estimate the cost of alternative programmes. Over time it should become clear which benefits packages attract the best applicants, which packages induce them to remain and what these packages actually cost. "Test and learn" strategies make it possible to improve performance, tuning packages to develop the desired response rate and to gain better control over costs.

Ideally, screening packages should seek to achieve a stable separation. That is, each set of customers should prefer the package designed and priced for them; when the packages are designed properly, smokers should decline the less expensive policy designed for their healthier companions and apply instead for the "smoker" policy.

Exploiting information advantage

Each of the three techniques for achieving an information advantage is used differently.

Data-mining is a targeted push strategy. The company develops a range of products and tries to infer enough information to determine which customers will find it attractive and which of those it should actually accept. It then pushes the offering out to them and hopes that the targeted customers will accept.

Both objectives of data-mining – to determine which customers will find a product attractive and which customers will be attractive if they accept the product offered – are essential. If a company does a poor job of targeting customers who will want its offerings, its acquisition costs will be too high. Equally, if it does a poor job of identifying which customers it should actually accept, the company will suffer from the "winner's curse"; that is, it will end up with too many customers that it should not want, and too many customers who accepted its offer because no-one else wanted them under the terms it has given them.

Signalling is a labor-intensive adaptive strategy, often combined with data-mining. That is, a company will use data-mining to identify prospects and try to bring them in, and then try to elicit a signal from them to determine what terms they should be offered. This is rarely used in large companies attempting to achieve mass customization as the costs of interpreting signals and designing appropriate responses are simply too high to allow much customization.

Screening is a pull strategy. The company designs an array of products with different combinations of price, features and service, makes all of these products available to its customers and potential customers, and hopes that all segments will locate an offering that they find attractive and that will make them attractive to the company. In its purest form, screening makes only limited use of data-mining for targeting but requires extensive design of product attributes and pricing strategy to attract and retain the best accounts.

An excellent example is the "balance transfer product" pioneered by Capital One to attract customers who pay finance charges. Such customers are profitable for credit card companies, while those who use their cards for convenience transactions and pay off their balances each month generally are not; equally importantly, only customers who pay finance charges should be interested in a card that offers them lower annual percentage rates for balances brought over from other issuers.

Although the idea behind this pull strategy appears simple – design the right product, with the right attributes and the right price, and the customers you want will come – execution requires careful calibration to achieve a stable separation. The product must discourage those who should be discouraged, perhaps with high fees for customers who do not incur finance charges. Careful calibration is also needed to ensure that rates are sufficiently low to attract desirable accounts and sufficiently high to achieve profitability.

Finally, screening is often augmented with data-mining to weed out customers who may be attracted by a product for a good reason but who would still be unprofitable. For example, customers who are likely to be unable to pay their credit card bills may still apply for a low-interest balance transfer promotion. Many of the characteristics of desirable customers who do not pay off their bills each month to avoid finance charges are similar to characteristics of customers who will ultimately declare bankruptcy. Skilled data-mining is essential to attract the first while eliminating the second.

Conclusion

Experience in a wide range of industries in the US, the UK, continental Europe and Asia – garnered over 14 years by Wharton's research programme in information – suggests that the transition from scale-based to skill-based competition is underway but that few companies have mastered it. The shift will accelerate as the cost of information falls and the expertise needed to exploit it becomes increasingly available.

Many companies understand that a customer profitability gradient exists but few understand the factors that contribute to customer profitability, fewer understand how data-mining can be used for targeting, and fewer still understand the art of designing product bundles to encourage customers to self-select. However, our experience does suggest that if you build the right product, the right customers will come.

With a proper information-based strategy, desirable customers can be attracted and retained. Just as importantly, less desirable customers can be repriced or their service mix can be renegotiated, transforming them into profitable customers. Alternatively, such problem accounts can be gently but firmly persuaded to go and cause losses for your competitors.

Summary

Service company managers have known for some time that some customers are more profitable than others. Indeed, in banking a relatively small proportion of customers may generate over 100 per cent of profits; unfortunately, these effectively end up subsidising the rest, some of whom are loss-makers. According to **Eric Clemons**, companies that fail to address this problem are vulnerable to new competitors that target the most profitable customers and – because their profitability is not hindered by loss-makers – offer them a better deal. It is therefore vital to identify profitable customers and to create offerings that are attractive to them. The three main techniques generally in use are data-mining, looking out for signals from potential customers that indicate profitability, and devising product ranges that screen out unprofitable customers. Companies that are able to master these techniques should thrive as the transition from scale-based to skill-based competition takes place.

Suggested further reading

Clemons, E. K. (1997) "Technology-driven environmental shifts and the sustainable competitive disadvantage of previously dominant service companies", in Day, G. and Reibstein, D. (eds) *Wharton on Dynamic Competitive Strategies*, 99–121.

Clemons, E.K., Croson, D.C. and Weber, B.W. (1996) "Market dominance as a precursor of companies' underperformance: emerging technologies and the advantage of new entrants", *Journal of Management Information Systems* (autumn): 59–75.

MANAGING IT IN THE BUSINESS

3

Contributors

 **Michael Earl** is professor of information management at London Business School.

 **Geneviève Feraud** is professor of information management at Theseus International Management Institute, Sophia Antipolis, France.

 **David Feeny** is vice president of Templeton College, Oxford, and director of the Oxford Institute of Information Management.

 **Peter Weill** is Foundation professor of management at Melbourne Business School, University of Melbourne.

 **Leslie Willcocks** is Fellow in information management at Templeton College, Oxford, and visiting professor at Erasmus and Melbourne Universities.

 **Marianne Broadbent** is head and research director of Gartner Group Pacific's IT executive programme.

 **M. Lynne Markus** is professor of management and information science at the Peter F. Drucker Graduate School of Management at Claremont Graduate University.

Contents

Introduction

In this module we move firmly inside the business and focus more on operational than strategic issues, and on the people who implement IT policy. A pivotal role, not least when it comes to managing internal and external alliances, is played by the chief information officer (CIO). The political skills required for this position are often in short supply, as are good IT professionals generally. Executives need to be clear about the scope of the IT function – what are the core capabilities and what can or indeed should be outsourced? A case study of BICC Cables illustrates some of these points and explains how customer behavior and changing technologies inspired a more centralized decision-making model. International comparisons are also presented in this module, showing how information and IT are managed in different countries. Some useful lessons are drawn from a study of IT infrastructure investment in more than 50 multidivisional companies.

Change isn't optional for today's CIO

by

Th... th... herit... Well, good s... Sev... with 10... to be 30... survivor... perhaps... factors" w... the results

Shared visio...
Survivor CI... vision of ho... banal piece o... have dominat...

- how can we
- how do we strategy?

d on organization charts in le synonym – has a longer preted as "career is over". mizations and command

ho were still in their job ing of the 1990s seemed that might distinguish cal to success – except Ten "critical survival listed below. I believe

romoting a shared may seem like a e twin issues that s have been:

ze? h our business

So the "shared v... drive the IT agenc... clearly has to wor... constantly reminde... you're gone," said or...

...emes which will ...nes. In this the CIO ...as to keep everybody goal. "The day you relax from this

In contrast a non-...vivor recalled that "the global IT vision was mine and mine only". It was perhaps no surprise that no one else owned or shared his enthusiasm for the massive IT investment programme he was seeking to implement.

Relationship with peers and superiors

In developing a shared vision, it is essential to work closely with peers and superiors not only to understand their problems but also to gather ideas and then build alliances. Survivor CIOs spent a lot of time doing this. Indeed, they would often make sure the IT department satisfied the IT needs of newly appointed senior executives so that a dialogue would start and a readiness to help the business be conveyed. "Serving but not being subservient" was how one survivor put it.

Contrasting behavior was typified by the non-survivor who admitted that "I did not enjoy the diplomacy and politics required in a corporate role." In other words, survivor CIOs managed upwards and across the organization as well as inside their own function. Non-survivors often were heroes in the eyes of their own IT staff – but they spent most of their time inside the IT department.

Relationship with the CEO

One relationship turns out to be critical: that with the chief executive. Often, of course, the CEO hires and fires the CIO and so a good relationship makes survival sense. However, if you get to know the CEO you have a much better chance of discovering that shared vision and getting the business on your side. You may even be valued for your non-IT contributions to the business. One CIO observed that "with each change of CEO I had to get to know his expectations of me and to let him know my expectations of him". In other words, a two-way understanding is required.

A non-survivor remarked that "with every change in organization, I became more remote from the MD. Then when we had a bad patch I had no support or sponsor." Of course, some CEOs do not want to play; it takes two to tango. However, savvy CIOs know just when and how to engage the CEO. In turn, the CEO who is competent to lead in the information age should be ready and willing to build a partnership with the CIO.

Credibility

Many CIOs know that you cannot talk strategy if the plumbing breaks down. In one CIO's words: "IT has a good reputation for delivering, which is why I am still here." So the survivor CIOs were notable for making sure that they spent time keeping on top of operational and project performance every day. If they were inexperienced in IT management, they made sure they appointed a very good technical number two.

One non-survivor reflected that "the function lost credibility and so did I". What distinguishes CIOs from many other directors is that they have very visible operational responsibilities. If the network goes down today, customers, supplies and your own executives – including the chief – notice very quickly.

Sensitivity

CIOs are in the business of change. However, they do have to be sensitive to the degree of change that is necessary, what will work and when to introduce it. They also need to be able to pick up signals that indicate when they themselves need to change. CIOs cannot march to a different beat . . . although it does pay to be one step ahead in thinking and preparing.

One CIO lost his job because he resisted decentralization of his IT function when the rest of the organization was decentralizing. Another went because he refused to accept the budget cuts everybody was expected to make in a recession. It sounds crazy, but IT people can sometimes believe that IT is "different".

Conversely, one survivor CIO observed that "you must be dynamic, but only in what the company is ready for". In other words, you must be able to read the weather. And in working out when your own function has to change in response to new corporate agendas you must be able to distinguish a passing squall from a sea change. These are the skills of the politician.

The model CIO

The model CIO (Figure 1) combines all of these qualities. But it is unlikely to be a stable model in the fast-changing world of IT. I am presently researching how the role of the CIO is changing. There have been four big developments in recent years.

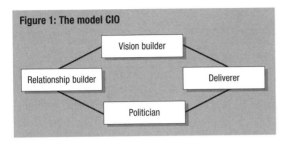

Figure 1: The model CIO

Change master

Several CIOs have taken on wider responsibilities, especially for business process re-engineering and business change. People often judge that CIOs have good understanding of business processes, have good ideas for change – often technology-enabled – and have experience of managing large projects, when few others do. So titles such as "director, business change" have appeared to embrace IT, process change and human resources. Some CIOs have assumed other titles and have added responsibilities such as HR and strategic planning or supply chain management and operations.

"Re-architect"

Many enterprises have been going through programmes of building new, global or enterprise-wide infrastructures. These include not only networks and new computing platforms (not to mention standard "desktops") but also common enterprise-wide systems. In other words, IT departments have been busy "re-architecting".

CIOs will not spend too much time on the complex technical details but they certainly have to ensure that the new architectures fit current and anticipated business needs. And increasingly they are expected to keep in touch with developments in new technologies and to advise on what to bring into the organization and when. As one CIO put it, "I am the group's technology watchtower".

Reformer

In the 1990s we have witnessed huge changes in the practices of many IT departments. Downsizing, outsourcing, quality programmes and new processes of systems development are typical examples. In other words, the winds of change that have hit most areas of business have hit the IT function as well. On top of this, newly converging technologies such as multimedia and the internet have placed new demands in terms of skills, methods and organization.

Thus CIOs of leading-edge companies have become reformers. They have to lead their own departments through change and they have had to work out some critical questions. Not least have been:

- what are core activities, and what non-core activities can be outsourced, run down or managed as legacy issues?
- how do we run a "new-paradigm" yet unstable IT activity alongside an older one which still underpins much of the business?

Alliance manager

Today's IT department has several interfaces and several rivals. The list of IT vendors grows daily and attempts to classify those that are strategic and need most managing are not easy because the IT environment changes so quickly. Some vendors can be seen as allies rather than suppliers, particularly if they provide out-

71

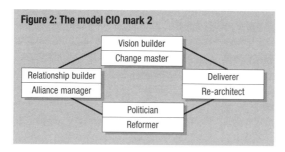

Figure 2: The model CIO mark 2

Vision builder / Change master
Relationship builder / Alliance manager
Deliverer / Re-architect
Politician / Reformer

sourced activities. And then there is the new breed of "power users", sophisticated users who are adept at using PCs and developing their own systems (even bringing in their own hardware and software). They can be seen as good news or bad news. They innovate, bring in new technologies and novel applications and build DIY systems. But they spend money, dislike standards and do not necessarily understand all the disciplines of building industrial-strength applications.

The CIO and his or her management team have to build alliances with all these stakeholders, as well as with the executive peers and superiors of old. They have to prioritize their time, decide which should be transactional partnerships and which more strategic – and they have to provide an information management philosophy that binds them all together. In short, the CIO is now an alliance manager.

We can superimpose these new roles on Figure 1 to illustrate the eight qualities of the new model CIO (Figure 2). One begins to see why the top CIO jobs command ever more attractive remuneration packages.

I am currently studying CIOs in some of the world's leading companies. Further developments in their work could be just around the corner. As IT is increasingly seen not just as supporting but influencing business strategy, CIOs may be assuming, or being given, a more strategic role. Over the next few years, their responsibilities look set to increase in scope. So CIO does not mean "career is over" – rather, it might more appropriately stand for "change isn't optional" or "challenge isn't over".

Summary

What qualities does a successful CIO have? A few years ago, **Michael Earl**'s research indicated that the most important were: a vision shared with the company's wider management, so that IT supported strategy; a close relationship with senior executives, especially the CEO; a willingness to pay attention to day-to-day IT performance; and an ability to judge the importance of political and organizational changes in the business. These qualities are still critical for CIOs who want to flourish in their posts. But IT and all things connected with it change quickly, and CIOs are now being confronted with new responsibilities. The perception that CIOs have a good understanding of business processes means that their job descriptions are now likely to encompass human resources and strategic planning. Like all managers, they have to be able to lead their departments through rapid change but they are often also expected to be the "corporate radar" for new technologies. Finally, today's CIO needs to manage relationships with an ever-growing range of external suppliers and contractors. It is little wonder that remuneration packages have grown.

Suggested further reading

Earl, M.J. and Feeny, D.F. (1994) "Is your CIO adding value?" *Sloan Management Review* 35 (3, spring).

Earl, M.J. (1996) "The chief information officer: past, present and future", in Earl, M.J. (ed.) *Information Management: The Organizational Dimension*, Oxford: Oxford University Press, 1996 and 1998.

Selective sourcing and core capabilities

by David Feeny and Leslie Willcocks

As the 20th century draws to a close, IT functions are receiving unprecedented levels of management attention. Some of this, of course, is caused by the need for information systems to be Y2K compliant; then there have been the systems required for the launch of the euro; and in many cases organizations have chosen to set up a new-generation systems infrastructure based on so-called "enterprise resource planning" (ERP) software.

All of these developments serve to emphasize the extent to which the operations of today's businesses are fundamentally dependent on the use of IT – and therefore on the professionalism of IT people and IT managers. Furthermore, we have the rhetoric of the "information age" and the "information superhighway", with its suggestion that technology is becoming a central factor in shaping the future strategies and fortunes of business. So have we entered a new golden age for the IT function? Is yesterday's Cinderella becoming today's Princess?

Certainly some IT functions – for example, those at BP Amoco and Safeway – are now demonstrably playing a critical role in the forward strategies of their companies. But IT staff everywhere are conscious of another factor in the evolution of their profession: the rapid growth of IT outsourcing companies, such as EDS, CSC and many more.

Many IT executives, instead of enjoying promotion to the top table, have seen their entire organizations outsourced. Their chief executives, skeptical of information-age visions, have signed long-term outsourcing contracts in the belief that they have secured low-cost provision of commodity support services.

Even chief executives who accept that IT is becoming a strategic resource can be tempted to outsource. If IT is becoming that important, the argument goes, why not form a strategic partnership with a world-class provider of IT services and thereby tap into economies of scale and scope that must be unavailable to an in-house IT function? Most of the UK government's IT activity has been contracted out on this basis. Perhaps the right issue, then, is whether the IT function has any long-term future.

At Templeton College's Oxford Institute of Information Management we have worked closely with dozens of companies during the past decade, researching appropriate responses to both the technology opportunity and the outsourcing phenomenon. We have come to the view that an in-house IT function is indeed a potentially critical future asset for any company – but that radical change in its shape, scope and staffing is often desirable.

The impact of outsourcing

In our experience the use of outsourcing is only one part of the long-term blueprint for a company's exploitation of IT. We prescribe a selective approach to the sourcing of IT activity, within which there are essential and complementary roles for both an internal IT function and for external providers. The central ideas of this approach are threefold:

20 Oct 1998

DIGITAL BUSINESS

Alan Pike on the UK passport agency's aim to outsource the mechanics of processing applicants

Financial Times

by Alan Pike

Traditionalist Britons, still disgruntled by the introduction of the standard EU passport, must come to terms with future applications being processed by the UK subsidiary of a German company, and printed at a privatised Stationery Office.

Most people would instinctively regard passports, like defence and policing, as core business of the state. The government's UK Passport Agency would not disagree. But technological change enables it to retain its truly core function – deciding eligibility to hold a passport – while outsourcing the mechanics of the process.

Siemens Business Services, the agency's private sector partner, has devised a world-leading automated processing system that, once fully established in the UK, has capacity to compete for business from other governments, and to develop an international market in passport production.

The system, launched this month, should provide a further flagship demonstration of business services companies' skills at devising innovative, IT-based solutions for big projects. But the increasing complexity of these companies' involvement in this customers' businesses is provoking change on both sides.

Gary Pusey, UK managing director of Siemens Business Services, says those who still regard business services companies as little more than places where clients can deposit IT problems misunderstand the way the market is developing.

He doubts whether conventional descriptions, such as outsourcing or facilities management, remain very illuminating of the relationship between IT-based business services companies and their customers. While it is often a search for IT solutions that brings the two together, this frequently acts as a key to far deeper involvement.

"What sort of company are we? We are involved in business integration and transformation, and process

and IT re-engineering. The range of skills among our staff illustrates it. We have people with backgrounds in change management, process re-engineering and a broach range of other business experiences.

"It is by no means all pure technology, because we are no longer engaged in purely technological solutions. IT is the starting point, but the focus of companies like ours is shifting to the design and management of change." He illustrates the point with the example of the modernisation of National Savings, another public sector project for which Siemens and one of its biggest rivals, EDS, are competing.

"National Savings will concentrate on the core activities of developing its product portfolio and handling its relationship with the Treasury. The private sector is being asked to handle an envisaged reduction in the 3,800 National Savings workforce, devise and implement new ways of working, organise the redeployment of staff and create opportunities for new work. That is a business transformation brief."

The passport project relies on a close, three-way partnership between Siemens, the UK Passport Agency and the Stationery Office. Application forms, signatures and photographs are scanned by Siemens into a data base, using equipment that has proved able to accommodate the quirks of individual handwriting.

The applications pass electronically from Siemens to UK Passport Agency staff and, after scrutiny, transfer again to the Stationery Office's security printing plant. If an application is urgent, printing can take place at any local passport office.

New digitally printed passports will be more secure against alteration and forgery. Other benefits include faster processing, better customer service and improved information retention and tracking, with

Continued

Siemens adding more than 35m back records to the electronic data base.

Mr Pusey describes the ideal relationship between business services companies and their clients as a state of mutual dependency, with managers from both organisations working as virtual teams reliant on each other. "Partnership is a word that has been around for a long while in the business services sector, and a lot of it is just marketing hype. But true partnership, based on mutual dependency in the sense that we both have something to lose if things go wrong, achieves results."

On one level, the implications of the necessarily close relationship implied by this form of partnership are straightforward. Passport office counter staff will work for Siemens rather than the UK Passport Agency. The agency must trust its partner to ensure it conveys an appropriate image on behalf of the agency.

On a different level, business services companies that achieve Mr Pusey's definition of true partnership acquire a sophisticated appreciation not only of their clients' IT requirements, but of their broad business philosophies. "We do not go into companies offering pre-designed solutions," he says. "We have no set of brochures to present. It is only when we understand fully what the customer is trying to achieve that we can work together to devise solutions."

1. **It is a mistake, potentially a very expensive mistake, to make an overall judgment that the IT function should be outsourced in a single contract; it is another mistake to decide that it should not be outsourced at all.**

   In any company the IT function is responsible for a wide range of activities, a portfolio of assets. Some activities – such as payroll system operation or desktop computer installation – are quite properly positioned as back-office commodities. Other activities – perhaps supply chain management systems or network management – may also be seen as necessities rather than order winners but their successful operation to a high standard is business-critical. Increasingly in organizations there are also IT activities that underpin competitive differentiation – online customer service support, for example, or a knowledge management infrastructure which enables more effective problem solving. A selective approach to IT sourcing recognizes these differences and identifies the arrangements – using external or internal resources – that will be effective for each part of the portfolio.

2. **Successful implementation of a selective sourcing approach brings a number of benefits.**

   Many established IT services may indeed be delivered at high quality and lower cost by external suppliers who operate scale-efficient facilities under world-class IT management practices. The IT cost structure can change from being predominantly fixed to being substantially variable as a smaller in-house IT function uses the external market to match supply with demand. The quality of projects that involve unfamiliar technologies or applications can be enhanced as skilled external resources are brought in to work with internal teams. But these benefits do not come for free.

   The IT function needs a new set of management capabilities to operate a selective sourcing approach, and in most companies the nature and extent of the management task has been poorly understood. IT outsourcing – selective or otherwise – is not a quick fix; it represents a transfer of activity, not of accountability. The IT function must adapt in order to fulfil its continuing responsibility for IT services in new ways. And penalty payments for contractual failures are a poor substitute for successful services.

3. **Selective sourcing allows the redirection of internal IT resources towards the highest value-added activity.**

At companies such as BP Amoco, ICI and Thames Water this has become the dominant theme. If future business success is increasingly dependent on exploiting new information technologies, the premier objective of the IT function is to help the business to understand what the opportunity is and how to grasp it. By deliberately outsourcing as much service delivery, support, and even development activity as possible, CIOs such as BP Amoco's John Cross have driven their IT functions to focus on the capabilities, activities and culture that are required to achieve this agenda. While external providers can be motivated and managed to deliver the IT services of today, an in-house IT function which is committed to the business can enable it to realize the opportunities of tomorrow.

Collectively these ideas provide the guidelines for designing an IT function fit for the future. This design should be based on establishing and developing what we call "the core IT capabilities" – those that are necessary and sufficient to fulfil the function's proper role within the business.

The core IT capabilities

Over the past few years we have worked with IT functions in a variety of contexts. Some have been strongly focused on the need to generate a more ambitious, creative and valuable agenda for IT in their business; others have set up task forces to consider how to respond to the opportunity (or threat) of IT outsourcing; quite a few have faced the challenge of rebuilding an in-house IT function after a total outsourcing decision had led to both operational and strategic difficulties. Drawing their various experiences together, we have identified nine core capabilities of the IT function. Figure 1 broadly indicates how each relates to the recurring challenges of exploiting IT.

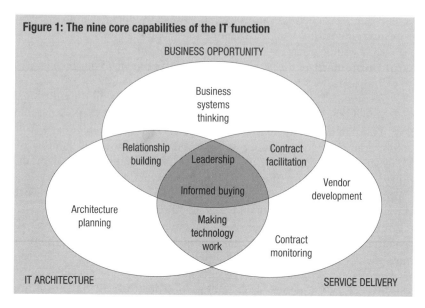

Figure 1: The nine core capabilities of the IT function

76

Business systems thinking allows the IT function to make a direct and effective contribution to the company's understanding of opportunity. As business contexts (probably) and technological capabilities (certainly) change over time, there is a continuous need to examine how best to move forward. Business systems thinkers are adept at understanding the connections and interdependencies between activities, and at communicating how existing processes work; they use that base to catalyze understanding of processes that technology can enable in the future. IT functions with people who possess such skills are sought-after contributors to new business initiatives.

Individuals with relationship-building capability facilitate the wider dialogue between business and IT communities. Comfortable in both business and technical domains, they act as bridge builders in achieving mutual understanding and trust. Gifted individuals, in our experience, can completely transform the climate for exploitation of IT.

As businesses' strategies and operations are increasingly dependent on IT for their delivery, the scope and integrity of the technical infrastructure over time becomes critical. While the construction and operation of such platforms can be effectively contracted out, the core capability of architecture planning safeguards the future ability of the business to keep its technical evolution in line with its business needs.

Making technology work is our innocuous label for the quite extraordinary capability some IT specialists show as they rapidly troubleshoot complex problems that have been disowned by others along the technical supply chain. A few individuals who excel in this respect, using their ability to "keep the show on the road", can ensure the credibility of the IT function's service arrangements.

Informed buying is the first of four core capabilities required to manage successfully a selective sourcing strategy. It provides the insight needed to determine and to shape the appropriate (external or internal) sourcing for each activity in the IT portfolio.

Contract monitoring capability then ensures that each service provider is held to account against existing contracts, and is more broadly assessed and benchmarked against the developing standards of the external market. Meanwhile, contract facilitation is a more action-orientated capability, which ensures that service users can have problems resolved promptly and fairly within the framework of agreements and relationships.

Last but not least of the service delivery capabilities is vendor development. The worst aspect of IT outsourcing is that changing suppliers generally involves substantial switching costs and considerable disruption; the objective of vendor development is to maintain motivation by creating win–win situations in which the supplier can increase its own revenues and profits through services that add value to the business.

The ninth and central capability is IT leadership. Effective IT leaders devise the organizational arrangements – structures, processes, staffing – that bring all the pieces together. As individuals they shape the values and culture which the IT function brings to the business, as well as influencing over time the perception at the top of the business of IT's role, potential and performance. They are also, of course, instrumental in determining the IT function's progress or otherwise towards the model we have described.

The challenge of transition

A fuller discussion of the core capabilities model and of the associated approach to IT sourcing can be found in the suggestions we make for further reading. We do not underestimate the degree of change represented by our prescriptions; there are major implications for structures, career paths, recruitment and development. Many organizations may wish to manage such changes gradually, over a long period of time. But we suggest that an IT function fit for the future is a considerable prize. Current evidence suggests that the pioneers have achieved dramatic improvements, in both business contribution and service, through "core" IT functions which employ roughly one-tenth as many people as their traditional predecessors.

Summary

Information technology is becoming more and more important to business. At the same time, it looks as if IT departments are being sidelined by the increase in outsourcing. But it would be wrong, argue **David Feeny** and **Leslie Willcocks**, to write off the corporate IT function; across-the-board outsourcing can often prove to be an expensive mistake. Instead, the IT function should be analyzed as a portfolio of activities to be selectively outsourced. Internal resources can then be focused on helping the business to grasp the opportunities represented by IT. Ultimately, the function needs to develop a set of core capabilities that will enable it to anticipate future developments in business and technology, maintain the IT infrastructure over time and manage outsourcing. Above all, it needs skilful leaders to build an organization that can achieve these diverse aims.

Suggested further reading

Cross, J., Earl, M.J. and Sampler, J.L. (1997) "Transformation of the IT function in British Petroleum", *MIS Quarterly* (December): 401–23.

Feeny, D.F. and Willcocks, L.P. (1998) "Core IS capabilities for exploiting information technology", *Sloan Management Review* 39 (3, spring): 9–21.

Lacity, M.C., Willcocks, L.P. and Feeny, D.F. (1996) "The value of selective IT sourcing", *Sloan Management Review* 37 (3, spring): 13–25.

These topics are also covered at length in chapters of *Managing IT as a Strategic Resource* (eds Willcocks, L., Feeny, D. and Islei, G.), New York and London: McGraw-Hill, 1997.

Organizing a better IT function

by M. Lynne Markus

The IT function exists to help organizations manage and use information and IT effectively. The effectiveness of the function itself depends on how it is constituted – its charter, structure and policies, which one might call its "hardware" – and how it operates – its processes, culture and human resources, which might be called its "software". Both the hardware and the software must fit the organization's strategies and cultures for the function to be successful.

Getting the "hardware" right: the case of BICC Cables

One of the primary IT management challenges in an organization is to set up an IT function to manage IT. How well the function is set up is a major factor in its effectiveness. Yet this requires highly effective IT management in the first place. And what constitutes a well-structured IT function can change over time with the strategic needs of the organization and with the characteristics of IT.

For many years BICC Cables had allowed its worldwide operations a great deal of local decision-making authority. Customers usually made local purchasing decisions. The company believed that managers of local operating units would make the best business decisions if they had responsibility for all factors affecting profitability – including IT.

Two issues caused the company to rethink its IT management strategy. First, managers anticipated a shift towards customers purchasing globally – a trend that would require greater interdependence among local operations. Second, they became aware of developments in IT that seemed to require a different management approach. The company's capital budgeting committee found itself simultaneously considering requests from two different operating units to replace ageing legacy information systems with an enterprise software package. The two had done a thorough evaluation to determine the best package for their needs – and had chosen two different packages.

Members of the committee asked themselves several questions. Did the two units do basically the same things? If so, how could two different packages both be best? How much would it cost to adopt different IT solutions in different parts of the company? And how would different IT solutions in different parts of the company hinder it from responding to likely future business trends? Preliminary investigations revealed that a corporate approach to acquiring enterprise software would yield major savings over a decentralized approach.

Of course, the committee's questions raised a number of red flags. How would local units react to any recentralization of IT management? Would this seriously undermine the autonomy that operational managers needed to control profitability? These were clearly serious concerns, requiring careful handling.

The committee put both requests on hold pending further study of the need for common systems, and Andrew Cox, the company's chief financial officer, hired his first chief information officer, Alan Harrison. To combat fears of "IT empire-building", Harrison operated for several years as a "department of one". He convened a company-wide task force to chart the major business processes of one of the local operations. Each site was then asked to review the charts, noting local differences. The results were quite compelling: the commonalities in business processes across local operations were far greater than the differences. Thus it looked possible to select a single enterprise package representing what was best for the company as a whole.

The next step was to form a company-wide software selection task force to evaluate several options, including the two first championed by local units. The evaluation criteria were rigorously defined in advance to forestall any criticisms from the "losers". When the committee completed its selection, Harrison negotiated a very favorable corporate contract with the software vendor.

The corporate purchase agreement was not the last of the new IT management decisions raised by enterprise software. Still to be decided were which units would adopt the software, how much local autonomy there would be in software configuration, and how implementation and support would be managed. To ensure local commitment to implementing the software successfully, units were still required to apply to the capital budget committee for funding. All were expected to justify their applications but they were granted freedom to justify their applications in locally relevant terms. Some cited business benefits such as inventory reductions; others emphasized IT cost savings.

To enable a co-ordinated response to customers in the future, BICC Cables decided to develop a common enterprise model. Local operations could request changes but these would be treated as changes to the core model rather than as changes in local implementations. But local operations were expected to implement the software themselves with consulting support from the vendor and from the still small (but no longer one-man) IT function. Because enterprise software involves a long-term commitment to a vendor's product family (and therefore a series of future upgrades), the local units were thought to require the capacity to manage implementations locally.

The case of BICC Cables illustrates several points about improving the effectiveness of the IT function. First, decisions about the "hardware" of the IT function (its size, structure, mission and tasks, including the activities to be outsourced) are critical. Second, these decisions must be revisited from time to time as changes occur in the nature of the business and in the opportunities and challenges posed by information technologies. Third, these decisions will not be the same for all companies but will depend on such things as the industry in which a company operates, the company's specific business strategies, and its size, structure and historical management culture.

The "software" question: a state of mind

The second key factor in the effectiveness of the IT function is how it executes its mission. The "software" of the IT function includes the attitudes, skills and behaviors of IT specialists as they interact with the organization's line managers and IT users. Even if the function's "hardware" is sound, the effectiveness with which a company manages and uses information and IT owes a lot to the function's culture and processes.

Unfortunately, in many organizations the relationship between the IT function and the line business units is poor. At one level, this is hardly surprising. Conflicts between the line and the staff components of organizations have existed as long as there have been line and staff. As in the case of BICC Cables, there is always the danger that line managers will view the activities of staff units as constraints on their freedom of action rather than as expert assistance.

But how IT departments and professionals do their jobs can make a big difference to the quality of the IT–business relationship. And the quality of this relationship can make a big difference to the quality of outcomes the organization receives from its investments in IT.

As a staff unit, the IT function cannot legitimately make decisions for the business, even about IT. Decision-making is the role of line management. Therefore the role of the IT function is primarily advisory or consultative. However, the relationship between an advisor and a client is difficult emotionally on both sides.

Clients may fear or be embarrassed by their own ignorance of the subject matter or they may wildly overestimate their own expertise. They may resent their dependence on experts and abdicate their legitimate decision-making authority to them, or they may take great pleasure in telling the experts what to do. Advisors may be anxious about their ability to satisfy clients' needs and may hide behind jargon. They may become arrogant about their own expertise and their clients' lack of it. And they may fail to listen to clients or dictatorially tell them what they need. Worse, they may recommend solutions that fit their own preferences, convenience or aesthetics but not the clients' needs. There are many ways in which relationships between advisors and clients can become dysfunctional and get in the way of an organization's ability to use information and IT effectively.

Compounding the problem are fundamental differences in worldviews among line managers, IT specialists and operational IT users. IT specialists have an engineering mindset that is not shared by many of those with whom they work. While working on a presentation with me, a colleague – Michael Ginzberg of Case Western Reserve University – asked CIOs about their views on organizational power and politics. One wrote: "Most [IT] practitioners . . . are introverted people focused on technology and almost totally binary on the 'right way' to do things. They generally try to avoid politics, thinking of it as a 'bad thing' rather than as an enabler."

By contrast, the action-orientated mindset of many managers is highly attuned to political realities and emphasizes expedience over technical excellence. From this perspective, the technical rationality of the IT specialist often appears wrong-headed. Some cartoons, recently published in *CIO Magazine*, illustrate how some US school students perceive IT professionals as socially inept geeks. One suspects that these images also reflect many managers' perceptions. Naturally the differences in worldview contribute to many miscommunications and conflicts.

The best solution to these difficulties is mutual understanding. But this does not come cheap. Both sides need to change. Line managers need to understand and appreciate technical issues and the people who manage them. And IT specialists need to learn the limitations of the technical approach.

The challenges of breaking through the technical mindset are many. The "almost totally binary" mindset of many IT specialists is a function partly of self-selection into the field and partly of educational preparation and professional socialization. Despite frequent claims that the work of IT specialists involves people as much as technology, the education of computer scientists and management information systems specialists is heavily weighted towards technical subjects. Treatment of the "soft issues" is usually inadequate. On-the-job training often reinforces technical bias. Students fully employed as IT professionals have told me of work assignments to develop systems with the explicit direction to "avoid bothering the users".

After years of technical education and enculturation, many IT professionals are unable to recognize sources of problems in their work and to take effective steps to correct them. Consider this statement by an experienced Japanese software engineer from a consumer electronics company after a course that emphasized the social and organizational aspects of IT work:

"Until recently I participated in many information system development projects as a software engineer, and also experienced a lot of project failures . . . It was not so difficult to code programs for users. But for some unknown reasons, the projects often went wrong. Users often complained about our jobs . . . I thought that improving productivity was the key to succeeding. If we had somehow completed our jobs more quickly, the projects would never have failed . . . But I feel that I have finally found a key to successful IS development.

"[A lecturer] stated a phrase, 'quality of IS–client relationships'. This phrase impressed me a lot. As a vendor, quality is the most important thing for us. And I was taught by my company that quality is always the first priority in order to get customer satisfaction. But there what we meant was 'quality of products'. Nobody mentioned 'quality of IS–client relations'. So this was totally a new concept for me.

"Now I remember that I had a tough time dealing with clients because I had never considered IS–client relations . . . At that time I thought that the result was due to our poor developing skills, that is, poor 'quality of products'. But actually it was mostly due to our poor dealing skills, that is, poor 'quality of IS–client relationships'."

The good news about this example is that it shows that poor IT-client relationships can often be turned around. Changes of mind can take place in carefully designed educational programmes both in school and on the job. And they can take place when the IT function engages in self-study and accepts the need for "transformation". Reprogramming the "software" of the IT function may be challenging but it is by no means impossible.

In many cases, "software" change follows naturally from "hardware" changes that are designed to make the IT function more responsive to business needs. Examples of such changes include decentralizing responsibility for IT applications and/or support to line units, or reducing the control tasks performed by the IT function. For instance, the organization might shift IT project approval authority from the IT function to a capital budgeting committee.

If structural change is inappropriate, interventions must target IT culture and mindset directly. A necessary first step is for IT specialists to recognize the need for change. Here, line managers can be helpful by providing constructive feedback about the effects of specialists' behavior and patiently working through any defensive reactions to the feedback. They can also help the IT function identify strategies for improvement.

In my work with IT specialists, I have found that training programmes can be very effective in changing attitudes and building "relationship management" skills. Good training programmes give IT specialists the opportunity to role-play difficult situations with clients (where the client is angry, say, or wants a different solution) and to observe others' responses to such situations. Practice of this sort helps build behavioral flexibility, which is essential when communicators have different worldviews and needs.

Summary

A critical factor in the successful management of IT and information, especially in multinationals, is the quality of the IT function. According to **M. Lynne Markus**, this should be assessed along two dimensions: the function's structure and remit within the organization, and its culture (including the personal skills and qualities of its staff). Using a case study, the author shows how, as industrial contexts change and new technologies develop, the IT function may need to change too – from a decentralized decision-making model, for example, to one that is more centralized. Such developments may cause friction between the function and the line managers with whom it has to work, and this is where the function's culture is critical. The problem is that too many IT professionals have not been educated to handle the political aspects of the organizations in which they earn their living; yet quality of relationships is perhaps as important as quality of product in this field.

What makes IT professionals tick?

by Geneviève Feraud

When asked to describe the ideal IT professional, most general managers insist on three points: an impeccable technical knowledge; familiarity with the business; and a high level of commitment to the organization. To get the best out of them and to ensure that they operate as part of a smoothly functioning team, however, general managers need to understand the behavioral characteristics of this unusual breed. Too often they do not. This article seeks to explain what makes IT professionals tick and offers advice on how they should be treated.

The problem

Given the demand for IT skills to sort out the millennium bug, implement enterprise resource planning systems and launch new web initiatives, companies can ill-afford high levels of turnover among their IT staff. Yet surveys and anecdotal evidence suggest that many IT professionals are dissatisfied with their jobs.

Reasons often given include long periods of overtime, inadequate remuneration, and task-orientated management, whereby managers exercise close control over the content of work at the expense of employees' autonomy. Above all, it seems that managers are failing to address the specific needs of their IT professionals. One explanation for this is that managers have tended to give priority to the IT users in their organizations (a bias reflected in much of the academic research into this area).

Loyalty is also being weakened by the recent spate of re-engineering and downsizing in big companies, while individuals are being encouraged (not least by business schools) to pursue more entrepreneurial avenues for their skills. The situation is so bad that some companies are trying to rehire retired IT professionals.

Offering higher salaries does not appear to be an adequate reaction to the increasing scarcity of IT professionals. One solution tried by some companies is to offer flexible hours or telecommuting: this can seem expensive until you weigh up the cost of losing an employee, hiring someone new, and investing time and money in teaching him or her about the company culture and the technical aspects of the job.

Staff turnover is always expensive, because staff members who quit are often the organization's best. When a company aspires to be the technological leader, moreover, competitors will be on the lookout and retaining the best staff is therefore a matter of survival.

Understanding IT professionals

We often use the expression "IT professionals" without really thinking about it. What is professionalism? Peter Drucker, the management writer, gave an excellent description of it more than 30 years ago when he said: "It is the essence of professionalism to apply objective standards of craftsmanship and accomplishment to one's work rather than business criteria."

Professionals have a high degree of expertise, a need for autonomy, a strong commitment to their field and high standards (both technical and ethical). These characteristics often find expression in their attitude to their job. There is a need for professional identification, for active participation, and for stimulation and support from colleagues.

IT professionals tend to look for and apply standards in the way they work, which guarantees rigor and precision but can lead to inflexibility. But, as Drucker points out, "the attitudes that cause the difficulties are in themselves desirable." The problems with IT professionals come not so much from the professionals themselves as from the fact that most companies do not understand their special characteristics and requirements.

Promotion

Nowhere can this be better seen that in the promotion system in many companies, which typically hold out a managerial position as the big reward for a job well done. For IT professionals this is dubious to say the least.

Compare, for example, a few aspects of a technical job on the one hand and of a managerial job on the other. The technical job usually generates measurable results and its content is extremely precise most of the time. Technical people tend to work in stable teams whose members are clearly identified.

In the managerial job, results often manifest themselves over the long term, can be difficult to appreciate and are sometimes impossible to measure. The job's content is very diverse, and often not well specified. Managers operate within a complicated web of relationships, with instability, change, evolution and fuzziness among the rules. When IT professionals find themselves in such an environment it is not surprising that they resent it or even find it strange, uncomfortable or hostile.

Interaction

One reason why IT professionals tend to be unhappy in managerial jobs may be that they tend have lower interaction needs. That is, they tend to enjoy solitary work more and mainly seek self-development through technical performance. Other employees pay more attention to the possibilities of team working in an environment where human relationships have to be managed. Evidence for this has been provided by research carried out by US academic and consultant Robert Zawacki.

I recently conducted a conference for high-level IT executives from different companies. More than 90 per cent of them had a technical background and they were a very quiet group. I discussed this "lower interaction need" with them but they insisted that IT people had exactly the same needs in this respect as anyone else.

I pointed out that even though it was the third day, they had hardly interacted with each other at all, even at lunch. This surprised me, given that a lot of the value of these professional events is in meetings between participants. People at this conference, however, would use breaks to make calls on their mobile phones and after lunch would hurry out of the dining room and disappear until the afternoon session.

This low need for interaction has two damaging consequences for IT professionals. First, it can be an obstacle to promotion where companies are looking for outgoing managers (although arguably this is a bonus for people who do not want to manage). Second, where a managerial position has been attained, the IT professional may find it difficult to fulfil the role satisfactorily – for example, by providing the feedback needed by subordinates.

Stress

The problems faced by IT professionals are made worse by the changing nature of their work. The time is long past when they could stay alone with the mainframe and its programs. Increasingly they have to forsake the intellectual comfort of their own department, cross the "organizational frontier" and work hand-in-hand with IT users – that is, the company's other employees.

This phenomenon is not specific to IT professionals but they often have to do it every day and for all their tasks, whether understanding user requirements or gathering information to design new applications. Such meetings generate questions and ambiguity. Users often have vague expectations and conflicting wants. The result can be a high level of stress.

Solutions

Fortunately, these difficulties are surmountable. Managers must try to meet IT professionals' need for personal accomplishment and growth. One way is to offer varied tasks with a high level of associated responsibility. At the same time, managers must respect their need for autonomy and trust them accordingly; they must delegate, letting them perform these tasks as they want to. This does not mean an absence of control – but IT professionals can have difficulties with hierarchical control.

Control can be exercised in two ways: it can focus on outcomes (which means controlling the way different tasks are accomplished) or on behavior (which means trying to influence employees' behavior to be consistent with company objectives). Research by US academics John Henderson and Lee Soonschul suggests that the best approach is a combination of the two, so that the IT team controls the outcome while the manager addresses behavior. Unfortunately, most managers tend to focus only on technical results.

An intriguing solution to the promotion problem is the "dual-ladder" system, in which promotion can follow two tracks: either a traditional managerial track or an "expert" track, where the person acquires the same rank and salary as a manager but remains a technical specialist.

Such solutions may seem troublesome to implement. But the growing importance of IT means that companies must pay attention to getting the best out of those who are expert in it.

Summary

With the dawning of the information economy, companies cannot afford to neglect their IT professionals. Yet many of these key employees are far from satisfied with their jobs. This is partly due to factors that affect all workers, such as re-engineering and inflexible working patterns. But other problems, says **Geneviève Feraud**, arise from the changing nature of IT and from the fact that companies fail to

85

recognize the needs of their IT professionals. Although they tend to prefer to work autonomously on clearly defined problems, promotional structures often reward them with more managerial posts – which have fuzzy responsibilities and entail political wheeling and dealing. IT professionals are also having to work more and more closely and frequently with IT users. The solution may be to focus managerial attention on team behavior and commitment while allowing a high degree of autonomy in technical matters.

Suggested further reading

Drucker, P.F. (1952) "Management and the professional employee", *Harvard Business Review* (May–June): 84–90.

Henderson, J.C. and Soonschul, L. (1992) "Managing I/S design teams: a control theories perspective", *Management Science* 38 (6, June): 757–77.

Zawacki, R.A. (1992) "Motivating the IS people of the future", *Information Systems Management* (spring): 73–88.

Local lessons for global businesses

by Michael Earl

In all aspects of management, it is easy to assume that we live in a homogeneous world – or, as Marshall McLuhan put it, a "global village". Information technology is one of the forces behind our sense of global intimacy as telecommunications collapse time and space.

In the world of information management, as corporations pursue global business strategies and build global IT infrastructures and enterprise-wide systems to match, there is a tendency to assume, perhaps unwittingly, that national cultures do not exist. Corporations build common systems that assume common industry structures and business practices. They develop e-mail facilities, groupware and decision support systems that assume that people everywhere communicate and make decisions in the same way. And they implement systems and manage IT as though there is one universal best form of organization and a single global set of values and preferences.

It is only when you travel around multinational corporations that you are pulled up sharp and are reminded of some crucial lessons of geography, history, anthropology and political economy. You can visit a corporate information systems group at headquarters to hear hand-wringing complaints such as "it was a great system but they simply wouldn't accept it in Japan". Or "they don't obey our standards in France".

Then you make a visit to China and the local management reminds you that "a

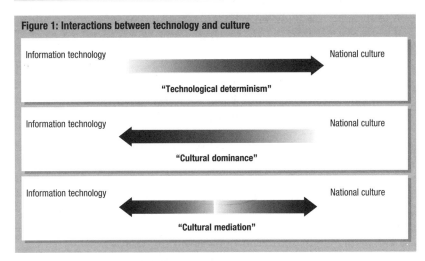

Figure 1: Interactions between technology and culture

Information technology → National culture

"Technological determinism"

Information technology ← National culture

"Cultural dominance"

Information technology ↔ National culture

"Cultural mediation"

logistics system built for North America is not a good fit with our methods of distribution and the transport infrastructure we currently possess". Or you go to a developing country to find that the automating goals of business process re-engineering do not always make sense in low-wage, low-employment economies. Equally, you may go just about anywhere and find an IT application in use that the rest of the corporation does not know about but could adopt to its benefit.

In reflecting on these issues, it is worth remembering that much of the IT industry – and the IT services industry – originates from the US. The IT business tends to spawn related business and management ideas. So has there been a global transfer of IT management philosophy from the US over the past 50 years? Do local, country practices and theories of management mediate such notions of apparent best practice? Or has there even been a conflict between technology and culture? These questions are summarized in Figure 1.

The generic issue is whether management theories and principles are universal, culturally dependent or culturally mediated. An important related question is whether IT itself has created a global village of management ideas, especially in the domain of IT management.

So with two colleagues, Moustafa Bensaou of Insead and Jack Rockart of MIT, I have been engaged in a four-country comparative study of IT management. However, most of what follows represents my own interpretation of this research.

From investigating companies in the UK, US, France and Japan it seems that:

1. Cultural differences exist and express themselves in the way IT is adopted and managed.
2. There are often strengths in local practices that other countries could learn from.
3. Multinational corporations are beginning, albeit often slowly, to adjust their global IT management philosophies and practices to a heterogeneous world.
4. Sometimes there may be worthwhile universal lessons hidden in local practices.

Cultural differences

Let us take two aspects of cultural difference which our studies suggest and which many executives may recognize. First, there is a common perception that the US is

87

a leader in technology adoption. You only have to experience computer retailers, bookstores and daily advertising in the US to get a picture of a certain degree of IT mania. The UK often seems about two years behind and you can draw a timeline across Europe which suggests that the curve of adoption goes from west to east.

Now to some readers' surprise, perhaps, we have found that US executives see such a lag of adoption between the US and UK but they also sense that companies in the UK are better at implementing new technologies and systems and realising the benefits. The "Brits" may be a little conservative but they worry about the returns.

On a completely different dimension, a key assumption in the Anglo-Saxon world is that information provision and analysis improves managerial decision-making. Companies may therefore have relaxed their views about who in the organization should have decision rights – IT has enabled them to distribute empowerment. In Japan, however, the traditions of consensus and participation are still deeply embedded in organizational decision-making. Considerable time and effort are invested in the early stages of information processing by floating ideas, seeking suggestions and accommodating compromises. The traditional hierarchy may mean that senior management signs off or even initiates decisions but much of the process of decision-making is middle-out.

The implications of these two observations are manifold. Two will suffice. First, beware expectations of rapid and common technology infrastructure programmes in global companies. Not only will local knowledge of new technologies vary but also so will local support services. Second, what is a good executive information system or decision support system in the US or UK could be suboptimal or dysfunctional in Japan – or in other countries.

Local strengths

Consultants may recognize the following experience. You go on an overseas assignment to visit subsidiaries of a parent multinational and are surprised by what you discover. I recall doing an "information systems audit" for a UK multinational and discovering local strengths which others may also have known about, but which were not formally recognized across the corporation. A subsidiary in the US was a leader in its sector at exploiting electronic data interchange. One in Spain could teach others about factory automation. One in France was pioneering process control systems.

Of course local circumstances could often explain these competences – particular threats or opportunities had inspired them. But the issue was whether the corporation was learning from them or whether the corporate IS team thought of itself as the center of excellence. Today in several corporations, we see centers of excellence being distributed; they need not be central. However, this should not be done just on a "fair share" basis of allocation. Managers need to be guided by two quite simple, but fairly rare, attitudes.

The first can be expressed as "seeing is believing". Whenever business or IT executives travel around the corporation they should look out for good ideas that may be hidden in, or ignored outside, the local unit. In other words, they should not travel with blind missionary zeal, but should be good observers and listeners, too. And then they should think about how the idea can be transferred. Equally, chief executives can help here. When they hear a divisional executive talk about something good that the division has done with IT, they should ask whether he or she has done anything to transfer it to the rest of the corporation.

The second simple corrective is not to be too cost-conscious on the travel budget. I have been to too many internal management conferences or meetings of IT policy committees where distant executives have been excluded, or have had to attend infrequently, because of the time and cost involved. If we believe in shared understanding and transfer of learning and best practice, the value loss of such behavior may be too great.

Multinational management

The two lessons above could be relatively informal, but useful, elements of a multinational approach to IS management. I use the term "multinational" advisedly here – that is, taking into account local or country differences even if some of the business imperative is a global (more uniform) logic.

There are at least four further measures that would add up to a multinational approach:

1. **Build a degree of federalism in the IT organization**.
   Often there will be strong reasons for considerable centralization of IT strategy matters, such as standards and vendor selection. The many multinationals that would like just one corporate e-mail system are testimony to this. And some IT applications may well need to be common and global – from financial reporting to order processing, depending on circumstances. However, some applications do not need to be common and others will only work if context-specific. Likewise, some IT management presence is often required locally if for no other reason than to look after and develop local IT professionals and ensure that IT matters are on local business agendas. "Subsidiarity" is a good metaphor in the business of managing IT globally.

2. **When implementing common systems globally, it can be a good idea to roll them out country by country**.
   This not only allows local adaptations to be made, it also enables one country to learn from another. Wiley, the publishing company, had good experiences with this strategy as it transferred common systems from Singapore to the UK to Australia and the US – and round again.

3. **Putting in scanning processes to learn about and transfer ideas is sensible**.
   This is not just transfer of best practice. For example, if you have a subsidiary in the US, why not make sure you learn about and exploit on a global basis a new technology which has so far only been tried there? It is an in-built advantage that multinationals can compete on.

4. **Moving IT staff around the world can be beneficial**.
   Obviously this should facilitate cultural sensitivity, but again it can accelerate transfer of ideas and learning. Indeed, companies can be quite deliberate in this respect. One multinational we studied installed a European IT director into its Japanese subsidiary not only because of a shortage of experienced IT directors in Japan but also more aggressively to export a Western technology which, if properly implemented, would steal a march on the local competition.

Best principles

Thus far, the spirit of the argument has been that cultural differences exist and therefore differentiation in managing IT in global organizations makes sense.

Figure 2: How Japanese and Western managers frame IT management

Issue	Western framing	Japanese framing
How do we decide what information systems our business needs?	**Strategic alignment** We develop an IT strategy that aligns with our business strategy.	**Strategic instinct** We let the basic way we compete, especially our operational goals, drive IT investments.
How will we know whether IT investments are worthwhile?	**Value for money** We adapt capital-budgeting processes to manage and evaluate IT investments.	**Performance improvement** We judge investments based on operational performance improvements.
When we're trying to improve a business process, how does technology fit into our thinking?	**Technology solutions** We assume that technology offers the smartest, cheapest way to improve performance.	**Appropriate technology** We identify a performance goal and then select a technology that helps us achieve it in a way that supports the people doing the work.
How should IT users and IT specialists connect in our organization?	**IS–user relations** We teach specialists about business goals and develop technically adept, business-savvy chief information officers.	**Organizational bonding** We encourage integration by rotating managers through the IT function, co-locating specialists and users and allowing executives who also oversee other functions to oversee IT.
How can we design systems that improve organizational performance?	**System design** We design the most technically elegant system possible and ask employees to adapt to it.	**Human design** We design the system to make use of the tacit and explicit knowledge that employees already possess.

Nevertheless, there may be some universal principles of IT management that transcend local cultures. Or there may be principles that require local interpretation. But where do we find these principles?

The Anglo-Saxon world has been a dominant source. This is not just because of the US domination of the IT and IT service industries. It is also because so much of the publicized management research and thinking in this area emanates from the same territory.

When Bensaou and I did our research in Japan we learnt (or relearnt) some lessons of anthropology. The questions we asked executives in Japanese corporations often were not understood – not at the level of language but at the level of meaning. Issues of IT management that were well known in the West raised puzzled eyebrows in Japan. Our interviewees recognized neither the problems behind our questions nor the implied solutions. There was a mindset difference.

Figure 2 portrays the core ideas. On the left-hand side are ideas or language about five aspects of IT management which should be familiar in the West. On the right-hand side are the "framings" we generally find in Japanese corporations. These represent – in our view – a much more down-to-earth, commonsense and "let's not treat IT as something special" approach to issues of IT strategy, investing in IT, technology adoption, organizing IT activities and designing systems.

Now one message of this model could be to think and act differently according to whether you are in the West or the East. We suggest another. The West can learn from the East – not least because we believe that the Western framing has not produced effective management practices. However, we are not saying that a

British or US company, for example, should transfer Japanese practices lock, stock and barrel. Rather, we suggest that the way we have described Japanese framing provides a set of best principles that can be transferred by adjusting them at the level of practices to suit local contexts and cultures.

Our model is, of course, high-level and needs detailed interpretation and practical development. However, I have been struck by some reactions to it so far. One reaction is to say: "Aha, this explains and emphasizes why Japan is backward in IT and how much Japanese corporate competitiveness has to catch up." Another reaction is to say: "Actually I don't think we have the issues in our business you imply, except for the second [or fifth or whichever]." Some therefore dismiss the ideas we describe and develop as aberrations or outliers. Others compare and contrast and look for the variance that could be instructive.

A few say: "You know, you've articulated an idea I had in the back of my mind but which would have been countercultural or politically incorrect to suggest." A paradoxical virtue of "cross-cultural" learning in a heterogeneous world is that it may release ideas that are already locked within one's culture.

Summary

One of the forces behind the sense that we live in a "global village" is the growing power of information technology. Hence it is tempting for corporations to assume global homogeneity in the way information and IT are managed. But according to research carried out by **Michael Earl** and his colleagues, significant local and cultural differences manifest themselves in this area of corporate activity. For one thing, adoption of new technologies is not instantaneous but diffuse across the world. And whereas Western companies have tended to see IT's decision support capabilities as a reason to spread decision making powers more widely, Japanese decision-making is still normally more organizational in nature. Such differences mean that companies should be on the lookout for best practices that may be hidden within local units. Perhaps the most important lesson that Western companies can learn from their Japanese counterparts is a more down-to-earth, more integrated view of IT strategy.

Suggested further reading
Bensaou, M. and Earl, M.J. (1998) "The right mindset for managing information technology", *Harvard Business Review* (Sept.–Oct.). (A fuller development of the mindset model summarized in Figure 2.)

Competing with IT infrastructure

by Peter Weill and Marianne Broadbent

Information technology infrastructure has become one of the most important investment decisions made by senior management. Companies' IT infrastructure investments will be as critical for creating long-term shareholder value as previous waves of physical infrastructure decisions about location, buildings and plant.

The merging of the computing, telephony, telecommunications, publishing and entertainment industries, and the pervasiveness of the internet and other vehicles for e-commerce, present strategic opportunities and threats for every company.

Business and technology managers are anxious to make smart use of this powerful combination of business unit, company, industry and public infrastructures. However, many struggle with their IT investments, grappling with a multitude of technical and business choices and trying to judge the optimal balance of capabilities at corporate and business unit levels. At the same time they need to consider how their companies' technology infrastructure will intersect with emerging industry and public infrastructures.

In the past there were fewer options, and infrastructures providing channels to customers were relatively limited. Today there are multiple options. As a growing proportion of companies' cash flows moves online, it is longer-term decisions about IT infrastructure investments that will differentiate competitive capabilities. The growing importance of the new infrastructures will test many organizational decision-making processes. Physical location will decline in importance. Identifying how to benefit from these changes is a critical challenge for senior management.

The new infrastructure

IT has become pervasive within contemporary organizations, where it is used to do business electronically and to connect to customers, suppliers, regulators and alliance partners. We define "IT" as a company's total investment in computing and communications technology. This includes hardware, software, telecommunications, telephones, myriad devices that collect and represent data (for example, supermarket point-of-sale and bank teller machines), all electronically stored data and the people dedicated to providing these services. It includes IT investments implemented by internal groups and those outsourced to providers such as IBM or EDS. We view the sum total of this investment as the "IT portfolio"; this must be managed like a financial portfolio, balancing risk and return to meet management goals and strategies for customer and shareholder value.

The foundation of the IT portfolio is the company's longer-term IT infrastructure investments. These in turn are linked to external industry infrastructures, such as bank payment systems, airline reservation systems, automotive industry EDI networks, and to public infrastructures, such as the internet and telecommunications networks. Together these infrastructures enable companies to perform business processes and to reach customers and suppliers, and provide governments with cost-effective ways of running public services.

The technologies in question provide the basis for new organizational forms, new products, new markets and new ways of working. The combination of a company's internal IT infrastructure and the external public infrastructures make up the total "new infrastructure" illustrated in Figure 1. The entire IT portfolio must be managed by a partnership of business and technical managers to create value. In many organizations IT is the single largest capital expense. In the US, over 50 per cent of all capital spending goes into IT.

Senior managers cannot afford to delegate critical decisions about the new infrastructure to technical personnel. All that managers need are well-developed skills to deal with IT issues with confidence and competence so that these complex choices – which combine strategic, technical, competitive, financial and organizational issues – can be made well.

The challenges of IT infrastructure

IT infrastructure investment accounts for about 55 per cent of the investments that companies make in their IT portfolios. Infrastructure provides the underlying

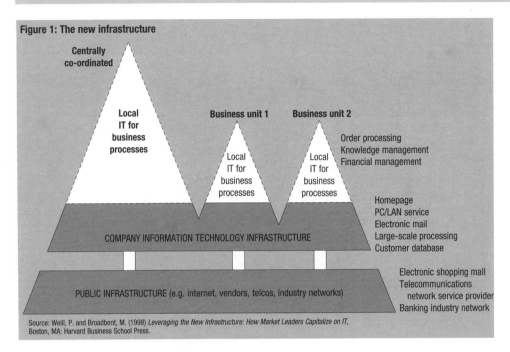

Figure 1: The new infrastructure

Source: Weill, P. and Broadbent, M. (1998) *Leveraging the New Infrastructure: How Market Leaders Capitalize on IT*, Boston, MA: Harvard Business School Press.

capability to apply technology to business processes, to link people and data through communication networks, and to manage increasingly demanding workplaces. Yet decisions about infrastructure capability and investments are often a "leap of faith" – or are not made until too late, by which time the lack of infrastructure has become a barrier to new initiatives.

Executives find decisions on infrastructure investments difficult because they often feel that they do not know what they are getting, what business capability will be provided and how it will lower costs or facilitate new business development. And taking a cue from other companies' decisions is apt to be confusing. For example:

- Johnson & Johnson is investing in shared IT services across previously autonomous businesses.
- Hong Kong-based conglomerates Hutchison Whampoa and Jardine Matheson make little or no company-wide investments in IT infrastructure.
- Citibank Asia is centralizing and standardizing all backroom IT processes into one location for its local Asian operations.
- Ralston Purina has no company-wide IT infrastructure investments.

Has each of these companies made the right decision? How did they arrive at their decisions? How can business and IT executives together identify the best choices for their businesses?

The challenge for companies is to know which infrastructure services are appropriate for their strategic contexts. Which IT-based business initiatives might they want to undertake in the future? Which should they implement as company-wide infrastructure and which should they leave to their business units? How will lack of an appropriate infrastructure hinder their competitive position?

Drawing on detailed analysis of over 50 multidivisional companies, we know that sound decisions about IT infrastructure must be based on deep understanding of the strategic context. This understanding needs to be articulated, communicated

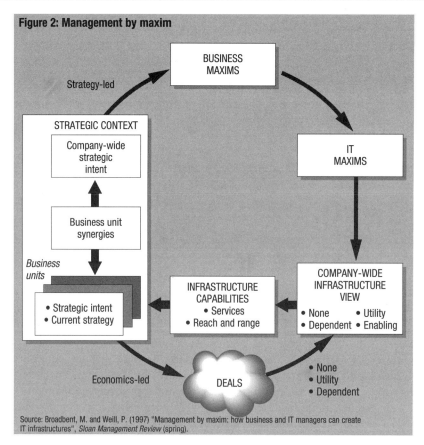

Figure 2: Management by maxim

Source: Broadbent, M. and Weill, P. (1997) "Management by maxim: how business and IT managers can create IT infrastructures", *Sloan Management Review* (spring).

and shared in terms of a clear body of evidence linking longer-term strategy and infrastructure capability. This capability is best depicted as a set of services offered across the company, with the electronic reach and range to ensure pertinent and timely support for the business.

Management by maxim

Successful companies often make decisions about IT infrastructure investments through a process we call "management by maxim". (Another approach is "management by deals", which we describe briefly later.) Decisions range from having no infrastructure services throughout the company to making extensive services available to the whole enterprise, including all business units, suppliers and customers. The essence of the decision is to choose infrastructure services that will readily support the family of applications required in future.

The framework begins with consideration of the company's strategic context, of synergies among business units, and of the extent to which the company wants to exploit those synergies (*see* Figure 2). For example, the strategic contexts of the international paper and packaging company Amcor and the vehicle manufacturer Honda are very different. Until recently, Amcor saw limited synergies among its businesses and had a strong focus on local autonomy. Honda, on the other hand, is seeking to gain synergies in both research and development (R&D) and production.

These two approaches have very different implications for how much company-wide infrastructure capability is necessary and appropriate. The framework helps to clarify IT investment in terms of the balance between short-term cost with minimum investment levels, and future options and flexibility, which might require over-investment relative to current needs.

Business and IT maxims

The strategic context can be expressed by what we call "business maxims", which encapsulate a company's future strategies. Business and IT executives need to work on these together to ensure that they are clearly articulated and to give IT executives insight into future business directions. We have found that this process is necessary because many companies do not have comprehensive and timely strategic statements, nor is their documentation sufficiently focused.

A business maxim for an insurance company with three business units might be: "All sales employees are decision makers about taking new policies and cross selling." This implies that the company's infrastructure needs to give all employees (regardless of location) access to the data and systems required to make decisions on insurance policies. This maxim should be one of five or six that together strongly and concisely state the company's business requirements. They should be reshaped in response to changes in the competitive environment.

From the business maxims, business and IT executives together identify "IT maxims", which describe how a company needs to deploy IT and connect, share and structure information. They identify how a company must:

■ lead or follow in the deployment of IT in its industry (for example, be a leader, fast follower or user of standardized applications)
■ electronically process transactions
■ connect and share data sources across different parts of the company
■ connect and share data sources across the extended enterprise (including, for example, customers, suppliers, regulators or strategic allies).

IT maxims specify the company's approach to:

■ the role of IT and levels of investment relative to competitors
■ transaction processing (standardization, common interfaces or local tailoring)
■ access to, and use and standardization of, different types of data (for example, financial, product or customer).

A given business maxim usually leads to one or more IT maxims, as shown in Figure 3.

The business and IT maxims identify the company's predominant view of infrastructure, which gives a context for decisions about funding specific services and about reach and range. For example, Amcor's previous emphasis on local autonomy and low synergy leads to an IT maxim such as "IT expertize and technological solutions are shared on an information basis", which implies no investment in company-wide infrastructure. This maxim was consistent with the company's strategic context and the decision to forgo IT-related synergies.

Honda's business maxim was, in effect, to "expedite global operations by maximizing synergies of production and operations in many countries"; this leads to a series of IT maxims, including:

■ information flow throughout Honda should allow all parts of the company to spot trends more easily and quickly and use these to Honda's advantage

Figure 3: Linked sample business and IT maxims

Sample business maxims	Sample IT maxims
Provide all the information to service client from any service point	Customer service representatives must have access to a complete file of each customer's relationship with the company
Drive economies of scale through shared best practice	We enforce standards of hardware and software selection to reduce costs and streamline resource requirements We centrally co-ordinate purchasing of IT from major vendors to minimize costs and ensure consistency
Capture the electronic delivery channel to customers	Our external communications provide channels to customers which are easy to access, particularly for electronic delivery of services and products
Ability to detect and respond to subtle shifts in the marketplace	Centrally co-ordinated information flow should allow all parts of the company to spot trends more easily and quickly and use these to the company's advantage
Management culture of information sharing to generate new business	The usefulness of data must be recognized beyond the area immediately responsible for its capture so it is not lost
Ability to develop resources for new products quickly and judiciously	New systems must provide a foundation upon which new products and services can be added without major modifications

Source: Weill, P. and Broadbent, M. (1998) *Leveraging the New Infrastructure: How Market Leaders Capitalize on IT*, Boston, MA: Harvard Business School Press.

- Honda R&D staff in different parts of the world must have ready access to each other to be able to communicate ideas and output to colleagues
- communication systems must facilitate high-quality person-to-person interaction among R&D staff and between R&D, production, operations and marketing personnel
- communication systems must support the transfer of sophisticated design concepts, data and documentation in a high-quality, cost-efficient manner to cut cycle time.

These and other IT maxims led to strategically driven investments in IT infrastructure.

Views of IT infrastructure and services

In our work we have found that companies take one of four views of company-wide IT infrastructure: "none", "utility", "dependent" and "enabling". Up-front investments and the number and depth of infrastructure services increase as the view moves from "no company-wide infrastructure" to an "enabling" perspective. None of the views is best for all companies, but each is appropriate for some, according to the strategic context and business and IT maxims.

The characteristics of the four views – in terms of investment and resulting capabilities – are compared in Figure 4. They are based on empirical research into 27 companies and 54 business units.

A utility view implies that expenditure on IT infrastructure is primarily a way to

96

Figure 4: Characteristics of the four views of infrastructure

VIEW OF INFRASTRUCTURE	CHARACTERISTICS				
	Investment in IT relative to competitors	Investment in company-wide infrastructure	Approach to justification	Reach and range	Extent of infrastructure services
None	Lowest	None	No attempt	Within business units	None
Utility	Low	Lower than average (37 per cent of total IT)	Cost focus	Within and between BU's for data and simple transactions	Basic
Dependent	Average	Just above average (45 per cent of total IT)	Balance cost and flexibility	Within and between BU's; some complex transactions; some customers	Basic plus a few services which are strategic
Enabling	Highest	Well above average (50 per cent of total IT)	Flexibility focus	Within and between BU's; some complex transactions; any customer	Extensive

Source: Broadbent, M. and Weill, P. (1997) "Management by maxim: how business and IT managers can create IT infrastructures", *Sloan Management Review* (spring).

reduce costs through economies of scale and sharing. IT is a utility which provides an essential service that incurs administrative expenses. Management must minimize the expense of the desired service. In companies with a utility view, maximizing current return on assets is critical.

A dependent view implies that infrastructure investments primarily respond to specific current strategies. Dependent infrastructure investments are derived from business plans that specify or imply information and IT needs. Companies with this view attempt to balance cost and flexibility.

An enabling view implies over-investment in IT infrastructure with respect to current needs. The purpose is to provide flexibility in achieving long-term goals and to enable quick, market-leading development of new IT-enabled products.

Changes in business maxims can mean that a change of view is needed, and thus greater or lesser infrastructure investment. This perspective is often unfamiliar to executive management teams – hence our focus on business and IT executives working together to understand the business drivers of infrastructure capability.

Infrastructure capability can be defined in terms of two factors:

1. **The infrastructure services offered across the company (for example, a shared customer database)**

   Each service can be offered at different levels. For example, the "multimedia operations and development" service in one company we studied was offered to a limited degree through provision of desk-to-desk video-conferencing facilities. However, another company in the same industry described its service in this area as "developing and managing multimedia operations to support high-bandwidth technical information and human communication across multiple countries". It used its bandwidth to transfer technical information swiftly between local area networks.

2. **Electronic reach and range**

   "Reach" refers to the locations and people the infrastructure is capable of connecting. It can extend from within a single business unit to the ultimate level of connecting anyone, anywhere. "Range" refers to the variety of business activities that can be performed across each level of reach.

In companies that gained real value from IT investment, the extent of infrastructure capability was clearly linked to specific business and IT maxims and to the company's view of infrastructure.

The maxims route: Johnson & Johnson

The maxims route assumes that both business and IT executives can view the company as a whole. This occurred in about half the companies studied.

In Johnson & Johnson, business maxims have changed over time due to changes in the healthcare industry and in how the company wants to compete. Its desire to leverage its strength with the healthcare industry's changing customer base resulted in the business maxim "to develop partnerships with customers on a worldwide basis". It therefore needed to identify large customers that were dealing separately with different autonomous business units, a requirement that changed the amount and type of information that operating companies needed to share worldwide. This led to a set of IT maxims that expressed the business need to have access to aggregated data in common systems, deliver customer profiles, reduce duplication of effort, and develop shared services as a foundation for IT systems that would foster personal interaction.

If a company takes the maxims route, any of the four views of infrastructure can result and any one might be appropriate, depending on the strategic context and maxims.

The deals route

Another way that companies make decisions about IT infrastructure investments is through deal making, which focuses on the more immediate needs of each business (*see* the base of Figure 2). In companies that take the deals route, IT managers talk with each business unit manager, often as part of a planning cycle, to understand units' current IT needs. After these discussions, the IT managers make company-wide infrastructure recommendations on the basis of the units' combined needs. After estimating costs, they go to each unit with a proposal, negotiate, trade costs and infrastructure services, and strike a deal.

In the companies of this type that we studied, we observed three possible views of infrastructure: "none", "utility" or "dependent". No company had an enabling view and few had a dependent view. The pressure of costs and the tendency for current strategies to dominate long-term strategic intentions in the deal process prevent an enabling view from emerging. This pressure prevents commitment to the flexibility inherent in an enabling view. Our observations suggest that only business maxims set by corporate executive management have the political weight to justify a company-wide infrastructure with extensive services.

Sharing responsibility

To achieve business-driven infrastructure both business and IT managers must share responsibility for its development. They must participate in a dialogue to ensure appropriate and timely capabilities and to reduce the likelihood of fragmenting resources among competing strategies.

Creating an appropriate infrastructure involves decisions based on a sound understanding of where a company is going, rather than of where it has been. This understanding starts with the company's strategic context and business units and leads to the articulation of business and IT maxims. Maxims provide a basis for deciding on a view of infrastructure that matches the company's competitive positioning. The final step is to identify specific infrastructure services with a reach and range appropriate to the strategic context.

IT infrastructure is such a critical resource that it requires special attention during the IT investment process. Companies that treat this part of their IT portfolio in the same way as other IT investments risk never having the infrastructure to support their business strategies.

Summary

IT infrastructure is a critical factor in companies' long-term competitive prospects, and decisions about investments in it are correspondingly difficult. Here **Peter Weill** and **Marianne Broadbent** present a framework for managers facing this challenge. The first requirement is a deep understanding of the strategic context and of the degree to which synergies between business units should be exploited. Business and IT executives must collaborate to distil this understanding into "business maxims", which clearly describe the company's strategic aims. From these, "IT maxims" are deduced, which specify how IT should be deployed and what level of infrastructure is needed. The maxim approach contrasts with the "deal" approach, in which IT managers negotiate with business unit managers about infrastructure requirements; the drawback of this approach is to make it unlikely that a flexible company-wide infrastructure will emerge, even if one is desirable in the long term.

Suggested further reading

Broadbent, M. and Weill, P. (1997) "Management by maxim: how business and IT managers can create IT infrastructures", *Sloan Management Review* (spring).

Weill, P. and Broadbent, M. (1998) *Leveraging the New Infrastructure: How Market Leaders Capitalize on IT*, Boston, MA: Harvard Business School Press.

THE SMARTER SUPPLY CHAIN

4

Contributors

 **Thomas E. Vollmann** is professor of manufacturing management at IMD.

 **Francis Bidault** is professor of strategy and innovation management, and dean of the MBA programme at Theseus International Management Institute, Sophia Antipolis, France.

 **Carlos Cordon** is professor of manufacturing management at IMD.

 **Donald A. Marchand** is professor of information management and strategy at IMD International, Switzerland.

 **Thomas H. Davenport** is professor of information management at Boston University's business school and director of the Andersen Consulting Institute for Strategic Change.

 **Eric K. Clemons** is professor of information strategy, systems and economics at the Wharton School, University of Pennsylvania.

 **Jukka Nihtilä** is a research fellow at Theseus International Management Institute, Sophia Antipolis, France.

Contents

Introduction

This module focuses on the supply chain – or as more than one writer describes it, the "demand chain" – and on those information and IT challenges faced as managers strive for closer relationships with suppliers, speedier product development with outside partners and, ultimately, better service for customers. Co-ordination of companies along the chain is more than just a question of everyone choosing the same software package – leading edge businesses can achieve large cost savings if they seek to eliminate ordering. Collaboration between companies via IT also facilitates effective product development, even if many businesses are instinctively reluctant to open communication channels about one of their core processes. ERP systems and how to make the best of them are discussed, as is a phenomenon widely expected to characterize the "information age": disintermediation.

Building a smarter demand chain

by Thomas E. Vollmann and Carlos Cordon

Supply chain management is about optimizing the overall activities of companies working together to create bundles of goods and services. The aim is to manage and co-ordinate the whole chain, from raw material suppliers to end customers, rather than to focus on optimizing a particular local business unit. By doing so it is possible to develop highly competitive chains and win–win outcomes for those who co-operate in the endeavor. The notion that improvements in one part of the chain will be offset by consequent problems elsewhere must be abandoned; supply chain management is not a zero-sum game.

A common view of the chain is as a streamlined pipeline which processes raw materials into finished goods and delivers them to consumers. But this is simplistic; the reality is a much more complex network. A network of vendors supplies a company which in turn supports a network of customers, with third-party service providers (such as transport firms) helping to link the companies.

For a business, the objective is to establish a portfolio approach to working with suppliers and customers. It needs to decide which to work with most closely and how to establish the infrastructure (processes and information systems) that will best support the working relationships.

Demand chain management

A fundamental shift in thinking is to replace the term "supply chain" with "demand chain". The critical difference is that demand chain thinking starts with the customers and works backwards. This breaks out of parochial approaches that focus solely on reducing transport costs. It supports a "mass customization" viewpoint, in which bundles of goods and services are offered in ways that support customers' individual objectives.

This does not necessarily imply product differentiation. In fact, it is often the service aspects that require differentiation. For example, a company such as Unilever will provide the same margarine to both Tesco and Sainsbury. However, the ways in which the product is delivered, transactions are processed and other parts of the relationship are managed can and should be different, since these two competing supermarket chains each have their own ways of evaluating performance.

The information systems required to support demand chain management necessarily focus on optimizing cross-company processes. This implies tailored business process re-engineering. The dictates of excellent demand chain management also require "flawless execution". Whatever the bundles of goods and services needed by particular customers, they must be supplied flawlessly and efficiently. The schedules for making and delivering goods need to be able to satisfy increasingly exact demands, such as shorter delivery times or more precise "windows" for delivery of materials. All of this puts major demands on information systems.

When Albert Heijn, the largest Dutch retailer, demanded less than 24-hour deliveries from its suppliers, Heineken found that it was not possible to provide

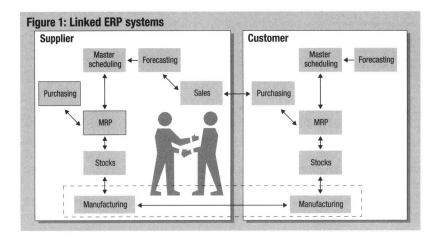

Figure 1: Linked ERP systems

this level of service simply by improving old processes and systems, which passed information and decision making through functional silos and batch processing systems. Instead, the brewery needed to overhaul totally its processes, its ways of working and its information systems to comply with the demand.

Weaknesses of present systems

The information systems needed to co-ordinate companies along the demand chain require a new and different approach to that required within individual companies. Some managers believe that if they and their suppliers choose the same standard software package, such as SAP, they will be able to integrate their information systems. In fact, most of these "enterprise resource planning" (ERP) systems are focused not on integration of the demand chain but on integration within a company.

Figure 1 shows how customers and suppliers work together with ERP systems. The customer has master production scheduling, which takes into account forecasts of demand. The outputs of master scheduling provide input into material requirements planning (MRP, a subsystem of ERP), which is also based on inventory data (including work-in-process). The result is a manufacturing schedule and information for the purchasing department to place orders with the supplier. The supplier in turn runs its own ERP-based system.

The time required for a problem in the customer's manufacturing department to go "up, over and down" through the functional silos of both companies – to the manufacturing department of the supplier – is typically measured in weeks. In fact, what is needed is the arrow shown connecting the two manufacturing departments directly – as well as the information systems (and thinking) to support this kind of supply chain relationship.

Elimination of ordering

The term "demand management" was coined in 1978 and is now a basic part of all ERP systems. Figure 2 shows the idea. Essentially, a company has a "pipeline" of capacity which is filled in the short run with customer orders and in the long run with forecasts of demand. The point is that order entry consumes the forecast, and demand management explicitly integrates both of these processes.

This was a great idea 20 years ago. Today we believe that connecting companies

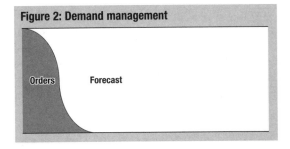

Figure 2: Demand management

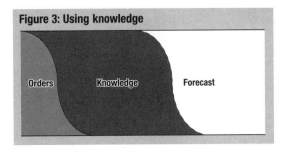

Figure 3: Using knowledge

in a demand chain through ordering is archaic. Figure 3 shows the practice we see in leading-edge companies, namely the inclusion of a band of "knowledge". If the supplier knows the needs of customers, it does not have to guess or forecast them, nor does it have to wait until these customers place orders. Philips Consumer Electronics has been able to work this way with several of its major customers.

However, in all too many situations, ordering still exists – and is further misaligned by accounting practices that fail to account for goods in transit. That is, when the books close at the end of the month, a company that has ordered goods to arrive on the first of the following month – the next day – will not include them in the inventory balance (which is deliberately reduced to low levels); but the company that has despatched them will count them as "shipped". The net result is that the goods do not exist as far as accounting is concerned – a peculiarity that can have expensive consequences.

If a supplier can work with customers in ways that allow it to use its discretion over when and how much to deliver, major savings can be achieved. But eliminating ordering again requires new processes, supported by new approaches to information systems, in both the customer and supplier. It also implies payments when the customer uses the materials (vendor-managed inventory) and flawless execution by both companies.

In many companies, large hidden costs arise because they have to respond to artificially tight demands from their customers. The result is spot buying of transport, from hauliers who necessarily have to be idle for a lot of the time in order to respond promptly. But some companies have made major improvements in this regard.

Skanska, the Swedish construction company, was able to reduce the cost of inbound freight to its building sites by 45 per cent by contracting with one haulier in 1995 to carry all inbound materials. It also went on to form partnerships with its suppliers, many of which also formed partnerships with the haulier to carry all their outbound freight. This enabled the haulier to optimise freight movements over a much larger area and to co-ordinate truck schedules more efficiently. Of course, it was also necessary to design and implement new information systems to connect each building site to the suppliers and the haulier, and to provide data on material requirements with a greater lead time.

Regionalization

Another key strategic issue that many companies face today is the regionalization of their activities. For example, fast moving consumer goods companies such as Nestlé, S.C. Johnson and Unilever traditionally set up factories in countries to serve just the local market. Sometimes this was desirable because of local tax, tastes or other conditions. Now, however, the competitive game is much more regional, particularly in Europe. Products are being harmonized, factories are being focused on shorter product lines run at greater efficiency, and physical distribution covers a much wider geographical area. In many cases the customer base is also becoming regional, as retailers combine and expand their bases of operation.

Regionalization in demand chain management is another reason why practices, processes and information systems need to be tailored to the needs of the marketplace. Co-ordinated scheduling implies some centralization of that activity. It also implies information linkages, so that actual demands in all areas can be seen quickly and integrated into the planning. Regional buying is often a major source of cost savings but again supplier companies need to be connected to customer companies with good information systems, and flawless execution is a must on all sides. The big savings have to come from true cost elimination – not from exercising muscle against suppliers.

Regional co-ordination of a network of factories requires new information systems but it first requires new thinking, new processes and new ways of working. Our experience with companies implementing these ideas is that one first needs to focus on behavioral issues. In far too many cases we find that plant personnel see sister plants as at least competitors and perhaps even the enemy.

Such parochial thinking needs to be replaced with a commitment from everyone to the overall maximization of company profits. If plant closures or other forms of rationalization are needed, the sooner they can be implemented the easier it is to focus on the right issues. These include new performance measures, transparency on issues such as transfer pricing, and an end to the "country disease", where local optimization comes at the expense of global optimization. All of this implies new information systems with new data elements, and new approaches to the business.

The internet

The internet is fast becoming a critical part of best-practice demand chain integration. We believe that every company must seriously assess the potential for using this technology in its management of the supply/demand chain.

One Swedish manufacturer of food products, for example, allows customers and suppliers to link up with its information systems through the internet. This allows suppliers to acquire up-to-date knowledge about the production schedules and the market forecast. The only requirement is to have an internet browser and a password. Some suppliers are using this access to react quickly to changes in their customer's factory and in the market. The internet has considerably lowered the investment needed to link processes.

If your company has not thought about how it can use the internet – particularly for order entry – then it surely needs to do so. Again, this requires new thinking about information systems, as well as changes in processes and working practices.

Transformation

In our Manufacturing 2000 research project at IMD, we have focused a great deal of attention on "transformation". Transformation is a matter not simply of doing things better – which is necessary but not sufficient – but of doing better things.

Transforming demand chains implies new ways of working with customers, new ways of competing, new and more powerful chains, new ways of working internally, and new information systems to link the processes of companies in the chain.

Demand chain partnering implies a meshing of the gears between companies, and a recognition that it is here – in business process re-engineering across the chain – that one can make the biggest cost savings and create new value.

Too many companies tend to see supply chain partnering as asking suppliers to do something new. This thinking is fatally flawed. What is needed is a transformation of the chain, which implies changes both in the ways companies work and in the systems that guide this work. This is not a one-time process. For a demand chain partnership to be a true partnership, the companies involved need to have an aggressive improvement agenda. The question is not "What have we done?" so much as "What are we going to do next?" And in all cases it is "we", not "they".

In practice, partnering is hard work and some significant projects have to be undertaken, both for developing new information systems and – more importantly – for changing the way people do their jobs. A typical project requires personnel from one company to work full time in the other, often for a year or two and sometimes even permanently, as is the case with Procter & Gamble and Wal-Mart. Sometimes there is an "exchange of prisoners", where people from each company are placed in the other. Such experience has proved to be amazingly beneficial in understanding what one's demand chain partners really believe to be important.

IT as "fast follower"

Our closing advice is to be quite clear about the role of management in developing new information systems to support the demand chain. Managers need to see information systems as a "fast follower", not the leader of their efforts. It is a serious mistake to believe that demand chain management is about information systems. Rather, it is about new ways of doing business. It is strategic, it requires choices, and the change in management issues must not be underestimated.

For example, telecommunications companies such as Nokia now realise that their traditional customers, such as the PTTs (post, telegraph and telephone companies), were very knowledgeable about telecommunications technology, with employees who could even create hybrid systems based on components from different manufacturers. Increasingly, however, new customers are entering the mobile telephone market who would scarcely know a telephone switch from a refrigerator – and could not care less. For these customers, Nokia needs to "move up the value chain" in the way it works, taking over issues such as the design of base stations, what kinds of antenna to use in particular situations and so on. This implies a new resource base for Nokia, new selling methods, new customer support activities and new information linkages. But the information systems must be driven by the business strategy. That is, new thinking drives new systems – not the other way around.

Summary

A first step in releasing the value locked away in inefficient supply chain practices is to pose the problem in terms of the "demand chain", say **Thomas Vollmann** and **Carlos Cordon**. Demand chain thinking starts from the customer's needs and works backwards, replacing narrow focus on transport costs with consideration of how to achieve "mass customization". This entails ever more precise, swift and efficient delivery of product/service bundles, which in turn places considerable demands on the information systems along the chain. But given good management of the right systems, suppliers should be able to anticipate customer companies' needs and deliver what is needed without the need for ordering. Internet technology – via which suppliers can hook up to customers' intranets at very little cost – can play a big part in this. Such approaches require companies continuously to transform the way they work together. Information systems are important but are best seen as a fast follower of this strategic process rather than as a driver.

Enterprise systems and process change: still no quick fix

by Thomas H. Davenport

In the early 1990s thousands of companies around the world began to redesign or "re-engineer" their business processes. While the idea was not entirely new, it combined several concepts that had not been put together previously: an orientation towards broad, cross-functional business processes, the notion of starting from scratch with a "clean sheet of paper", and the use of IT as an enabler of process change.

Through the decade, some companies succeeded at this form of process change. Many others – perhaps the majority of those that undertook re-engineering, though there are no good data on the topic – experienced considerable difficulty with their projects. The desire to start from scratch, to "think out of the box" with no constraints on new process designs, led to the need for many new information systems. Since each company designed its own business processes, it had to build its own systems. And constructing an entirely new set of systems to support cross-functional processes in an integrated fashion proved simply impossible for most companies.

Re-engineering is not dead but it is substantially different today. Companies still aspire to create efficiencies across broad processes such as order management, supply chains and new product development but few clean sheets of paper are in evidence.

Re-engineering and enterprise systems

Instead, companies today largely re-engineer on the back of software called "enterprise resource planning systems", or "enterprise systems" (ES) for short. These are packages of computer applications that support many or all aspects of a company's (or nonprofit's or university's or government agency's) information needs. From accounting to manufacturing, from sales to service, ES modules support thousands of business activities. Apart from personal productivity applications on personal computers such as spreadsheets and word processors, ESs may be the only business systems an organization requires. This breadth is one of the key factors that distinguishes ESs from earlier systems.

But the primary connection to re-engineering comes from another aspect of ESs: their support of broad, cross-functional business processes. Unlike previous information systems, ESs are able to pass information freely across an organization's key business functions. There need be no functional "stovepipes".

For decades companies have wanted to integrate their information systems across broad processes; for just as many decades they have built or installed systems that address only a single part of the organization's needs. Salespeople have been unable to find out what inventory is available for sale because that information resides inaccessibly in a manufacturing system. Manufacturing cannot build only what the salespeople have sold because there is no link between the manufacturing function and the systems used by the sales force. ESs, by resolving this problem, have been the single most important factor advancing a process view of business since the decline of "clean sheet" re-engineering.

In the early days of re-engineering, ESs were not widely known; only a few companies (Dow Chemical, for example) in the early 1990s made explicit links between their re-engineering projects and ESs. I referred to ESs only briefly, for example, in my 1993 book on re-engineering, and I know of no other mentions in the re-engineering literature of the time. Since the mid-1990s, however, ESs have increasingly been viewed (by their creators and by their users) as the savior of re-engineering and major process change.

What processes does an ES support? Most major operational processes are supported by the larger and more sophisticated ESs, including those from the vendors SAP, PeopleSoft and Oracle. Though there is some variation across vendor packages, some of the processes typically supported by an ES are listed below.

Processes that ES can support

- all financial and accounting processes, including treasury, controllership, accounts payable and receivable, investment management and financial reporting
- all supply chain processes, including sourcing, procurement, shipping, billing and payment, as well as planning and optimization in the most sophisticated ESs
- all manufacturing processes (although many companies have separate shop floor systems that are interfaced with their ES)
- customer/order fulfilment processes
- customer service processes (either integrated within a vendor's ES or in interfaced but separate systems)
- sales force management (again, integrated or interfaced)
- human resource management
- maintenance of plant and equipment
- construction and project management
- some management processes (reporting, ad hoc analysis and so on).

This includes the great majority of processes that companies aspire to improve or re-engineer and support with information systems (as well as some that are rarely improved in explicit projects, such as management processes). Support for some processes, such as sales force management and customer service, has been added only recently to ESs, so these functions are not yet in wide use. The only major process that has generally been untouched by most ESs is new product development, and its addition is only a matter of time.

So adopting an ES definitely predisposes a company to manage itself along business processes. Is the process orientation encouraged by ESs achieved automatically upon implementation of the system? The answer is "no".

Process management is much more than process-orientated information systems. It includes process-orientated management and leadership styles, process-orientated remuneration and evaluation structures, organizational structures that reflect process ownership and management, and many other facets. Putting in an ES does not bring about any of these other changes. All that an ES really does in the context of process management is to remove a major barrier to it. If an organization wants to manage and measure itself along process lines, it will have to undertake a broad change effort in addition to implementing an ES.

One that has done so is Owens-Corning. The Ohio-based maker of fiberglass insulation and other building materials made multiple changes as soon as it installed its SAP system, including adopting a process orientation. Key processes were identified, including "sourcing", "finance" and "customer fulfilment", and re-engineering projects were started for each of these three. "Process executives" were appointed to own the processes and lead the change projects. One responsibility of the process executives was determining how the SAP system would support their respective processes.

In addition to re-engineering the three processes mentioned above and establishing process ownership, Owens-Corning managers undertook such process-orientated steps as changing the headquarters building to allow more cross-functional communication, creating a new process measurement system, and even developing a new product strategy. This strategy – "System Thinking" – took advantage of the company's ability to configure building material solutions across products and company functions.

"Advantage 2000", as the overall project was called, involved radical changes in virtually every part of the business and was supposed to take place within an ambitious timeframe of two years (the project has already taken considerably longer; five years is more accurate). The information systems changes alone have cost roughly $200m; re-engineering and reorganization costs have added considerably to that total. There is no question that these changes were necessary at Owens-Corning but they might have been undertaken more gradually, particularly in the case of human resource and organizational changes.

The new re-engineering

Owens-Corning did not start from scratch in redesigning its processes. Companies are increasingly using a new approach to process change that quickly and simultaneously deals with both the opportunities for significant process improvement and the constraints of a packaged information system. Owens-Corning called its approach "good enough" re-engineering; like many other companies, it simply wanted to get a system in place quickly without having to modify its ES to suit close-tailored process designs.

In ES-enabled or "good enough" re-engineering, companies commit themselves to an ES early in their projects. Then, armed with some high-level principles for how their processes should eventually work, they must then begin to compromise. The complex and difficult task of "configuration" involves reconciling how the organization wants to work with how the system will allow it to work.

In fact, the actual mapping of the system to the desired process used to be much more difficult than it is today. In the early days of ES, companies had painstakingly to decide how each of thousands of "switches" within the system needed to be set. But configuration is now much easier, in part because of the availability of process and industry templates. These constitute a predefined set of answers to the many questions that used to bedevil companies when configuring systems to their processes.

Templates are often structured by industry, so that if I work for an oil company I can start with a set of configuration decisions that are typical for that kind of company. If certain aspects of the template do not fit, then I can perform a detailed analysis and change particular aspects of the template.

Even with these templates, by the time most companies finish configuring and installing their ES they are quite ready to wash their hands of the whole thing. But configuration is never finished. First, there is the fine (or in some cases, gross) tuning of the system over time to adapt to changes in the way the organization works. The organization itself may change through acquisitions, divestitures or restructuring; external events (customers, regulations and so on) may force a change; perhaps the system never really fitted the company's processes in the first place. Maybe the company jammed the system quickly into place and now does not want to live with the result.

The system itself will also change over time. ES vendors are always announcing new releases or bringing out new modules, and ES-related software will come out continually. Each new release or module will require a certain amount of configuration or reconfiguration.

In short, fitting information systems to business processes is a matter of business-driven continuous improvement. But that is what process management is all about in the first place. And in addition to creating better information support for their processes at all times, companies should also be continually re-evaluating and readjusting the other factors that lead to good process management. Reporting structures, evaluation and remuneration systems, people skills, and other aspects of the organization also need continuous refinement and should themselves be modified to fit with new processes and information systems.

The promise of the extended enterprise

Up to now, ESs have been all about internal efficiency – not strategic differentiation. (Indeed, even internal efficiency is elusive for some users, and often requires add-on modules from third-party vendors.) But ESs become a more strategic investment when they allow a company to connect with other enterprises.

Consider the case of Adaptec, a US-based hardware and software company, which outsources its production to manufacturers in Asia. As the company was beginning implementation of SAP's R/3 software, it realised how much better it would be if the information integration it was putting in place could be extended to those critical partners. Using bolt-on software, it achieved just that; now the orders keyed into Adaptec's SAP system – and even ancillary information such as complex engineering diagrams – flow directly into its partners' systems, over the internet. Several days have been cut out of the supply chain. By extending its enterprise system, Adaptec has been able to get the same responsiveness from its "virtual factory" as it would from a wholly-owned one.

Increasingly, cross-enterprise integration like this will become the norm – it will have to, given companies' needs to compete on a new set of imperatives:

- manufacturing flexibility
- supply chain adaptiveness
- flexibility in configuring products
- lean production
- time-to-market and design chain management
- supplier relationship management
- global inventory management.

Continued

In the face of such challenges, companies will be driven to share information with other enterprises as far as possible. Once managers throughout the enterprise have the advantage of complete, accurate and timely information in their decision-making, it will seem increasingly absurd to deny it to important customers and critical suppliers. The power of ESs simply will not be contained within corporate walls.

"Son of EDI"?

The dream of closer links with supply chain partners is not new. It was the impetus behind EDI, the standard for data exchange over the past decade. But EDI led only to surface-level integration between companies, and the exchange of only the most prosaic forms of information, such as purchase orders and bills of lading. In some instances, EDI actually slowed down processes because of lack of integration between the supplier's processes and those of retailers; this happened at Gillette, the large shaving and consumer products company.

Going beyond EDI means going beyond simple data transmission to exchanging richer forms of information. It also means creating live links between systems managing related goods or information in different environments. In other words, it means taking what enterprise software does so well within companies, and extending it across larger expanses of the supply chain.

A harbinger of things to come is the successful collaboration between Nabisco Foods and its customer Wegman's Food Markets. To test a new approach called CPFR ("Collaborative Planning, Forecasting and Replenishment"), the two are sharing unprecedented amounts of information about sales and promotions. In a recent 13-week test of the new approach, they achieved a 36 per cent increase in product sales.

Where EDI allowed only a one-way flow of transaction data, the new system provides a "common visibility network" among trading partners that facilitates collaboration. Armed with the same insight into demand, they can develop their sales forecasts jointly. Companies using this approach will increasingly look like one entity, not several.

Today, this kind of collaboration takes place on the margin of ESs. CPFR, for instance, is only possible thanks to a software product (called Syncra Ct) that extracts and compares information from the different companies' enterprise applications and/or spreadsheets. Every major ES vendor, however, is beginning to build such functionality into their packages. All see it as an essential new area for development as customers, now millions of dollars into their implementation efforts, look for greater business benefits from their enterprise applications.

How soon?

There is no question that ESs will provide the foundation for true extended enterprises, and that this will be a key source of strategic advantage. But how rapidly will this happen? Both vendor and user companies have technology issues to resolve; what happens, for example, when supplier and customer have different ES packages, or very different configurations of the same one? Will companies within a given "value network" be compelled to go with the vendor selected by the most powerful member of the network, or will "middleware" make communication seamless across packages? Will the internet prove sufficiently secure and reliable to act as the connection between different companies' ESs or will third-party networks still be necessary?

Political, organizational and behavioral factors will be even more difficult to surmount. For this level of integration to work, companies and their employees will have to diminish their sense of "us" versus "them". Giving suppliers and customers access to confidential information will have to become routine; trust will have to replace suspicion. The companies that thrive will not be those that have the best technology – because that will be broadly available – but rather those that are most adept at organizational, and inter-organizational, change.

Companies that overcome such challenges, however, stand to reap many rewards. This is what is motivating Colgate-Palmolive in its latest ES efforts. Now that the company has successfully implemented its SAP software, it is wasting no time in integrating supply chain partners. With the help of the internet, the company is giving key suppliers access to such essential data as manufacturing production schedules and inventory levels. The goal is vendor-managed inventory. Colgate will no longer have to perform a task that has always involved redundant effort with suppliers. Finally, one hand will know what the other is doing.

Julia Kirby of Andersen Consulting's Institute for Strategic Change co-authored this section.

Summary

Enterprise resource planning systems are software packages that enable companies to meet the information needs of all their functions. Because they are fully integrated across functions – so marketing can access production data, say, as readily as manufacturing – they facilitate a "process" view of business. But as **Thomas Davenport** points out, while these systems remove a substantial barrier to process management, other measures are needed, such as changes in styles of leadership and in organizational structures. The eventual cost can be very high. Unlike the early days of business process re-engineering, however, at the beginning of the 1990s, the availability of "off-the-shelf" enterprise systems means that companies have a template against which to work. Even so, there are no quick fixes; process management must always be responsive to changes in the business environment and in the technology available.

Sensitivities of shared product development

by Jukka Nihtilä and Francis Bidault

Distributed product development has become standard practice in many technology-intensive industries. Telecommunications, information technology and even entertainment, for example, are increasingly characterized by rapid technological advances and the need to develop products to meet increasingly sophisticated customer needs – all on a global basis. It is clear that product development in such an environment cannot be carried out by one company in a single location. The process is inherently multifunctional, multisite and multiorganizational.

Information and communication technologies play a fundamental role in dispersed product development. Much of the work related to product development is bound to documents – most of which are now produced in a digital format of some kind – and to managing them (that is, finding, retrieving, manipulating, mediating and storing them). As products increase their technological complexity, the amount of technical documentation needed to describe them increases too. E-mail, intranets, engineering or product data management systems, and other knowledge management applications have made it technically possible to share information across functions, sites and organizations rapidly and efficiently.

A reluctant consortium?

According to our research, having the technology in place is in many cases only the starting point. A few months ago, we studied a consortium of companies charged with designing and delivering a piece of industrial machinery. The IT for sharing data across the collaboration was all in place. All the information in the project was produced by a variety of applications and computerized testing systems and stored in digital format either on engineers' desktop machines, on a network file server, in a legacy system or in a database.

115

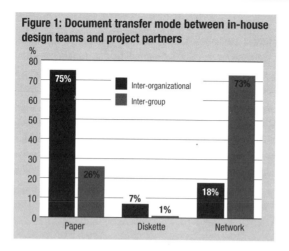

Figure 1: Document transfer mode between in-house design teams and project partners

An investigation into the way information was transferred revealed significant differences between the practices inside the companies and across organizational boundaries (Figure 1).

The transfer or sharing of documents within and even between the design groups within any particular company mainly took place via the network. In 73 per cent of cases the document was either transferred or accessed via the network. In 26 per cent of cases hard copies (paper printouts) were still used. The case of inter-organizational document transfer was quite different: 75 per cent of documents were transferred in hard copy and only in 18 per cent of cases was a network connection used.

The language barrier

In many cases, one of the first stumbling blocks in inter-organizational information sharing is the "language barrier" – the simple fact that different organizations have different operating procedures, including standards for naming, numbering and structuring documentation. Often these are strongly rooted in a company's history, people and its way of doing business. Any changes in the way documents are numbered, for example, are likely to face strong resistance.

Nevertheless, in order to facilitate information sharing, documents must be linked to a structure which is common to all organizations involved. A common vocabulary of some kind has to be in place. Information needs across organizations have be made explicit and understandable.

One way of achieving this is to visualize the document interdependency network as an essential part of the plans for each stage of the project. A regular assessment of document interdependencies could form a solid basis for a common understanding of the whole development process. Sharing a holistic picture of the project's information flow could help all the organizations and individuals involved to understand their role in the total delivery process.

Admittedly, some of the reasons for the information gap between companies are technological. Yet these problems are often exaggerated. It is true that different companies are apt to have different IT systems, which makes tight integration difficult. However, the recent emergence of platform-independent applications that rely on internet standards should make it possible to share information effectively across multiple systems. Moreover, most information needs within a dispersed product development project can often be met by being able to view and print the content.

The managerial challenge is paramount. Organizations – especially profit-seeking corporations – are instinctively reluctant to open communication channels that could affect a core process such as innovation.

Buyers and suppliers

Over the past ten years there has been a significant change in product development processes, with the growth of "early supplier involvement" (ESI). Suppliers have become increasingly involved at the earliest stages of development, a practice pioneered by Japanese carmakers and later emulated by their Western competitors. Today there is a widespread tendency in most industries to ask key component suppliers to contribute product-specific engineering studies. This obviously requires tight co-ordination between the buyer and the supplier.

Recent research by Michigan State University investigated the differences between the most successful and the least successful development projects that relied on supplier integration. The researchers' list of key success factors is representative of the issues that managers face in distributed development activities generally.

The following 12 factors – listed here in decreasing order of importance – were top of the list:

1. **Employees of the supplier were members of, or participated in, the buyer's project team**
2. **There was direct cross-functional, inter-company communication**
3. **The two companies shared education and training**
4. **The two companies set up common and linked information systems (for example, electronic data interchange, Cad/Cam, e-mail)**
5. **There was co-location of some of the buyer's and seller's personnel**
6. **Technology was shared**
7. **Formal trust development processes had been set up**
8. **Information about customer requirements was exchanged**
9. **Information about technology was shared**
10. **The two companies shared physical assets (plant and equipment)**
11. **There were formalized agreements on the sharing of risk and rewards**
12. **There was agreement on the measurement of performance.**

A further 10 factors had been hypothesised to play a role but they did not prove to discriminate significantly between the most and least successful projects.

The list illustrates a logic which we also found in our own research: IT applications are not a substitute for but a complement to organizational solutions such as co-location or joint training.

It is interesting to note that the three most important factors all relate to people. Technology-related factors only make it to fourth place. Companies that practise ESI have observed that effective teamwork across company and functional boundaries is of the utmost importance to joint development. And teamwork depends primarily on how people get on together – hence the importance of proper team-building, training, and communication channels. Once the context is set, then technology can contribute effectively.

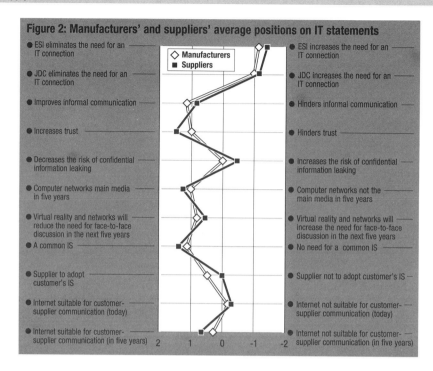

Figure 2: Manufacturers' and suppliers' average positions on IT statements

The other way round is fraught with pitfalls. We have heard countless anecdotes of e-mail- or groupware-mediated disputes between engineers who have often simply misunderstood one another. One occurred when a manager thought a colleague was angry with him because the colleague wrote certain words in capital letters in e-mails to him. The two had never actually met or talked on the phone about the matter. One of them simply misinterpreted the other's messages.

This highlights the fact that joint innovation requires cautious design of the relationship, careful preparation of human resources, and patient follow-up on these matters once the project is up and running. The importance of such preparation becomes even more evident when we consider that staff and management often have lots of concerns and even prejudices about other companies coming in on confidential product development activities.

Further evidence of the complementarity between organizational solutions and IT applications was gathered in another recent survey, in which we collected opinions from engineers involved in the development of automotive products. We surveyed both the customer and supplier side of co-operative projects (see Figure 2).

In particular, we asked respondents whether they thought "joint development centers" should "increase the need for an IT connection". Joint development centers – where engineering staff from the customer and the supplier work together on the same site (typically the customer's) – could be seen as a substitute for IT connections. Instead, respondents from both sides overwhelmingly agreed that such centers should increase the need for IT connections. This is probably because only part of the supplier's staff is "co-located", so much of the design work still has to be conducted on the supplier's premises.

Information brokers

Dedicated resources are needed if inter-organizational information sharing is to take place smoothly. But it is likely that none of the organizations directly involved in a product development process will want the responsibility of setting up (let alone maintaining) the required IT infrastructure.

Rapid advances in internet and worldwide web technologies have opened interesting opportunities for a new type of service provider, the so-called "information broker". These companies do not just take care of IT infrastructure, they also offer value-added services to multi-company projects. For example, at McDonnell Douglas a spin-off company, AeroTech, takes care of the inter-organizational system. In addition to providing access to information on the network servers,

AeroTech offers a service for Cad file conversion, a shared scheduling application and is even planning to sell McDonnell drawings for the spare-parts business.

Other examples of the information broker approach are the "private internets" developed for equipment manufacturers and suppliers in the automotive and aerospace industries. However, according to our own observations, manufacturing companies are still quite skeptical about the suitability of such networks today, even though most are optimistic that they will be more suitable in the future (see Figure 2). Their skepticism might be due to the fact that internet solutions do not as yet provide satisfactory security for the transfer of sensitive information.

Back to trust

Trust is one of the most important factors in successful technological collaborations between companies. Fundamentally it is a belief that another person (or organization) will behave in ways that will not be detrimental to us even if unforeseen circumstances should arise. Yet in this day and age, when technology is so pervasive, trust may look like a throwback to a time when ignorance prevailed, a time when traders had to "believe" in the honesty and competence of the other party because they did not have enough information about them. But now parties to a transaction have a wealth of information on one another's capabilities and reputations (and on alternative partners); surely information makes trust unnecessary because it can replace faith with knowledge.

On the contrary, many pieces of research – including the Michigan State University survey mentioned earlier – point to the renewed importance of trust. And this is quite consistent with what we know of ESI partnerships. These relationships are quite complex from an organizational standpoint, let alone a technological one.

As companies enter ever more ambitious relationships, which involve a great number of competences, to address markets with innovative, immature technologies, they expose themselves to a very high level of risk. And trust is vital in risky situations. Consequently, companies are treating trustworthy partners as assets of enormous value because the development of trust between companies is a lengthy, risky, and thus very expensive, process.

Summary

Development of high-technology products in today's global market is an expensive, complex process, so it is not surprising that many projects involve collaboration between companies, using information technology to share technical documents among managers and engineers. Research by **Francis Bidault** and **Jukka Nihtilä** suggests that even where there is a common IT infrastructure there are significant differences in the way project information is shared within and between partners. These stem partly from the "language barrier" – the fact that companies have different standards and procedures for handling documents – and partly from a natural desire to protect core processes. Careful planning of the desired information flow at all stages of the project is therefore vital. The authors also consider research into "early supplier involvement" (ESI) initiatives which shows that success depends as much on organizational solutions as on IT applications. Despite the abundance of information about the capabilities of partners and possible partners, trust is essential.

How to keep up with the hypercompetition

by Donald A. Marchand

When you meet with a group of senior managers from manufacturing companies today, the question usually arises of how many are implementing new information systems for supply chain management. Most indicate that their companies in Europe, North America and, to a lesser extent, Asia are currently planning or in the middle of implementing large projects lasting several years.

In most cases, the applications are financial, production planning, distribution and inventory management systems. Usually they add that it will take four to five years and tens to hundreds of millions of dollars in direct expenses to get the new systems into place. For large global companies, the estimates reach the $1bn mark.

Finally, when asked about the impact of these projects on competitive strategy, the managers usually say that their companies will be more customer-responsive and better able to share consistent and accurate information across functions. They will also operate at lower cost. Other managers, whose projects started several years ago, say that the Y2k problem led their companies to modernize their supply chain software and that they hope to complete these projects just in time for the date change.

While such long-term views sound reasonable, the same senior managers are beginning to raise concerns about the competitive value, the costs, the complexity and the large time frames of these projects. They are beginning to ask whether they can get more business value by undertaking less time-consuming, less complex supply chain management projects.

Moderate competition and hypercompetition

Most companies today are moving from markets in which competition is moderated by the competitive moves of industry leaders to markets in which companies position themselves aggressively against one another.

In "moderate" competition, companies position themselves around rather than directly against each other. Barriers are used to limit new entrants. Sustainable advantage is possible so long as industry leaders co-operate to restrain competitive behavior. Many traditional industries, such as chemicals, construction, cement, industrial equipment and petrochemicals, have operated this way in the past.

In "hypercompetition", companies constantly seek to disrupt the competitive advantage of industry leaders and to create new opportunities for competition. Competitive advantage is sustainable only through continuous short-term changes that create new bases for profitability and growth. This type of competition has in the past been closely associated with high-tech industries such as computers, mobile phones, microprocessors, software and telecommunications.

In the context of moderate competition, manufacturing companies can seek sustainable advantage through large-scale re-engineering projects and through database and application projects that take four to five years to implement. If the context – in terms of customers and the market – is stable enough, then highly integrated supply chain management projects of this type are likely to succeed.

However, in hypercompetitive markets, where customer loyalty is challenged continuously and where companies must transform their capabilities and processes to match or exceed those of their competitors, the pursuit of re-engineering, application and database projects that require four to five years to complete is questionable. In hypercompetition, companies change their strategic capabilities in increments of 6 to 12 months.

"Time-to-implementation" is therefore a key variable in designing supply chain management initiatives for competitive success. If the business "window" is 6 to 12 months, then re-engineering and software projects that require four to five years to complete are inappropriate. On the other hand, projects that take only 6, 12 or 18 months offer substantial flexibility; they either achieve business results rapidly or, if their competitive value shifts significantly, they can be discontinued relatively easily. In hypercompetitive industries, the windows for competing and for realizing business results from supply chain improvement projects coinciding.

Supply chains and demand chains

The operational focus of supply chain management projects is likely to differ in moderate and hypercompetitive markets (see Figure 1). In moderate markets, investment in upstream projects such as financial systems, production planning and control systems or inventory management systems can bring substantial operational benefits. These may include consistent information sharing and better cross-functional co-operation around market forecasts and production planning.

Figure 1: Competing with demand/supply chain management

Type of competition	Moderate competition	Hypercompetition
Competitive strategy	Align processes and systems over years	Align processes and systems in many small continuous steps
Demand/supply chain management	Product/supply focus Maximize volume and reduce costs	Customer/demand focus Create value (ROI) and reduce costs
Demand/supply chain process priorities	Financial management Market forecasting Production planning and control Inventory management	Customer/account management After-sales service Service management Order fulfilment and payment

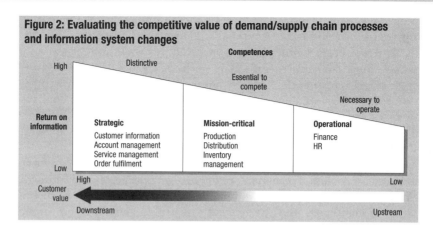

Figure 2: Evaluating the competitive value of demand/supply chain processes and information system changes

However, in hypercompetitive conditions, the focus needs to be on processes and information systems with a high "return on information" (ROI) and added customer value. In these cases, as Figure 2 shows, the operational focus of supply chain projects will shift to demand chain management and will emphasize customer interaction, account management, after sales service and order processing.

To sustain competitive advantage in hypercompetition, a company may also seek to eliminate the need for detailed management reporting and controls, or for market forecasts and production plans. Instead, it may substitute real-time, online product movement information from dealers and retailers, or simplify controls and management reporting by "delayering" the organization and empowering staff to improve process quality continuously.

The strategic value of information systems will vary according to the competences a company competes on in its demand or supply chain versus its marketplace. For example, chemical companies in moderate competitive environments focus on supply chain improvements in production, distribution and financial systems, while retailers in hypercompetitive markets are investing heavily in customer information, service management and order fulfilment systems.

Data standardization

As well as selecting the right processes and information flows to automate, general managers must also consider the business impact of the ways in which they are automated. The tradeoffs and choices that managers need to make about information management, information systems and IT are different in moderate and hypercompetitive markets.

In moderate competition, companies are concerned with the consistency and accuracy of information in the supply chain, especially between market forecasts and production planning and control, as well as in financial management, inventory management and distribution. Improvements in information management usually focus on achieving consistent data definitions among disparate functions and on removing unnecessary costs of paper handling, old, inefficient software applications and labor.

Moderate companies select projects where defining common databases and definitions up front are critical to the required level of process and information integration. Supply chain management improvements are directed at making relationships with suppliers and distributors faster and more consistent, and at lowering the cost of working capital by using inventory as the buffer of last, rather than first, resort.

In hypercompetition, information management focuses on creating value primarily by improving information use and quality in customer data, after sales service and order fulfilment; defining more consistent information for upstream processes such as financial reporting and controls is a secondary concern. In this context, creating value with customers and improving "sell through" of products with retailers and dealers is more important than standardizing the meaning and use of operational data, which may shift dramatically over time as the competitive focus of the supply chain shifts from the product to the customer.

Changing standards

The greatest changes in supply chain management during the 1990s have taken place in the implementation of software applications. First, over the past 10 years, packaged software for manufacturing companies has become a major growth market. Companies such as SAP and IBM now offer packaged software on mainframe or more distributed platforms, such as the AS 400.

There has also been significant growth in new companies such as BAAN, PeopleSoft and QED, which offer software packages on client/server platforms with versions of Unix or Microsoft's NT operating system. These new players have begun to challenge established companies on the speed of implementing applications and on the cost of hardware. They have made their software more "open" and easier to connect to other packages. In effect, they have sought to undermine the proprietary databases and integrated software applications of industry leaders such as SAP.

The good news is that these new players have brought innovations and choices to their manufacturing customers; the bad news is that many have yet to establish enough market share to be assured of being long-term players in this field.

The second major change in the supply chain software market has been a shift in the dominant pattern of software development and package adoption. This development started in the US some six or seven years ago and is now extending to Europe.

For most of the 1980s and 1990s, the dominant "waterfall" approach to implementing software projects was a complex, sequential process in which companies' needs were investigated and applications developed over four or five years (or much longer for major projects). Typically, these projects were billed on "time and materials" for both internal and external IS support personnel. Failure rates were high, sometimes exceeding 80 per cent. As package providers (such as SAP) which specialized in manufacturing company software came along, IS and functional managers recognized the value of successful implementation of integrated databases and applications, even if the cost – in time and money – was high.

Such norms have been challenged by companies that provide more adaptable software on lower-cost platforms, such as PeopleSoft, BAAN and QED, or by companies that specialize in rapid implementation on a fixed-cost, fixed-time basis, such as US company Cambridge Technology Partners. By committing themselves to a fixed cost and time, these companies share the risk of overruns with their clients. They usually emphasize the "customer value" side of the demand chain and focus on completing projects within 6 to 12 months.

As a result of these two developments, general managers today have a wider choice of software sources and implementation times than 10 years ago. Companies

22 Oct 1998

DIGITAL BUSINESS

Many retailers make the costly mistake of not preparing for the impact the internet will have on consumer habits, writes Vanessa Houlder

Financial Times

by Vanessa Houlder

The rise of the 'consumer society' has been accompanied by momentous changes in the industries that serve it. New winners and losers have emerged every few decades as shopping habits have changed and different marketing techniques emerged.

Gary Hamel, the business strategist, believes the retail industry is about to face yet another convulsive development. Aided and abetted by the internet, consumers are poised to exert an unprecedented degree of control over what they buy. "It is the ultimate triumph of consumerism," he says. Prof Hamel is exploring the consequences of this shift with Jeff Sampler, an associate professor at London Business School. Together, they are trying to construct a coherent picture of the changing relationships of producers, retailers and consumers.

The main threat facing companies is that prices will be driven down by consumers' ability to shop around using the internet. This phenomenon, dubbed "frictionless capitalism" by Microsoft chairman Bill Gates, will make it harder for companies to make money using traditional business models, says Prof Hamel.

"Money comes from knowing people won't comparison shop. People make enormous money out of friction," he says.

The implications are stark. "When information is immediately accessible there will be a huge premium on innovation. That is the only way you can resist the relentless pressure for prices to descend to variable cost," he says.

The arrival of electronic commerce will require a shift in thinking in the retail industry. Until now, the industry had concentrated on improving the efficiency of its distribution arm. Sophisticated supply chains allowed retailers to bring an enormous range of products under one roof and pass on distribution economies to customers.

We are moving, says Prof Hamel, from a distribution economy to a "search economy". In this world, consumers will want to shop over the internet and have goods delivered – even if that means paying a premium.

He rejects the notion that only affluent people are prepared to spend money to save time. Ordinary dual-income parents "who are stressed and stretched beyond belief" are the ones for whom it will have greatest appeal, he argues.

Skeptics argue that it will be too expensive to deliver goods to homes. But Prof Hamel points out that huge numbers of people are willing to pay, for instance, for pizzas to be delivered. "The impact will be a lot more ubiquitous than people think."

These changes will force companies to build new competences, he says. One example might be an ability to deal with consumer queries online. DIY stores, for instance, could allow customers to investigate their inventory online before they visit the store. If the customer wants to build a conservatory, it should be possible to go online to enter the dimensions and materials required, along with credit card details. The goods could then be selected and packaged for the customer.

This demonstrates how companies could use the web as part of a hybrid marketing strategy, says Prof Hamel. Another example is provided by Charles Schwab, the leading online broker. One reason Schwab is able to charge much bigger fees than some of its rivals is that it combines its online service with a low-cost branch network and a telephone service.

"They have recognised the web has certain virtues and weaknesses," says Prof Hamel. "The web is lousy if you have a complex question. Likewise, it does not allow for people's need for relationships. Not everyone feels happy about sending a cheque to a broker they have never seen."

Continued

For some companies, success will come from incorporating the web into their marketing strategy. But, in Prof Hamel's view, companies that currently dominate the retail industry will struggle to adapt to new ways of doing business.

This conclusion is based on experience. Every time there has been a big change in the retail industry – such as the growth in out-of-town shopping or the arrival of the huge "category killer" megastores – the arrivals have undermined the leaders.

"With each of those shifts, never did the leaders in one paradigm become the leaders in the next," he says. "I think it is just as unlikely that the winners in out-of-town shopping centres will be winners online." This conclusion will be rejected by many businesses. But complacency is unwise, Prof Hamel warns.

"Even if only 10 per cent to 15 per cent of the market migrates to the web, the impact on the rest of industry will be immense," he says. "I think most companies have a bigger danger of under-estimating than overestimating the impact."

Professor Gary Hamel is chairman of Strategos, a San Francisco-based consulting firm, a distinguished research fellow at Harvard Business Shool and a visiting professor at London Business School.

whose hypercompetitive environment demands new supply/demand chain systems are no longer forced to choose among systems whose costly, lengthy implementation periods are better suited to moderate environments.

Dynamic stability

Most large manufacturing companies today are trying to leverage their supply chains on a global, regional and local basis simultaneously. To implement application software systems quickly and effectively, companies such as Hewlett-Packard, Procter & Gamble and BP Amoco have sought to standardize their IT infrastructures on a regional and even global basis. The principle that these companies have employed is "dynamic stability". That is, against a background of a standardized global IT infrastructure, there is considerable scope for customizing local and regional applications.

A company can enjoy the cost-reducing, value-creating advantages of consistent computer platforms, operating systems, database software, and voice, video and data networks regionally and globally, and still tailor software packages for localized content where it is strategically important. As the large manufacturers just mentioned have moved to client/server technology and more robust voice, data and video networks, they have sought to institute global standards for IT infrastructure and to reduce costs as a proportion of sales. But at the same time they have rapidly implemented applications software in their demand/supply chains on a regional and local basis. As the president of a leading European manufacturer has said: "We must localize those parts of our supply chain that face the customer and regionalize all other parts of our supply chain to lower costs and improve speed of operations."

Manufacturing companies that are still debating the merits of centralization versus decentralization in IT are missing the competitive opportunity today. Their colleagues in hypercompetitive markets have standardized the commodity aspects of their IT infrastructures and services, while focusing on the 10–20 per cent of applications and information flow that adds 80 per cent of the value in their demand/supply chains.

Conclusion

Many general managers of leading manufacturing companies today are committing tens to hundreds of millions of dollars to IS and IT projects whose benefits – if any – will take four to five years to reap. To reduce the time to needed to implement IS and IT projects in demand chain management and to reap their full competitive value, managers should keep in mind the following guidelines:

■ understand the types of competition that you face and the competitive value of demand/supply chain improvements

■ shift your thinking towards demand chain management to achieve a higher return on IS improvements

■ to gain competitive advantage, define a time scale for implementing IS/IT projects in the demand chain that is consistent with the windows of opportunity in your industry

■ make sure that your people use the 80/20 rule for redesigning demand chain processes and information systems. Customize only what adds value and standardize the rest.

■ implement the right mix of business flexibility (to create value) and standardization (to lower overall costs) globally, regionally and locally.

More than one large manufacturing company in Europe has committed between $200m and $300m to integrated supply chain management projects whose implementation risks are high and whose business payoffs are perhaps low for the hypercompetitive markets of the late 1990s and the next decade. Fast, flexible, modular implementations of software systems and databases will differentiate manufacturing companies over the next two to four years in hyper-competitive markets.

Companies that embark on IS and IT projects with the wrong competitive assumptions are likely to find that their approach has placed them at a disadvantage and created significant business risks. These problems will appear just as their competitors are creating value with customers through rapid, focused and continuous improvements in demand chain processes and information management.

Summary

Many manufacturing companies are implementing new information systems to improve their supply chain management. These projects typically cost tens or hundreds of millions of dollars and take four or five years to complete. This is fine in moderately competitive markets, says **Donald Marchand**, but in hypercompetitive markets, where competitive advantage is sustained by continuous short-term changes, the cost in time and money is likely to be excessive. Such markets require a "demand chain" approach, which focuses on fast, responsive interactions with the customer; unlike moderate markets, standardization of data upstream – in financial and inventory management systems, say – is not the main source of advantage (and may even be a hindrance as the competitive environment evolves). Fortunately, over the past 10 years, companies have begun to offer flexible software packages that can be rapidly implemented and are thus well suited to fast-changing hypercompetitive markets. The author concludes with a look at the "dynamic stability" strategies being pursued by major global manufacturers, which are establishing standard global IT infrastructures to lower costs while customizing local systems to maximize customer value.

Suggested further reading

Boynton, A.C. (1993) "Achieving dynamic stability through information technology", *California Management Review*, 58–77.

Marchand, D.A. (1998) "Balancing flexibility and global IT", in *Mastering Global Business*, London: Financial Times Pitman Publishing, 91–96.

Oliver, D. and Marchand, D.A. (1997) "Hewlett–Packard (HP): competing with a global IT infrastructure", IMD International, Case Study GM 653.

When should you bypass the middleman?

by Eric K. Clemons

The internet has the power to change drastically the balance of power among consumers, retailers, distributors, manufacturers and service providers. Some participants in the distribution chain may experience an increase in their power and profitability. Others will experience the reverse; some may even find that they have been bypassed and have lost their market share.

Many strategic uncertainties are associated with consumer-orientated electronic commerce. Which products are appropriate for electronic distribution? Which consumer activities will be supported by which channel participants? Which consumer segments are likely to adopt electronic distribution? How quickly will adoption proceed? But the most important strategic question is: "Will my role in my industry increase or decrease in power and profitability as consumer's adopt e-commerce?" The framework presented below is intended to help companies address this question.

The basic framework

Any company considering launching an e-commerce attack on an established industry, whether it is a financial service such as insurance or the sales and distribution of a physical product, must consider the following questions:

Is it possible to attack?
Can I do so in a way that was not possible previously? That is, is there really an opportunity and is there really a reason to believe that it was not exploited earlier because it did not exist earlier?

Is it attractive to attack?
Assuming that it is now possible to enter, why should I want to be in this industry?

Can established players defend themselves effectively against my attack?
Will I gain share and profitability or merely force current players to alter their strategy or structure?

To see how this framework can be applied, we will consider the distribution channels for two very different industries, grocery shopping and air travel. Both have similar formats; that for grocery shopping is as follows:

- manufacturers
- wholesalers/distributors
- retailers
- and, of course, consumers.

Manufacturers – Coca-Cola, Cadbury's, Unilever and Procter & Gamble, for example – produce the products that consumers purchase. Wholesalers and distributors break bulk and ship products from manufacturers to smaller retailers while helping them with planning and promotions; most consumers cannot name any wholesalers and may be unaware of their role. Retailers, such as Wal-Mart, Kroger's, Carrefour, Tesco or Sainsbury's, are familiar to consumers and may seem as vital to them as the manufacturers themselves. We have highlighted manufacturers and consumers because they have the most vital roles: someone has to make baked beans or detergent, while someone else has to eat baked beans and use detergent; the roles of other players in the distribution channel are less fundamental.

The structure of air travel distribution is less familiar, even to frequent flyers:

- airlines
- vendors of computerized reservation systems (CRS) services
- travel agencies
- and, of course, passengers.

Airlines – such as British Airways, United Airlines and Lufthansa – operate flights and offer the seats that travellers occupy. CRS vendors – such as Galileo and Worldspan – maintain global inventory management systems and communicate enquiries and booking requests between airlines and travel agents; most travellers cannot name CRS operators and are unaware of their separate role from airlines or agencies. Travel agencies – such as American Express or Thomson – are familiar to travellers, to whom they may seem as essential for their advice or expense management support as the airlines themselves. But we have highlighted airlines and travellers, because once again they have the most vital roles: someone has to fly a 777 between Washington and Frankfurt, while someone else has to sit in the seats and watch the movies.

Now let us use this framework to assess how vulnerable the players in these distribution channels are to e-commerce attacks.

Channel power in air travel

Some players in the distribution channel for air travel are extremely vulnerable to bypass and disintermediation. While airlines and passengers will always have a role, agencies and CRS vendors are less essential. Internet-based search agents can locate flights and lowest fares; these same services can be used to book flights and to generate tickets or electronic ticket surrogates ("e-tickets").

Ease of attack

Online search agents, tied to e-ticketing, could be part of a strategy that would make it easy to attack established agencies. Airlines would start by developing systems for e-ticketing, and would make them available directly to travellers for last-minute changes, especially changes en route. This could be part of a stealth strategy to prevent agencies feeling threatened; agencies could initially be encouraged to use e-ticketing, since it would reduce their expenses, and travellers could be encouraged to use agencies for the sake of familiarity.

Since agencies would not feel threatened they would not punish airlines that introduced e-ticketing by booking as many flights as possible on competitors (a tactic they have used in the past). And airlines would not make e-ticketing too attractive to passengers during the stealth period to avoid alarming the agencies. When there was enough acceptance among business travellers, however, airlines could more actively promote e-ticketing.

Attractive to attack

The distribution channel for air travel is indeed attractive to attack. There is a large difference between profitable customers, who are easy to serve and pay high ticket prices, and less profitable leisure customers, who require more advice and pay lower fares.

The agency distribution system emerged because in the 1950s and 1960s airlines viewed all leisure travel as incremental business, but as business that required a lot of coaching and advising; this was the segment originally served by agencies. When in the 1980s and 1990s airlines noticed that they were paying commission to agencies for serving not only incremental leisure travellers but also business travellers, they began to resist. What had started as the cheapest distribution channel for incremental leisure had become an expensive distribution channel as well.

changing attitudes in the mid-1990s were the promotion budgets that they gave to airlines used marketing funds to bond previously they had provided funds to agency commissions have been cut substan-

they can encourage rapid adoption of payment" to their best accounts. This frequent flyer miles or cash rebates.

customer" we examined mechanisms for data-mining, signalling and screening. or agencies, airlines need not resort to their best accounts; most frequent flyers nature of their flights and the cost of made clear at check-in.

by the best corporate accounts will as; the business that agencies would them will no longer be routed through redirect it. Agencies will still have a serving passengers that airlines do not

their easiest corporate business to and agencies are already responding these corporate clients as rebates, profitability.

ies, but they will not be easy to

to retain corporate business, they strategy. It will be possible to survive strategy and charging corporate travel

for services.

Agencies will need to supplement their reduced commissions for serving the labor-intensive leisure market. They will need either to impose charges directly

129

upon the customers, or to introduce a service charge to be paid by the airlines themselves. Otherwise they will fail, and the cost of serving these accounts will ultimately have to be borne by the airlines.

The grocery channel

As in air travel, discussion of channel power in grocery retailing is driven by the threat of bypass, in this instance of grocery stores. As before, direct consumer interaction, in the form of home shopping, can greatly facilitate this.

We first address the concerns that might motivate a consumer packaged goods manufacturer to bypass major retailers. Many consumers today exhibit levels of brand loyalty that are extraordinarily low by historical standards. In a physical store the retailer must stock all popular brands to ensure that he has the product that a particular brand-loyal consumer might want; he cannot run ahead when I enter the store and restock the Surf detergent if that is my preferred brand, and then pull it off and replace it with Tide, my neighbor's favourite, just before my neighbor walks in. But in an electronic shopping system this is quite simple; the merchant can retain data on my shopping patterns and can readily reconfigure his displays for each consumer. Thus he can show me Surf and can display Tide prominently for my neighbor.

What will the merchant do for the vast majority of consumers who are indifferent about their choice of detergent? In all likelihood he will actively promote whichever brand has paid him the larger rebate; he will impose a positioning charge, or a rental fee for electronic shelf space, appropriating the manufacturers' margins for himself.

Ease of attack

It may appear straightforward to develop computer systems for home shopping. Upon further reflection, however, the number of dimensions that consumers will want to examine has made matters difficult. Some consumers will want to ascertain freshness, at least for some products; other consumers will want to compare price per ounce, or calories per serving, or the salt content, or the fat content, or the number of chocolate chips per cookie; still other consumers will have other concerns. This has contributed to the slow adoption of home grocery shopping.

Problems exist in physical distribution as well. Until sufficient market share has been obtained, it is expensive for manufacturers to break bulk and distribute directly to consumers; higher prices have likewise slowed adoption. Finally, unless there is a broad enough range of products available, from a sufficient number of manufacturers, consumers will not be interested in dealing with manufacturers or their electronic home shopping systems; this, too, has discouraged manufacturers' attempts at direct distribution.

Attractive to attack

Unlike air travel, where there are corporate travellers who purchase expensive tickets and need little advice, and leisure travellers who purchase cheap tickets and need a lot of advice about destinations, there does not appear to be a basis for manufacturers to distinguish between attractive and unattractive buyers of detergent or peanut butter. Although every airline has its million-mile travellers, there are no million-sock detergent users; as importantly, although airlines know their million-mile travellers, only the supermarkets know the manufacturers' best customers and they do not share this information with manufacturers. Thus manufacturers have no basis on which to pursue strategies that target their best consumers for direct distribution.

Difficult to defend

Again, unlike air travel, where corporate travellers can be encouraged to adopt airlines' bypass strategies quickly, in grocery distribution there will be slow consumer adoption of any manufacturer-initiated bypass strategy, for the reasons outlined above.

During this lengthy consumer adoption period, traditional retailers will retain considerable market share and thus a significant ability to punish the first manufacturer in any category which attempts to bypass them. This punishment will be analogous to that used by travel agencies against airlines; that is, retailers will promote the brands of manufacturers they consider their allies, and will reduce shelf space, reduce promotions and increase their own margins on brands from manufacturers that they consider to be hostile to their interests.

Predictions for grocery distribution

Ultimately, traditional stores are vulnerable. In the US, consumers view grocery shopping as a hateful and time-consuming activity. Although other activities, such as taking the family car in for a service or sitting in the dentist's waiting room, are considered even less pleasant, they take far less time out of the average consumer's week; weighted by the time it consumes, grocery shopping is by far the most unpopular consumer activity.

Thus it seems likely that online shopping and electronic consumer interaction will eventually replace much of consumer shopping in traditional physical stores. However, the analysis above suggests that alternative forms of electronic shopping will come from a source that cannot easily be punished by current retailers during the considerable period in which they are still able to punish. The threat will come from electronic intermediaries outside the current grocery distribution channel, such as Microsoft or AOL. Alternatively, if they can manage the necessary cultural transition, home shopping systems may be developed by current retailers themselves.

Conclusion

Although it looks inevitable that electronic distribution will come rapidly to air travel and eventually to grocery retailing, there remains considerable uncertainty about prospects for bypass within all distribution channels. In particular, it remains uncertain who will control the new channels, and how quickly they will emerge. Comparing air travel with grocery distribution enables us to make the following general observations:

- power gets paid. Where the intermediary or retailer can influence consumer choice it has power and can earn profits, while if the manufacturer enjoys significant brand loyalty it will have power and earn profits
- electronic distribution enables more information to be captured and can benefit the primary supplier (airline) or retailer (grocer); this increase in information produces a shift in power, which will result in a shift in profits
- established intermediaries can lose their profits without actually being bypassed; the plausible threat of bypass may be sufficient to allow manufacturers to pull out profits that had previously been retained by intermediaries

- where there is a sufficient difference between the best and the worst accounts, and where this difference can be observed, there is an opportunity for a new channel entrant. It is attractive to attack
- where the cost advantage from bypassing the existing distribution channel is sufficient, there is an opportunity for new channel entrants
- where consumer adoption will be slow and where it is difficult for new entrants to identify the best accounts and encourage their adoption of new channels, retailers will retain the ability to punish any supplier that attempts a bypass strategy
- where retailers are able to punish manufacturers that attempt to bypass them, the attacker developing an alternative form of distribution is unlikely to come from among current manufacturers.

Summary

The internet gives companies an opportunity to boost profits by selling directly to consumers. But before embarking on such a strategy managers should ask themselves three questions: is there really a new opportunity to bypass intermediaries? Is it possible to do so profitably? And what resources do the middlemen have to defend themselves? To see how these questions might be answered in practice, **Eric Clemons** looks at air travel and grocery distribution. In the case of air travel, airlines have a motive to bypass travel agencies, which take up profitable corporate business that airlines could easily handle directly – and which they can easily target given all the customer information they have. But matters are less straightforward in grocery distribution. Retailers hold detailed information about customers that manufacturers lack, and, until e-shopping is established, can punish "enemy" manufacturers by not co-operating in promotion. Ultimately, online grocery shopping may come from companies over which retailers have no power, such as internet service providers.

NEW ORGANIZATIONAL FORMS

5

Contributors

Thomas W. Malone is the Patrick J. McGrath Professor of Information Systems at the MIT Sloan School of Management.

Geoffrey McMullen is chief executive of Ukerna and vice-president (professional formation) of the British Computer Society.

Robert J. Laubacher is a research associate with the 21st-Century Initiative at the MIT Center for Co-ordination Science.

David Feeny is vice-president of Templeton College, Oxford, and director of the Oxford Institute of Information Management.

David Oliver is a research associate at IMD, Switzerland.

John C. Henderson is professor of management information systems and director of the Systems Research Center at Boston University School of Management.

Johan Roos is professor of strategy at IMD.

N. Venkatraman is visiting professor of strategy and international management, London Business School, and David J. McGrath, Jr, Professor of Management at Boston University School of Management.

Bart Victor is professor of organizational behavior at IMD.

Contents

Introduction

The main theme of this module is organizational structure and the possible shape of companies in the information age. The "networked revolution" certainly means large companies can combine the resources of being major players with the adaptability more associated with a start-up. But will the big battalions dominate or will they fragment into flexible, temporary networks of electronically connected freelances? This is still the stuff of speculation, yet convergence – between banks and insurance companies, for instance – is an organizational phenomenon now a familiar part of corporate life. Issues affecting such businesses are discussed here, as are the challenges facing newly global organizations. For the latter, as ABB has emphasized, standardized systems are an important "enabler" – but what can one learn from the experience of other large global businesses which have embarked on similar IT projects?

All change for the e-lance economy

by Thomas W. Malone and Robert J. Laubacher

In October 1991, Linus Torvalds, a computer-science student at the University of Helsinki, made available on the internet the kernel of a computer operating system he had written. Called Linux, it was a rudimentary version of the ubiquitous Unix operating system. Torvalds encouraged other programmers to download his software – for free – and to use, test and modify it as they saw fit. A few took him up on the offer. They fixed bugs, tinkered with the original code and added new features, and they too posted their work on the internet.

As the Linux kernel grew, it attracted the attention of more and more programmers, who contributed their own ideas and improvements. The Linux community soon encompassed thousands of people around the world, all sharing their work freely with one another. Within three years, this informal group, working without managers and connected mainly through the internet, had turned Linux into one of the best versions of Unix ever created.

Imagine now how such a software development project would have been organized at a company such as IBM or Microsoft. Decisions and funds would have been filtered through layers of managers. Formal teams would have been established and assigned tasks. There would have been budgets, milestones, deadlines and status meetings – along with the accompanying turf wars, overruns and delays. The project would have cost an enormous amount of money, taken years to complete and quite possibly produced a system less valuable to users than Linux.

For many executives, the development of Linux is easily dismissed as an arcane tale of hackers and cyberspace – a neat *Wired* magazine kind of story, but one that has little relevance to the serious world of big business. This interpretation, while understandable, is short-sighted. Many respected observers of the high-tech world view the Linux approach to software development – known as "open sourcing" – as a greater threat to Microsoft's hegemony than the US Justice Department's antitrust suit or the AOL–Netscape merger.

What the Linux story really shows is the power of a new technology – in this case, electronic networks – to change fundamentally the way work is done. The Linux community, a temporary, self-managed gathering of individuals engaged in a common task, is a model for a new kind of business organization that could form the basis of a new kind of economy.

The fundamental unit of this economy is not the corporation but the individual. Tasks are not assigned and controlled through a stable chain of management but rather are carried out autonomously by independent contractors. These electronically connected freelancers – "e-lancers" – join together into fluid, temporary networks to produce and sell goods and services. When the job is done – after a day, a month, a year – the network dissolves and its members become free agents again, circulating through the economy, seeking the next assignment.

Far from being a wild hypothesis, the e-lance economy is, in many ways, already

137

upon us. We see it not only in the development of Linux but in the evolution of the internet itself. We see it in the emergence of virtual companies, in the rise of outsourcing and telecommuting, and in the proliferation of freelance and temporary workers. Even within large organizations, we see it in the increasing importance of ad hoc project teams, in the rise of "intrapreneurs", and in the formation of independent business units.

All these trends point to the devolution of large, permanent corporations into flexible, temporary networks of individuals. No one can yet say exactly how important or widespread this new form of business organization will become, but judging from current signs, it could conceivably define work in the 21st century, just as the industrial organization defined it in the 20th. If it does, business and society will be changed utterly.

The hollow corporation

A future of temporary networks would seem to run counter to the wave of mergers sweeping the global economy. The headlines of the business press tell the story: "Compaq buys Digital"; "WorldCom buys MCI"; "Citibank merges with Travelers"; "Daimler-Benz acquires Chrysler". Yet when we look beneath the surface of all merger and acquisition activity, we see signs of a counter-phenomenon: the disintegration of the large corporation.

Twenty-five years ago, one in five US workers was employed by a Fortune 500 company. Today, the ratio has dropped to less than one in 10. Large companies are far less vertically integrated than they were in the past and rely more and more on outside suppliers to produce components and provide services. While big companies control ever larger flows of cash, they are exerting less and less direct control over actual business activity. They are, you might say, growing hollow.

Even within large corporations, decisions are increasingly being pushed to lower levels. Workers are rewarded not for efficiently carrying out orders but for figuring out what needs to be done and doing it. Many large industrial companies – ABB and BP Amoco are among the most prominent – have broken themselves up into numerous independent units that transact business with one another almost as if they were separate companies.

What underlies this trend? The answers lie in the basic economics of organizations. Business organizations are, in essence, mechanisms for co-ordination. They exist to guide the flow of work, materials, ideas and money, and the form they take is strongly affected by the co-ordination technologies available. When it is cheaper to conduct transactions internally, within the bounds of a corporation, organizations grow larger, but when it is cheaper to conduct them externally, with independent entities in the open market, organizations stay small or shrink.

The co-ordination technologies of the industrial era – the train and the telegraph, the car and the telephone, the mainframe computer and the fax machine – made internal transactions not only possible but also advantageous. Companies were able to manage large organizations centrally, which provided them with economies of scale in manufacturing, marketing, distribution and other activities. It made economic sense to control many different functions and businesses directly and to hire the legions of administrators and supervisors needed to manage them. Big was good.

But with the introduction of powerful personal computers and broad electronic networks – the co-ordination technologies of the 21st century – the economic equation changes. Because information can be shared instantly and inexpensively among many people in many locations, the value of centralized decision-making and bureaucracy decreases. Individuals can manage themselves, co-ordinating their efforts through electronic links with other independent parties. Small becomes good.

In one sense, the new co-ordination technologies enable us to return to the pre-industrial organizational model of small, autonomous businesses – businesses with a workforce of just one or a few – conducting transactions with one another in a market. But there is one crucial difference: electronic networks enable these microbusinesses to tap into the global reservoirs of information, expertise and financing that used to be available only to large companies. The small companies enjoy many of the benefits of the big without sacrificing the leanness, flexibility and creativity of the small.

In the future, as communications technologies advance and networks become more efficient, the shift to e-lancing promises to accelerate. Should this happen, the dominant business organization of the future may not be a stable, permanent corporation but rather an elastic network that might sometimes exist for no more than a day or two. We will enter the age of the temporary company.

The temporary company

From the 1920s to the 1940s the movie business was controlled by big studios such as MGM and Columbia. They employed actors, directors, writers, photographers, publicists, even projectionists – all the people needed to produce a movie, get it into cinemas and fill the seats. The film industry was a model of big-company, industrial organization.

By the 1950s, however, the studio system had begun to disintegrate and power gradually shifted from the studio to the individual. Actors, directors and screen-writers became freelancers and made their own choices about which projects to work on. Today, independent producers initiate projects, assemble financing and bring together teams of freelancers to join temporary companies. Once a film is finished, the company that made it goes out of existence, but its members, in time, join together in new combinations to work on new projects.

The shift in the film business from permanent companies to temporary companies shows how entire industries can evolve rapidly from centralized to network structures. Such transformations are by no means limited to the idiosyncratic world of Hollywood. Consider how manufacturers today are pursuing radical outsourcing strategies and letting external agents perform more of their traditional activities.

An extreme example is the fashion accessories company Topsy Tail, which has revenues of $80m but only three employees and never even touches its products through the entire supply chain. It contracts with injection-moulding companies to manufacture its goods; it uses design agencies to create its packaging; and it distributes and sells its products through a network of independent fulfilment houses, distributors and sales representatives.

Another, broader, example is the textile industry in the Prato region of Italy. More than 15,000 small textile firms, averaging fewer than five employees, are active there. These tiny firms operate state-of-the-art factories and warehouses and have developed co-operative ventures in such areas as purchasing, logistics, and research and development, where scale economies can be exploited. Brokers, known

139

as *impannatori*, act as conduits between the firms and textile buyers. The *impannatori* help co-ordinate design and manufacturing by bringing together appropriate groups of businesses to meet the particular needs of a customer. They have even created an electronic market which allows textile production capacity to be traded like a commodity.

Prato, however, is a relatively small and homogeneous region. How would a complex, diverse industry operate under the network model? The answer is: far more easily than one might expect. As a thought experiment, let us take a brief journey forward in time, into the middle of the 21st century, and see how cars, the archetypal industrial product, are being designed.

General Motors, we find, has split into several dozen separate divisions, and these divisions have outsourced most of their traditional activities. They are now small companies concerned mainly with managing their brands and funding the development of new models of car. Numerous independent manufacturers perform fabrication and assembly on a contract basis. Vehicles are planned by freelance engineers and designers, who join together in small, ever-shifting coalitions. One coalition may, for example, focus on engineering an electrical system, while another may concentrate on managing the integration of subsystems into complete cars. These design coalitions are autonomous and self-organizing, and all depend on a universal, high-speed computer network for communication and transfer of money. A highly developed venture-capital infrastructure monitors and assesses the various teams and finances the most promising.

Such a vision may strike some as far-fetched. But in our research at the Massachusetts Institute of Technology (MIT), we have discussed this scenario with managers and engineers from big car companies. They have not only agreed that it is plausible but also pointed out that the industry is in some ways already moving towards such a structure. Many carmakers have been outsourcing more and more of their basic design work, granting ever-greater autonomy to external design agencies.

A shift to an e-lance economy would bring about fundamental changes in virtually every business function, not just product design. Supply chains would become ad hoc structures, assembled to fit the needs of a particular project and disassembled when the project ended. Manufacturing capacity would be bought and sold in open markets. And independent, specialized manufacturing companies would undertake small batch orders for a variety of brokers, design shops and even consumers.

Marketing would be performed in some cases by brokers, in other cases by small companies that would own brands and certify the quality of the merchandise sold under them. In still other cases, the ability of consumers to share information on the internet would render marketing obsolete; consumers would simply "swarm" around the best offerings. Financing would come less from retained earnings and big equity markets and more from venture capitalists and interested individuals. Small investors might trade shares in ad hoc, project-based enterprises via the internet. Business would be transformed. But the greatest changes would be in the function of management itself.

The transformation of management

In the mid-1990s, when the internet was just entering the consciousness of most business executives, the press was full of disaster stories. The internet, the pundits

140

proclaimed, was about to fall apart. Traffic was growing too fast; there were too many sites and too many people online. Demand would outstrip capacity and it was only a matter of months before the entire network crashed or froze.

It never happened. The internet has continued to expand at an astonishing rate. Its capacity has doubled every year since 1988 and today more than 30m people are connected to it. They use it to order books, check the weather in distant cities, trade stocks, send messages and discuss everything from soap operas to particle physics.

So who is responsible for what is arguably the most important business development of the past 50 years? No one. No one is in charge of the internet – it grew out of the combined efforts of all its users, with no central management. When we ask people whether they think the internet could have grown this fast for this long if it had been managed by a single company, most say no. Managing such a massive and unpredictable explosion of capacity and creativity would have been beyond the skills of even the most astute and capable executives. The internet had to be self-managed.

The internet is the greatest model of a network organization that has yet emerged, and it reveals a startling truth: in an e-lance economy, the role of the traditional business manager changes dramatically and sometimes disappears completely. The work of the temporary company is co-ordinated by the individuals who compose it, with little or no centralized direction or control. Brokers, venture capitalists and general contractors all play important roles, initiating projects, allocating resources and co-ordinating work, but there need not be any single point of overall supervision. Instead, the results emerge from the individual actions and interactions of the different players in the system.

Of course, this kind of co-ordination occurs all the time in a free market and we usually take for granted that it is the most effective way for companies to interact with one another. But what if this kind of decentralized co-ordination were used to organize all the different kinds of activities that today go on inside companies?

One of the things that allows a free market to work is the establishment and acceptance of a set of standards – the "rules of the game" – that governs all transactions. These standards can take many forms, including contracts, systems of ownership, and procedures for resolving disputes.

Similarly, for an e-lance economy to work, whole new classes of agreements, specifications and common architectures will need to evolve. We see this already in the internet, which works because everyone involved with it conforms to certain technical specifications. But standards do not have to take the form of technical specifications. They may also take the form of routine processes, such as those which allow a group of doctors and nurses to collaborate in an operating room. Or they may simply be patterns of behavior that are accepted as norms – the "culture" of a company or "the way things are done" in an industry.

Thinking about the future

Most of what you have just read is, of course, speculative. The future of business may turn out to be far less – or far more – revolutionary than the one we have sketched here. We are convinced, though, that while the e-lance economy may be a radical concept, it is by no means impossible or even implausible. Most of the necessary building blocks – high-bandwidth networks, data interchange standards, groupware, electronic currency, venture capital micromarkets – are either in place or under development.

What is lagging behind technology is our imagination. Few people are able to conceive of a completely new economy, where much of what they know about business no longer applies. Mitch Resnick, a colleague of ours at MIT, says that most people are locked into a "centralized mindset". When we look up and see a flock of birds flying in formation, we tend to assume that the bird in front is the leader and is determining the organization of the other birds. In fact, biologists tell us, each bird is simply following a simple set of rules – behavioral standards – from which the organization emerges. The bird in front is no more important than a bird at the back or a bird in the middle. They are all equally essential to the pattern.

To meet the challenges of the future, it will be essential for us to recognize and to question the bias of our existing mindset. An e-lance economy might well lead to a flowering of wealth, freedom and creativity but it might also lead to disruption and dislocation. Free-agent workers, separated from the communal safety nets of today, may find themselves lonely, alienated and separated into "haves" and "have-nots". To seize the opportunities of this possible golden age of business – and to avoid the potential problems – we need to think as creatively, and as wisely, as we possibly can.

Summary

Despite the wave of big mergers and acquisitions over the past year or two, the days of the big corporation – as we know it – are numbered. While the cash flows that they control are growing, the direct power that they exercise over actual business processes is declining. Because modern communications technology makes decentralized organizations possible, control is being passed down the line to workers or outsourced to external companies. In fact, say **Thomas Malone** and **Robert Laubacher**, we are moving towards an "e-lance economy", which will be characterized by shifting coalitions of freelancers and small firms. Although this recalls preindustrial economic models, dominated by large numbers of competing microbusinesses, a critical difference is that these small, agile companies will enjoy the information resources traditionally associated with large corporations. The power of e-lancing can be seen in the explosive growth of the internet, which is taking place without any overall management. The role of the manager will change dramatically as companies see the virtue of achieving results by allowing them to emerge rather than by controlling them at all stages.

This article is adapted from the authors' "The dawn of the e-lance economy" (*Harvard Business Review* 76 (5, Sept.–Oct.), 1998: 144–52).

Strategies for converging industries

by David Oliver, Johan Roos and Bart Victor

The financial service industry is in the throes of significant change. To cite just one example, in August 1997 – after eight years of joint-venture activities with Swiss Reinsurance – Zurich-based bank Credit Suisse merged with Swiss insurer Winterthur. Just four months later, rivals Union Bank of Switzerland and Swiss Bank Corporation (which had previously formed partnerships with insurance companies Swiss Life and Zurich Insurance respectively), joined forces to create the fifth-biggest bank in the world, with a market capitalization of $60bn. What is going on in the tradition-bound Swiss banking and insurance industries?

The term increasingly used to describe what is happening within banking and insurance (as well as between telecommunications and information technology, road hauliers and railroads, and companies in the emerging "multimedia" industry) is "convergence". As traditional boundaries separating these industries fall, it is becoming more and more difficult to predict around which business models companies will eventually settle. For example, will the winning multimedia business model more closely resemble that of the IT, cable TV or film industry? Will companies in the new bancassurance industry more closely resemble banks, insurance companies or something completely different?

We do know that different kinds of information are going to be necessary to make sound business decisions in converging industries. It makes little sense to try to understand these industries by analyzing the "parent" industries in isolation. For example, unlike in stable industries, mergers and acquisitions in converging industries lead to the development of entirely new business systems and value chains. We have to throw away the old merger and acquisition rulebook to capitalize on the very different opportunities found in converging industries.

Just what kinds of information will we need in order to win in converging industries? In this chapter, we explore one new source of information – intellectual capital profiles – which we think can help managers do just that. But first we will review what we already know about convergence.

Two types of convergence

Two different forms of convergence appear to be occurring in many industries. The first – which we refer to as "demand-driven convergence" – occurs where customers start to consider products offered by separate industries as interchangeable. For example, in the 1970s mainframe computers and minicomputers each performed separate tasks: mathematical computation and repetitive processes respectively. However, in the mid-1970s, changes in technology meant that these two types of computer started to compete against each other in the emerging market for powerful, large-system computers.

The second form of convergence occurs when products from different industries work better together than they do separately. We call this "supply-driven convergence", and it occurs when each of the components increases the marginal

143

value of the combined whole. For example, the development of video games has increased the value of the computer, film and cable TV industries, and vice versa.

A different rationale lies behind each type of convergence. Demand-driven convergence is often driven by the need to acquire particular resources to provide broader-based products to increasingly demanding clients. These resources might include knowledge, capital or tangible non-financial assets. For example, IBM paid $3.5bn for Lotus in 1995 largely to gain access to its highly successful Lotus Notes groupware, into which IBM was able to bundle some of its existing products (such as image-processing technology). Where demand-driven convergence is occurring, companies with broad scope – operating in many different areas – can creatively bundle diverse products together and win against larger but more narrowly focused competitors.

Supply-driven convergence is often driven by industry dynamics such as "network effects" or attempts to set an industry standard. The more members a network has – that is, the more companies providing technically compatible products – the more valuable it becomes, particularly if you can set the standard. Once a technology "locks in" it is extremely costly for customers to switch, and companies providing "locked-in" products reap major benefits. Many of the alliances now forming are efforts either to be part of the "locked-in" technology or at least to avoid being "locked out". Nobody wants to be stuck with millions of dollars invested in the next Betamax technology.

How are companies trying to win in such industries, in which few signposts exist? Let us look at the world of financial services, in particular, the emerging bancassurance industry.

Bancassurance

Our research has focused on a significant convergence that has been taking place on the boundary between banking and insurance – the development of bancassurance. There is as yet no English equivalent for this French neologism but this may change before long; as regulations governing banking and insurance change around the world, the boundaries between these two industries can be expected to continue to fall.

Switzerland has recently seen a flurry of activity in the area of bancassurance. In 1996, after eight years of alliances with Swiss Reinsurance, Credit Suisse – the country's second largest bank – began collaborating with Winterthur, its third-largest insurer; the two companies merged the following year. The resulting Credit Suisse Group had a market capitalization of over $33bn and briefly became the largest player in Swiss financial services.

It was eclipsed just four months later when the Union Bank of Switzerland and Swiss Bank Corporation, the country's first and third-largest banks, announced their merger. This put an end to speculation that the two would acquire insurance companies; the speculation had been driven by the fact that UBS had a joint venture with Swiss Life and SBC a cross-selling agreement with Zurich Insurance.

The Swiss banks have tried three different approaches to enter the new, converging bancassurance industry: acquisition/merger (Credit Suisse), joint venture (UBS) and cross-selling agreement (SBC). These activities are part of a larger effort to create the industry itself. If the players succeed in doing this, they will be able to dominate the new industry; if they fail, the convergence point in financial services will be found elsewhere. How can these companies avoid being counted among the numerous convergence failures, such as IBM's acquisition of ROLM, Sony's acquisition of Columbia Pictures, or AT&T's acquisition of NCR? Let us see how intellectual capital profiles can help us grasp what is going on.

Profiling intellectual capital

Organizations have value that does not appear on any balance sheet. When IBM bought Lotus, it paid seven times Lotus's published book value because of its millions of customers, intensive research and development, strong market position and brand name. Measuring these non-financial indicators – or "intellectual capital" (IC) – may give us a better understanding of where companies are investing their money. It can help us glimpse what is going on in organizations behind their financial statements.

Are there any ways to compare IC investment across companies? We believe there is. We can think of companies and entire industries as profiles of different kinds of non-financial capital. Some companies focus a great deal on their customers, some on their internal processes, some on long-term investments, some on their employees and some on how they appear in their financial statements.

Skandia, the Swedish insurance company, has developed a framework for measuring its IC, called the Skandia Business Navigator. It breaks down the company's capital into the following five categories or "focus areas".

1. **Financial: value creation on the balance sheet**
   Financial results such as profitability, growth, operating income and shareholder value.
2. **Human: value creation by individual employees**
   Individual competencies and capabilities important in providing solutions to customer problems; includes training and development related to individuals, employee satisfaction and turnover.
3. **Process: value creation through processes**
   The efficiency of internal processes, for example, cycle times, productivity, critical technologies, information systems, administrative systems and processing time.
4. **Customer: value creation through customer relationships**
   The strength of relationships with existing clients, including market share, customer partnerships, service and customer satisfaction.
5. **Renewal and development: value creation through investment in the future**
   Investments made to develop future human and structural capital, such as the ability to innovate and learn, number of new products launched, and expenditure on long-term competence development.

The human, process, customer, and renewal and development focus areas make up a company's IC. Each area has a range of managerial tools and prescriptions for improving it (such as total quality management to improve processes, total customer service to improve customer relationships and so on). Organizations have to pay at least some attention to all of the focus areas.

We tracked all publicly announced change actions made by organizations in the Swiss banking and insurance industries between 1992 and 1996 and classified each action into one or more of the IC categories, depending on which focus area it addressed most closely. We then developed an "IC profile" of each company based on the emphasis it placed on each focus area during the period studied. These profiles – which we call "IC-DNA" – were different for each company. We studied the mergers and alliances that have occurred in the light of the IC-DNA of the companies concerned.

What is happening in bancassurance?

Our early results reveal some interesting patterns in the emerging Swiss bancassurance industry, as both demand- and supply-driven convergence appear to be taking place. The Credit Suisse–Winterthur merger can be considered an example of demand-driven convergence. The goal of this merger clearly was not cost savings, which were estimated to be a modest $100m (mainly generated through better use of office premises, reduced IT and telecommunications costs, and the ability to develop businesses jointly in high-growth markets). All 500 predicted job losses were to occur through attrition.

The real motivation for the merger appeared to be the two companies' desire to share their customer bases and to be able to offer larger corporate customers new products that they could not offer separately. For example, they could combine the insurance company's employee benefit services with the bank's asset management skills. According to this perspective on convergence, the key success factor for the new company will be its ability to offer products that extend across the former industry boundary between banking and insurance.

The UBS–SBC merger, on the other hand, represents supply-driven convergence. These companies appeared to be following a business model whose objective was to generate economies of scale in core businesses, which would lead to lower costs and ultimately feed major increases in market share. These economies of scale could then be leveraged to gain entry into adjacent markets, including lucrative side businesses such as derivatives trading. Economies of scale are necessary to service each company's huge installed base, which for banks consists largely of branch networks. According to this perspective on convergence, the key to success will be the ability to set a new low-cost "standard" in the new industry through sheer size.

In our study, we looked at whether merger and alliance activity tended to occur between companies with very compatible (similar) or complementary (different) IC profiles. We observed evidence of both patterns. In the merger of Credit Suisse and Winterthur, the two companies had the most different IC-DNA of all the companies in our study. They had concentrated on very different IC focus areas over the five years before their merger. In the case of UBS–SBC, the two companies had the most similar IC-DNA of all.

Each of these two IC patterns appears to be linked to a different convergence perspective. If the Credit Suisse–Winterthur merger was motivated by demand-driven convergence, it makes sense that "opposites attract" with regard to IC-DNA. The case of UBS–SBC seemed to be linked to supply-driven convergence, so it follows that "like attracts like".

What management issues does our study of IC in bancassurance bring to light? What happens when you put complementary IC systems together in a converging business environment?

Management implications

Here are two points to consider when taking action in converging industries:

1. When operating in a demand-driven convergence environment, you have to find ways to extend your competences across industry boundaries. This involves forming partnerships with companies that have complementary assets (or, as we put it, companies that have IC-DNA patterns very different from yours).

   In the Credit Suisse–Winterthur merger, the identities of the two businesses in the merged company have been retained. The merged company even folded Credit Suisse's old life insurance business (Credit Suisse Life) into the Winterthur Life business unit to strengthen the company's insurance arm. The objective should be to capitalize on the merged company's diversity.

2. When operating in an industry characterized by supply-driven convergence, you have to find ways to gain scale in all parts of your value chain (for example, distribution systems). This can most effectively be accomplished by choosing alliance partners that have compatible assets (that is, with similar IC-DNA to yours).

   In the UBS–SBC merger, the merger itself proceeded quite quickly, and the two banks immediately moved to adopt a single name (United Bank of Switzerland) and identity. The objective should be to make the merger as fast and painless as possible to reap the economies of scale quickly.

Summary

Boundaries between industries are blurring. This process, known as "convergence", is taking place not only in high-tech industries but also in more traditional sectors, such as banking and insurance; in Switzerland, for example, a new bancassurance industry is emerging. According to **David Oliver**, **Johan Roos** and **Bart Victor**, there are two types of convergence. "Supply-driven convergence", in which products from one industry enhance the value of products from another industry, occurs when companies strive to shape (or at least conform to) emerging technical standards. "Demand-driven convergence", in which products from different industries come to be seen as interchangeable, happens when companies attempt to provide broader products to increasingly demanding customers. A useful way to understand corporate strategy in converging industries is to examine companies' "intellectual capital profiles", which indicate the degree to which they focus on customers, internal processes, employees and long-term investments. Generally, companies seek mergers and alliances with companies with dissimilar (and therefore complementary) intellectual capital when convergence is demand-driven; but when it is supply-driven, "like attracts like".

Suggested further reading

Greenstein, S. and Khanna, T. (1997) "What does industry convergence mean?" in Yoffie, D. (ed.) *Competing in the Age of Digital Convergence*, Boston, MA: Harvard Business School Press.

Oliver, D. and Roos, J. (2000) *Striking a Balance: Complexity and Knowledge Landscapes*, Maidenhead: McGraw-Hill.

Roos, J. et al. (1997) *Intellectual Capital: Navigating in the New Business Landscape*, Basingstoke: Macmillan.

Victor, B. and Boynton, A. (1998) *Invented Here: Maximizing Your Organization's Internal Growth and Profitability*, Boston, MA: Harvard Business School Press.

The authors are extending their analysis to the US financial services industry. If you have questions or are interested in a dialogue on this topic, just send an e-mail to oliver@imd.ch

Is standardized global IS worth the bother?

by Geoffrey McMullen and David Feeny

For the corporate management of any multinational, the idea of common, standardized information systems (IS) across national subsidiaries and product businesses has long had an intuitive appeal. At the very least, the argument goes, it must be cheaper and simpler to solve the same problem once rather than many times. More importantly, as the world becomes a "global village", the achievement of a consistent and coherent IS platform is seen as imperative. For example, accounts of ABB, which has been widely admired throughout the 1990s, consistently cite its standardized systems base as one enabler of its innovative global organization.

It is clear that the efforts required to achieve such standardization are formidable. Virtually all attempts of the 1970s and 1980s – based as they were on in-house development of systems that addressed the combined needs of multiple business units – ran expensively and embarrassingly into the sand.

More recently the picture has brightened, with the emergence of sophisticated "enterprise resource planning" (ERP) software from a number of suppliers. It has become the norm for multinationals to adopt such software as the vehicle for global standardization across business units, as well as the means of integrating information across functions within units. Projects to deploy global standards are now regularly reported as completed rather than aborted. But the investment required apparently remains large – tens or even hundreds of millions of dollars of external expenditure on software and consultancy. Is this inevitable? And in what terms should we evaluate the prize that may have been won?

In pursuit of these questions, we recently studied common IS projects in seven different companies. Six were large corporations – Black & Decker, BOC, Ford, Grand Metropolitan, Shell, Zeneca; the seventh, Thomas Miller, has only a few hundred staff but operates worldwide and is a market leader in its chosen sector of the insurance industry.

In all seven, we studied high-profile projects that involved implementing standard IS support worldwide for one or more major business activities. Five companies had chosen software packages as the systems base, from SAP, J.D. Edwards and MFG Pro. One had decided to take as the standard a system already operating in one of its business units; another had committed itself to developing a new system. All had reached a point at which implementation had been successfully achieved in at least some of the target theatres of operation. Their experiences highlight a number of issues for any manager considering global IS initiatives.

Project success factors

Issue number one is understanding why these projects of the 1990s seem to be so much more successful than their predecessors of the 1970s and 1980s. This is not so much a story of technological advance as one of project management learning.

Six factors are crucial to success in any IS project (see Figure 1). These

Figure 1: Success factors in global IS projects

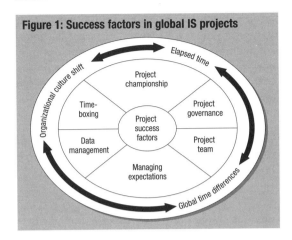

are predominantly managerial rather than technological in nature and recognize that:

- most "IS projects" are in fact properly positioned as business change projects; they must therefore be visibly championed by senior business line managers who have authority across the domain of change
- the "project champion" should be part of a wider project governance structure which can ensure the involvement and commitment of all stakeholders affected
- project teams need to be multi-disciplinary in nature and staffed by the most able (rather than the most available) people from the business and from the IS function
- the expectations of all those who will be affected by the project need to be actively managed to ensure that they understand the nature, extent and timing of change
- very few projects are delivered to "green field" sites; most must be designed to connect to a heritage of other systems and processes, and so data definitions and data management across boundaries are essential
- the business is usually best served by delivery of an adequate system sooner rather than of an all-embracing one later; mandating short time scales – "time-boxing" – drives a project culture which reflects the business priority.

In the context of global IS projects, achievement of these success factors is made much more difficult by the intrusion of the factors depicted in the outer rim of Figure 1. Consider the following:

- when new and complex systems are implemented across multiple product businesses (or scores of national subsidiaries) the time required will be measured in years not months. It is therefore unrealistic to assume that a single executive will stay the course as project champion; instead, a succession of champions must be planned. And how many able volunteers will be found to join the project team? Whereas being part of a high-profile, six-month local project can be career enhancing, disappearing to another country for several years is a different prospect
- global time differences are a daily problem in addressing such success factors as team-working and managing stakeholders' expectations. While technology such as video-conferencing can help, there is no mutually sociable working hour that links Europe, the US and Australia

149

- global IS projects are usually associated with shifts in organizational power that are more easily embedded in organizational charts than in organizational mindsets and culture. Project governance and championship arrangements may be exhaustively scrutinized for various shades of political correctness. The implementation of data standards, so dear to head office in London, may be obstructed as officious meddling or a costly irrelevance by the Brazilian factory management.

While project management learning has dramatically improved the track record of global IS projects, they continue to demand high levels of management ability, time and attention. They clearly are not to be undertaken lightly.

Software packages

Although package software has little obvious impact on these success factors, it is clear that most global IS projects are based on the available ERP systems. Comments from our research suggested several advantages to this approach:

- it short-circuits potentially lengthy debates about functional requirements; what is required is what is in the package
- it frees people to focus on the challenges of project implementation rather than programming
- it emphasizes and assists the creation of standard global business processes
- it assists the achievement of data standards (interestingly, this related more to older centralized software such as SAP R2 rather than distributed software such as SAP R3).

These advantages arguably increase the chances of successful project completion. However, none of the companies in our study claimed that the emergence of ERP systems has reduced project costs (indeed, we find no evidence for this anywhere). Issue number two for managers, therefore, is to understand that, with or without ERP, global IS projects require massive investment.

Business benefits

Issue number three is to establish what business benefits have been and can be achieved through such investments. As projects move towards conclusion in many corporations, this is the issue most under scrutiny at present.

Our research case studies were all self-reported successes but in most of them "success" was not sharply defined. Benefits reported included "integrated information", "year 2000 compliance", specific operational improvements and a general expectation that future software maintenance costs would be lower.

These may be useful benefits but they surely do not match the scale of investment and resources required to achieve them. For most, it seems, the implementation of a common systems base has been something of an act of faith (or "broad strategy"). There may be a belief that it is a necessary enabler of some yet-to-be-defined future method of global management, that benefits will emerge once the new infrastructure is in place, or that the business will be competitively vulnerable without such a capability in place. We question such a stance.

Two of our case studies were distinctive, and could provide much more definite responses to the business benefit question. Rather than defining their projects in terms of new systems infrastructure, each of these companies had targeted a specific and compelling business requirement.

Targeting global IS initiatives

Our evidence suggests that investments in common global IS have most value when they are targeted on specific business ideas within the broader agenda of "globalization". In earlier research we used Michael Porter's "configuration/co-ordination framework" to facilitate managerial discussion of the most important targets. In the example shown in Figure 2 (of a global electronics business) management concluded that:

- there would be a major business advantage if research and development, which was centralized, could be devolved to create a "close-to-the-market" presence in each region; but close co-ordination across the regions remained imperative to avoid wasteful duplication

- no value had been added by the centralization (in the name of globalization) of the logistics function. It needed to be devolved to the regional level

- the consolidation of manufacturing from national to regional level had been appropriate. There would be some advantage in increased co-ordination, focused on the transfer of learning

- while the sales function inevitably had to operate close to the customer, it was becoming essential to establish key account managers to co-ordinate activity with customers who were becoming global.

With these directions clarified, the implications for IS were relatively straightforward – a common computer-aided engineering (CAE) infrastructure for regionalized R&D, groupware-type facilities for account managers, and so on. It was clear to executive management that organizational changes would have to accompany each IS investment.

Figure 2: Targeting global IS initiatives

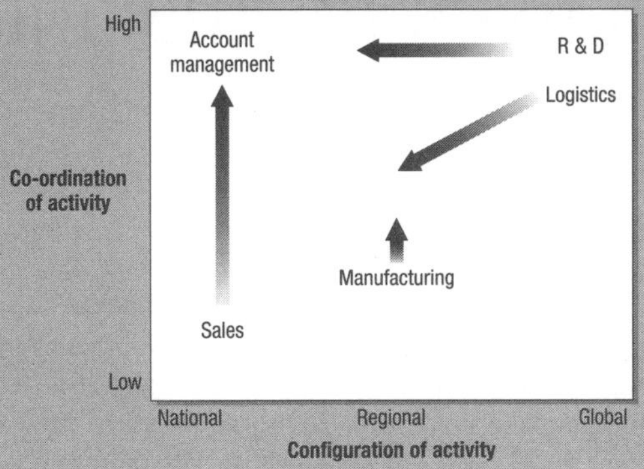

In one case, the chief executive had identified the globalization of procurement as a critical lever for product cost restructuring; this company's project was therefore defined as providing the means by which the new function could operate. In the other case the company had an even clearer imperative: it had been told that it would lose its biggest customer unless it put in place the capability to serve that customer in a standard way around the world.

With clear business imperatives, it is not surprising that these two companies were more articulate about their achievements. They also completed their (more limited) projects in much less time than the other companies. And there is one final point of difference: neither used package software as the base for its efforts. We would not want to suggest that there is a real causal relationship here. But promoting to all concerned that this is the "Global Customer Project" or the "Global

Purchasing Project" – rather than the "SAP Project" – must help to concentrate the mind.

Global information systems and decentralized cultures do not mix. These IS investments need to be components of phased and targeted plans to achieve a more global corporate mindset.

Summary

Managers in multinationals have long recognized the desirability of standardized global information systems. But it is only in the 1990s that projects to put such systems in place have had much success. According to **David Feeny** and **Geoffrey McMullen**, this is primarily due to better project management; among other things, companies now recognize the need for senior business managers to support such projects and for stakeholders' involvement and expectations to be carefully managed. The emergence of "enterprise resource planning" systems has also helped managers to focus on implementation instead of debating data standards and common business processes. The authors conclude with a discussion of the business benefits. Strikingly, of seven multinationals that they studied recently, only two – which undertook their global IS projects to support specific strategic objectives – were able to articulate substantive benefits.

Five principles for making the most of IT

by John C. Henderson and N. Venkatraman

We are in the midst of profound shifts in how corporations are structured, how markets function and who delivers superior value to customers and shareholders. We need to rethink the role of information systems and technology: from merely supporting business operations to being central to core capabilities; and from an internal, operational focus to an external, customer focus.

Jack Welch, chairman of General Electric, put it well in his 1996 letter to shareholders: "Information technology is making the huge transition from the 'function' it was in the 1980s – with its own language, rituals and priesthood – to the indispensable competitive tool, the central nervous system of virtually every operation in the company." Managers across a wide variety of industries and markets now realize that information systems and technologies will be an important driver of strategies and organizations in the 21st century.

However, companies are confounded by the complexities and subtleties involved in leveraging IT resources. How best to extract value from IT is unfortunately not an analytical issue of figuring out the most appropriate value metric. It is a question of creating a new management approach that is suited for the information age, rather than simply overlaying IT on industrial business models.

Realizing IT's potential to create value has emerged as a senior leadership issue and cannot be delegated to lower operating management levels. Senior

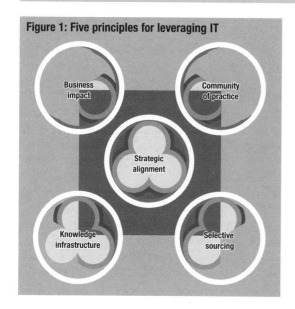

Figure 1: Five principles for leveraging IT

management teams and boards of directors are giving more attention to IT than ever before.

Based on our research and consulting experience with large companies on both sides of the Atlantic, we have distilled a set of five principles for effectively capitalizing on the value of IT. These are schematized in Figure 1.

1 Business impact

Value realization lies in the design of new business models that are enabled by IT and in the design of product/service platforms for the information age.

Every company's products and processes will become increasingly information-intensive and linked through communication and data networks. So we cannot and should not look at the value of IT just from an operational efficiency perspective. Some IT resources will be directed at enhancing operational efficiency while others will be directed at creating business differentiation. Product or service features will be fused with underlying information system capabilities and every business process will be anchored in unique information attributes. The executive challenge will be how best to trade off the different ways in which IT can have an impact on the business.

Products

As products become more information-intensive, the power of IT consists of enhancing product/service features. Think of the potential for enhanced service when appliances such as toasters, refrigerators, televisions and copy machines are connected to a (domestic) network. Take the case of the latest Lego product – the MindStorms robot. It is a programmable 8-bit computer housed within a large Lego brick. Its software runs under Windows 95 and the user can program it to perform an endless variety of tasks.

Or consider the OnStar system that General Motors is installing in many of its vehicles. This is an information service, available for a fixed fee, that uses Global Positioning System satellite technology and a hands-free, voice-activated cellular phone to link the driver and vehicle with a call center. Advisors provide real-time,

27 Oct 1998

DIGITAL BUSINESS

More car buyers are using the internet and as a result are better prepared for their deal, writes Nikki Tait

Financial Times

by Nikki Tait

At least one-quarter of new car buyers in the US use the internet at some stage in the purchasing process, according to recent estimates. So does this mean that the days of haggling on a dealer's lot, or rustling through pages of over-hyped advertising and small print in newspapers are over? Nice thought – but not quite the reality, although matters may be moving that way. What the internet has created is a group of savvier, better-informed buyers. But try to find the best price – even for a new car – and you will still burn up energy.

Alex Simons, group product manager for Carpoint, the internet-based car-buying service run by Microsoft, sums up the customer problem. "What we found through our research is that there are four or five big purchases that people make in their lives that they generally are uncomfortable with – and automotive purchasing is number two after buying a house," he says. "It's unpleasant for two reasons. It's hard to get all of the information on what kind of car is right for you, how much you should pay for it, what the right features are. It's also hard because traditional dealerships have not been very customer-friendly organizations – there's been a lot of back and forth, game-playing."

On the first score, the internet is already a big help. A raft of car-buying services – including Carpoint – now post useful consumer reports and background information on vehicles. Most big car manufacturers have also clambered on the bandwagon, providing online product details, suggested list prices, and local dealer details. As Mr Simons puts it: "It's not that those things weren't available before, but it was work to get them. Now they're available for free on one website."

But the buying process itself is less easily tackled. Take Carpoint. It has a network of about 2,000 vetted dealers, made up of both independents and members of some bigger chains, such as Wayne Huizenga's Republic group. Each dealer pays Carpoint a flat monthly fee, averaging around $1,000 (£586), and is required to have a dedicated Carpoint service person on site.

The customer, meanwhile, e-mails Carpoint with model requirements and a personal address and telephone number, and is notified in return of one or two dealers in his/her location. Providing a telephone number is obligatory – a requirement which Microsoft justifies on the grounds that not all Carpoint dealers have e-mail facilities. The dealer then contacts the customer.

Carpoint admits that the service does not aim to give the customer a wide range of alternative purchasing outlets. "You're right – there's no case where you could access more than two dealers from your area," says Mr Simons. "The object is to ensure that you are getting to a dealer who is going to service you."

Still, would not a glance through the local paper actually give a typical customer a better idea of competitive sales offers for what – in the new car market – is essentially a standard product? "We're not trying to set up a situation where you're bidding among multiple dealers," Carpoint stresses. "The customer who is looking for absolutely the best price can plan to spend five or six weekends driving all over town. It's the customer who values their time highly, but wants to find a good price with no work, who Carpoint is trying to service."

The online service adds that its dealers are required to quote "best prices" immediately, and that any negotiation is grounds for removal from the service.

Admittedly, not all internet-based services work this way. A few provide a bigger range of dealers in response to a customer query, most of which actually

Continued

post prices for the vehicle in question. This leaves more of the initiative in the customer's hands. And, either way, the online buying process does have the big advantage of reducing time spent in a showroom. At present, these services tend to be the focus of new car buyers. "About two-thirds of our users are looking for new cars and about one-third for used cars," says Mr Simons, for example. "That is really a reflection of the demographics of the internet right now. We expect that over the next two years, we'll see that flip. In the US, about 35m used cars sell each year, and only about 15m new cars. We're still early in this. We think the used will grow substantially faster."

But running an online used car service would also seem to present more challenges – simply because the products are not standardized. Mr Simons

acknowledges: "We already allow more for exactly that reason. Any day we hav 100,000–120,000 used cars listed."

Perfected or not, online car-buying has become a big growth area. Carpoint says that about 1.69m customers came to its site in August alone. Based on follow-up discussions with users, it believes that about 5–6 per cent of the daily hits resulted in a request form being sent off. "We're driving over $300m in car sales a month now," it claims.

Mr Simons makes the point that much of this growth has occurred in the past 12 months. "It really is taking off. In January our estimates were that about half a per cent of all of the new car sales in the US were being sold through an online buying service. In six months, that number increased to 6 per cent."

The shift has already got the attention of the "Big Three" car manufacturers. GM plans to launch its "GM BuyPower" online service next year.

person-to-person services such as automatic detection of air bag deployment (and alerting of emergency services), stolen vehicle tracking, route finding, remote diagnostics and remote door unlock.

Processes

Business processes are also becoming more information-intensive. Companies can achieve greater supply-chain efficiency through better use of information. Wal-Mart, Dell Computers, National Semiconductor, Gap, Motorola and others are continually improving their operating efficiency through knowledge-intensive logistics. These allow rapid modification of supply-chain processes through real-time processing of information.

Superior customer service is still focused on person-to-person interactions but is considerably enhanced when supported by appropriate information systems. Customer service in British Airways, for example, is supported by its Caress system. Ritz-Carlton uses high-tech systems to support its personalized hospitality service.

IT's strongest impact on processes is its capacity to fundamentally change business capabilities, leading to the creation of new business models. Encyclopedia Britannica is in the midst of a serious business shift, as it attempts to transfer its dominant position in print media to electronic media. Hallmark Cards is trying to straddle the physical space and the virtual space. New entrants such as E*Trade (www.etrade.com) and Ameritrade are challenging traditional stockbrokers. New-style auctioneers (such as www.ebay.com and www.priceline.com) are challenging the traditional assumptions of supplier–buyer relationships. Amazon.com has rocked book retailing. Television network NBC is trying to create an entertainment platform that is seamless across network television (NBC), cable (CNBC) and the internet (www.msnbc.com).

2 Communities of practice

Value realization requires an organizational architecture that is able to co-ordinate a community of professionals with complementary expertise.

The second principle for value creation focuses on the need for organizational co-ordination. Value maximization is not simply a matter of allocating some resources and waiting for results to appear. Nor is it a matter of restructuring the IT organization with greater decentralization and autonomy – many companies still find themselves swinging back and forth on the centralization–decentralization pendulum.

As IT becomes more important to business operations, the roles and responsibilities of those managing this critical resource should be reconceptualized. Successful companies are designing communities of professional practice that are different from traditional hierarchical and rule-bound organizational structures, which often isolate IT professionals from one another and their business clients.

Consider an organization that is seeking to implement an enterprise resource planning system (such as SAP or Oracle) for a supply chain or for global new product development. It is unlikely that all the professionals involved will work for the same manager or even the same company (given the use of external vendors and consultants). Or consider the development of global transaction processing systems in banks such as ABN-Amro. The teams responsible cut across organizational boundaries and different types of expertise and organize themselves as networks rather than hierarchies.

Companies are developing ways in which experts involved in such tasks can feel part of a larger system bound by shared goals and incentives. The power of networked organizations is high when traditional "command-and-control" is minimized and expertise is shared. We suggest that IT organizations should explore the benefits of creating a professional context that fosters trust, innovation and knowledge sharing – a community of practice.

An example is the "transition alliance" developed inside Xerox for deploying a new global IT infrastructure. This professional community included important IT infrastructure managers across Xerox's many business units. Working together, they were able to provide Xerox with a new, coherent infrastructure in minimal time with significant cost savings. The community became the forum in which project requirements were interpreted and relayed to widely distributed operating groups for implementation. While each member of the community ultimately acted within the context of his or her business unit, the alliance was the foundation for the broad commitment needed to accomplish the project.

A similar strategy is being used by BP Amoco in its efforts to improve its ability to find and drill for oil. Building upon initial experiments with "virtual teams" – experts working together via video conferencing – it has developed a global community of practice. Involving over 250 of BP Amoco's own drilling professionals and more than 500 from partner companies, the community uses internet-based systems to share best practices and lessons learned. It has proved to have significant business value; after all, effective problem-solving in the short term boosts long-term cost-effectiveness.

3 Selective sourcing

Value realization is enhanced by assembling the required IT capabilities through a portfolio of relationships that is adapted over time.

The third principle for value creation focuses on the need for selective outsourcing of IT through a variety of alliances and partnerships. This complements the communities-of-practice principle.

Given the tremendous growth in IT products and services (estimates suggest over 50,000 new product/service introductions per year), it is unrealistic to expect any company to maintain the required expertise in-house. The principle of selective sourcing stipulates that every organization should articulate a strategic approach to sourcing and assembling its required capabilities. A rule of thumb is that a company should direct internal expertise to IT-enabled capabilities that differentiate its operations, while allowing partners to see to those capabilities that at best provide competitive parity.

Take the case of J.P. Morgan. In 1996 it set up a consortium, Pinnacle Alliance – in which CSC was the primary partner, but which also included AT&T Solutions, Andersen Consulting and Bell Atlantic – to manage its data centers and voice, data and software services. The company has redirected its internal resources towards the development of complex computer programs needed for securities trading and other financial services.

J.P. Morgan is not unique. ABN-Amro, BP Exploration, Shell, Volvo, General Dynamics, Xerox, DuPont and others are all trying to optimize their IT capabilities through outsourcing. The challenge they face is to avoid thinking of outsourcing as a means of abdicating responsibility for this critical resource. Instead it requires them to orchestrate a portfolio of different types of relationships for different levels and types of capability.

Some relationships are set up simply to get communications networks or data centers up and running. Others are more strategic, in that they drive business differentiation. Although it is preferable to keep differentiating activities in-house, companies may lack the necessary expertise, decide that it is not cost-effective to do so, or want to experiment and reduce the risk by outsourcing.

Bankers' Trust is selectively deploying a "venture capitalist" model to seed the development of technology-based capabilities. Identifying IT-enabled capabilities that might be possible in future and entering into strategic relationships early on is a big challenge.

4 Knowledge infrastructure

The new economy is likely to reward intellectual assets more than physical assets; value realization requires the creation of a business platform suited to this environment.

There is widespread view that a new type of economy is emerging, in which organizations will be less characterized by their ability to make, store and move physical assets than by their ability to create, share and use knowledge and expertise. Vincent Barabba of General Motors, for example, has described this as a shift from "make-and-sell" to "sense-and-respond". James Wolfensen of the World Bank has proclaimed that his organization needs to become "the Knowledge Bank".

If such aspirations are to be realized, companies will need to have the right information infrastructures in place. However, current infrastructures – which are designed to support operational efficiency – are proving to be inappropriate. Thus the challenge is to design and deploy infrastructures that will serve as the backbone for the management of intellectual capital. Far beyond static databases for structured numerical data, these will enable virtual work and the sharing of context-rich information. They will link individuals to an array of experiences, documents and lessons learned, blurring the distinction between "doing" and "learning". Companies will be able to mobilize their expertise anywhere in the world and bring it to bear on a specific problem or training opportunity.

While the community-of-practice principle focuses on the importance of expert teams, this one is about leveraging the knowledge contained in the whole organization. We can see it in practice already, as many organizations develop the knowledge infrastructures that will sustain them well into the next century.

Schlumberger's Information Network (SINet), for example, allows employees rapidly to download updated design tools (and tips for their use), enhancing their ability to solve customers' problems. The network has also been of benefit in training the company's young professionals. The US army has established the Center for Army Lessons Learned to spearhead its efforts to share knowledge. As it increasingly has to undertake "peacetime" operations, it wants to codify and transmit the lessons it is learning. Training increasingly involves multimedia simulations. Sainsbury's, the UK supermarket chain, has an "innovation center" in which managers can explore new work environments designed to promote innovation through better knowledge sharing and team collaboration.

5 Strategic alignment

Value creation through IT rests on strategic alignment of the four principles discussed above; this is a dynamic process, as the changing business environment drives the evolution of new organizational models.

An overarching principle of value creation is that senior management should be able continually to align business and IT operations. An organization's leaders should be able to integrate the four principles discussed so far in a way that is unique to the organization. Otherwise, the four principles taken individually could lead to different approaches to value maximization or even conflict with each other. Accordingly we have placed strategic alignment at the center of Figure 1.

Alignment needs to be seen in dynamic terms, as helping to guide the organization into the information economy as well as guaranteeing efficiency today. Senior managers must ensure that actions guided by the four principles above are constantly adapted in response to a turbulent, intensely competitive environment.

Strategic alignment is made more important by the growing emphasis on managing intellectual capital. Thus there is a shift towards creating knowledge infrastructures that also serve as platforms for superior product/service delivery. IT investments cannot be decoupled and managed independently from other business investments.

Dell Computer's business model cannot be designed and implemented without IT (business impact principle). At the same time, one of the reasons for its success is its ability to learn about customer preferences and to redefine product/service offerings accordingly (knowledge infrastructure principle). Indeed, the rapid growth of the internet and of electronic commerce creates major opportunities for integrating the four principles.

Not analysis but leadership

Realizing the value of IT is not a matter of fine-tuning the IT budget process. Neither does it involve more refined calculations of cost-benefit ratios, nor looking for new metrics. Instead it is a matter of leadership, of recognizing the new and powerful role of IT – not for greater operational efficiency through re-engineering but for value creation through new business designs. Value realization is also a question of leading the organization into the 21st century, where information and knowledge will be much more important drivers of business value than they are now.

Just as obtaining value from globalization requires more than simply establishing a set of overseas subsidiaries, obtaining value from information means more than just buying powerful applications and systems. We hope that the five principles discussed in this chapter will generate constructive dialogue. They should allow managers responsible for IT leadership to move discussions of value realization away from the selection of metrics and towards ways of creating and appropriating business value under uncertain conditions.

Summary

IT has gone from being a separate, rather arcane business function to being a central part of competitive strategy. But how can companies maximize its potential to create value? According to **John Henderson** and **N. Venkatraman** they need to adhere to five principles. First, they must understand that IT is far more than just a means of boosting operational efficiency. It can profoundly change the nature of products, services and business processes. Second, successful implementation of IT systems requires the establishment of cross-functional "communities of expertise", for which "command and control" management is inappropriate. Third, as we have seen earlier in this book, the growing complexity of the IT market means that selective outsourcing is essential. Fourth, companies must ensure that their IT infrastructures maximize the knowledge locked within them and focus it where needed. Finally – and most importantly – managers must strive to align these principles with one another and with their corporate strategies in a fast-changing world.

KNOWLEDGE MANAGEMENT

6

Contributors

Thomas H. Davenport is professor of information management at Boston University's business school and director of the Accenture Institute for Strategic Change.

Michael Earl is professor of information management at London Business School.

Donald A. Marchand is professor of information management and strategy at IMD International, Switzerland.

Ian Scott is a visiting research fellow at the Centre for Research in Information Management, London Business School.

Charles Despres is professor of organization at the Graduate School of Business, Marseille, France, (ESC-MP) and affiliated professor at the Theseus Institute, Sophia Antipolis, France.

Larry Prusak is executive director of IBM's Institute for Knowledge Management in Cambridge, Massachusetts.

Danièle Chauvel is director of the Information Centre at the Theseus Institute, Sophia Antipolis, France.

Peter Murray is a research fellow in the Information Systems Research Centre at Cranfield School of Management.

Contents

Introduction

This has been one of the hottest business topics of the late 1990s. Few these days deny the immense power of knowledge, but how do you share and apply it? How do you make tacit knowledge implicit and convert one person's insights and wisdom into another person's awareness? How do you turn individual experience into organizational learning? These questions have become more urgent at the same time as "delayering" and "downsizing" have robbed many companies of valuable corporate memory. However, a range of technologies – such as the internet, groupware and teleconferencing – offer dynamic organizations the opportunity to gather and exploit knowledge profitably.

Is KM just good information management?

by Thomas H. Davenport and Donald A. Marchand

The concept of "knowledge management" emerged several years ago at a time when managers' skepticism about business fads seemed to be at an all-time high. Was KM, they wondered, merely a different, more up-market label for information management? Their suspicions about the origins of KM were nurtured by several remarkable "coincidences":

- many early writers and speakers on KM (including the authors of this article) had previously written and spoken on information management
- many tools deemed useful for KM (the internet, Lotus Notes, search and retrieval software) had also been widely used to manage information
- much of the "knowledge" found in KM repositories looked remarkably similar to information resources previously held in paper form (for example, directories of experts in companies).

An observer with an historical perspective might have been even more suspicious. For the previous 30–40 years of computer use in business, the information that had counted most was that which could be "automated", which was usually called "data" – highly structured, quantitative shorthand for real events and human attributes. What could be programmed and processed by modern computers in the form of "data" or "transactions" seemed more important than information confined to paper records and documents (which was nevertheless where most information resided).

In the 1970s and 1980s, as computer technology combined with networks and new software tools became available, businesses moved from data processing to information systems and document management. No sooner had people and organizations got the hang of dealing with data than managers began to aspire to "information management". Suddenly, when they were starting to master that, "knowledge management" appeared.

The skeptic could easily conclude that nothing more significant than terminological inflation was happening. After all, people had been talking about the "information age" since the advent of data processing; perhaps by the time organizations really got to the point of managing information, they needed to dignify it with the term "knowledge".

The issue we address in this chapter, then, is whether KM is really different from information management. We will argue that there is a large component of information management in KM, and that much of what passes for the latter is really the former. However, true KM goes well beyond information management in several ways.

A question of value

It may be useful to try to shed some light on these overlapping terms. Generations of philosophers have wrestled with the deep meanings of "knowledge"; as business school professors we feel obliged to offer a pragmatic definition.

Data, information and knowledge are points along a continuum of increasing value and human contribution. Data – the signals about human events and activities that we are exposed to each day – has little value in itself, although to its credit it is easy to store and manipulate on computers.

Information is what data becomes when we as humans interpret and contextualize it. It is also the vehicle we use to express and communicate knowledge in business and in our lives. Information has more value than data and, at the same time, greater ambiguity – as any manager will attest who has ever argued over how many interpretations the terms "customer", "order" and "shipment" can have inside the same company.

Knowledge is information within people's minds; without a knowing, self-aware person there is no knowledge. Knowledge is highly valuable, because humans create new ideas, insights and interpretations and apply these directly to information use and decision making. For managers, knowledge is difficult to "manage" in other people because (being mental) it is invisible and its extraction, sharing and use relies on human motivation.

In practice, it is difficult to determine exactly when data becomes information and when information becomes knowledge. We usually advocate spending little energy on classification and a lot of energy on adding value to whatever you have and advancing it along the continuum.

What is managed in KM?

For a 1996 research project Thomas Davenport and colleagues examined 31 different "KM" projects, as they were called by their managers. What companies actually managed in these projects appeared to be a mixture of information, knowledge and perhaps a little data. Eighty per cent involved the creation of some kind of repository, which held a wide variety of items that employees might find useful: best practices, competitive intelligence, sales presentations, product documentation and even cafeteria menus and bus schedules.

Many companies explicitly strove for "one-stop shopping" – a single location for all the useful content anyone could desire. Certainly, much of it would need further digestion and interpretation before being considered high-value knowledge; therefore, it was probably information. But simply locating desired information in a large collection is one means of adding value.

Some repositories included what might be called "information about knowledge". This is information that guides the seeker to knowledge, whether in the form of a document or an expert. So-called "knowledge maps" and "knowledge yellow pages" or expertise directories describe a set of knowledge categories, the location of the knowledge and, in some cases, its condition and value. If one believes (as we do) that the most important knowledge is in people's heads, facilitating access to it through improved information management is an important part of KM.

The primary reason for this close link between information and KM is that people in organizations are constantly converting knowledge into various forms of information (for example, memos, reports, e-mails and briefings) and acquiring information from others to improve their knowledge. This continuous conversion of knowledge into information and information into knowledge is required because people cannot always share their knowledge person to person. There are constraints involving personal time and attention as well as the number of people who must be kept informed across time zones and geographical locations.

In addition, since organizations exist to achieve predictable results, their members are encouraged to share their knowledge. This occurs through improved management of information about where knowledge resides, how it can be deployed and reused, and when it can create greater business value through new ideas and innovations.

Previous approaches to KM benefit from the use of IT and improved information management practices. Some companies excel by developing their capabilities to collect and organize information about knowledge, to provide broad access to it, and distribute it over distances. But there are other aspects of KM that distinguish it from information management and do not rely on computers or telecommunications networks at all (or at best only tangentially). Unfortunately, these are its most difficult aspects, and they are the ones that most strongly differentiate organizations. The truly distinctive aspects of KM fall into two key categories: the creation of knowledge and the use of knowledge.

Knowledge creation

Knowledge creation is not a new subject, but it has recently been the subject of renewed investigation in the context of business. Books such as *The Knowledge-Creating Company* and *Wellsprings of Innovation* demonstrate a strong connection between knowledge creation and innovation in product and service development. Large Japanese companies such as Canon and Sharp and a few Western companies such as Chaparral Steel and Oticon of Denmark have relied on knowledge creation to foster long-term innovation and strong business performance.

However, there are bracing messages for companies wishing to replicate these companies' approaches to innovation. The Japanese companies that excel in this regard have a strong focus on tacit knowledge (essentially knowledge that is difficult to express in words); they motivate knowledge creation through bold visions of products and strategies coupled with organizational cultures that promote sharing, transparency and active use of knowledge and information. Honda, for example, used the phrase "Let's gamble" to guide the creation of a new city car model. Japanese companies also have human resource policies (such as rotation of employees around different functions) that support their emphasis on tacit knowledge. Western companies are not likely to adopt such practices easily.

Among the few Western companies that specialize in knowledge creation and innovation, the sobering lesson is the pervasiveness of these orientations within their cultures. At Chaparral Steel and Oticon, for example, there is no "division of knowledge labour"; knowledge creation is everyone's job. Even the lowest-level worker is considered capable of designing production experiments and of working with customers to create new products and processes. There are no time clocks, no limits to sick leave, no special perks for managers, no specialists in knowledge creation.

Both companies have been very successful in their industries, but their growth may be constrained by finding workers who want to be "knowledge creators". Other Western companies could try to emulate Chaparral and Oticon but doing so would require highly committed executives and large-scale change.

Knowledge application and use

The other aspect of KM that differentiates it from information management relates to the way people apply and use knowledge in contrast to information. Knowledge, like information, is of no value unless applied to decisions and actions in a purposeful business context. Many companies have worked diligently to "stock the shelves" of repositories with information about knowledge. However, they have paid far less attention to how effectively employees apply and use their knowledge not just for operating today's business, but for generating new ideas about tomorrow's business.

Knowledge application and use is a complex issue with several different dimensions. One is cultural. Does an organization's culture reward decisions and actions according to how people use and share their knowledge? Or is it content with widespread use of intuition and guesswork at the expense of organizing people and processes to apply the best knowledge, experience and skills to projects and tasks?

Are new employees hired in part because they are willing and able to apply knowledge to their decisions and actions? Basic intellectual curiosity is difficult to inculcate if it is not already present, and hiring policies should reflect this. If, for example, a prospective employee has not reviewed material about a company before going to work there, it is unlikely that he or she will begin to consult information about knowledge resources after arriving.

Another determinant of knowledge use is the design of processes for "knowledge work". Planning, marketing, product design and development, consulting and other business activities depend heavily on knowledge. If knowledge workers feel that they have no time to use knowledge in the course of their work, or that it is inconvenient to do so, even the best repositories will not be used.

Essentially a company must create links between these knowledge work processes and its KM processes. Every key activity should be examined to see how knowledge is imported from human brains and information sources. Conversely, managers should look carefully at how knowledge acquired by people in the course of their work can be exported and shared in the form of reliable information with the rest of the company.

There are several ways to help ensure that knowledge is used in knowledge work processes. One is to create specific roles for importing and exporting knowledge. Some professional services firms, among the most aggressive of industries in adopting KM processes, have created such roles. Ernst & Young calls them "knowledge stewards", Accenture "knowledge champions"; in both cases they work on client projects and facilitate the application of knowledge.

Another strategy is to design knowledge-orientated analysis into the phases of a knowledge work project or process. Johnson & Johnson's Pharmaceutical Research Institute and W.L. Gore, the chemical company that makes Gore-Tex, have inserted reviews of knowledge already gained and knowledge still required into key points of the product development process.

A third approach to facilitating knowledge use is to program it into the IT systems that support knowledge workers. This approach was tried a decade ago in the "expert systems" movement; the most successful applications of that era had the objective not of replacing workers but supplementing their capabilities.

At General Motors and DaimlerChrysler, for example, designers of new car and truck models use a "knowledge-based engineering" system that embeds a set of design rules into the computer-aided design system. The rules might specify the relationship of the width of the vehicle to its wheelbase or might suggest that an existing component be used instead of designing a new one. The challenge in this type of project is to bring the entire organization's design knowledge to bear while preserving room for individual creativity and innovation.

The human element

There is no doubt that KM incorporates a strong dose of information management. The continuous conversion of knowledge into information and information into knowledge is a key element of what companies must do to develop and apply knowledge successfully. The use of IT to collect, organize and process information about knowledge is important in developing KM capabilities.

This is not a problem, as long as managers recognize the differences between information and KM and do not assume that one is interchangeable with the other. But if all of your KM efforts just involve better information management or use of the latest IT, then you may be limiting your company's potential to use its collective knowledge to innovate and expand the business. If knowledge resides primarily in people and it is people who decide to create, use and share their ideas to attain business results, then KM is as much about managing people as it is about managing information and IT. If you have not already come to this important conclusion about KM, there is a lot you may be missing.

Summary

Over the past 20 years or so, managers have had to master data processing, information management and knowledge management (KM). The more cynical among them – noting that KM has the same advocates and often uses the same tools as information management – suspect that nothing more substantial than "terminological inflation" is taking place. Part of the problem is that there is no hard and fast distinction between information and knowledge; information may be (theoretically) public and knowledge locked in people's minds, but for the purposes of KM they occupy a continuum of increasing value. And as **Thomas Davenport** and **Donald Marchand** point out, many KM projects have a significant element of information management; after all, people need information about where knowledge resides, and to share knowledge they need to transform it into more or less transient forms of information. But beyond that, KM does have two distinctive tasks: to facilitate the creation of knowledge and to manage the way people share and apply it. In the end, the companies that prosper with KM will be those that realize that it is as much about managing people as information.

Suggested further reading

Davenport, T.H. and Prusak, L. (1998) *Working Knowledge: How Organizations Manage What They Know*, Boston, MA: Harvard Business School Press.

Leonard-Barton, D. (1995) *Wellsprings of Knowledge*, Boston, MA: Harvard Business School Press.

Ikujiro Nonaka and Hirotaka Takeuchi (1995) *The Knowledge-Creating Company*, Oxford: Oxford University Press.

Davenport, T.H., DeLong, D.W. and Beers, M.C. (1998) "Successful knowledge management projects", *Sloan Management Review* (winter): 43–57.

How to map knowledge management

by Charles Despres and Danièle Chauvel

Hughes is a successful US high-technology company that launched 11 satellites last year. But Arian Ward, Hughes' "leader of learning and change", claims that the company suffers from "islands of knowledge", deep pockets of expertise that have trouble developing synergies among themselves. Accordingly he has helped to establish a "knowledge highway" to link these isolated islands. The highway, which is at the centre of Hughes' approach to knowledge management, is an IT-supported network of company experts. The aim is to capture and share their knowledge in order to reduce product development cycle times.

Dow, the US chemicals multinational, has created a "patent tree" that maps the company's presence and business opportunities in a market in terms of the patents it holds. Since a major source of income for the company is to license its technology, it makes sense for clear information about its patents to be readily available to all departments. The company also monitors competitors and other researchers in the areas in which it does business, and has developed a "knowledge tree" that includes intellectual assets other than patents. Dow's objective is to understand its internal stock of expertise in order to exploit hidden business potentials.

Buckman is a speciality chemicals company whose frontline employees spend 80 per cent of their time in the field. Ideally, it would like to bring the full weight of its collective expertise to bear on each meeting with a client, so that its associates are more productive and its clients more satisfied. This has spurred a shift towards a more client-focused system of management, in which the sharing of knowledge is a fundamental imperative. Buckman is devoting significant resources to a worldwide intranet ("K'Netix") that distils its technical and customer knowledge in a continuously updated knowledge base. The objective is to develop more responsive, and more profitable, customer relationships.

The simple fact is that more and more companies are moving towards knowledge management (KM) in one form or another. Lew Platt, chief executive of Hewlett-Packard, has articulated the motivation for most in a now-familiar phrase: "If HP knew what HP knows, we would be three times as profitable." This is a persuasive argument, particularly as managers grapple with burgeoning networks of information and academics proclaim that intellectual capital is essential to wealth generation. Arguments abound to the effect that we operate in a knowledge economy, work for knowledge-intensive companies, and are all knowledge workers in one form or another.

All of this has three discernible effects on managers:

- some become anxious as time-honored principles (such as the chain of command or the sanctity of one's "own" files) fall into disrepute
- some dismiss "the fad" and claim that they practise KM without employing the term (through IT systems, quality programmes, business process re-engineering)
- some are convinced that their knowledge infrastructure is the only way to succeed in future.

Managers' anxieties will not be eased by the fact that companies in the KM limelight, such as Hughes, Dow and Buckman, are developing very different approaches. There appears to be no universal way to adopt KM; those presented with the task are instead faced with a mosaic of options. If 21st-century management is on a knowledge-intensive journey, then those on the path are taking very different routes.

KM is a turbulent, noisy field. Over the past decade, business and academic journals have recorded a 100 per cent per year rise in new KM articles, according to our research in UMI's ABI/Inform database. There are currently more than 1,800 different software products that carry the KM label according to John Blackwell, head of IBM's KM practice for Europe, the Middle East and Asia. E-commerce has even entered the scene: managers can now visit knowledgeshop.com to browse for search engines, document management systems, gurus, consultants or conferences (http://www.knowledgeshop.com/).

Something old, something new

The first step in sorting out this bedlam is to recognize that there is, in fact, something important afoot. In 1991, for the first time, US expenditure on computers and communications equipment outstripped expenditure on all other industrial goods combined. Arguably, this marked the passage from one age to another – from the industrial era to the information era. Managers will increasingly confront the proposition that information and the creation of knowledge are the stuff of 21st-century enterprise. From this overwhelming conclusion there is no return.

The second step is to understand a sociological fundamental: when the principles that regulate a community are challenged, part of the community will cling to established ways while another part will embrace the new framework. No management group leapt wholeheartedly into management by objectives or business process re-engineering or any of the other organizing themes in recent history. Instead, there was a period of uncertainty as advocates on both sides of the matter struggled to win the day.

KM is the latest challenge to established business principles. But the uncertainty surrounding it is compounded by the fact that it appears to be a manifestation of a profound economic shift. This uncertainty expresses itself in four main ways.

Diversity

There are dozens of different approaches to KM, including document management, information management, business intelligence, competence management, information systems management, intellectual asset management, innovation, organizational learning and others.

Relabelling

Some companies have a confusing tendency to affix the KM label on previously familiar activities such as team building, career management, training and development, re-engineering, business process design, and so on.

Broad remits

The American Productivity and Quality Center (APQM) has tried to clarify matters (in a survey published in September 1996) by outlining six KM strategies for

171

29 Oct 1998

DIGITAL BUSINESS

Roger Taylor talks to one of the pioneers of a new way to buy and sell goods and services – by auction on the internet

Financial Times

by Roger Taylor

Behind a glass security wall, in the middle of a cavernous room, a woman sits in front of a bank of about 50 computer screens housed in a matt-black metal frame. The loudest noise is the hum of the air conditioning as she wheels her chair from screen to screen to check the constant flow of information.

It looks like the control centre for a nuclear power station or a set from a James Bond film. It is, in fact, a shop. "It can handle about $1 billion (£600,000) of business – equivalent to about 100 retail outlets," explains Jerry Kaplan, chief executive of Onsale, the company that owns this impressive bit of technology.

Onsale is normally described as an internet auction business but Mr Kaplan dislikes the term.

"We are not an auction house. We are a 'real-time retailer'," he explains. Onsale's customers are not bidding, they are involved in "group price negotiations".

Such tortuous language is inevitable when you are trying to define an entirely new mode of business. Mr Kaplan says the so-called internet auction businesses, of which there are now several, did not exist when he first developed the idea for Onsale.

He started with two observations about retailing on the internet. Firstly, retailers could change prices "in real time".

Secondly, they could collect almost instant feedback from customers about what was selling and what was not.

Mr Kaplan tried a number of ways to turn these musings into a business operation, some of which worked and some of which failed. One system involved allowing the price of goods to fluctuate according to demand. The quicker the goods sold, the higher the price would move. If demand slackened the price would fall.

This proved a failure. The reason, Mr Kaplan says, was the lack of a "call to action". If anything,

there was an incentive for buyers to hold off in the hope that this might help the price to come down.

Since then, he says, a fundamental element of any offer the company makes has to be to create a "sense of urgency".

The most successful model has been the auction, in which goods are put up for sale with an opening price of as little as $1. The auction then runs for a fixed period of time, with bidders informed by e-mail as higher offers come in.

The result is a business that has doubled sales in the past 12 months. In the last quarter it sold $63 million of mainly surplus computers and electrical hardware.

Mr Kaplan points out that Onsale does not just use auctions. Ten per cent of its sales now come from fixed price transactions, using methods such as time-limited special offers. Furthermore, the company continues to experiment with different types of offer.

Despite the use of competitive bidding, Mr Kaplan says his business is very different from a traditional auction operation.

He says Onsale models itself much more on the direct marketing industry and has recruited many senior executives from the sector.

A key strength is Onsale's ability to know its customer's buying habits and make exclusive offers by e-mail.

The result has been a high number of repeat purchases, with 77 per cent of sales going to existing customers.

Onsale has developed in ways Mr Kaplan did not initially envisage. For example, when he started the company, it owned no stock but acted as an intermediary between manufacturers and customers.

However, Mr Kaplan has since decided he needs to own and distribute its stock in order to have

Continued

control over the "post sale experience" and ensure satisfaction.

The types of goods have also changed. Originally it sold wine and collectables – the fare of traditional auctions – as well as computers. These have now been replaced by sporting goods, holidays and even rental property.

Another unexpected development has been the customers. Onsale originally aimed to attract the consumer market.

As it turned out, it now sells more to small businesses. The company has had to respond by adjusting its product range.

Perhaps the biggest surprise, however, has been the lack of resistance from existing retailers. Mr Kaplan says when he started he had concerns that established retailers and surplus stock auction houses would quickly move onto the net and try to crush him.

But non-internet companies have been far too sluggish in their response to present any serious threat. Indeed, the competition he now fears most is from internet companies operating in other areas which might choose to expand into his business.

The rapid pace of change on the internet, which has helped Onsale to prosper, could just as quickly turn against him.

Already analysts are talking about new models of customer-driven retailing in which buyers band together on the web in order to bargain for what they want.

Mr Kaplan says he wants his company to be one of the leading retailing organizations of the next century.

If he succeeds, it will no doubt be with a business which looks very different from the one he runs today.

companies: as an overall business strategy, as best-practice transfer, as personal learning, as customer intelligence, as intellectual asset management and as innovation. Is this clear? While we do not want to criticize APQM as a whole, and we acknowledge that it has said more on the subject, its six strategies exemplify the fuzziness and "scatter" that characterizes the KM field.

Vagueness

Finally, even casual conversations on KM stumble over the definition of knowledge itself. The next time a consultant speaks to you on the subject, ask him or her to define knowledge. As a follow up, question the implication that knowledge was previously unmanaged. The results can be enlightening.

Emerging phenomena are always fuzzy – particularly when their importance is fundamental – and KM is among the fuzziest to have arisen in recent times. But if one takes a bird's-eye view, KM's contours begin to emerge and the practical implications become clearer.

Mapping KM

Beginning in September 1997, we undertook a research programme that explored the various aspects of applied KM in three specialist literatures: academic, consulting and practitioner. Our approach was to analyze the reports, cases, analyses and projections in the field and to make sense of the disparate programmes and areas of concern. Building on this, we developed a classification system that articulated the basic assumptions beneath the rhetoric. Our proposition is that the bulk of current thinking has four dimensions: "process", "type", "level" and "context".

Process

Thought does not spring into existence out of nothing; it is the result of a series of

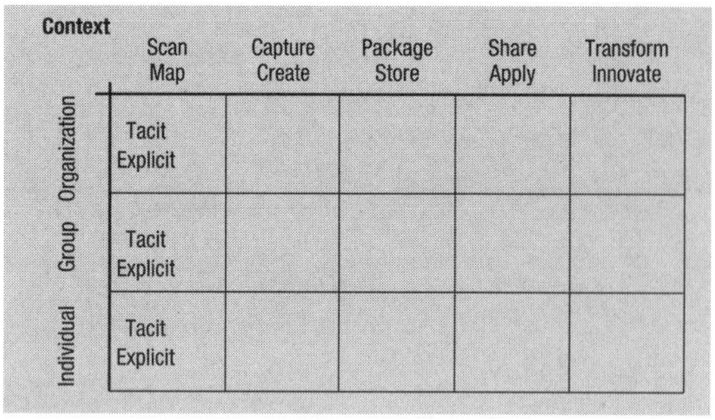

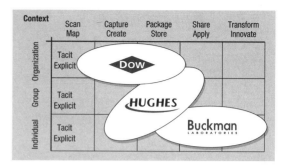

Figure 1

Figure 2

factors that come together over time. Of course, cognition is a highly interconnected, multi-causal process but we can simplify it to extract the issues relevant to KM (*see* "The knowledge process").

Type
The field of KM struggles with the fact that knowledge is not a simple, stable quantity. Different schools of philosophy and sociology give different accounts. Currently, the importance of tacit and explicit knowledge is recognized by managers and is the subject of considerable work within KM.

Level
The idea that companies have three levels of social aggregation – individuals, groups and organizations – is familiar in management studies. Individuals are the fundamental building blocks, particularly in knowledge-intensive systems, but most individuals accomplish their work in groups, using resources provided by the organization.

Context
The importance of an organization's context – which influences its systems, structures and expectations – is increasingly cited in the KM literature. More fundamentally, nothing has any meaning outside a context – hence, whether a piece of information is meaningful or not depands on its context. KM efforts should begin by specifying their meaning-making context(s) and build from there.

Reading the map
These four dimensions create a map that positions most of the KM practices that companies, consultants and academics are now applying. Each cell is partitioned to include both tacit and explicit knowledge, and the overall framework is embedded in a context which varies according to the analysis being carried out (*see* Figure 1).

The map appears to embrace most programmes and practices in KM today. As shown in Figure 2, the activities of Dow, Buckman and Hughes can readily be positioned on it. While there are overlaps, those in the thick of things (such as KM officers at Buckman and Dow) say that the map accurately represents their central concerns.

Dow, for example, is primarily concerned with capturing and organizing the patent-related information that exists at the organizational level; Hughes is trying to make the expertise of its teams available across boundaries; Buckman is packaging its associates' product and customer expertise.

Whether implicitly or as a result of conscious deliberation, most companies are

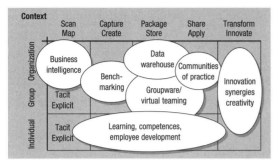

Figure 3

navigating some parts of the map and ignoring others. This is good, in so far as programmes need to be tailored to a company's specific needs but it is less desirable if companies assume that some part of the map (such as construction of an intranet) is the entire domain itself.

By plotting various KM activities on the map it becomes possible to define regions in which the different practices and processes cluster (*see* Figure 3). Since few companies or vendors restrict themselves to a single cell, these regions correspond to the way companies actually use KM.

The central point is that KM is the entire range of activities depicted in the map. Managers should realize that KM comprises more than groupware or an intranet (group level/package-store and share-apply), more than business intelligence

The knowledge process

Mapping
None of us, collectively or singly, is able to embrace the universe of information around us. Instead, we search for comprehensible nuggets of information in corners of the universe that we are familiar or comfortable with. In effect, individuals and organizations map out information environments of their own making.

Acquire/capture/create
From these environments we appropriate (and subsequently, perhaps, recombine) the most valuable nuggets of information. This stage includes personal or organizational search routines which locate the information that becomes the stuff of one's work.

Bundle
A variety of media are then available to bundle this information: paper, e-mail, voice, multimedia and so on. Before information can be bundled it must be interpreted by an author who seeks to infuse it with a coherent meaning before making it public. The critical

issue is the meaning that others are able to extract and this is anything but an absolute.

Store
Individuals and organizations stockpile information in memory systems of various kinds. These range from brains, to hard disks, filing cabinets, libraries and data warehouses.

Apply/share/transfer
The field of KM implicitly recognizes that information is social. There is no way of recognizing data as information or knowledge outside some kind of social context. The field is also beginning to validate the notion that the value of knowledge depends on the actions to which it gives rise.

Innovate/evolve/transform
Knowledge must evolve to keep step with changes in the environment or else it will lose its value. This necessitates R&D programmes that build on experience in the marketplace, creativity processes that broaden intellectual horizons (such as those espoused by Edward de Bono), and so on.

(organization level/scan-map) and more than a "yellow pages" database of employee CVs (individual level/package-store).

A company that chooses to set up a yellow pages database via an intranet should know where it is on the map to understand what ground remains to be covered. Our research indicates that most companies implement such KM projects on a small, experimental scale and then expand into other areas. The map is a chart of the feasible options, a navigation tool.

It seems clear that KM has, for most of its existence, been rooted in the individual and his or her behavior. With the formalization of this field, attention is shifting towards the systems and structures that encourage knowledge-intensive behavior in a company – the generation, transfer, application and reinvention of knowledge. Much of this movement has been occasioned by new information technologies.

Generally, successful KM programmes are process-based rather than static structures. The map should help managers at all levels to visualize the ground that their programmes are covering.

Summary

Knowledge management is a puzzling field. Companies that claim to be implementing KM programmes do very different things. And every year the number of KM books, articles and software products increases massively. The result is confusion over the definition of KM and vague, contradictory prescriptions as to what managers need to do. To clarify matters, **Charles Despres** and **Danièle Chauvel** undertook a research programme in which they closely analyzed the academic, consultancy and business literature. They concluded that KM can be analyzed along four dimensions: the process of cognition; the type of knowledge (tacit or explicit); the level of activity (individual, group or organizational); and the context in which the knowledge is used. These dimensions define a map of KM, on which companies' different activities can be plotted; in the end, KM is the map is KM. Companies implementing KM initiatives can use the map to find their current position and to suggest how they might develop in the future.

The role of the chief knowledge officer

by Michael Earl and Ian Scott

In several large organizations, and some small ones, a new corporate executive is emerging – the chief knowledge officer, or CKO. This is quite a different role, so far, from the chief information officer, or CIO, who oversees the IT function. CKOs are being appointed to initiate, drive and co-ordinate knowledge management programmes. In 1997–98 we studied 20 CKOs in North America and Europe both to understand their roles and to gain insight into evolving knowledge management practice.

The rise of knowledge management

But what is knowledge management and why are corporations investing in it? Most of our CKOs would agree on three points:

1. Today knowledge is a sustainable source of competitive advantage, and one that it is essential for companies to tap. In an era of rapid change and uncertainty, companies need to create new knowledge, nurture it and disseminate it throughout the organization, and embody it in technologies, products and services. Indeed, several sectors – for example, the financial services, consulting and software industries – depend on knowledge as their principal means of value creation.

2. Most companies are not good at managing knowledge. They may undervalue the creation and capture of knowledge, they may lose or give away what they possess, they may inhibit or deter the sharing of knowledge, and they may underinvest in both using and reusing the knowledge they have. Above all, they may not know what knowledge they have.

3. Knowledge management programmes may be a means of galvanising companies to develop knowledge as a source of value creation, redirecting their attention away from capital, natural resources and labor as the only economic resources that matter.

Knowledge management programmes, therefore, are explicit attempts at:

- designing and installing techniques and processes to create, protect and use explicit knowledge (that is, knowledge that the company knows it has)
- designing and creating environments and activities to discover and release tacit knowledge (that is, knowledge that the company does not know it has)
- articulating the purpose and nature of managing knowledge as a resource, and embodying it in other initiatives and programmes.

Knowledge management programmes are being developed in a variety of industries, from financial services and consultancy, through IT- and science-based companies, to fast-moving-consumer-goods (FMCG) manufacturers and food and drink companies.

The rise of the CKO

The people who drive and co-ordinate knowledge management programmes are not necessarily called CKOs ("the most pretentious title in the company", as one of the CKOs we interviewed put it); they may enjoy kindred titles, such as "director of intellectual capital", "vice-president, intellectual assets" or "director, organizational learning". But for the purposes of our study, our subjects had to be corporate executives with "knowledge" in their title. On this definition, we reckoned there were about 25 CKOs in the world. By the end of 1998 this number may have doubled. Those we studied came from the financial services, IT, consultancy, utility, petrochemical, media services and FMCG sectors.

None of the people we looked at had been in the job for more than two or three years. They had small staffs and small budgets and did not expect their role to be permanent. In some ways, they were like the executives who led "total quality management" (TQM) initiatives, appointed to achieve change but with few direct resources.

However, most had considerable influence and status – initially at least –

because they had been appointed by the chief executive, to whom they reported. They were normally appointed from within the organization and so were familiar with its culture and character. But no obvious route to becoming a CKO was apparent. Our CKOs came from a variety of backgrounds, often with a mixed career profile. For example, one had experience of consultancy, IT and organizational learning. Typically, our CKOs were in their forties, with a track record of achievement, particularly in change, behind them, and apparently an excellent career ahead of them. Forty per cent of those we studied were women.

A question of character

In most of the cases we looked at, the chief executive appeared to have made an intuitive decision to appoint a CKO. These decisions were bold but not worked out in detail, with the result that most CKOs had to work out their own job specification. However, given what the CKOs were seeking to do and the way they were going about it, the chief executives seem to have had an eye for appointing the right people.

What struck us early on in our research was the CKOs' distinctive personalities. They were lively, enthusiastic and able to transmit their enthusiasm to others. They were curious and reflective, seeking to learn as they evolved in their role. They had great belief in knowledge management and were ambitious for the success of their company. They were flexible, looking to work with anyone on anything that could advance the cause of knowledge management. They were content to sponsor projects or to let others take the lead and the praise.

A striking quality was the breadth of their interest. They were not obsessed solely with the ideas and products of the IT industry for knowledge management, but they did not dismiss them. Indeed, they saw themselves as designers of social environments and events, new business processes and organizational development initiatives. This is why we suspect that a rich and wide previous career helps. However, to judge what will work in a company and at what pace, deep experience of that organization is also likely to help.

So striking were these personalities – and the high proportion of female incumbents – that we applied a psychometric test to those CKOs who would respond. The resulting profiles tend to reinforce our descriptions. However, we were particularly keen to derive a picture of the CKO in terms of role.

The model CKO

From the interviews and subsequent workshops with our CKOs, we derived a model which seems to us to capture the four critical capabilities of the CKO (Figure 1). There are two "leading" and two "managing" qualities.

"Leading" qualities

The CKO needs to be an entrepreneur, a self-starter who is excited by business development and by creating something. All our CKOs saw themselves as builders, starting a new activity or function. They recognized the personal risks involved in taking on a newly created position, especially one with a title that invites ridicule (although most valued having the word "knowledge" in their titles). However, all seemed stimulated by the risks.

A critical attribute of such entrepreneurship is being a strategist who can understand the implications of using knowledge management to transform the

178

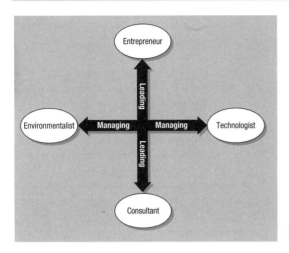

Figure 1

organization. To a degree, the CKO is a visionary, able to see the big picture that the chief executive has in mind but also able to translate it into action. He or she can think of new ways of doing things and yet focus on deliverable results. In short, the CKOs we have met are driven by building something and seeing it through.

However, vision and determination are not enough. The CKO is also a consultant. He or she has to listen to other people's ideas and bring them in and nurture them if they make sense and fit the knowledge vision. Without practical ideas and projects, knowledge management is likely to be little more than rhetoric. So, as in classical management consulting, a valuable skill is matching new ideas with managers' own business needs.

Managing relationships is therefore an important capability. The CKO can operate only through influence, persuasion and demonstration. At the same time he or she must be willing to let others take centre stage and receive the credit.

It is also important to be able to read the company's appetite for change and appreciate how to connect to, and work along with, other change initiatives. One CKO said that she was "driven to make a difference to performance" but added that such goals are to no avail unless the CKO "understands the organization's business model and is clear on the kinds of knowledge that are relevant and will create value". This reads like the central competence of a good strategy consultant.

"Managing" qualities

CKOs also need two principal design competences as they encourage, initiate and manage investments in IT and the social environment. First, as a technologist the CKO has to understand which technologies can contribute to capturing, storing, exploring and, in particular, sharing knowledge. Some of these technologies are just emerging. The CKO has to be sufficiently informed to evaluate what technologies work, what opportunities they open, whether and when to adopt them, and how easy implementation is likely to be.

On some occasions the CKO is the sponsor of the IT project and nearly always has to work with the CIO or a senior IS executive. Thus the CKO needs to be able to have credible discussions with these colleagues. Among the CKOs we studied this was more likely to come from past involvement with IT projects than from formal IT training.

Such technical understanding is not optional: the CKOs we studied recognized that they could not operate in the more social and often tacit domains of knowledge management alone. Indeed, their first initiatives were often based on IT, such as creating knowledge directories, developing knowledge-sharing groupware or building an intranet. And re-engineering knowledge-intensive management and business processes, such as new product development or sales planning, often requires development of a knowledge-sharing IT application (such as groupware to record experiences and ideas). In other words, much codification of knowledge, particularly explicit knowledge, requires the help of IT.

The second design competence is "softer" in character and relates more to the management of tacit knowledge. Here our CKOs stressed their role in creating social environments that stimulate both arranged and chance conversations, or in developing events and processes that encourage more deliberate knowledge creation and exchange. The CKO is therefore also an environmentalist, which implies several things. It includes the design of space, such as offices and relaxation areas, and sometimes even the acquisition and furnishing of retreats and learning centers. It also involves bringing together communities with common interests that rarely interact with each other. For example, people in different functions who serve or have information on important customers may be brought together to exchange knowledge (especially experience and gossip).

Being an environmentalist also means redesigning performance measurement and executive appraisal systems to break down incentives centered on the individual. It means encouraging people to develop knowledge collectively, to share knowledge with one another, to be prepared to take risks and to learn through experimentation. More basically, being an environmentalist means advocating management education and organizational development initiatives that increase the company's capacity to create knowledge. Examples include experience-sharing events for fast-track managers and career development programmes that allow participants to acquire broad and deep knowledge.

CEO, CIO and CKO

The model CKO needs multiple competences. More particularly, the model in Figure 1 suggests how the CKO's responsibilities differ from those of other executives. The "leading" entrepreneur/consultant axis combines the strategic, integrating, enterprise-wide qualities of the chief executive with the catalyzing, selling and implementing qualities expected of the change agent. The "managing" environmentalist/technologist axis covers the softer, organizational, process-oriented perspective of the human resources specialist as well as the technological, information systems perspective of the CIO. In these respects, the CKO is perhaps deeper than the chief executive often is expected to be and broader than the CIO wants or has the time to be.

When we add our personality data to this descriptive analysis of what CKOs actually do, we conclude that they are a different breed from the typical CIO. CKOs are more extrovert, more tolerant and probably more relaxed than CIOs, and have a broader range of skills and interests. This is not a value comparison of the two roles. The CIO's role is very demanding, as described in the chapter "Change isn't optional for today's CIO", and in particular it demands more functional leadership, technological knowhow and obsession with daily operational performance. The qualities required of the CKO are an unusual and perhaps rare mix, in which coping with ambiguity and helping others to change are key attributes.

A transitional role?

The CKOs we studied saw their role as temporary, coming to an end when knowledge management was accepted by their company and embedded in its daily life. Again, this recalls the TQM movement, which was needed to focus companies' attention on quality as a competitive necessity. Success was achieved when "quality" was no longer a special issue, at which point some of the TQM change processes could be taken away.

Likewise, our CKOs saw their goal as working themselves out of a job. However, they were generally finding that the changes required in organizational and managerial behavior to manage knowledge as a normal, daily activity – and the environmental and technological investments required – were going to take longer than they or their chief executives expected. So we do not believe that CKOs will be "here today and gone tomorrow" – they may be required until at least the day after.

Summary

The growing popularity of knowledge management is reflected in the fact that more and more companies are employing chief knowledge officers (CKOs). Unlike the chief information officer, whose task is to oversee the deployment of IT, the CKO's job is to maximize the creation, discovery and dissemination of knowledge in the organization. Recent research by **Michael Earl** and **Ian Scott** indicates that the broadness of this remit is echoed in the personality of the typical CKO: he or she tends to be lively, infectiously enthusiastic, flexible, willing to work with anyone anywhere, and interested not only in the latest IT but also in "soft" organizational mechanisms for promoting knowledge. The best CKOs fulfil four roles: entrepreneur (willing to champion risky new initiatives); consultant (able to match new ideas with business needs); technologist (fully IT-literate); and environmentalist (able to design settings and processes to maximize knowledge). While most hope that once knowledge management becomes ingrained in the company their role will be finished, the transitional period is taking longer than expected.

Suggested further reading

Davenport, T.H. and Prusak, L. (1998) *Working Knowledge: How Organizations Manage What They Know*, Boston, MA: Harvard Business School Press.

Earl, M.J. and Scott, I.A. (1998) "What on Earth is a CKO?" Research Report, London Business School and IBM, August.

Earl, M.J. and Scott, I.A. (1999) "What is a Chief Knowledge Officer?" *Sloan Management Review* (winter). (Discusses the results of psychometric tests carried out on CKOs.)

Making knowledge visible

by Larry Prusak

Since the beginning of the recent "knowledge management" movement, a small but vocal chorus of detractors has argued that the idea is an oxymoron. Knowledge cannot be managed, they cry; it is found only within the minds of human beings, and is therefore entirely inaccessible to managerial approaches and techniques. At the same time, large numbers of large companies have proceeded to build large repositories of what they describe as "knowledge". How can this controversy be resolved?

Knowledge is undeniably a difficult thing to manage because it is invisible and intangible and thus unmeasurable. We do not know what knowledge exists within a person's brain, and whether he or she chooses to share knowledge is entirely a matter of volition. This presents problems for those undertaking knowledge management (KM) programmes within organizations, since by their nature such programmes imply a certain tangibility – that something of demonstrable benefit will get done that will improve the organization's performance.

Identifying that something leads managers into a difficult set of choices. They can admit that knowledge is indeed invisible and go forward on faith alone. Or they can focus management programmes on helping people to acquire knowledge, to share it with others in conversation and direct interactions, and to use it effectively in decisions and actions.

These steps may not feel very tangible but then we deal with many intangible entities in our lives. After all, there are no reputable measures for the expected return on other "invisible" things by which we tend to live our lives, such as family, patriotism, piety and altruism. Within corporate environments, we spend a lot of money and energy on such intangibles as organizational learning, customer and employee satisfaction, and corporate culture.

Yet this approach to knowledge runs counter to the tendency of organizations to select projects that are based upon some form of quantifiable benefit. It is important for those involved in KM to find ways of making knowledge "visible" if they wish to justify the projects that they feel will benefit their organizations.

Let us consider three aspects of knowledge that are, or can be made, visible. They are activities involving knowledge, outcomes based on knowledge, and investments in knowledge. These visible manifestations of knowledge seem to be the most useful proxies for the role of knowledge in organizations; they enable comparisons of knowledge projects within and across companies, as well as providing a base set of numbers (of people, currency, time, and so forth) from which to derive metrics for evaluating knowledge efforts.

It is important to state that none of the following ideas are conclusive; we cannot say that so much of this activity will result in so much knowledge being generated or transferred. The business world does not yet know how to make such correlations. However, we only have been studying the role of knowledge in organizations since around the time of the second world war. As we grow more familiar with this asset, we will have a better sense of its benefits and perhaps less need to make it visible.

Knowledge activities

It is possible to describe many everyday activities – from reading a newspaper to chatting with colleagues at the water cooler – as knowledge-orientated. However, such activities, valuable as they may be, cannot easily be used to develop concrete measures of the prevalence of knowledge in organizational processes. Let us instead examine some knowledge activities that can be made visible.

One important knowledge activity is the identification and development of informal networks and communities of practice within organizations. These self-organizing groups number around 50 to 300 people in large companies and share common work interests and passions, usually cutting across a company's functions and processes. Knowledge tends to "clump" in these groups – people exchange what they know freely and develop a shared language that allows knowledge to flow more efficiently.

At Ford, for example, a virtual community of several hundred employees focuses on the development and adoption of new braking technologies. Within IBM, there are at least eight distinct communities concerned with differing aspects of KM itself.

We know that communities exist when we observe direct or electronic conversations between members. We can measure the number of members, the level of participation in knowledge sharing, and even the number of bits of information that flow across the network.

These networks can be made even more visible through various IT tools. There are several network analysis tools that collect responses to specific questions and highlight knowledge flows and connections. These tools can describe who talks to whom about a particular type of problem, and can also be a guide when searching for expertise. In other words, they tell a user who to contact in order to get an answer to a particular question.

With a large set of responses, one can then "map" a knowledge network and make it visible to others in the organization. Knowledge maps are valuable guides that can assist employees of large or medium-sized companies to ascertain who knows what. Corporate "yellow pages", skills inventories and expert databases are versions of maps, albeit difficult to maintain and update. As organizations grow larger, more complex and more dispersed, the problems associated with locating and benefiting from expertise – and hence the value of maps – grow accordingly.

Knowledge maps can be useful even when very simple. At American Express, a mid-level systems analyst decided to draw up a map showing the locations of the company's data centres and what was in them. The project was done independently and with little corporate support. Not surprisingly, though, this low-cost aid was a huge success in the company.

Another type of knowledge activity that is often neglected by management is the development of symbols and signals that highlight the importance of knowledge. These activities legitimize the work of knowledge practitioners by making visible the company's commitment to knowledge-based work.

In the last annual reports of the World Bank and IBM, for example, both organizations publicly highlighted the value of their knowledge activities. BP Amoco's chief executive, Sir John Browne, publicly advocates the value of knowledge as a crucial lever for company performance. His speeches and articles in business publications serve as a signal of the importance and value of knowledge at the company.

Other common knowledge symbols and signals include allowing employees to attend conferences, evaluating employees in part on their knowledge-sharing behavior, and giving employees unstructured time in which to reflect on their work and what they have learned from a recent project or task. Financial and nonfinancial incentives for knowledge creation and sharing, as offered by many consulting firms, also lend visible support to knowledge activities.

Knowledge outcomes

There are several categories of knowledge-related business outcomes that organizations use as measurable indicators of knowledge. Again, it is possible to treat this category as a catch-all and assume that almost all organizational activities translate into knowledge outcomes. One should be careful to ensure that whatever outcomes are used can, at least anecdotally, be tied to genuine knowledge-based activities. Without this connection, such efforts will simply generate cynicism. For example, improvements in the speed of a knowledge work process (new product development, for example) should be linked to evidence of increased sharing of knowledge across the relevant community.

Consider a company's accumulation and use of patents. A company cannot have an approved patent without new knowledge being generated and utilized. Many organizations overtly make this connection between knowledge and patents through advertisements, analyst briefings and other public relations efforts.

Similarly, new drug approvals and product introductions are the pharmaceutical equivalent of patents and should be considered part of companies' visible knowledge assets. These knowledge outcomes provide imperfect but tangible evidence of substantial knowledge inputs and effective knowledge creation and transfer.

Another viable category is product development and service innovation. Companies such as Sony, 3M and Baxter, which introduce hundreds of new products into the marketplace every year, see these products as direct outcomes of creative knowledge activities. While the knowledge embedded within these innovations is invisible, the products/services themselves are tangible. The frequency and speed at which these innovations come forth from an organization can be viewed as a measure of its success in dealing with knowledge.

Other knowledge outcome measures that companies could use include cycle time, customer retention and measurable corporate reputation. For example, a company could measure the impact of improving access to expertise by examining the effect on cycle time in relevant business processes. Similarly, a company's ability to capture and apply useful knowledge from mass sales could be measured in terms of the rate at which future sales are won or the speed with which new salespeople become effective.

Knowledge investments

Every day companies make substantial investments in improving their employees' knowledge and enabling them to use it more effectively. Analysis of these investments is a useful way of making KM activities visible. For example, how much technical and nontechnical training are individuals consuming? What is the rationale for purchasing groupware and collaboration technologies other than to improve knowledge flows? How much is invested in competitive and environmental scanning, and in other forms of strategic research? The most obvious knowledge investments are basic and applied R&D expenses, which in some cases reach more than 10 per cent of gross earnings.

Investments in knowledge, of course, may be misspent like any other type. But the level of investment indicates how seriously a company views knowledge, its ability to support knowledge-orientated activity, and its intention to produce knowledge-related business outcomes. Investment levels suggest, however roughly, the cost of knowledge in the organization; such measurement may then inspire a company to assess how the money is being spent.

When we know what types of knowledge an organization is spending money on, we get a sense of what knowledge it feels is important. When we see what kinds of training and education an organization buys for its employees, we begin to understand what knowledge managers feel employees should acquire.

Assessing knowledge investments makes more apparent (both to organizational insiders and to any outsiders who can get the information) the priority given to knowledge acquisition, development, codification, transfer and use. If an organization is not investing in knowledge, it is unlikely that it will be good at knowledge-related activities or that it will achieve the knowledge-related business outcomes it desires.

Summary

Cynics argue that knowledge management is impossible: knowledge is invisible stuff that resides in people's heads, whereas management deals with what is tangible and measurable. But this conclusion is too stark, says **Larry Prusak**; after all, we value many things without expecting to be able to measure their value. More importantly for KM, knowledge in companies can be made visible if we focus on knowledge activities, outcomes and investments. Analysing these three manifestations of corporate knowledge is a critical step for companies that want to create, share and apply it. Activities include networks of experts (which can be "mapped" by network analysis software to benefit the whole organization), pronouncements by senior management, and incentive schemes that reward knowledge sharing. Outcomes include things such as patents, product launches and cycle-time reductions; however, knowledge managers need to make explicit the connection between these and knowledge activities. Finally, knowledge investments – in training, for example, or groupware – reveal the importance that companies attach to different sorts of knowledge.

Tools for knowledge management

by Philip Manchester

Knowledge management may be a product of the information age but there is far more to it than IT. Ideally, it involves employees sharing "tricks of the trade" with each other via networked databases. But in the real world this is not so simple. Pioneers of expert systems and knowledge-based technology in the early 1980s found that people do not surrender their knowledge easily – often because they are unaware that they have it in the first place.

At the annual Institute of Personnel Development conference in Harrogate in October 1998, for example, Professor Karen Stephenson of the University of California noted that the key to KM was analysis of the "human networks" at work within an organization: "As

well as holding the key to understanding organization, networks are the key to unlocking the knowledge in people's heads. An organization's knowledge capital is invested in the invisible networks that connect people."

She went on to explain: "In all but the smallest organizations, no-one can understand the millions of communications and decisions that get made through the networks because people only see those immediately connected with them. What I am saying is that organizations need to find their DNA."

The range of technology to support this quest for corporate DNA is wide, although at this early stage there are no clear market leaders. The three main threads of development – information retrieval, document management and workflow processing –

Continued

have each spawned products that point in the direction of KM.

Information retrieval – from the internet, corporate networks and other data sources – is the most important of these technologies and can form the basis for comprehensive KM strategies. Microsoft's Index Server, for example, builds on traditional information retrieval techniques to provide a method for searching many different text sources, including Microsoft Word and Adobe Acrobat. It is bundled free with Microsoft's NT operating system and can be extended to other formats.

Verity's Search 97, Fulchrum's Knowledge Network and Excalibur's Retrievalware also build on traditional information retrieval concepts to provide the advanced search and analysis functions needed for KM applications.

Products such as Sovereign Hills' InQuery and Autonomy's Agentware use a more advanced approach. InQuery not only searches for specific word patterns, but also weighs them according to their value in a particular search. After scanning a collection of documents, it produces a score to indicate the relevance of specific texts.

Autonomy's Agentware works in a similar way. It creates "concept agents" that can analyze new data and classify them according to the dynamic rules that they "learn". It also makes new connections with old information by continually modifying its network of relationships.

Agents – self-contained software programs that refine themselves in the light of their "experience" – provide a powerful mechanism for overcoming many of the current problems of information retrieval. Other approaches rely upon "keywords" and "filters". However, keyword scanning – which often produces more unwanted than useful "hits" – is a much more limited method for analyzing unstructured data than pattern recognition by agents. Furthermore, keywords are language and syntax dependent. Autonomy's

agents are not concerned with specific words – they deal with patterns and data strings in natural languages.

Similarly, filters are a crude method of refining data. They can take a lot of time to set up and can be difficult to tailor to idiosyncratic subject areas. Agents provide much richer results, which can be further analysed by other agents.

Agents are dynamic; the more they are used, the more effective they become. They allow for change and the introduction of new concepts because they can "learn". Agentware can, for example, monitor an individual's interests by extracting "concepts" from documents read online and, in doing so, can build a profile of the user. Once it has picked out patterns it creates appropriate concept agents. As interests change, then so do the concept agents to reflect the change in the user's profile.

Another advantage of agents is that they can be shared among users on a network or corporate intranet. An employee working on a project to, say, look at marketing possibilities in eastern Europe, can be put in touch automatically with employees who might have worked there or have special expertise stored in their user profile.

Information retrieval products such as those described so far form the foundation for KM applications. But they are only the beginning. Context-sensitive document management tools (that can, for example, work with the "content" held in a document image) and workflow processing software (to manage business processes) are also required. Increasingly, vendors in these sectors are incorporating information retrieval engines into their products. Lotus and Netscape, for example, use Verity's Search 97 package in their products.

At the same time a new breed of comprehensive KM package is beginning to emerge. Open Text's web-based package Livelink, which includes information retrieval, document management and workflow processing, is an example.

186

How smarter companies get results from KM

by Peter Murray

First and foremost managers want results. Once they have defined the desired results the next issue is to determine what actions are needed to get them. With an action plan laid out the question then arises "What do we need to know to perform the actions?"

This approach of starting at the "results end", identifying the business pull-through and locating KM within that context, was recently used in the "knowledge survey" carried out by Cranfield business school in association with *Information Strategy* magazine. The survey examined what European businesses are thinking, planning and doing in the area of KM; we will look at some of the results later in this chapter.

The "results end" approach also provided the framework for judgment in *The Economist*'s annual KM Awards. Entrants were awarded most points for a clear statement of the business benefit they had achieved through KM, for demonstrating that the benefit was obtained by managing knowledge, and for showing how they measured the benefits. Many entrants failed at the first hurdle because their case for seeking an award was purely from the knowledge supply side; they failed to start by identifying the business benefit arising from KM.

A results-driven KM model

Figure 1 (which is based on earlier work by Professor N. Venkatraman at Boston University School of Management) expands the above reasoning. Moving from left to right – the conventional interpretation of the model – indicates a useful aggregation of value, starting with basic data and leading to "informed actions" which in turn generate business results.

The Cranfield approach takes the opposite view. It starts with the desired business results and moves back from there. Besides preventing "technology push" (where strategy is blindly driven by technology) this approach avoids the creation of seas of unfocused data and information. The only information collected is that required for the actions.

Different views of "knowledge" create different scenarios for knowledge managers. "Knowledge" encompasses a range of meanings – from the philosophical to the commonsense. Confining the area of investigation to business narrows the range but still contains at least two working definitions: knowledge as a "body of

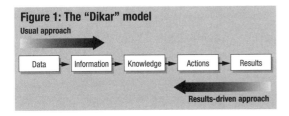

Figure 1: The "Dikar" model
Usual approach

Data → Information → Knowledge → Actions → Results

Results-driven approach

information" and knowledge as "knowhow", often referred to respectively as explicit and tacit knowledge.

Knowledge as a body of information

Starting from the knowledge box in the "Dikar" model and looking towards data and information, the knowledge manager has a set of issues to contend with which are different from the "upstream" view. An example would be where a worker at a research establishment has knowledge that the knowledge manager's company could benefit from in its own research or market planning. This could be knowledge about laboratory or survey work or something similar; it can be thought of as a body of information, formally written down and capable of being readily assimilated by the interested company's systems.

The issues of KM here are: identifying the knowledge and its location; validating it and verifying its value; obtaining it in a useful form at a reasonable cost; determining where it is most useful in the business; making it available there in an appropriate form, using suitable technology; and ensuring that the knowledge is used beneficially. Knowledge defined this way is amenable to being processed by information technologies.

Knowledge as knowhow

Looking "upstream", the knowledge manager is concerned with the kind of knowledge that determines actions, and actions that need certain knowledge. This is the domain of knowhow, a more elusive form of knowledge which resides in peoples' heads.

An example could be a business which wants to move into a new overseas market. It will need someone who knows how to set up supply chains into that market quickly, who knows the business scene there, the relevant legal and tax factors, the culture and so on. This is primarily experiential knowledge, although some of it can be made explicit to a degree (for example, tax laws). Someone who knows the working relationship between businesses and a country's civil servants has knowledge that is hard to code.

In dealing with knowhow, the knowledge manager has to operate in a much more personal domain. The motivation to share hard-won experiential knowledge is not usually high; the individual is "giving away" their value and may be very reluctant to lose a position of influence and respect by making it available "to everyone".

Some managers are hopeful that as the information software and systems become more "intelligent" it will be possible to capture such knowhow. Suppliers of "knowledge systems" are keen to feed this hope. But the assumptions that all knowhow can be captured may be too simplistic. While at one level it is clear that rules that have evolved over time can be encoded, some behaviors owe more to "chaotic", intuitive factors than to predictable, universal reason.

A more complex variation on knowhow is the situation where knowledge is distributed among a team of people. Teams can be an effective way of generating learning and of marshalling and disseminating knowledge. Here the knowledge manager has to facilitate team activities, provide frameworks for more formal knowledge handling and ensuring that knowledge is recorded so that learning can take place.

Barriers to team-working are numerous. Two important factors that a knowledge manager has to address are geography, especially in global companies, and team members' perceptions that their real job lies elsewhere, which means that they ration the time they devote to teamwork. This leaves no space for formal steps such as recording and disseminating learning.

Benefits arising from KM

As part of the Cranfield knowledge survey, European companies were asked to rank eleven possible benefits of KM programmes. Strikingly, "competitiveness" was ranked way above any other benefit. The only other contender was "profitability", which was ranked second or third in all countries (except Germany, which ranked it eighth). "Revenue growth" was consistently ranked last. Taken together, this suggests that businesses are looking for high-margin market niches; these can only be sustained by companies that have something unique to offer, and this in turn requires companies to leverage knowledge.

So what should businesses do in the way of KM if they are aiming to be competitive? And what are the obstacles to achieving this? One message is clear from the Cranfield survey, case studies and current research: do not look to technology for the solution. Installing an intranet will not turn your organization into a "knowledge company" (whatever one of those is). That is not to say that technology does not have a role; it does, but it is never the primary role. Above all, KM is a "people and process" issue. Organizations that are reaping benefits from KM activities are those that have identified the agents of knowledge and have in effect embedded the "Dikar" relationships into their business processes.

Global companies, especially those that also have global customers, are making serious – and successful – attempts at this. Often such organizations have the necessary expertise to crack many issues but geography and organizational structure make it difficult to assemble all the relevant knowledge. Many organizations are certain that they have the knowledge but are unsure as to where.

One solution is "virtual teams". Properly constructed and focused, they can act as communities of best practice, something that many KM proponents advocate. Successful organizations are also insisting that the team runs with a formal learning loop as part of its activity, irrespective of whether it has succeeded or failed (there are lessons from both situations).

One obstacle to this is that project teams are often disbanded as soon as the project has delivered, largely because of time pressures on the members. This is wasteful because immediately after the project the team probably knows more about the issue in question than anyone else in the organization. And the team itself may be in an excellent position to leverage further this knowledge.

A good example of an organization that has brought together the various elements discussed so far is Zeneca, in the area of product licensing. Like all major pharmaceutical companies, Zeneca invests heavily in its own research and development (R&D). Increasingly its portfolio of drugs contains products that are under licence from other companies. Typically, around 20–30 per cent of revenue in the industry comes from "licensed-in" products.

The "route in" for a licensed product can be varied and complicated. During the Cranfield survey, Roger Lloyd of Zeneca's business development group reported that there were up to 15 legitimate contact points between Zeneca and prospective licensors. Approaches to Zeneca can run to thousands a year. The process for handling all this lacked focus and was vulnerable to duplication and misunderstanding. It was also too slow.

Just under two years ago, Fred Brown, Zeneca's internal KM consultant, initiated a KM approach to the issue. There were two bodies of knowledge that needed managing: the scientific and commercial knowledge, and the knowledge scattered all around the company about the status of any particular product under consideration.

The first step for Brown and Lloyd was to understand fully the process of transferring products and technology into the company's R&D and commercial activities. The next step was to secure agreement on the roles of knowledge owners and experts within that process. Clarifying ownership of each stage of the process and its key knowledge components was vital; only when they had fully understood the process, its owners and the knowledge required, did Brown and Lloyd employ technology.

They created, in effect, a virtual global department – a community of the various experts needed to manage external investment activities. While they now act in concert with each other, the experts remain in their previous functional and geographical locations, where they are most valuable. The supporting technology (named "Concert") allows structured and managed contact to occur among the relevant experts and the project manager at each stage of the external investment process.

The results have already been rewarding. The weeding-out process is much sharper – serious evaluation which might lead to contractual commitment can involve up to 60 or 70 people, so making sure unsuitable candidates do not get far means that scarce expertise can be focused on what really matters. The Zeneca case also illustrates another important feature of KM – knowledge ownership. With a clear process, agreed ownership, and demonstrable security in the Concert technology, vital knowledge is now quickly available to the groups that need it.

In a true knowledge process, learning is critical. Zeneca intends Concert to be the basic repository of this learning. The company asserts that everyone in the investment process is now better informed; that corporate vulnerability arising from knowledge residing in one individual has been reduced; that knowledge and best practices are being shared; and that as a result individuals' contributions are becoming more valuable.

The way ahead

Cranfield's current work on KM is based on a model that charts how well a business can manage information and knowledge. Basically there are three linked competences to consider: knowledge supply, knowledge exploitation, and knowledge strategy.

These link together in a "virtuous circle", in which the connections are themselves organizational competences. For example, there is a two-way relationship between knowledge exploitation and supply: exploitation needs should drive the supply agenda and supply opportunities should inform and enhance exploitation activities.

Early work indicates that many organizations are placing almost sole emphasis on supply issues; attempts to exploit knowledge are often made out of context (that is, they are not linked to company strategy) or are over-determined by technology-push. Another common weakness is that supply lacks strategic direction. This can lead to the undirected accumulation of information in the hope, say, that a data-mining technology will reveal the knowledge.

KM in Europe: no more "need to know"

Cranfield's KM research is based largely upon survey work carried out by the Information Systems Research Centre at Cranfield School of Management during 1997 and 1998, in association with *Information Strategy* magazine and Xerox.

After a review of the KM field a survey questionnaire was piloted with a number of multinational organizations then sent to companies across Europe. Information in the report is based on 260 responses plus additional analysis, interviews and related research. There was also collaboration with the Fraunhofer Institute in Berlin.

Half the survey respondents classified themselves as either chief executive, managing director or chairman.

The main findings

The management of knowledge is expected to move steeply up the agenda of European corporations in the next three years.

Knowledge management emerges primarily as a people and process issue. Ninety-four per cent believe it requires people to share what they know with others in the organization. Traditional "need-to-know" cultures are becoming obsolete – 85 per cent did not agree that people should only be informed on a "need-to-know" basis.

There will be a significant increase in European corporate KM spending – by an average of almost 70 per cent – in the next three years. There is also a consistent belief that the number of knowledge workers will increase significantly during that period.

Gaining competitive advantage is ranked as the most important application of knowledge to business objectives. Second comes increasing profits.

Around 85 per cent of companies believe a value can be attached to business knowledge and over 90 per cent claim to have plans to acquire and exploit knowledge assets. There is increasing awareness of the need to address KM in a more formal way than at present.

European companies believe knowledge is primarily an integral part of business processes, with 85 per cent asserting that knowledge is not an extension of IS/IT. IT will nevertheless have an important role in future for integrating knowledge-sharing.

Businesses need more knowledge about customer needs and preferences than anything else. Eighty-nine per cent ranked this as "very important", while the remainder judged it to be "important". Most organizations (61 per cent) believe that much of that knowledge is already inside the organization.

"People" and cultural issues dominate as both the necessary means for – but also the key obstacles to – sharing and exploiting knowledge. Forty per cent of respondents do not rate their company at all as a "learning organization".

The survey identified up to seven overlapping approaches to KM. The main ones are knowledge as an intellectual asset, teams in virtual organizations, and process approaches (usually assisted by technology); others are strategic, technological or philosophical, and knowledge as an HR activity.

Sixty-two per cent of respondents believed that KM is not a fad, while 14 per cent are still waiting to make up their minds. Nevertheless, knowledge managers' actions will be crucial if the early good work is not to be dismissed as a passing fashion.

Organizations are taking KM very seriously. According to the Cranfield survey, most chief executives reject the notion that it is a fad and spending on KM is set to rise by over 60 per cent in the next three years. The first companies to benefit from this expenditure will be those that locate KM within a balanced framework of competences.

Summary

Knowledge management can be plausibly broken down into five stages: data becomes information, which in turn becomes knowledge; knowledge results in informed actions, and these produce business results. According to **Peter Murray**, many knowledge managers make the mistake of "going with the flow", of concentrating on the supply of knowledge rather than the desired results. They would do better to start with the results and deduce what knowledge will be needed to achieve them. This falls into two categories: knowledge as a body of information (which can be readily processed by suitable IT and resides at the "data/information" end of the flow) and knowledge as knowhow (which requires good people management and is found at the "action" end). Reporting on Cranfield School of Management's recent survey of KM in European businesses, the author argues that KM is primarily a "people and process" issue. A particularly effective strategy is to create and nurture "virtual teams", which can leverage knowledge across geographical and organizational boundaries.

Copies of the survey report (which also includes details about *The Economist* awards) are available from the Information Systems Research Centre at Cranfield School of Management (+44 (0) 1234 754 477).

ELECTRONIC COMMERCE

7

Contributors

Sirkka L. Jarvenpaa is professor of information systems at the University of Texas at Austin.

Jan Stallaert is a visiting assistant professor at the University of California, Los Angeles, and a researcher at the Center for Research in Electronic Commerce at the University of Texas in Austin.

Stefano Grazioli is assistant professor of management information systems at the Graduate School of Business of the University of Texas at Austin.

Robert Plant is associate professor of computer information systems at the University of Miami, Florida, and a research affiliate at Templeton College, Oxford.

John Walsh is professor of marketing at IMD, Switzerland.

Leslie P. Willcocks is a fellow in the Oxford Institute of Information Management, Templeton College, Oxford, and visiting chair at Erasmus University, Rotterdam and the University of Melbourne.

Nirmalya Kumar is professor of marketing and retailing at IMD, Switzerland.

William J. Kettinger is director of the Center for Information Management and Technology Research at the Darla Moore School of Business, University of South Carolina.

Andrew Whinston is a professor at the University of Texas in Austin and a researcher at the University's Center for Research in Electronic Commerce.

Gary Hackbarth is a research associate at the Center for Information Management and Technology Research at The Darla Moore School of Business, University of South Carolina.

Manoj Parameswaran is a doctoral candidate at the University of Texas in Austin and a researcher at the University's Center for Research in Electronic Commerce.

Contents

Introduction

Electronic commerce is probably *the* hot management topic of the moment. Indeed, the manner in which transactions (both business to individual and business to business) are moving rapidly to a digital platform raises issues affecting all functions and departments within a company. Executives are naturally frightened because e-commerce disrupts distribution channels at the same time as transforming them. Economists are excited, though, because digital networks make possible their dream of "markets for everything". The softer issues, meanwhile, should not be overlooked. Trust, for example, is a particular concern in cyberspace and companies' efforts will come to nothing if they do not win consumer confidence. Customer satisfaction is no less important than in traditional face to face exchanges so companies must work hard to customize their communications with the marketplace.

Surfing among sharks: how to gain trust in cyberspace

by Sirkka L. Jarvenpaa and Stefano Grazioli

An IBM commercial shows a couple of American tourists visiting a small-town pottery shop in rural Italy. When they introduce themselves as coming from Illinois, the elderly shopkeeper replies: "Ah, Illinois! We sell there. And in Florida, California, New York, Arizona, Colorado, Alaska . . . " The commercial fades as the list of markets grows longer and longer but the message is clear: an internet presence allows retailers to reach potentially millions of consumers worldwide.

Greater choice, lower prices and the creation of entirely new product categories are among the other advantages cited by enthusiasts for this form of commerce. Yet unless such electronic store-fronts can convince consumers that the seller has the ability and motivation to deliver goods and services of the quality they expect, internet shopping will not reach its full potential. Indeed it risks becoming discredited.

The US Department of Commerce already reports widespread distrust among consumers about internet-based merchants. This (as we shall see) is partly due to the special characteristics of the medium compared to traditional retail formats. Lower entry and exit costs have encouraged many "fly-by-night" operators who have established sites and marketed their wares fraudulently to an unwary public.

Trust

Because of the nature of the medium, internet merchants have a much harder time when it comes to fostering consumer trust than their brick-and-mortar counterparts. In most cultures, consumers grant their trust to business parties that have a close physical presence: buildings, facilities and people to talk to. On the internet, these familiar elements are simply not there.

Decades of academic research have shown that trust is most readily established when both parties share similar backgrounds, are governed by the same social and legal systems, and expect to interact with each other in future. The seller's reputation, the size of his business, and the level of customization in product and service also engender trust.

Take customization, for instance. Customization implies willingness on the part of the merchant to commit resources, effort, and attention to a specific customer relationship. As a precondition, customization requires some prior knowledge of the customer, including his or her identity. Yet many customers avoid sites that ask them to identify themselves too closely. And to put it simply, one cannot truly personalize for an anonymous buyer.

As we consider the other factors that foster consumer trust, we find that it does not get any easier for the internet merchant. Store size and reputation can be hard to convey on the internet and are relatively easy to forge. The information on many websites about their legal (and physical) location, consumer legal protection and remedies is often incomplete or ambiguous.

Risk

From the consumer's standpoint, trust is the antidote to perceived risk in a business transaction. Internet consumers will inevitably wonder whether a merchant will deliver the goods that they have paid for. If goods are delivered, will they be the ones that they have ordered? Can they be returned? To whom? At what cost? The perceived risk depends on the likelihood of default by the other party and on the extent of the loss deriving from that default.

Internet merchants need to elicit consumer trust when the level of perceived risk involved in a transaction is high. This is not always so. In the case of the purchase of books over the internet, for instance, consumers are likely to perceive relatively little risk when the transaction is unlikely to involve more than a few tens of dollars. Air travel, by contrast, can cost hundreds of dollars and can have a large number of variables (such as routing, scheduling and penalties for changes) which have to be agreed upon. The more significant the purchase and the more unfavorable the perceived outcome if things go wrong, the more the merchant needs to develop trust.

Security and privacy

Although it is often said that security and privacy considerations can hamper internet commerce, recent research has found that consumers who have built up trust in an internet merchant will ignore such concerns. Studies of internet consumer behavior show that consumers who go online, find something interesting and competitively priced to buy, and perceive the seller as trustworthy, will buy.

Nevertheless, internet merchants need to address issues such as fear of privacy invasion and abuse of customer information (about their credit cards, for example) because they stop people even considering the internet as a shopping medium.

Earlier this year, one of the present authors received an e-mail from a student residing in Brasilia, but enrolled in her University of Texas course. The student wrote: "I ordered the textbook over the internet, and I was certain the transaction was encrypted, but I discovered last week that my order submission was likely side-tracked. [A well-known internet bookstore] did not have any record of my order, and within a few days, someone had purchased a stereo system in the United Arab Emirates using my Visa card."

Technological progress, legal remedies, and user education are helping address these issues. Communications between customers' web browsers and web servers (the information hubs operated by internet merchants) can now be automatically encrypted, so that no unauthorized person can easily eavesdrop. Browsers are becoming more resistant to viruses and other kinds of electronic attack. Technologies such as firewalls and digital certificates which control and audit access to information about customers contained in a web server have become more robust.

Misrepresentation and fraud

While tampering and eavesdropping are being tackled, the problem remains that it will always be possible to have a perfectly secure transaction with a crook. As a New Yorker cartoon once put it, "On the internet nobody knows that you are a dog."

There are signs that the risk of e-fraud is increasing with the growth of internet commerce. Internet Fraud Watch, a site sponsored by a consumer organization with ties to the US government, receives an average of 100 fraud reports per month, up 200 per cent with respect to the same time last year. As the internet continues to be cluttered by small and start-up companies, concerns over merchants' reliability and reputation are increasingly in the minds of consumers.

Some frauds are old, some new. The old risks include pyramid schemes, phony initial public offerings, "pump and dump" price manipulations of securities, scholarship scams, deceptive travel programmes, false weight-loss claims, questionable business opportunities, work-at-home schemes, prizes and sweepstakes, and credit card offers. These frauds are the electronic equivalents of ruses that have been practised for years by telemarketers and junk-mail swindlers.

Among the old scams, the pyramid scheme is one of the better known. Pyramid schemes are based on the idea of generating an ever-expanding base of recruits, who are in turn requested to find new recruits. Since the expansion cannot continue forever, pyramid schemes eventually collapse, causing most of those involved to lose money.

The enormous potential for reach offered by the internet makes it an ideal medium for pyramid schemes. According to the US Federal Trading Commission (FTC), tens of thousands of consumers have already lost millions of dollars.

"Pump and dump" consists of artificially inflating the price of a security and selling it immediately afterwards. The US Security and Exchange Commission (SEC) has taken action against an internet newsletter that recommended the purchase of several stocks and predicted that their market price would double or triple. According to the SEC, in making these recommendations the newsletter failed adequately to disclose that it received substantial compensation from profiled issuers of securities, and that it had sold securities shortly after recommending them.

New scams for the consumer are made possible by the distinctive features of internet technology. For instance, internet-enabled interactivity makes it possible to conduct online auctions, an exciting new development in retail commerce. Risks in this area include bid-price manipulation, false product descriptions, and failure to deliver merchandise. Recently, the FTC brought a suit to stop a seller who offered for sale personal computers on several auction sites and collected money from "successful" bidders without delivering the auctioned goods.

Another distinctive risk is the possibility that opportunistic merchants will take control of a customer's computer – for instance, by downloading a virus during a transaction – and perform some unauthorized action. The FTC alleges that one internet merchant "highjacked" the modems of unsuspecting consumers. The modems were then instructed to sever the phone connection between the consumers' computers and their internet service providers, and to re-route them towards a high-price international line. According to official sources, an estimated 38,000 people were swindled by the scheme.

Honest internet merchants face what economists call the "lemons market" dilemma: when it is difficult to tell the difference between good products and a bad one, the bad one poisons the market and drives away the good products (and eventually, of course, the consumers).

The rise and decline of pay-per-call services in the US over the past decade is an instructive example. According to governmental data, US consumers bought $6bn in pay-per-call products and services in 1991. The vast majority of merchants who adopted the new technology were honest but a few were not. As the industry and the government were slow in reacting to the fraudsters, the reputation of this means of payment became tarnished and aggregate yearly business dropped to just $300m.

Reputation building

Building a good internet reputation is obviously critical for success in e-commerce. The Amazon.com story is repeated over and over again in corporate board rooms as well as MBA classrooms. But it is worth mentioning here because that company's continued losses can be attributed in large part to the huge investment it has had to make to build its credibility as an efficient low-cost provider. At least in the eyes of the company's shareholders, these investments are paying off.

How can an internet merchant build customer trust? As mentioned above, scores of academic research studies have shown that trust is most readily established when parties have similar backgrounds, are governed by a common social and legal code, and expect to interact with one another again. Although most of this research is not specific to the internet, it is almost certainly germane. Websites designed to emphasize cultural homogeneity with the customer (for example, translated into the customer's language), references to adherence to local regulations and business practices, as well as promotional campaigns designed to stimulate repeat business, are all techniques that may encourage the formation of trust.

Some websites have started to include photos and video clips of store owners and staff to overcome the perception that electronic storefronts are too impersonal. But this can prove to be a double-edged sword. What appeals in one part of the world may be off-putting in another. To reinforce the perception of quality service and to boost the number of interactions, some internet stores have started emphasizing post-sales contacts, such as order confirmation, stronger product warranties, and customer support.

Specific results about internet consumer trust have been obtained by a group of researchers drawn from the University of Texas, Ben Gurion University in Israel, the Helsinki School of Economics, and the University of Melbourne. The group has studied ways in which online retailers can increase consumer trust and thereby increase the willingness of prospective customers to shop in this new cross-border retail environment.

The researchers have found that consumers recognize differences in size and reputation among internet stores, and that those differences influence their assessment of store trustworthiness, their perception of risk, and their willingness to shop on a particular site. A consumer who believes that there is a physical store (or chain) behind a website is more likely to trust the site on a first encounter.

Reputation looms particularly large in consumers' minds when a site appears to be run by a small player. Interestingly, though, being the largest site in a particular category (for example, being the world's largest music store) does not by itself seem to affect consumer trust. Seller size has much more influence on trust when it is coupled with a good reputation. Hence there appears to be little payback from banners boasting about a web merchant's size unless they are accompanied by stories from credible third parties or customer testimonials attesting to the seller's reputation.

Reputation, in short, is far more important in global internet selling than in local retail store marketing.

To an extent, trust can be transferred. Merchants seeking to enhance their reputation might therefore consider cross-linking their sites with other reputable, well-known sites. Trust, however, can also be quickly destroyed. Internet merchants should be wary of applying marketing tactics that could undermine consumer trust. Consider, for instance, the practice known as differential pricing, which consists of offering different prices to different customers. If customers realize that the price they are offered is greater than the price offered to their neighbor, trust in the merchant can quickly fade.

Finally, we would argue that things which traditionally engender consumer trust can change in the light of experience in an electronic environment. At least initially, customers who flock to the internet will assign trust to internet merchants on the basis of the same cues that they use when they interact with their brick-and-mortar counterparts. But positive and negative experiences, both personal and shared, will shape attitudes thereafter. Successful merchants will be those who learn to send the appropriate signals, so that the buying public can surf safely among the sharks.

Summary

Internet merchants face an inherently bigger challenge than their brick-and-mortar counterparts when it comes to winning the consumer's trust. As **Sirkka Jarvenpaa** and **Stefano Grazioli** explain, reputation and size are harder to convey and close customer relationships more difficult to develop in cyberspace than in a traditional physical setting. Tampering and eavesdropping continue to discourage some electronic shoppers, although technology and the law are coming to the rescue. A more serious problem is fraud and the growing number of "fly-by-night" operators attracted by the internet's low entry and exit costs. The authors document some recent scams and draw on fresh research to advise companies on the best ways to gain customer confidence. Seller size, they stress, is not enough on its own but needs to be coupled with a good reputation and endorsements from independent third parties.

Websites with a personal touch

by John Walsh

From the birth of commerce, knowledge of the customer has been a precondition of a successful enterprise. Early vendors won a customer's patronage by forming a relationship with him, knowing his likes and dislikes and thereby making transactions easier and more pleasant.

In the last quarter of this century, the corner stores that offered this level of service have been dying off in the face of competition from hypermarkets and shopping malls. These impersonal businesses knew their customers too – they guessed correctly that when faced with a choice between low price and attentive service consumers would opt for the former.

As we look forward to the next century, internet retailers – inevitably dubbed "e-tailers" – will dominate their brick-and-mortar foes. How? By offering service more personalized than corner shops could ever contemplate at a price lower than the largest chain stores could profitably charge. In doing so they will use a broad range of high-tech methods to understand each and every customer's individual desires.

On the record

Transactions taking place on the web are effortlessly, costlessly and automatically recorded as a collection of bits and bytes. The anonymity of cash-based transactions has not made its way onto the web. (Although the concept of "e-cash" has been discussed it is unlikely to retain the anonymity of notes and coins.)

To make a purchase on the web a consumer has to give personal information. Typically, the minimum is credit card details and a postal address although sometimes a short questionnaire may need to be completed. Even where no purchase is made, information may be required.

For example, newspaper websites such the *Financial Times* and *The New York Times*, which are free, ask visitors to use the same username and password when they visit. This information can subsequently be used to analyze reading patterns. How many people read only the headlines but do so every day? How many read each and every article but visit infrequently? The anonymity of browsing through periodicals at a newsstand does not exist on the web, and the information that is recorded can be used by managers to great effect.

For a glimpse into the future, the reader should visit Peapod.com, an online supermarket and one of the more sophisticated recorders and users of customers' personal data and shopping behavior. With over 100,000 customers in eight US cities, Peapod's website sells groceries that are then delivered to customers' homes. A list of previous purchases (including brand, pack size and quantity purchased) is kept on the site, so that the customer can make minor changes from week to week, saving time and effort.

Peapod creates a database on each shopper that includes their purchase history (what they bought), their online shopping patterns (how they bought it), questionnaires about their attitudes and opinions, and demographic data (which Peapod buys from third parties). A shopper's profile is used by the company to determine which advertisement to show and which promotions/electronic coupons to offer. Demographically identical neighbors are thus treated differently based on what Peapod has learned about their preferences and behavior over time.

Shoppers seem to like this high-tech relationship marketing, with 94 per cent of all sales coming from repeat customers. Manufacturers like it too. The more detailed customer information enables them to target promotions at customers who have repeatedly bought another brand, thereby not giving away promotion dollars to loyal customers.

We can expect to see many more supermarkets in a variety of countries offering a similar service. Peapod has recently divested its software division, appropriately named SplitPea, and its goal is to license the technology within the supermarket industry and in other industries with a similar structure. It has already signed a deal with Cole Myers of Australia.

Reading the clickstream

Given the potential advantages for consumers and vendors alike, the manager's challenge is twofold: (1) to develop a website that collects the relevant data in an unobtrusive way to which customers will not object; (2) to determine how to analyze

202

the vast quantity of data that will be collected and integrate it into decision-making. For companies with a mass-production mindset, addressing these issues may prove too difficult.

So how do websites collect this useful information? First, people who visit a site for the first time are asked to register, which typically involves giving a name, physical address, e-mail address and perhaps some other demographic data (such as age and income). From the customer's perspective, this is all that needs to be done; he does not have to answer any more questions.

When the customer comes to the site in future, he either types his chosen username and password or more commonly these days, if he is using the same computer, the website recognizes him using a "cookie", a small file that uniquely identifies the computer. In either case, we can associate each subsequent visit with the answers the customer gave on the registration form.

From the manager's perspective, the work is just beginning – the website has to be personalized for the user. How? From the initial survey, we may have learned that the user is male, young and British. If we are running a news site, we can provide information that typically appeals to this demographic profile. If we are selling clothes, we can feature items that are usually bought by people fitting this profile.

As the user repeatedly visits our site, we learn more about him as we record his series of "clicks", the information he requests using his mouse. His sequence of clicks (or "clickstream") will be central to personalizing the site. Clickstreams reveal what he is really interested in. Perhaps on news sites he always goes to the sports section first and immediately reads about Manchester United's latest victory. Advertisements for Man U's most recent strip could be shown to him with some effect.

Clickstreams allow the website to add behavioral information to the answers given at registration. They are at the heart of Amazon.com's personalized book suggestions. CDNow, the compact disc vendor, is convinced of the value of clickstream data. It analyzes instances where shoppers look at information about a CD but choose not to buy – not only purchases reveal what a person is interested in.

Learning from purchases will not be new to many companies. Consumer goods companies employ armies of analysts to apply advanced statistical models to sales data taken from in-store barcode scanners. However, on the internet, purchase data is a tiny fraction of the total clickstream data to which companies have access.

Clickstream data are analogous to data that follow a shopper's eye movements in a store, as he or she considers one brand and, on seeing the price, rejects it in favour of the cheaper generic. Perhaps some brands are never looked at.

Mere purchase data do not reveal the process consumers use to buy a product, they simply yield the outcome. Companies that use clickstream data to understand the way consumers make decisions will be the market leaders of the future.

Do consumers mind being asked to part with information in order to receive personalized goods and services? Most early research would suggest that they do not, so long as they perceive a benefit, such as reading a newspaper for free or saving time.

However, it is worth keeping in mind catalogue retailer L.L. Bean's experience. Using caller ID, a technology that allows one to know the phone number of the person calling, L.L. Bean was able to answer the phone with a personalized hello. Consumers reacted negatively, offended by what they considered an invasion of privacy. The benefit of not having to state their name and address was apparently not enough.

Is it worth it?

In a recent study by Jupiter Communications, 35 per cent of surveyed internet executives said personalization capability was the most important determinant of who they use to develop their website. Clearly this is an issue that is capturing their attention. But have the collection and analysis of clickstream data, and the subsequent website personalization, been worthwhile? Have companies profited from it or is it all hype?

The addition of personalization capabilities can add up to $3m to the cost of a website. Yet *Business Week* reports that personalization pays for itself within a year. It does so by increasing the loyalty of users to a site. When people recognize that an offering is targeted at them – or, indeed, when they have a hand in its creation – they are more likely to return again and again.

Companies selling information rather than products over the internet have been able to charge advertisers more as their advertising becomes more targeted. Internet advertising has grown explosively, mostly because of the growth of the internet itself, but in part because advertisers can get their ads viewed by more specific groups of people. There have recently been some extraordinary manifestations of this enthusiasm for targeting; for example, some companies have offered free computers to people who agree to have their online behavior recorded and advertisements beamed at them.

How will business be affected by personalization? Treating customers as individuals will become more prevalent and, since we are talking about the internet here, this is likely to happen soon. Essentially, personalization will become just another cost of doing business.

In the early part of this century, Henry Ford built a very successful company by offering customers a car in any color they wanted as long as it was black. Early in the next century, personalized communication and offerings will be so common that current impersonal business practices will look as outmoded as Henry Ford's color choices do now. The web will cause this revolution.

Summary

Internet retailers are set to dominate consumer markets. According to **John Walsh**, they have the potential to combine "corner shop" service with hypermarket prices. Much of their advantage will come from their ability to profile individual customers by tracking their pattern of clicks online. This will enable them to tailor the site to the customer, boosting revenue from consumers and advertisers. The challenge for managers is to collect and use "clickstream" data in a way that people do not consider obtrusive.

Internet distribution strategies: dilemmas for the incumbent

by Nirmalya Kumar

The internet is a radical new distribution channel. Consequently, many established incumbent companies fear that the internet has the potential to harm them: to be competence-destroying instead of competence-enhancing; to devalue their distribution network assets rather than leverage them; to turn their core competences into core rigidities; and to disrupt their industry leadership positions rather than reinforce their dominance. To assess the disruptive capacity of the internet as it relates to distribution strategy, incumbent companies should ask the following three questions:

- to what extent does internet distribution complement or displace existing industry distribution channels?
- to what extent does internet distribution enhance or destroy the company's core competences and distribution network assets?
- how will internet distribution strategy interact with the company's existing distribution strategy?

Existing channels and the internet

Innovations in distribution channels may take two forms – those that complement current distribution channels and those that displace existing distribution channels. For example, supermarkets in the US displaced "mom and pop" convenience stores. The supermarket's value proposition of better assortment, one-stop shopping and substantially lower prices for a little more travel was considerably better than that offered by the mom and pop store. The result was both an absolute and relative decline in the number of mom and pop stores. In contrast, television and later the home video extended the distribution channels available to the motion picture industry.

In the face of the current media hype regarding the internet and how it is going to destroy existing retailing systems, it is perhaps useful to spend some time understanding the dynamics between film producers, cinemas, television, and home videos.

When television first appeared in the 1950s, it was seen as a great threat to the Hollywood studios. As a result the market value of Hollywood studios fell dramatically. A similar story was repeated with cinemas when home video first appeared. In each instance, two important issues were overlooked.

First, the value proposition of the new distribution channel (television and home video) was not superior to but rather different from that of the existing distribution channel (cinema). Home video, on the one hand, offers greater assortment, time flexibility, informality and lower prices. On the other hand, cinemas have the excitement of a "date" or "an evening out". They overwhelm you with a big screen and big sound while providing opportunities to see and be seen. The two distribution channels have clearly delineated value propositions, attracting different segments of customers, and can therefore coexist.

Second, home video gave consumers the opportunity to watch movies when tired, disinclined to dress up, wanting to be alone or unable to get a baby-sitter, as well as when cinemas were closed or had stopped running a particular film. The new distribution channel made it much easier for the consumer to buy and consume the product, thereby greatly expanding its total market.

This changed the economics of the movie industry because producers did not need to rely solely on cinema revenues to break even. The new distribution channels were hungry for product. Television and video expanded the market for motion pictures and provided substantial additional streams of revenues for the industry.

What the supermarket and home video examples show is that whether distribution through the internet will complement or displace existing distribution channels depends upon the industry. To take another case – that of travel – the effect of the internet will be to replace many existing players in the current distribution channels.

The ability to purchase airline tickets or to make hotel and car reservations over the internet is not going to increase the number of vacations or business trips consumed. Instead many customers will see little need for a travel agent if all necessary information is available over the internet and is accessible faster than through a traditional travel agent who promises to call back but never does. Furthermore, there is no product with air travel that needs to be physically delivered, since confirmation numbers and e-mails are adequate for most travellers. (Those who prefer having the traditional ticket before departure can receive it by post at a small cost compared to the price of the ticket.)

Not surprisingly, over the past two years, the share of US domestic airline reservations booked through independent travel agents has declined from 80 per cent to 52 per cent. Travel agents are in decline as increasing numbers of travellers elect to buy their tickets directly, either via airlines' websites or over the telephone after a search of those sites.

In contrast to what is happening in the travel industry, the internet has empowered and encouraged more individual investors to buy and sell stocks and mutual funds. Information such as past financial statements, earnings estimates, analyst recommendations, customized portfolio analysis, and real-time quotes, which was previously unavailable or available only through full-service brokers, is now freely available through internet brokerage houses. Furthermore, trading over the internet is much cheaper, with investors benefiting from the reduced transaction costs. Consequently, both the frequency and number of transactions conducted by individual retail investors has dramatically increased.

This does not mean that there is no replacement effect: clearly some of these internet trades would have gone through traditional stockbrokers. However, by offering, for the first time, an attractive value proposition for those individual investors who are willing to help themselves, the internet has extended the market.

Figure 1 helps in assessing the extent to which internet distribution will have a complementary or a replacement effect. Most of Figure 1 is based on the discussion above except for the questions related to product standardization and customers' desire for variety.

Some products, such as branded cereals or white socks for men are easier to standardize because they can be mass produced. Others, such as agricultural products or antiques, are either more difficult to standardize or exist only as unique objects. If products cannot be standardized then it is harder to communicate their quality through the internet and consumers will consequently have a greater need to touch, feel and see in order to reduce the perceived risk of purchase. Furthermore, even if a product can be standardized, customers may prefer variety in consumption. For example, the production of men's suits can be standardized but few customers desire multiple units of the same suit.

Core competences and network assets

Regardless of whether it complements or displaces existing distribution channels at an industry level, the internet tends to affect the core competences and distribution network assets of existing players in different ways. Therein lies a large part of its disruptive nature: internet distribution may help some companies leverage their core competences and distribution assets, while it may have the opposite effect for other companies within the same industry. How it affects these things depends on how a company competes within an industry.

In the personal computer industry, the worldwide market leaders are Compaq and Dell. However, the business model of the two companies differs dramatically, as Figure 2 demonstrates.

Compaq has business systems of the type traditionally associated with branded products. It has high R&D expenditures; low-cost, low-variety, large-run manufacturing systems; one-month finished-products inventory; and it distributes primarily through third-party resellers. In the early days of the industry – when IBM, with its large direct sales force, was ambivalent about selling through third-party resellers – Compaq dedicated itself to PC sales through resellers. This endeared Compaq to resellers, whose subsequent push was partially responsible for catapulting Compaq into the market leadership position.

Dell primarily targets corporate accounts but with built-to-order, customized PCs at reasonable prices. In pursuit of this strategy, Dell invented a radically different business system. This combines minimal R&D expenditures, made-to-order, flexible manufacturing systems (which give Dell a slight manufacturing cost disadvantage compared to Compaq), one-week parts inventory, and an efficient direct distribution system.

The emergence of the internet pushed Compaq and Dell to explore how to exploit this new distribution channel. What makes the internet so exciting is that in its

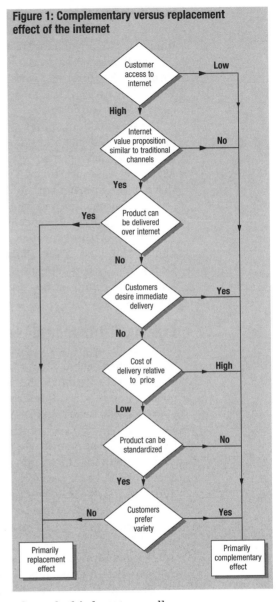

Figure 1: Complementary versus replacement effect of the internet

207

most advanced form it offers companies the opportunity to have a one-to-one dialogue with the customer (interactive capacity) and then to respond with a unique, customized offer (responsive capacity). Thanks to its business system, Dell was well positioned to exploit these unique features of the internet, and sales through the internet were a natural extension of the "Dell Direct Model". Consequently, Dell is a pioneer in PC sales through the internet and website sales currently exceed $14m a day.

However, Compaq has struggled to exploit the internet, because to do so properly would mean building customized PCs and bypassing its distributors. It is difficult to deliver customized products at competitive prices with high-volume, low-variety manufacturing systems. And it is difficult for Compaq to promote sales through the internet without upsetting its resellers and jeopardizing its historically strong relationships with them.

In order to limit direct competition, Compaq has had to design a new line of PCs, Prosignia, for sales through the internet. As a result, Compaq has lagged Dell by almost three years in adopting direct sales in this way. The internet turned Compaq's core competences and distribution network assets – low-cost manufacturing systems and strong relationships with third-party resellers – into core rigidities.

Existing distribution strategy and the internet

Most manufacturers who adopt the internet as a direct sales channel find that it places considerable stress on their existing distribution network. As a global network, sales through the internet impinge on a manufacturer's existing pricing policies and territorial restrictions. Furthermore, direct sales through the internet lead manufacturers to compete with their resellers, which results in channel conflict. The extent to which these effects are salient depends upon which of the following four approaches to internet sales are adopted by the manufacturer.

First, manufacturers may decide not to sell their products through the internet and prohibit their resellers also from using the internet for sales. Only product information is provided on the internet, with any customer queries being passed on to the appropriate channel member. In industries, such as aircraft manufacturing, where sales are large, complex and customized, this may be an appropriate strategy.

A second strategy for the manufacturer (for example, Oneida tableware) may be to leave the internet business for resellers and not to sell directly through the internet. How effective this strategy is depends on the existing distribution structure. It can be effective when manufacturers assign exclusive territories to resellers, since resellers can be restricted to either delivering only to customers within their assigned territory or can be compensated through profit pass-over agreements if they are adversely affected. Any leads generated by the manufacturer's website are passed on to the appropriate regional reseller.

By contrast, for intensively distributed products where resellers have no assigned territories, resellers simply compete with each other as they would do in the normal, physical marketplace. The global nature of the internet creates price transparency, which may conflict with differential prices charged by the manufacturer in various markets. Another limitation of this approach is that most consumers search for manufacturers' websites (sony.com, say) rather than resellers' websites. Inability to purchase from the manufacturer's website can be

Business models of Dell and Compaq

	Dell	Compaq
Target customer	Knowledgeable customer buying multiple units	Multiple customer segments with varied needs
Value proposition	Customized PC at competitive price	"Brand" with quality image
Business system		
● R&D	Limited	Considerable
● Manufacturing	Flexible assembly, cost advantage	High-speed, low-variety, low-cost manufacturing system
● Supply chain	Made-to-order; one-week, primarily through-component inventory	Made-to-stock; one-month, primarily finished-product inventory
● Marketing	Moderate sales response advertising	Expensive brand advertising
● Sales and distribution	Primarily through sales force and telemarketing	Primarily through third-party resellers
Value capture	Through pushing latest component upgrades ("up-selling") and low-cost distribution system	Through premium for the "brand" and reseller push

Figure 2

frustrating for the consumer and can result in lost sales for the manufacturer.

A third strategy for the manufacturer (Levi Strauss, for example) is to restrict internet sales exclusively to itself. This strategy is only profitable if the manufacturer has a business model that is aligned with sales through the internet. The business system of most manufacturers (such as consumer packaged goods companies) is not set up for sales to end users who place numerous small orders. Alternatively, by selling through the internet a manufacturer may aim not to generate profits but rather to learn about this new channel of distribution, collect information on consumers, or build its brand. But regardless of a manufacturer's objectives, resellers dislike having to yield the marketspace to manufacturers.

Finally, a fourth strategy is to let the market decide the winners and open the internet to everybody – for direct sales and resellers. Manufacturers who have ventured online, either through the third or the fourth strategy, usually sell at retail prices and/or provide only a limited line because of their desire not to compete with their resellers. However, this limits the attractiveness of the internet's value proposition.

The fear of cannibalizing existing distribution channels and potential channel conflict requires manufacturers to trade off existing sales through the traditional distribution network and potential future sales through the internet. Unfortunately, history suggests that most companies tend to cling to declining distribution networks for too long.

Summary

Like all innovations in distribution the internet can disrupt businesses as readily as it can transform them. Different industries – and different companies within the same industry – have been affected in different ways. Just as television and later home video extended the film industry's distribution channels, so the internet looks to be expanding the market for retail investment brokers. Travel agents, on the other hand, are suffering as airlines reach out directly to consumers. According to **Nirmalya Kumar**, manufacturers have four choices: not using the net for sales at all, letting resellers use it exclusively, using it themselves, and opening it to everyone in a market free-for-all. Cannibalization is a danger – but history suggests that most companies cling to declining distribution networks for too long.

Markets for everything in the networked economy

by Andrew Whinston, Manoj Parameswaran and Jan Stallaert

The advent of digital technology marks the beginning of a period of profound economic change. Radically new economic institutions will emerge; existing institutions will be transformed. Most of these changes will be information-driven.

The information infrastructure has the reach and ease of access to bring large numbers of buyers and sellers together with great efficiency. It also extends the scope of the economy beyond the restraints imposed by political and geographical barriers. These factors, together with digital technology's inherent capacity to convey information, imply the availability of extensive information on trading opportunities.

Unfortunately, most of this information is not organized, verified or standardized. It therefore becomes prohibitively expensive for economic agents to search and co-ordinate trading opportunities. Thus the need for a new set of agents arises: intermediaries.

Intermediaries will provide sound and convenient information to economic agents, furnish trading mechanisms and ensure reliable transactions. They will also act as trusted third parties and certification authorities. Other ancillary functions include co-ordinating agents, negotiation mechanisms, catalogue services and yellow page services.

E-commerce intermediaries will exist to process demand, supply information and facilitate trades. Modern economic theory contends that markets are the best way to process chaotic information and allocate resources; hence e-commerce intermediaries will be designed around market mechanisms (as current trends clearly indicate).

Model markets and real markets

Economic theory holds that markets are the best way to allocate resources, under two assumptions: perfect and symmetric information, and equality of market power among individual agents. In such conditions, allocations are efficient and readily stabilize themselves at equilibria.

By and large, the real world does not follow economists' assumptions of perfect competition. Asymmetries of information yield market power to sellers, and consumers find it unrealistic to acquire information about the wide range of goods that they purchase. This leads to monopolistic competition, where sellers offer "take-it-or-leave-it" prices and consumers rely on such factors as brand recognition, reputation and advertisement. Digital technologies are drastically changing this scenario.

With ease of entry and broader scope, electronic markets bring many more sellers and buyers to the marketplace. Further, the infrastructure makes available extensive information about these agents. The e-commerce environment allows efficient dissemination of this information, both between consumers and via inter-mediaries. Information is richer and better distributed, which creates a much better environment for markets.

Market mechanisms in the physical world are limited by many factors. These include scope, scalability, problems with estimating demand and the difficulty of dynamically updating prices. Digital technologies can go a long way towards overcoming these limitations. They significantly relax the bounds of scope and scaleability. They facilitate collection and processing of demand information. Most importantly, they make possible fast and scaleable algorithms that can dynamically compute prices on the basis of supply and demand schedules; these in turn can give rise to sophisticated market mechanisms (for example, various types of auction) which dramatically improve the efficiency of allocations.

Market applications

These benefits are not restricted to existing markets. The real world abounds in problems of resource allocation that are not resolved by traditional market mechanisms. Examples include energy resource allocation, flight scheduling, traffic management, distributed databases, radio frequency allocations, knowledge sharing, class scheduling, and many more.

The traditional view is that markets are a means for exchanging resources whose value is expressible in money terms. Most of these allocation problems tend to be complex, with participants and resources distributed over various locations. Valuation can be difficult, and may need to be updated constantly.

Digital technology's ability to collect information from distributed sources and to process it through fast algorithms opens the possibility of using market mechanisms to handle all sorts of problems more efficiently. Indeed, new electronic markets are being increasingly used in the fields of electric power, radio frequency allocations, flight scheduling and traffic management.

The potential scope for market mechanisms extends far beyond these current trends. For instance, consider a corporate information system that is used by personnel from different departments. The flood of complex queries is served on a

3 Nov 1998

DIGITAL BUSINESS

Richard Waters finds the group has learned a lesson on purchasing from suppliers via the internet

Financial Times

by Richard Waters

General Electric, which buys $35bn (£21bn) of materials and services each year, certainly has the muscle to nudge its suppliers into line when it comes to developing online purchasing systems. That is apparent from its use of electronic bulletin boards and extranets to harness its buying power and bring down purchasing costs.

But even GE cannot use technology to shift the relationship between a company and its suppliers as much as it might want. That appears to be one lesson from the US group's early experience with GE Marketplace. GE had hoped to use the system to get suppliers to bid against each other in real-time auctions, says Randolph Rowe, a manager in GE's corporate initiatives group. That would guarantee GE the lowest price available at the time, and allow suppliers to bid aggressively to raise their volumes against competitors.

In the event, the idea, launched in 1995, did not take off in its original form. Suppliers did not take to the format, and GE found that some suppliers made promises they could not fulfil. Technology may make it theoretically possible to turn a supplier network into a virtual marketplace, but that does not guarantee that it will happen.

Despite that, the use of electronic bulletin boards like GE Marketplace could become a significant factor in GE's electronic commerce armoury, and could have a profound impact on its suppliers.

GE set out to apply the technology of the internet to its dealings with suppliers in the mid-1990s as part of an effort to bring down purchasing costs.

The aim was to improve "speed, cost, quality", says Gary Reiner, chief information officer. Much of GE's purchasing power is fragmented, with buying decisions devolved to people around the group. Also, processing orders was fraught with human error: more than a quarter of the 5m invoices processed by

GE each year have to be reworked, adds Mr Rowe.

A large part of the solution could come from doing away with the group's patchwork of purchasing systems. GE's industrial controls business, for instance, had seven: by combining them, the benefits of standardization become possible. A common system will allow the division to "create a virtual business", combining orders from different sources to harness the group's buying power.

Combined with the technology of the internet, standardized purchasing systems stand to transform relationships with suppliers.

Take the latest incarnation of GE Marketplace, now known as TPN (Trading Partner Network). The system acts as a web-based noticeboard: suppliers post their catalogues on a master database maintained by TPN. GE buyers can then use a standard web browser to compare prices or products, and make purchases online. A purchase triggers an automatic purchase order and shipment from a supplier.

The system, being rolled out first in GE's lighting division, will be used for buying indirect materials – those not used in GE products – and for items as small as screwdrivers or batteries.

"It forces our employees to use the contracts that have been negotiated centrally, where there is much more leverage," says Mr Reiner. GE is now opening the TPN network to buyers in other companies. The information that suppliers post on the central database is sliced differently for different buyers, enabling a supplier to charge various prices, depending on the buyer.

TPN is also being used for online bidding – though not the sort of real-time auctions of the GE Marketplace days. Suppliers are invited to tender for contracts online, then they are subjected to a compressed round of bids that squeezes the normal

Continued

process of competitive bidding into as little as two days, according to Mr Rowe. The efficiencies that come from automating this process have brought price reductions of 5 to 15 per cent, he adds. GE also plans to create a series of extranets that act as private information networks for its suppliers. The first, used by the group's aircraft engine division, is being rolled out now.

The extranet, a secure part of the internet, carries a broad range of information to help suppliers, "whether it's drawings, information

about orders or anticipated volumes that they should gear up for", says Mr Reiner. GE can use the system to direct information to specific suppliers – it plans, for instance, to post supplier scorecards on the extranet – or to broadcast its needs to a wide group.

The implications of all of this for suppliers are clear: only those prepared to make their own investments in technology and training will be able to benefit from the closer relationship that developments like TPN and the use of extranets imply. And they will have to be prepared to fight harder over price to survive.

first-come-first-served basis with no differentiation based on the relative importance of requests. But with token valuations and a market mechanism, queries can be differentiated and computing resources allocated more efficiently.

Another example would be a supply chain system, where markets can be set up to determine inventory sizes and allocations dynamically. A crucial advantage of using markets in these scenarios is the fact that markets do not just process information, they also provide it. In all these allocation problems, feedback about demand and usage patterns will be provided by the market. These can lead to the design of systems that make better use of the resources in question.

Types of market

A striking feature of the digital economy is the variety of market institutions that it supports. In business-to-consumer and consumer-to-consumer e-commerce, a mix of posted price systems and various types of auction markets are currently in existence.

Posted price systems, by and large, represent a quick migration of mail order shopping to the internet. However, many companies are realizing the advantages of the more complex mechanisms that can be supported by electronic markets (see HotMail and eBay examples at the end of this chapter). Innovative business models have come into existence; these include novel uses of bundling and customization, the "free" bundled good (see Yahoo) and, most significantly, the market-based intermediary that conducts auctions for a variety of goods.

Many of these intermediaries are driven by expediency; they aim to make quick, short-term profits by exploiting the immense potential of the market. Theoretical or practical initiatives to identify sustainable, long-term market mechanisms – on which the future of electronic commerce will depend – are yet to emerge.

Currently, the markets predominantly use English auctions. In an English auction buyers submit bids for (multiple units of) an object. However, the fact that the internet brings together a high number of buyers and sellers, whose valuations can be processed and matched quickly by software, argues the case for double auctions as a sustainable digital market mechanism.

In a double auction, buyers as well as sellers submit prices at which they are willing to buy or sell goods. A useful analogy is provided by financial markets, where large number of buyers and sellers converge, and demand and supply change

213

HotMail

Several successful internet businesses make their products freely available to consumers and rely on revenues through advertising supplied with the content. The business model can be understood by viewing advertising as having a negative price. The consumer receives a bundled good, with a positively priced digital product or service, and negatively priced advertising. The price of the advertising offsets the price of the content, thus giving the consumer the illusion of a free good.

HotMail is a classic example of this approach. HotMail's innovative idea was to offer web-based e-mail to consumers, which implied that they did not have to procure a specific e-mail application, and could send and receive e-mail from any desktop with web access.

The success of the idea depended on capturing a large customer base quickly, and the entrepreneurs decided to offer the service free. The "free" good is in effect the e-mail service bundled with advertising. HotMail can be viewed as an intermediary that buys advertising from companies at a negative price, and resells it to customers. Further, each e-mail sent by a HotMail user serves as an advertisement for the service itself, a powerful way of exploiting the internet's connectivity. The growth of HotMail's customer base has been extraordinary, and the company has been bought by Microsoft for a hefty sum.

The success of the free bundled good strategy depends on the number of customers that the advertising can reach; if the product is valuable, the fact that it is "free" ensures that this number grows rapidly. With an innovative and useful product, this strategy can reap huge benefits.

dynamically. Double auctions have come to provide efficient markets for financial assets. The current predominance of English auctions on the internet is largely due to the fact that companies are simply transferring the most popular real world auction mechanisms to the digital world. However, as the potential of the digital environment becomes apparent, so to will the efficiency of double auctions.

Double auction markets will be built around intermediaries, as they require a "marketmaker" to match trades. These intermediaries will compete on several dimensions, such as trust, the number and reputation of participants they bring in, efficient matching algorithms, reliable and secure transactions, post-purchase customer service, scalability, the target product group, efficiency of user interfaces, and catalogue services.

Types of product

The products sold over electronic markets can be roughly grouped into two categories: purely digital goods and services, and physical products.

Digital goods and services

The first category includes information goods and services, such as financial information, news services, reference and learning material, entertainment and multimedia products, software distribution services, distributed database services and remote computation services. In addition, the internet has spawned innovative digital products such as online gaming, chatrooms, search engines, online advertising, yellow pages and certification services. These products are characterized by being difficult to value and easy to copy; related issues are disputes over copyright, zero marginal costs and uncertainty over quality.

Companies use different strategies to price and market these goods. They include customization and bundling, bundling valuable content with advertising to

eBay

The eBay website (www.ebay.com) provides a forum for sellers to put up goods for auction, and for buyers to bid for those goods. In effect, it hosts numerous single (English) auctions at a time; it is a little like a huge flea market.

eBay demonstrates a basic feature of successful internet enterprises: an idea, however simple, that exploits the unique characteristics of digital networks.

The net represents a large community of buyers and sellers, with numerous goods to trade. Online newsgroups and classified ads provided forums for trading before; eBay took this further by introducing auctions. The internet enables it to run hundreds of them at once at relatively little cost.

Like other successful internet businesses, eBay's growth is linked to a fast growth in its user base. But unlike most others, eBay directly earns revenue from users, by collecting percentage fees for auctions. This could make eBay vulnerable to competitors that could charge lower fees or no fees at all; its customer base is not necessarily locked in and could defect to cheaper alternatives.

provide "free" goods, introducing different versions of the same product to suit different users, charging subscriptions and, most importantly, using market mechanisms to help set price.

Physical products

Marketing physical products over the web has led to some of the biggest success stories in e-commerce. The key to success is marketing that takes advantage of the interface and the networked environment. Transferring a conventional mail-order business to the web adds little value.

The potential advantages of the internet include the scope for real-time interaction within a vast networked community, the possibility of using sophisticated market mechanisms, and the illusion of almost infinite inventory (when an intermediary acts for many suppliers). Businesses that exploit these opportunities, such as Amazon.com and eBay have met with enormous success.

Customization and bundling

The virtual environment makes possible unprecedented customization of products and services. In the real world, sellers specialize in highly standardized, individual products. Customers try to co-ordinate purchases across a broad spectrum of products on the basis of posted prices. The digital world, in which information can be acquired and processed with ease, lets sellers tailor their products to individual customers. Further, the electronic environment allows companies to respond quickly to consumer feedback.

The ease of customization, and the ability to cater to variations in consumer preferences, lead to the possibility of bundling goods in the electronic markets. While most sellers specialize in individual products, customers' preferences range over sets of products. Because the products in these sets complement each other, value is added. Each consumer will prefer a different product bundle, and the perceived value of the same product will vary from bundle to bundle.

In the physical world, it is unrealistic for sellers to establish these valuations. But in the digital economy the situation is different. Negotiated trading mechanisms can allow consumers to bid for bundles according to their preferences; efficient algorithms can match bundles to facilitate trades that increase the value for both sellers and buyers. In securities markets, for example, the bundle trading

Yahoo!

Success in the digital economy often depends on business models that exploit the unique features of the networked environment. This is in contrast to business initiatives built around the transfer of conventional business models to the internet. For example, many telcos have maintained yellow pages on the net for a long time without achieving conspicuous success.

Contrast this with Yahoo! which identified the need for yellow pages tailored to the digital world. It exploited the internet's connectivity to let users register their websites and choose for themselves the category in which to list them; in effect, the directory built itself.

First-mover advantage can be critical. With established brand equity and a strong customer base, Yahoo! has been able to stay ahead of the competition by adapting to newer trends such as personalized internet portals and free web-based email. The advantage conferred by being the first to innovate can offset competition from better technologies.

mechanism (patent pending) developed by Omega Consulting allows traders to submit a valuation for a complete portfolio of assets, instead of requiring asset-by-asset pricing.

In markets characterized by product complementarity, bundle trading using double auctions offers substantial benefits: it can facilitate price discovery and simplify trading. Possible applications extend over a wide range. These include commodity trading, financial assets trading, trading of knowledge and information goods, electric power and other energy markets, radio frequency spectra, network resource allocation, corporate information systems, supply chain management and enterprise software systems.

Summary

Digital technology will have far-reaching impacts on economic markets. Here **Andrew Whinston**, **Manoj Parameswaran** and **Jan Stallaert** provide an overview of the likely developments. Perhaps the most important will be increasing use of market mechanisms to solve resource allocation problems; this will be made possible by the internet's capacity to carry information swiftly among large numbers of economic agents. At the same time, a new breed of e-commerce intermediary is emerging to supply information and facilitate trades; over time, various forms of auction may displace the conventional posted price system. The virtual environment makes possible unprecedented customization and bundling of products, and companies that leverage these and other features will be more successful than those that try to mimic traditional business models.

Suggested further reading

Whinston, A., Choi, S. and Stahl, D. (1997) *Economics of Electronic Commerce*, Basingstoke: Macmillan.

Moving to the net: leadership strategies

by Robert Plant and Leslie P. Willcocks

If you were to ask investors what the major events were on Wall Street in 1998, two issues would be raised – the "mini-crash" (or "necessary correction") of August and the internet. It appeared that all you had to do was put ".com" on the end of your name and your stock price would go up 10 or 20 per cent or more. Ironically, the autumn run-up in the Dow and Nasdaq was due in part to online trading, which allowed retail traders access to the markets like never before; the internet stock bubble was in part fuelled via the net itself.

With the glare of e-commerce activity in the media and public eye, no executive in the US could escape its shadow. Even the 1998 Superbowl, the most sacred sporting event in the US with the most expensive advertising time on television succumbed: Victoria's Secret, the lingerie company, took a 15-second slot to promote a live supermodel fashion show on the internet.

The message is clear: the internet is here to stay. But beyond the start-up legends, the intermediaries, infomediaries and service providers, the internet is challenging established corporations' relationships with customers. The question they face is: "what does the net mean for our business, our competitive strategy and our information systems strategy?"

Our detailed interviews with senior executives in 38 major US and European corporations have revealed diverse approaches. Some companies feel that they can ignore the internet, that it does not concern them yet (to which our response is "How quickly could you respond if your strongest competitor came out with a powerful e-commerce strategy tomorrow?"). Other companies, however, are determined to have the best e-commerce branding on the planet.

In the face of a barrage of new rules for the information economy, business is finding that the boundaries of strategic thinking, and of competition, have vastly expanded. The challenge is to keep up with the rapid growth in converging technologies and to translate their potential into a business vision and a dynamic competitive strategy.

Unfortunately, many executives do not know what their strategic options are. They react by purchasing the necessary hardware and software and setting up a vanity website: "Look world, here we are!" is the statement. This is often followed by a bigger site and then perhaps a catalogue. But this is not an effective e-commerce strategy.

Corporate strategy can be defined as the formulation of a set of directives which, when effectively executed within the organization, fulfil the competitive vision set by executive management. Our consistent finding has been that, to be effective, an e-commerce strategy has to be integrated with the strategic vision of the company as a whole. As a respondent from American Express put it: "The net has to integrate into your core business."

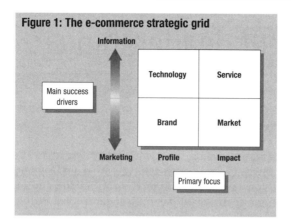

Figure 1: The e-commerce strategic grid

Four e-strategic directions

In creating an aligned e-commerce strategy we have found four main areas of strategic focus: technology, brand, service and market. These areas can be viewed in relation to two main issues: the primary focus of the strategy – gaining a market profile, or making a significant impact on the bottom line; and the main success drivers – a focused information or marketing strategy (*see* Figure 1).

Several generic points can be made immediately:

- there is a real sense among the e-commerce leaders that the internet is a foundation stone for a new network-centric business era. In many ways they are following the advice of Carver Mead, a pioneer of the microprocessor: "Listen to the technology. Find out what it is telling you."
- however, technology changes and is never sufficient. Enduring advantage comes not from the technology but from how information is collected, stored, analyzed and applied. As the director of corporate communications at one high-technology company put it: "We really need to manage this from an information perspective."
- not just technologies, but competition, opportunities and customer expectations are all evolving very fast. Time-based competition has become critical. Companies now need to be able to develop a strategy in "internet time".
- leading organizations learn quickly and are able to shift their strategic focus. Development of an integrated information and marketing platform is likely to pay off; over time it should enable deeper understanding of technological capabilities and business possibilities that can be converted into revenue streams.

The transience of technology leadership

E-commerce strategies that are focused on technology are found in all industrial sectors. Technology leadership involves early adoption of an emerging technology to achieve a pre-emptive position in its application for competitive advantage. Many companies we studied, including Citicorp, BMW, Pratt & Whitney, W.R. Grace and Genentech, began in this quadrant in the mid-1990s.

However, developing technology just to be in the race does not pay off. Companies with good e-strategies learned the technology in the course of developing an information and/or marketing strategy; this enabled them to shift their focus over time to other quadrants. Another effective approach was to develop the technology further for internal use as an intranet or to apply it to supply chain management in the form of an extranet.

An example of shifting focus is provided by the US power utility industry, which uses the internet to buy and sell natural gas, and to make bids for gas and pipeline capacity. This is mandated by the Federal Energy Regulatory Commission through a system called Oasis (Open Access Same Time Information System).

The utilities see their technology leadership strategy as a ploy to increase and lock in market share, for both residential and corporate consumers. While their mandate is to reduce their customers' power consumption, they balance this with a strategy of increasing their market share, which is made possible at dramatically lower cost by the internet.

Internet technology boosts the utilities' ability to monitor customers' usage (eventually even individual appliances could be monitored) and to offer suggestions on energy-saving. Their strategic focus is therefore moving from "technology" to "market". Competition in the industry is no longer based on the cheapest solution per kilowatt but on the use of technology to add value; the ultimate aim is to allow the utilities to get closer to customers and to create wider market coverage.

Brand as strategy

According to Lou Gerstner, chief executive of IBM, "branding in a network world will dominate business thinking for a decade or more". This arises from the unique branding opportunities provided by the internet, which are epitomized by the often-quoted example of Amazon.com. Although it only started to sell books on the web in July 1995, its revenues for the nine months ending September 1998 were $357m.

However, many established companies do not wish to develop a new sales channel at present. Instead they pursue a "brand" focus, reinforcing the customer's awareness of and regard for their brand. To do this, a company must add value by providing information to customers and developing a quality relationship with them. This is not a static information interchange but a dynamic one, in which the customer will expect change and continual value from the relationship.

BMW's is a good example of an advanced brand reinforcement strategy. The company has moved astutely from a "technology" to a "brand" leadership strategy, bridging both; its mission, it says, is to make its site "drive and feel like a BMW". It allows customers to build their own dream cars and even to hear the sound of its M series engine in the Z3 Roadster. But unlike Amazon.com, BMW would prefer potential new owners to visit a traditional dealer, not because it lacks the technology to sell via the internet, but because it feels that the relationship between customer and company is best served by face-to-face interaction and bonding.

Even though such internet channels do not directly generate revenue, they do bring tangible benefits for companies – such as BMW, Citicorp, Land Rover and home financier and builder Lennar – that understand the "marketspace". All four confirm tangible returns through feeding insights from the internet into their retail operations. According to one respondent, "What makes the internet such a wonderful marketing tool is that it shows fairly quickly what works and what does not work."

The service payoff

An obsessive focus on information and the customer is the most effective way to establish service leadership via the internet. Service should not always be expected to translate immediately into purchases by customers. Its value often consists simply in building relationships with, and gathering information about, potential customers.

The value-adding effects of building virtual communities have been well documented by management consultants John Hagel and Arthur Armstrong in their 1997 book *Net Gain*. Over time, a group of internet service providers, advertisers, potential customers and sellers can build a web-based community of interest that shares information and buys and sells goods and services. A fundamental feature of such networks is that their value increases exponentially even as they grow incrementally. Over time, the companies that nurture them can look forward to more customer transactions and greater revenue.

Other companies have taken less radical – but nevertheless profitable – approaches to service over the internet. Consider UPS, the world's largest package distribution company, which transports more than 3bn items a year. It is currently (1999) using the internet to position itself as a deliverer not just of packages but of information. UPS's "Document Exchange" service aims to enable businesses to transmit documents cheaply and securely over the internet, with the same benefits – such as package tracking and delivery confirmation – that it offers with physical packages. The internet also makes it easier for the company to customize logistics for its customers – for example, by ensuring that parts from different countries arrive where needed at the same time.

The internet is allowing organizations to offer innovative service variations to more and more customers. We found examples in most industries: utilities such as Entergy and the US-based FPL Group analyze their customers' bills and power usage; biotechnology companies such as Genentech support community activities; American Express provides tools for customers to carry out their own financial portfolio management; and companies across the board provide annual reports to shareholders. It is becoming possible for multinational companies to offer a level of service previously restricted to their home and major markets to all markets.

In search of market growth

Still other corporations have combined marketing, service and information to achieve disproportionate market growth via the internet. Office Depot, a US-based company, receives 300,000 orders for office products a day through its straightforward, user-friendly internet site. The company aims to retain customers by providing a convenient and efficient service, and also provides real-time inventory checking and customer call centers.

Car rental company Alamo is aggressively pursuing a strategy of being the first to facilitate wider market coverage and closer relationships with customers. Naturally this has influenced the speed at which it is developing its internet activities. The company reports that the internet is not only more profitable than traditional channels, but that it tends to receive a fairly constant amount of use, even when demand is less steady elsewhere. In Japan, Alamo's internet revenue has been eight times that from traditional channels.

Royal Caribbean Cruises, one of the world's largest cruise lines, evolved from a "technology" web presence in 1997, through enhancing its brand, to a more recent "market" focus, achieving significant market growth through on-line sales. By contrast, American Express first focused on brand reinforcement. As one marketing executive stated: "The internet is where the home run is – when you leverage what you are good at already and you use online in a way that cannot be duplicated. It reinforces what your products and services are, makes them better, and reinforces your brand and what it means." But more recently it has moved into market growth through the internet, for example through helping customers to trade stocks online.

Finally, US broker Charles Schwab had no exposure on the internet before 1996. But now over 58 per cent of its trading takes place on its website – that is, $4bn in securities every week. The internet has allowed Schwab to reduce its prices and, more importantly, to provide real-time, individualized information to customers at very little cost. It is now the largest single internet broking company.

Companies with this level of success clearly see the new business model which the internet makes possible for them, and commit to the hilt on the financial, technical and management resources needed. As Richard Lichfield of American Bankers Insurance Group remarked: "It's a bit like ATMs [automated telling machines]. Everybody was getting them and if you didn't you lost customers. But the internet also reinforces organizations, adds new channels. It is a real transition in business, one of those points where huge differences can be shown and made."

Succeeding on the internet

Strategic focus is not enough to guarantee success in e-commerce. Further drivers, some quite traditional, are required. The most important are:

- a senior management champion, preferably the chief executive
- a strong and flexible IT infrastructure
- active support by the organization's "content owners" (that is, groups and individuals that have a direct stake in the information on the website)
- the ability to climb the learning curve quickly – what struck us about the companies that are making the best use of e-commerce was the speed at which they developed online projects and the wealth of future online options that they considered
- belief that R&D for online activities is a strategic investment – we found that funding for internet projects sparked no serious "return on investment" questions in leading online companies
- adoption of a sourcing option that reflects the mission-critical nature of the internet. Although companies often start with an in-house group thrown quickly together (often dubbed a "skunk works") or complete outsourcing, the technology rapidly becomes too critical. It needs to be either established in-house with a centralized core and marketing heavily involved, or a strategic alliance has to be sought with a technology partner
- focus on areas other than the business-to-consumer channel. We found that leading e-commerce companies had made or were making heavier investments in intranet, extranet and supply chain applications.

Summary

Managers are confused by the way the boundaries of competition and strategic thinking are expanding in the information economy. The result is often failure to implement an effective e-commerce strategy. Where companies do have a strategy, say **Robert Plant** and **Leslie Willcocks**, they focus on four key areas: technology, branding, service and market growth. Developing technology just to be in the race generally does not pay off – companies with good e-strategies simply "pick up" the technology in developing an information or marketing strategy. The authors' interviews with executives in US and European corporations indicate that the most important success factors include strong leadership, a flexible IT infrastructure and active support by the corporate website's "content owners".

Suggested further reading

Hagel, J. III and Armstrong, A.G. (1997) *Net Gain*, Boston, MA: Harvard Business School Press.

Plant, R. and Willcocks, L. (1999) "Internet-based business strategies: the search for leadership", Oxford Executive Research Briefing, Templeton College, Oxford, December.

Willcocks, L., Feeny, D. and Islei, G. (eds) (1997) *Managing IT as a Strategic Resource*, Maidenhead: McGraw-Hill.

Reaching the next level in e-commerce

by William J. Kettinger and Gary Hackbarth

In the classic 1947 movie *Miracle on 34th Street*, Macy's Santa Claus advises parents to purchase hard-to-find toys from Macy's competitors. While the store loses some sales, this results in droves of satisfied customers seeking Santa's advice, increased store traffic and, ultimately, lots more sales for Macy's.

To achieve this win–win approach in today's age of e-commerce, Macy's must do more than employ a friendly Santa. It must consider a transformational business model based upon information asymmetries. These exist wherever a company leverages customer, supplier or consumer information unavailable to or unusable by its competitors.

Today we can go one step further by sharing business information with competitors in a reciprocal relationship to build a "virtual ecosystem". Introduced by James Moore, virtual ecosystems create "co-opetition", where companies co-operate with suppliers (who may also be their competitors) to offer complementary services.

A virtual ecosystem could exploit Macy's brand recognition and sizeable customer base by allowing competitors to sell complementary products and services through portals on Macy's website; this would increase the competitors' own traffic and brand equity. Likewise, a competitor could build a complementary web presence that sells Macy's products and services to enhance its own image.

Rethinking a business model by exploiting information asymmetries, leveraging customer and partner relationships and finding the right fit of "co-opetition" requires a company to break with prevailing ways of thinking about e-commerce. To achieve this level of sophistication, managers must be able to implement effective e-commerce "breakout strategies".

Nowadays products are more standardized and more alike in terms of quality than ever before. Therefore consumers find it difficult to distinguish between products simply by comparing physical attributes. They base buying decisions on the information value added to a product and on the customized service associated with it.

For example, the personal computer has grown to be a commodity product. Yet, Dell Computer has managed to differentiate its PCs by using an e-commerce model in which mass customization is supported by detailed customer information. The company also continually leverages superior customer support.

222

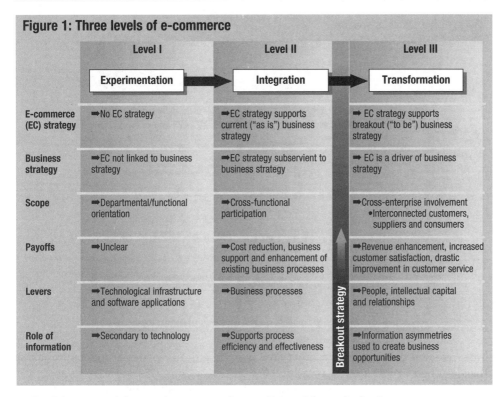

Figure 1: Three levels of e-commerce

	Level I — Experimentation	Level II — Integration	Level III — Transformation
E-commerce (EC) strategy	No EC strategy	EC strategy supports current ("as is") business strategy	EC strategy supports breakout ("to be") business strategy
Business strategy	EC not linked to business strategy	EC strategy subservient to business strategy	EC is a driver of business strategy
Scope	Departmental/functional orientation	Cross-functional participation	Cross-enterprise involvement • Interconnected customers, suppliers and consumers
Payoffs	Unclear	Cost reduction, business support and enhancement of existing business processes	Revenue enhancement, increased customer satisfaction, drastic improvement in customer service
Levers	Technological infrastructure and software applications	Business processes	People, intellectual capital and relationships
Role of information	Secondary to technology	Supports process efficiency and effectiveness	Information asymmetries used to create business opportunities

Breakout strategy (arrow spanning Level II to Level III)

In this competitive environment, the traditional boundaries between customers, suppliers, partners, information, goods and services begin to blur. In the new business ecosystem, partners do not merely add value at each stage of a chain but work together to create new value for the customer. Together they provide an integrated, seamless offering of products and services that extends each of their capabilities.

Three levels of strategy

E-commerce strategy and implementation pass through three levels of increasing sophistication (*see* Figure 1).

Most companies are at Level I, where individual departments take the technological lead in developing specific internet applications. These disparate applications are not tightly tied to business or e-commerce strategy. For example, the marketing department may create a public relations website while research and development uses an intranet for sharing designs and the purchasing department links its largest suppliers with EDI (electronic data interchange). While these applications serve parochial interests, senior managers have little idea of the payoffs.

Many industry leaders (such as Wal-Mart, Seagram's, Cisco and Tesco) have successfully moved to Level II. These companies incorporate e-commerce into their business model by integrating across functional departments. They focus on direct support of existing business processes.

Level II companies are driven by the promise of cost reductions, better business support and improvements in current operating models. Using technologies such as EDI and EFT (electronic funds transfer) these companies create cross-functional links with customers and suppliers. Large retailers such as Tesco and Wal-Mart

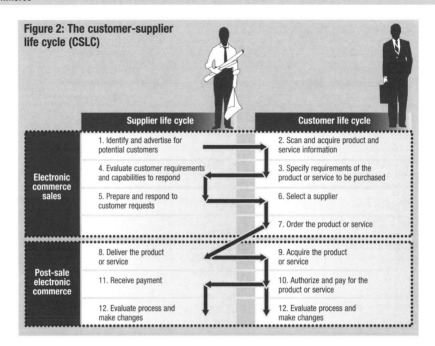

Figure 2: The customer-supplier life cycle (CSLC)

	Supplier life cycle	Customer life cycle
Electronic commerce sales	1. Identify and advertise for potential customers	2. Scan and acquire product and service information
	4. Evaluate customer requirements and capabilities to respond	3. Specify requirements of the product or service to be purchased
	5. Prepare and respond to customer requests	6. Select a supplier
		7. Order the product or service
Post-sale electronic commerce	8. Deliver the product or service	9. Acquire the product or service
	11. Receive payment	10. Authorize and pay for the product or service
	12. Evaluate process and make changes	12. Evaluate process and make changes

have created substantial competitive advantage in logistics and purchasing through their proprietary networks.

What is the common denominator in these successful Level II companies? A business process view tied to the bottom line and a culture that continually uses technological advances to hone process efficiency.

To move from Level I to Level II, companies must make a deliberate effort to align their business strategy with the e-commerce initiatives dispersed throughout the organization. The vehicle for this integration is business process. It has been our experience that a thorough review of the "customer–supplier life cycle" (CSLC) pinpoints those areas that are poorly integrated (*see* Figure 2).

The CSLC characterizes the buying and selling of products and services within a company as an integrated process. We take this process view of e-commerce because buying and selling include a number of activities that must be effectively managed to maintain strong customer–supplier relationships.

Companies must continually focus on (1) the nature of products and services bought and sold; (2) the type of value exchanged by buyers, sellers and other members of the value chain; and (3) the very definition of a buyer or a seller.

The CSLC isolates a company's buying and selling activities in a single transaction. It evaluates the extent to which people, information, processes and technologies are integrated; it looks at the relationship between customer and supplier as well as between pre- and after-sale activities. Thus a CSLC analysis recognizes the importance of using e-commerce technology to find and satisfy customers before as well as after a sale.

Clearly, an integrated CSLC demands increased collaboration and knowledge-sharing between customers and suppliers, as well as standardized policies. The result is an integrated process that shortens transaction times, lowers the cost of expertise, builds trust, and increases customer satisfaction with products and services.

Leapfrogging from Level I to Level III is only possible for a few start-up companies that are not burdened by an existing business model. Companies such as Amazon.com can quickly move from being a bookstore to a drugstore to an internet entertainment portal. However, most companies are not internet start-ups. They have existing business processes, pre-internet business strategies and people that are not always quick to make the transition to the information age.

Some excellent Level II companies may make the transition to Level III by the sheer weight of market dominance and a programme of incremental process improvement. Federal Express initially designed its VirtualOrder software to support its existing business processes, including order placement, billing, invoicing and inventory management. A master at customer satisfaction, FedEx went on to enhance customer relationships through its InterNetShip software, which allows companies to initiate and track shipping transactions online. It also recognized a valuable business opportunity in helping affiliated companies publish and maintain their catalogues online. FedEx has further extended its services by providing facilities to handle payments.

In essence, FedEx is evolving from its business process efficiency perspective (Level II) towards a new internet logistics and transaction management portal for its customers (Level III). It leverages its strong brand and logistics capabilities to achieve new levels of information asymmetries by closely linking its core competences in virtual and physical value chain activities.

Strategic breakout

While some market leaders such as FedEx may incrementally evolve to Level III, most companies will not get there without major intervention on the part of senior management. If they are to achieve drastic increases in revenue and customer satisfaction, companies must capitalize on the intellectual capital in their employees and external relationships. Level III business leaders will need to disrupt the status quo by proposing Level III "breakout strategies". However, breakout is only possible if information asymmetries can be exploited and the company has the will, knowledge, talent and technological infrastructure to change course.

How can senior executives position themselves to take the lead? By recognizing that e-commerce has changed the rules. Effective leadership demands that senior executives have a greater technological knowledge than in the past. Most importantly, they must develop an "information orientation"; in essence, this involves being attuned to the company's strategic information holdings, so that these can be leveraged to improve business relationships.

Where in Level II it was appropriate merely to align IT strategy with business goals, Level III requires executives to align business strategy with the dramatic developments now taking place in information and technology. Executives need a new mindset; they must realize that e-commerce strategy is business strategy.

Breakout strategies begin with executive commitment to an e-commerce vision. This vision is rooted in the belief that the company is not doing all it can to leverage customer information to build market share and increase profits. An executive taskforce should systematically gather information about customers, suppliers, business partners and e-commerce technologies as they relate to the CSLC. This industry assessment can be systematically compared to the company's current business strategy.

Using a variety of brainstorming techniques to break away from stereotypical

225

thinking, a breakout strategy is then envisioned. The aim is to alter the course of the company by leveraging asymmetrical information so that it will emerge as a leader in specific products or services.

Breakout strategies use industry best practices (in terms of processes and technology) to establish an ambitious, but theoretically obtainable, strategic target. To cope with the turbulence of the information economy, this strategic reinvention must be done habitually to maintain the company's forward course.

Around the world, senior executives have begun to focus on Level III transformation of their companies and industries. Ford's experience is typical. In 1995 it launched an electronic brochure (website) as an advertising medium and source of intelligence (Level I). Its success encouraged Ford to intergrate its business activities further via internet/intranet applications that connected employees and suppliers by extending existing EDI. However, major competitors quickly followed this strategy and Ford's advantage was not sustained.

Ford, General Motors, Chrysler and Toyota broke out towards Level III when they created the Automotive Network Exchange (ANX). ANX connected automotive suppliers through a common communication infrastructure of interactive tools.

Business strategies were transformed by co-opetition as ANX's members recognized that they could leverage the commonality of parts and designs to reduce costs. Companies benefited by building a web of alliances that extended the scale and scope of the automotive community. Co-opetition also had the effect of deepening the commitment and loyalty of automotive community members to each other.

Finding the level

For many companies an immediate jump to Level III may prove difficult. For some, a radical breakout strategy is too much, too fast in terms of change. Clearly, a company must first decide if it is at Level I, II or III. To help with this decision, it should ask the following questions:

Does the company have the technological infrastructure to support e-commerce? Do its e-commerce applications reside within specific departments or functional units? Is it experimenting with e-commerce or attempting to integrate its business processes? Answering "yes" to these questions would suggest that the company is at Level I.

Does the company have an e-commerce strategy and does it support the business strategy? Does it integrate e-commerce technologies throughout the CSLC? Does it include customers and suppliers within its automated business processes? Here "yes" would indicate a company at Level II.

The next set of questions is germane to companies at Level III.

Does the company have customer information it is not using to build market share and increase profits? Are competitors able to field products and services with a higher degree of quality and customer satisfaction in its target market segments? Can the company share specific customer information with competitors without security breaches, and can it withdraw from some markets and enter others with a competitor's tacit consent? Are there synergies in the development of products and services that the company and its competitors can jointly agree on and leverage to lower costs, improve efficiency and increase quality? Is its strategic focus on building relationships, developing intellectual capital and cultivating knowledge workers? Is it prepared to alter its business model radically to remain successful?

Virtual ecosystems, co-opetition and electronic markets are going to be at the heart of companies' breakout e-commerce strategies. The companies that will succeed as the 21st century gets under way will focus on building relationships and exploiting intellectual capital to create opportunities. The real question is, if you do not move to the next level, and do so quickly, how long will you remain in business?

Summary

Companies need to break with prevailing ways of thinking about e-commerce if they are to exploit information asymmetries and fully leverage relationships with customers and partners, argue **William Kettinger** and **Gary Hackbarth**. There are three levels of strategic sophistication. At the most basic, individual departments take a lead in developing specific internet applications; the result is disparate "islands" of e-commerce initiatives not tightly tied to business strategy. At level two, companies incorporate e-commerce to support their current business models by integrating across functional departments. To reach the third level, however, a "breakout" strategy which disrupts the status quo is likely to be necessary. Such a change may be too radical for many companies to undertake immediately. The authors conclude with a list of questions to help executives determine at what level their company is operating.

THE HUMAN FACTOR

8

Contributors

M. Lynne Markus is professor of management and information science at the Peter F. Drucker Graduate School of Management at Claremont Graduate University.

Wanda J. Orlikowski is associate professor of information technologies and organization studies at the Sloan School of Management at the Massachusetts Institute of Technology.

Thomas H. Davenport is professor of information management at Boston University's School of Management and director of the Accenture Institute for Strategic Change.

H. Jeff Smith is associate professor at the Babcock Graduate School of Management, Wake Forest University, North Carolina.

Chun Wei Choo is associate professor at the Faculty of Information Studies, University of Toronto.

Contents

Introduction

This theme has cropped up many times in other modules but here it takes center stage. Research and anecdotal evidence confirm that one reason why so many IT investments fail to achieve positive results is companies' failure to understand the people who actually use new technology. There is an important distinction, for example, between "espoused" technologies (what companies install) and "technologies-in-use" (what employees actually use). Human behavior is an important factor in the success – or otherwise – of many telecommuting, homeworking and hotelling initiatives launched by large organizations. A good way to start is to understand how people acquire and process information.

How workers react to new technology

by M. Lynne Markus

Where you stand depends on where you sit. Nowhere is this truer than in people's reactions to new information technologies. The people who make decisions about adopting new technologies – usually line managers and executives – often react favourably, since they play such a prominent role in acquiring technology. In fact, influenced by vendor and media hype, they might have unrealistically high expectations – essentially assuming that technology is a magic bullet to cure all organizational ills.

Technology specialists too are often enthusiastic about new technologies, not only because they like technology, but also because their career success may depend on knowing about the latest developments. Surprisingly often, however, specialists may resist pressure from decision-makers to acquire new technologies. These may differ sharply from those already in use in the organization, raising the specter of integration challenges and performance problems. The shakedown phase of any new technology often requires long hours from specialists already stretched by other projects or staff cutbacks. Finally, they may be unwilling to stake their reputations on the need to make an unknown technology work.

But the most varied reactions to new information systems and technologies come from those who are expected to use them. Here reactions range from phobia to enthusiastic acceptance, with resistance and apathy somewhere in between.

Actions and reactions

Explanations for the reactions of technology users are as varied as the reactions themselves. It is common to claim that resistance to change is a fundamental human trait. A second explanation focuses on the process of making the change: whether people have had a say in selecting the technology or in the way it is introduced and used, how the new technology is communicated, how much training and support are provided, and how carefully the rollout is planned and executed.

A third account centers on the technology itself: how well suited it is to users' work, how easy it is to learn and to use, how "forgiving" it is of user errors, how reliable, and so forth. Yet another explanation focuses on group and organizational dynamics: the perceived or actual effects of the technology on social relations, the distribution of power, and existing job skills; the degree to which the technology is promoted by supervisors, managers and fellow workers; and the degree to which use of the technology is reinforced by human resource policies, such as pay and promotion.

Finally, new technologies often accompany other organizational changes, such as changes in job design or conditions of work. It can be difficult to distinguish people's reactions to the technology from their reactions to other changes. New technology is a convenient scapegoat for many workplace dissatisfactions.

Clearly, any or all of these factors may play a role in how people react to a new technology. Nevertheless, there are some relatively predictable aspects.

Appearances deceive

People's initial reactions to new technologies do not always last. Negative reactions due to fear and uncertainty often evaporate after experience with the technology. Also, early reactions are often heavily conditioned by start-up problems such as downtime, data conversion errors and mistakes by novice users. When these problems are resolved during the shakedown phase, people tend to become more accepting. (However, failure to resolve start-up problems promptly can lead to rejection of the technology.)

Another important point is that people's acceptance of a technology does not mean that they are using it effectively or achieving adequate benefits for the organization. A fair body of research suggests that few organizations get full value from their IT investments, either because people have not learned how to use technology well or because managers have not learned how to manage its benefits.

Individual skill

Some years ago, one of my doctoral students conducted an experiment on the effectiveness of IT training approaches. She selected 60 people who had at least two years of word processing experience then tested their actual level of skill. Two of the 60 experienced users had never learned the basic feature of "word wrap" (in which the software automatically positions text on a new line when the typist reaches the end of a line).

These two people had learned their text-handling skills on manual or electric typewriters, which require users to return the carriage or typing mechanism manually when they reach the end of a line. Regardless of their training in word processing, they still had mental models of word processors as typewriters. When they reached the end of a line, they automatically hit the return key – and so never learned that this action is both unnecessary and dysfunctional.

This example is not as extreme as it appears. In studies that I and colleagues have conducted on the use of voicemail, we have found that few experienced voicemail users know about or use the features that allow one to send voice messages like e-mails. Most users treat the technology as an answering machine. If the person they are calling does not answer the phone they leave a message. Similarly, they retrieve their own. But they do not know that it is possible to send a voice message without ringing the other person's phone or to send the same message to multiple parties via a distribution list. Many people bring to voicemail their mental models of answering machines and do not learn the technology's new features.

Consider these additional research findings:

- a study by Ronald Rice (Rutgers University) and a colleague showed that most users of a new digital telephone system knew only a handful of its hundreds of features. The best users knew perhaps 10 features. The average user could not transfer a phone call
- studies of spreadsheet use show that user errors in designing and testing spreadsheets abound
- research in human–computer interaction has found individual differences in task-completion times ranging from 7 to 1 in text editing to 50 to 1 in programming, with data retrieval somewhere in between.

Some readers may not be bothered by these statistics – after all, how could any one person possibly benefit from all the thousands of features in a product like

Microsoft Word? But this response ignores the fact that many people simply do not use their IT tools well, even after years of routine use.

Organizational use of IT

It is a mistake to think of IT skill solely in individual terms. Organizations also must learn how to manage IT so that benefits are achieved. There is some evidence that organizations, like individuals, have IT learning curves – and that some organizations learn more and better than others do.

A study by Wanda Orlikowski and Marcie Tyre published in *Organization Science* in 1994 found that technology projects are characterized by short bursts of adaptation and learning followed by much longer periods in which technology use is routine and relatively unchanging. Unless something happens to unfreeze the situation – such as a retraining programme or a technology upgrade – technology usage stabilizes, often at levels far short of ideal. The researchers concluded that there are "windows of opportunity" for intervening to improve the effectiveness of IT use.

Researchers at the Nanyang Business School in Singapore found similar patterns of organizational technology use in small Singaporean businesses. Companies usually computerized in "waves", with a burst of initiatives at the beginning followed by a decline in activity. Some organizations had subsequent waves of computerization. Intriguingly, the researchers found evidence that patterns of computerization were related to organizational performance. High-performing organizations tackled more projects initially and appeared to have more waves of computerization, with higher levels of activity and shorter gaps between waves.

These studies suggest that effective organizations do not leave IT projects simply to run their course. To combat fall-offs in IT learning and enthusiasm for change, they demand results from IT projects and create opportunities for continuous improvement. Organizational learning about IT is a process that must be managed.

Managing people's IT skills

The two most obvious ways to improve individuals' skill at using IT are training (and retraining) and making technology easier to use. While both of these methods are important, neither is a sure-fire cure-all. And there are many barriers to these strategies, a fact that underscores the need for IT learning management.

Training

Skilful IT users need three kinds of knowledge: knowledge about the IT products and services they use (what they do and how they work); knowledge about when to use them and why; and knowledge about how to use them to enhance personal and organizational effectiveness. Most IT training materials address only the first goal, although research has shown that many people have insufficient job knowledge to apply IT effectively. For instance, because they may not know how their work affects others, they may be cavalier about data accuracy.

It is often thought that people can and do learn about their work from information technologies designed to support it. The weight of evidence suggests, however, that managers should not count on this happening. People rarely learn much about an unfamiliar work domain by using an IT tool designed for that domain unless the technology has been consciously designed as a learning tool. (But lack of computer skills can prevent domain experts from using a relevant new technology effectively. They cannot apply their work knowledge while using IT without adequate technology skills.)

Why do companies not make a better job of IT and job skill training? The simple answer is that the training required for effective use of new technologies often far exceeds managers' willingness to pay. A recent article in *Computerworld*, for example, pegged the average cost of organizational training in a new IT application area (sales force automation) at $400,000. Analysts estimate that organizations should allocate 15–25 per cent of the cost of enterprise resource planning (ERP) projects to training. With ERP project budgets of hundreds of millions of dollars in large organizations, an adequate training budget can be very large indeed.

Compounding managers' unwillingness to fund training are the sales pitches of technology vendors, who understandably bill their products as easy to use and requiring little training. Training may also be a victim of funding policies that locate it in operational budgets rather than including it as part of the initial capital outlay. And because training necessarily comes late in technology projects, it is very likely to be cut when the schedule slips.

And if these barriers are not enough, there is always the problem that technology training is often not as effective as we educators would like to believe. Research shows that some approaches are better than others, but even with the better approaches people may still come away with a limited or incorrect idea about the technology.

Many packaged training courses do not meet the needs of either novices or more advanced users. Most novices prefer to learn new technology through one-to-one coaching on the job instead of in a classroom. But this method can be very expensive for large numbers of trainees and its effectiveness depends on coaches' IT skills. Even in well-designed formal training programmes, novices can absorb only a limited amount of information about a new technology before they are overwhelmed. Experience shows that it is best to plan for advanced training later as well as for periodic refreshers – which, of course, adds to training cost.

Ease of use

There is ample evidence that the quality of the interface between technology and the user makes a difference in IT learning and use. But there is still a great deal to be learned about interface design. And organizations wishing to maximize interface quality may face formidable barriers. The "best" interface for a particular user may be a function of his or her skills, job type and experience. But the best interface for an organization may have to be a common standard to minimize training and support costs.

Today, IT is more powerful, flexible and customizable than ever. At the same time, there are strong pressures for organizations to adopt standard technologies with minimal customization. Most organizations used to develop bespoke systems to fit exactly the way they did business. This strategy maximized user acceptance because it made minimal demands for change. But the downside was that organizations rarely achieved improvement in performance. (No pain, no gain.)

Today, many organizations recognize that their work practices may not be effective relative to benchmark companies. In addition, software packages have become widely available, and are much cheaper than bespoke software. But the long-term benefits of packaged software require companies to adapt their work practices to software rather than the other way round. Customizing package software to a business's needs usually makes upgrading difficult and costly. The net effect of these trends is that organizations may find themselves installing new software that is harder for employees to use than the software they used before.

For example, I recently studied an equipment manufacturer implementing an ERP package. In many parts of the organization the package was expected to streamline work. But this was not the case in the maintenance department. Customers typically collected defective pieces of equipment and returned them for service in batches of 10 or more. The old software allowed maintenance workers to enter multiple repair items on a single customer repair order. The new software required a separate order for each item, which meant re-entering customer information each time.

Managers estimated that the new software would effectively increase each worker's daily workload from 8 to 11 hours. Fortunately, corporate executives approved an increase in staff to accommodate the change. They expected that the total benefits of the system would outweigh an increase in local costs and that the software vendor would eventually improve the maintenance module. Unfortunately, many package-using organizations do not provide for such problems and the reactions of users are predictably negative.

Ever faster learning?

As software vendors improve their products over time, problems like those of the maintenance department may well disappear. However, organizations will only reap the benefits of new releases if they do, in fact, upgrade. And here we have perhaps the most interesting challenge new IT poses today. People in organizations will be expected to assimilate new technologies at ever greater rates.

One large company I know of plans to have no more than three versions of ERP software "in play" at any given time: the old version; the new version (being rolled out to sites still using the old version); and a future version (being configured to replace the new version). Given the rate at which ERP vendors produce new releases, the company estimates that any one site might remain with a release for no more than 12 to 18 months!

Such plans create enormous requirements for individual and organizational learning. The benefits of adopting new software must surely be related to how quickly people can learn to use it well. The longer and the less effective the learning cycle, the less chance the organization has of achieving payoffs. If, through human resistance, inadequate training or bungled change management, it takes six months or more for users to assimilate software and job changes, the chances that the organization could benefit in a 12–18-month implementation cycle are slim. Conversely, achieving the benefits in this time will require organizational and individual commitment to rapid learning, with all this entails for training and support budgets.

It is often said that all IT adoption and use problems are transitional – they go away with improvements in technology and user skill. Most people in the workforce today did not grow up using computer technology but learned it as adults. So we do not have the awesome dexterity, confidence and computer knowhow of the Nintendo generation. And technology is improving every day. Does this mean that all companies will soon be able to forego the costs of technology training and change management? Or does it simply mean that companies that learn how to learn about IT will gain a bigger, more durable edge?

Summary

As the pace of technological change accelerates, workers are expected to learn more and more new IT applications. Unlike managers and IT specialists (who naturally support the systems they buy) their reactions to new technology vary greatly; although in some cases they are enthusiastic, in others poor communication, organizational power shifts and a host of other factors can lead to hostility or apathy. Fortunately, says **M. Lynne Markus**, negative reactions usually die down as people become accustomed to new systems and glitches are ironed out. But the bad news is that many people simply "get by" with IT applications and do not use them with maximum effectiveness. Worse still, many companies fail to push for continuous improvement and do not treat training as a priority. Another issue is the rise of standardized enterprise resource planning packages, which may entail more work for some employees in spite of overall benefits.

One cheer for the virtual office

by Thomas A. Davenport

Two years ago, a co-author, Keri Pearlson, and I completed a study on "virtual offices" – alternative work arrangements in which information technology replaces direct contact with co-workers and/or a physical office location. Our study revealed both positive and negative aspects to virtual offices, both of which I will describe below. Towards the end of the period in which we did the research, some early adopters of virtual offices were beginning to question and even reject their new arrangements. This development, and several other troublesome aspects of the phenomenon, led us to entitle the article "Two cheers for the virtual office", suggesting that these work arrangements are less than optimal.

For the past seven months, I have worked regularly in a virtual office. As a result of this "participant observation" I am more negative about virtual offices than before, at least for knowledge workers such as researchers and consultants. In most cases, I do not think the financial savings equal the human costs. In this article I will describe both my academic research into the area and my personal experience of this kind of environment.

It is important to note that neither I nor anyone else knows the implications of virtual offices for productivity and performance at either the individual or the organizational level. It is difficult to show the direct effects of almost anything (including IT in general) on worker or company performance. As with the question of closed offices versus cubicles or suburban versus city-centre offices, we have only preferences, not performance differentials, as the basis for deciding which arrangement to adopt. In today's labor market, however, preferences may be enough. If good workers are hard to find, and if workers prefer – all other things being equal – nonvirtual offices, perhaps they should have them.

What is a virtual office?

The concept of the "virtual office" actually refers to a range of alternative work

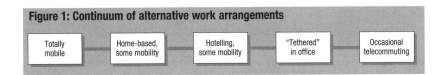

Figure 1: Continuum of alternative work arrangements

Totally mobile → Home-based, some mobility → Hotelling, some mobility → "Tethered" in office → Occasional telecommuting

arrangements, with varying degrees of presence outside a physical office. The different virtual office environments are displayed on the continuum in Figure 1.

Telecommuting

At the most stationary extreme, the term "telecommuting" usually (but not always; there is little precision in the language of virtuality) refers to workers with fixed offices who occasionally – often one day a week – work at home. This arrangement was the most common that we found in our research into virtual office policies in US companies.

The primary benefit of telecommuting is worker flexibility, and perhaps increased productivity (but this is seldom measured) for individual employees. Because no office space is freed up, there are few cost savings; because the virtual work is only occasional, there is little need for new management approaches. It is a low-risk, low-reward option.

Tethered in office

Further along the continuum is the tethered worker, who has some mobility but is expected to report to an office on a regular basis. These workers have no fixed office but they do have a fixed work location. When the advertising agency Chiat/Day opened new offices in New York and Los Angeles, for example, it initially adopted the tethered arrangement. Workers checked into the building in the morning and received a mobile phone and laptop computer. They were then free to wander around the office or nearby.

This type of arrangement is not common enough to yield generalizations about its success, but it led to problems at Chiat/Day. The company's innovative virtual office design received acclaim from architectural critics. But some workers found it difficult to be creative and to work with – or even locate – their teams in tethered mode. And when Chiat/Day was bought by another agency, new managers were concerned that workers who could not find productive spaces in which to work were simply staying at home. As one manager put it, "We didn't want people thinking that they didn't have to come to the office any more." The space in the merged company was redesigned, more private spaces were added and workers were given their own phones and computers.

Hotelling

Hotelling is another type of virtual work which is often coupled with work-at-home or work-at-the-customer programmes. Workers come into the office occasionally but because they are often absent they are not given a fixed office space. Instead, they can reserve a hotel "room" (more likely a cubicle) where they can receive and make phone calls and link their laptop computers to the network. The hotel space may be in a city-centre building previously used for traditional offices, or it may be in some suburban location specifically selected for mobile work. IBM calls its suburban hotels "productivity centers". Hotelling is popular with professional services firms (including my own), primarily because their personnel are frequently working at client sites.

Home

Home workers have no office at all other than a room in their homes. They may go to customer sites on some days. Company programmes such as those at AT&T and Hewlett-Packard have equipped such workers with furniture, computing equipment and high-speed phone lines. The work in this situation is largely performed on the computer and the telephone; typical activities are customer service, telemarketing or computer programming.

The benefits of this arrangement are work flexibility and freedom from commuting for workers, and reduced office space costs for employers. Of course, it is not an easy solution for individuals who face obstacles posed by children, at-home spouses and small dwellings without adequate space for the computer, fax, desk and files. Home offices reduce costs by replacing the company's real estate with the employees' – a proposition of questionable fairness. Some research has suggested that home offices are popular with workers for a year or two but often fall from favor after that, perhaps because home workers eventually become too disconnected from their jobs and co-workers.

Fully mobile

Finally, fully mobile workers may not even have home offices. They are expected to be on the road or at customer sites during the working day. Most workers of this type were already mobile before the virtual office era but were just not as well connected to their companies. Typical fully mobile workers include field sales and customer service employees.

For example, pharmaceutical representatives, such as those at Astra and Pfizer, view their offices as their portable computers and files kept in their cars. Otis Elevator service personnel have been fully mobile for several years. The virtues of this approach center on the ability of mobile workers to spend more time with customers, and the flexibility of total mobility in dispatching workers to customer locations.

While most of the companies we surveyed used only one or two types of virtual work, a large corporation might eventually employ all the types for different workers. In our survey, we found the most common combination beyond casual telecommuting was a home programme coupled with a company hotelling arrangement.

How prevalent are virtual offices?

Two years ago, when we completed our survey of large US companies, virtual offices of one type or another were quite popular, and becoming more so. At that time about 30 per cent of these companies had a formal programme for some sort of alternative work arrangement in place, and another 15 per cent were planning to institute one. Many more companies allowed occasional telecommuting on an informal basis.

My informal analysis since then suggests that the number of virtual workers continues to increase – companies committed to virtual offices are rolling them out to more locations, and more informal programmes are taking effect. But the rate of adoption of formal programmes has slowed. Like Chiat/Day, a few companies have abandoned virtual offices altogether.

The industries that made the greatest use of virtual work in our study were the IT industry (for example, IBM, AT&T, Pacific Bell, Hewlett-Packard, Compaq, Xerox), which had a reason to showcase the use of its products, and the professional services industry. The consumer products industry (Frito-Lay, Procter & Gamble) was also active because its sales forces travelled frequently to large grocery chains.

The most popular business functions for virtual work (in order of popularity) were field sales and service, technical support, staff functions (MIS, human resources, procurement, legal), product development, engineering, research and general management. Almost all of the jobs involved substantial use of electronic information.

The benefits of virtual offices

In our study companies adopted virtual work arrangements for two main reasons: cost and worker convenience. Cost-orientated programmes tended to involve hotelling, home-based programmes or total mobility. They were generally mandatory, either prohibiting or strongly discouraging fixed, permanent offices. These programmes were generally applied to all members of a particular function within an office, and sometimes to all people within an office or geographical area.

While workers were often unhappy with these arrangements, they did reduce costs. One professional services firm, for example, reported 30 per cent reductions in real estate costs in offices where hotelling had been adopted. Other companies cited reductions in office space of between 25 and 67 per cent; overall a big company might save $50m–$100m per year, according to AT&T. However, these savings are offset in some cases by increased costs for technology and home office furnishings, and by the inability to renegotiate leases quickly. Some Xerox sales offices adopted virtual office arrangements expressly to create savings to pay for laptop computers for the sales force.

The other major benefit is worker convenience. Some companies, such as Hewlett-Packard, adopted virtual offices on a voluntary basis for workers who wanted the convenience of virtual offices, or who found themselves living in a location with no HP facilities. The overall goal is to increase employee satisfaction, productivity and retention.

Such voluntary, convenience-orientated programmes are naturally popular with workers – they do not save as much money in office costs but their long-term value in terms of increased employee retention and personal productivity levels could be substantial. It is difficult to measure such benefits, particularly in comparison to the "hard" savings from lower office leasing costs.

Problems with virtual offices

Virtual offices have some benefits, but the shortcomings often outweigh them. Below are a list of potential problems resulting from trading technology for offices, and some suggestions for how to address them:

Corporate culture

Offices are a place to socialize and be socialized into the culture of the organization. New workers in virtual settings have little opportunity to learn the "HP Way" or the "AT&T ethos" by example, which is the best way to receive tacit knowledge. If virtual offices are established, they should be restricted to employees who have already absorbed the culture.

Loyalty

Offices create an identification with a company. During an era in which corporate allegiance already seems at an all-time low, the absence of a place to go to work probably further weakens loyalty. This is particularly problematic for home-based or fully mobile workers. If workers do not have offices, other sources of loyalty – social events, evidence of concern for the whole person, and high remuneration – should be introduced to boost retention.

Communication

Offices make possible frequent, unplanned communications. Face-to-face conversations convey not only information content, but also attitudes, levels of motivation, and concerns. Companies that adopt virtual offices need to created planned events for communication and rely on electronic distribution of key information. The company Verifone, now a subsidiary of Hewlett-Packard, managed to create a high degree of information flow through electronic means even though its workers were scattered around the globe.

Access to people

Offices are also a place where people can find one another. Technology is addressing this problem, but it is still hard to find people when they are not in the office. Virtual office-orientated companies should make special attempts to keep track of workers without being too invasive.

Managerial control

Office presence tells the world that one is working. Many managers are only comfortable if they can observe their subordinates at work. Virtual offices require shifts in performance cultures to emphasize delivered results, rather than observation of the work process.

Access to materials

Offices are normally situated near the physical artifacts of work. Computers and telephones are now portable, but filing cabinets, books and other documents, and large, expensive examples of products (such as large office equipment or industrial machines) – all key sources of learning and information – are less so. Contrary to popular opinion, not all information and knowledge resources are on the internet or in electronic form. Access to documents is particularly important for research- and marketing-orientated workers.

None of these issues is impossible to overcome, but together they can add up to an ineffective work environment. In labor markets where skilled knowledge workers are difficult to hire, the fact that many workers do not like virtual offices may be the biggest shortcoming of all. Perhaps the desire for a place of our own is embedded in our genes. In any case, companies that offer fixed, desirable offices may be more able to attract talented workers. At a minimum, the variations in fit between virtual offices and different types of job and worker situations suggest that virtuality should often be voluntary rather than mandatory.

Personal experiences

For the past few months I have worked in a hotelling environment. Every day I am in the office, I must reserve a space; most of the time I get a different office each day. I plug my laptop into the network; my phone rings wherever I happen to be that day. At the end of each day I must clean up my assigned office, remove all evidence of my presence and put my belongings into my briefcase.

As a relatively senior person in this office, I receive the maximum allocation – three file drawers – for storage, but they are two floors away, so I rarely use them.

My firm's implementation of virtual offices is relatively advanced, with appealing architecture, sophisticated information systems for office reservations and phone assignments, and extra subsidized services (massages, car washes on Fridays, dry cleaning drop-off) as compensation for the lack of a fixed office.

I am not particularly happy with this arrangement; nor are the co-workers I have canvassed informally. I have used none of the available services and the fact that I cannot leave things (work in progress, coffee mugs, message slips, and so on) in my office overnight is a major inconvenience. Along with many of my colleagues, I prefer to work at home rather than coming into the office, which of course hinders our ability to communicate. When I do come in, the odds that I will know my neighbors are small and I usually do not bother getting to know them, since they will be sitting in some other neighborhood tomorrow.

My work is unlike that of many others in my office in that I do little consulting work (and am hence in the office often), and need to use many physical documents (books and articles, for example) on a daily basis. Nevertheless, policy prohibits an exception in my case.

To their credit, the local management recently allowed me to trade my luxurious, closed, free (to my research center's budget) hotel office, and those of my fellow researchers, for an open, overcrowded, featureless big room costing several thousand dollars a month. I accepted this deal because I could have a place of my own in which I could leave my things on my desk in disarray. I am in close proximity now to the people with whom I work. My briefcase is lighter, as is my mien.

To their further credit, the space managers have been quite supportive in helping me and my colleagues find a building of our own, where we can make our own rules. I like my job and my employer, and I would not change them because of a virtual office environment. But the prospect of having a real office is wonderful. And when we do make our own rules, you can be sure they will not include hotelling.

Summary

The concept of the virtual office covers a range of working arrangements from occasional telecommuting, with perhaps one day a week spent at home, to full mobility of the kind practised by field sales and customer service types. According to **Thomas Davenport**, the IT, professional services and consumer products industries have been quickest to introduce "virtual" programmes – but informal analysis suggests that the rate of adoption has slowed in the last couple of years. Cost and worker convenience are the main benefits of virtuality but shortcomings such as lack of contact with the corporate culture, communication difficulties, and poor access to people and materials often outweigh them. These can be overcome but, as the author points out, desirable offices may be a good way to attract talented staff and, where possible, companies should try to make virtual arrangements voluntary. He concludes with some observations arising from his own experience in a "hotelling" environment.

Suggested further reading
Davenport, T.H. and Pearlson, K.L. (1998) "Two cheers for the virtual office", *Sloan Management Review* (summer).

5 Nov 1998

DIGITAL BUSINESS

Serving the online consumer: John Willman looks at precisely how Unilever markets spaghetti sauce and toothpaste in cyberspace

Financial Times

by John Willman

Spaghetti sauce, laundry detergent and toothpaste – none of them obvious candidates for websites on the internet. Yet Unilever, which spends $6bn (£3.6 billion) a year on advertising and marketing brands such as Ragu, Persil and Mentadent, believes even such everyday consumer goods need a presence in cyberspace.

The Anglo-Dutch group has launched more than 40 websites worldwide for these and other leading products including Fabergé cosmetics, Bird's Eye frozen foods and a spread called I Can't Believe It's Not Butter!

Its aim is to reinforce consumer loyalty, building direct links with customers by using digital technology to address them individually. Niall Fitzgerald, co-chairman of the group, explained the rationale behind its launch into cyberspace to the European Association of Advertising Agencies in Dublin at the end of last year.

"Twenty years ago, you could reach almost 80 per cent of your target audience – say, women between 18 and 49 – with one 30-second off-peak television commercial. Today to reach the same amount, you would need 250 prime-time slots.

"Digitization, the new technology, the convergence of computing and telecommunications sciences, the plunging costs of equipment, rising levels of disposable income and the deregulation of the airwaves all mean that simple, one-way mass com-munication has its best and biggest days behind it." The group has always prided itself on being at the forefront of marketing its consumer brands, launching Lux Radio Theatre in 1934 to promote its soap flakes and moving it on to television in 1950.

In 1995, it established a website for Ragu spaghetti sauce, which it claims was the first consumer food product site on the worldwide web. It now draws tens of thousands of visitors each day,

attracted by recipes, tips and Italian language lessons.

Others followed, including one offering samples of Mentadent toothpaste which led to almost 40,000 requests and boosted the group's database of consumer names and addresses.

"The challenge facing us is how can these consumer sites compete for the eyes, ears and eventually the pocketbooks of online consumers," says Richard Goldstein, Unilever's US chief executive who is responsible for the group's interactive operations. "We have learned that building brands in an interactive environment often requires using non-branded but related information of value to the consumer."

The Mentadent site, for example, offers lots of information about oral health, including access to an online hygienist who can answer questions. There is also an appointment reminder which prompts users when their dental checkups are due – or any other family occasion – in return for filling in a questionnaire about which products they use.

One lesson the group has learned, says Mr Goldstein, is that it needs partners to make a success of interactive marketing. One partnership signed in July is with America Online (AOL), the leading internet service which is received in 12m households and has 20m adult users.

Unilever can produce its own websites and advertise on other organisations' pages. But the alliance gives it the opportunity to experiment with new forms of promotion on AOL pages, such as general cooking advice and health promotion.

Another partner is Microsoft, which Unilever hopes will help improve database management to increase cross-selling of its products. For example, it wants to try selling Breyers ice creams to consumers who have registered for information on Ragu, or even

Continued

jump product categories from a personal care product such as Dove soap to a foodstuff like Lipton's tea.

None of these marketing efforts will achieve their potential, however, unless Unilever can deliver its products to the consumer. An alliance with NetGrocer, the first nationwide online supermarket in the US, gives it a stake in a market expected by Morgan Stanley to reach sales of $20 billion a year for groceries alone within the next seven years.

The tie-up also means US consumers can "click-to-buy" on Unilever websites with the products delivered to their homes using the NetGrocer

distribution system – giving the group an alternative distribution channel to the supermarkets.

Unilever admits it cannot predict the impact of the digital revolution on its markets. But it believes that only by getting involved can it hope to reap the benefits, and has established its own Interactive Brand Center in New York to explore the opportunities.

"The real value of interactive marketing is that information flows both ways," Mr Fitzgerald has said. "It will be formidably difficult to learn to use this well, addressing each consumer as an individual person, not as a member of admass.

"The key is to be able to use the information that flows back to focus on potentially fruitful relationships and save on the ones that aren't."

Closing the cognitive gaps: how people process information

by Chun Wei Choo

We often see "information" described as a "resource". This implies that information is a "thing" that resides in documents, information systems or other artifacts. The information is assumed to be constant, unchanging. Its meaning is fixed by its representation in the artifact.

A complementary view is to look at information not as an object but as the outcome of people constructing meaning out of messages and cues. Information resides not in artifacts but in individuals' minds. Individuals actively create the meaning of information through their thoughts, actions and feelings.

When we treat information as an object, we are concerned with how to acquire the information that we need, and how to represent the information that we have in order to make it easier to use. When we treat information as constructed by people, we are concerned with understanding the social and behavioral processes through which it is created and used. The social settings in which information is encountered determine its value. A fuller understanding of information seeking as social behavior helps us design better information processes and information systems.

As shown in Figure 1, we can divide information seeking into three processes: experience of information needs, information seeking, and information use. In this article we will examine the cognitive, affective (emotional) and situational factors that influence each of these processes.

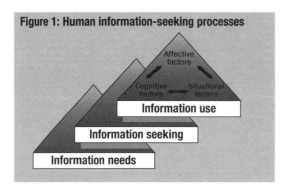

Figure 1: Human information-seeking processes

Information needs

Since the second world war, many studies have attempted to understand how different groups of people – including scientists, engineers, doctors, academics, civil servants, managers and public sector employees – experience and meet information needs. A convincing recent model of such behavior is the "sensemaking" model developed by Brenda Dervin of Ohio State University.

In the sensemaking approach, a person moves through space and time, taking steps through experiences. As long as he or she can make sense of these experiences, movement ahead is possible. But from time to time, movement is blocked by the perception of a "cognitive gap" – a situation that the person is unable to make sense of. To bridge this gap, the person seeks information to make new sense so that he or she can continue the journey.

Dervin and her associates have completed over 40 studies in the past two decades based on the sensemaking approach. Their research suggests that the ways in which people perceive cognitive gaps and the ways that they want information to help are good predictors of their information-seeking behavior. Better yet, the ways people define these gaps fall into categories that apply across different groups of information users. Dervin has identified eight such categories (*see* Table 1).

Cognitive needs are as much felt as thought about. When sense runs out, the lack of understanding creates uncertainty. Carol Kuhlthau of Rutgers University, New Jersey, has found that uncertainty causes anxiety, apprehension, confusion, frustration and lack of confidence, among other symptoms. These affective states in turn direct the way people seek and use information.

Affective responses influence, and are influenced by, individuals' ability to construct meaning, to focus on what information they need, to manage moods and expectations, and to feel personal interest in the search. People cope with the stress of uncertainty in different ways. Research into health information seeking by Tom

Table 1: Dervin's eight cognitive gap categories

Category	Situation
Decision stop	Person sees two or more roads ahead
Barrier stop	Person sees one road ahead but it is blocked
Spin-out stop	Person sees self as having no road
Wash-out stop	Person sees self as on a road which suddenly disappears
Problematic stop	Person sees self as being dragged down a road unwillingly
Perceptual embeddedness	Person judges how foggy the road ahead is
Situational embeddedness	Person judges how many intersections are on the road
Social embeddedness	Person judges how many people are also travelling

Table 2: Information needs and problem solving

Information is typically needed to solve a problem. Users therefore value information that is not just about the topic in question, but that also helps them deal with the specific requirements of the problem situation. Susan MacMullin and Robert Taylor of Syracuse University have identified 11 problem dimensions that amplify information needs. These dimensions also form the criteria that people apply to judge the value of information.

#	Problem dimensions: problems lie on a continuum between...	Information needs (examples)
1	Design Discovery	Options, alternatives, ranges Small, detailed sets of data
2	Well-structured Ill-structured	Hard, quantitative data Probabilistic data on how to proceed
3	Simple Complex	Path to the goal Ways to reduce problem to simpler tasks
4	Specific goals Amorphous goals	How to achieve and measure the goal Preferences and directions
5	Initial state understood Initial state not understood	Clarify unclear aspects of initial state Soft, qualitative data to define initial state
6	Assumptions agreed upon Assumptions not agreed upon	Information to help define problems Views of the world, definition of terms
7	Assumptions explicit Assumptions not explicit	Range of options, frames to analyse problems Information to make assumptions explicit
8	Familiar pattern New pattern	Procedural and historical information Substantive and future-orientated information
9	Magnitude of risk not great Magnitude of risk great	Cost-effective search Best available information: accurate, complete
10	Can be analysed empirically Cannot be analysed empirically	Objective, aggregated data Experts' opinions, forecasts, scenarios
11	Internal imposition External imposition	Clarification of internal goals, objectives Information about external environment

Wilson at Sheffield University contrasts "monitors", who prefer high levels of information to cope with stressful events, with "blunters", who prefer less information.

At the situational level, information needs arise from the problems, uncertainties and ambiguities encountered in specific contexts and experiences. These relate not just to the subject matter, but also to such things as whether objectives are clear and agreed, the magnitude of risk, the amount and structure of control, professional and social norms, time and resource constraints, and so on.

As a result, the determination of information needs must not stop at asking "What do you want to know?" but must also address questions like: "Why do you need to know it?" "What does your problem look like?" "What do you know already?"

"What do you anticipate finding?" and "How will this help you?" Susan MacMullin and Robert Taylor of Syracuse University, New York, suggest that situations should in fact be analyzed in terms of 11 "problem dimensions" (*see* Table 2).

Information seeking

Experiencing information needs may lead to information seeking. This resembles a problem-solving or decision-making process. An individual identifies possible sources, selects which ones to use, locates or makes contact with them, and interacts with them to obtain the desired information.

In today's rich information environment – where human attention is a scarce resource – how do people allocate time and energy when searching for information? Research suggests that they weigh the amount of effort required to use a source against its anticipated usefulness. This cost/benefit evaluation is affected by the individual's personal interest and motivation, and by the complexity of the task at hand.

At the cognitive level, an individual selects a source that he or she considers most likely to provide relevant, usable and helpful information. Relevance and usability in turn may depend upon how up-to-date and comprehensive the information is. Another important factor is the perceived reliability of the source. Research into information seeking often groups some or all of these attributes under the rubric of "perceived source quality" in order to examine their effect on source use.

At the affective level, an individual's personal interest in a problem determines the amount of energy he or she invests in seeking information. Carol Kuhlthau has noted that as information searches progress, initial feelings of uncertainty and anxiety fall as confidence rises. If a clear theme is developed to focus the search, the individual may become more highly motivated.

Drawing on social learning theory, Tom Wilson argues that since a feeling of personal mastery about using a source leads to greater use of that source, doubt about one's ability to use a source would conversely lead to that source not being used. This may be the case even if the source is perceived to contain relevant information.

Selection and use of sources is influenced by the amount of time and effort required to locate, contact and interact with them. At least three different kinds of effort or costs may be pertinent: physical effort (to travel to the source, say); intellectual effort (for example, to learn a classification system or computer application); and psychological effort (for example, to deal with an unpleasant source).

These situational attributes can be bundled together as "perceived source accessibility". The selection of sources then depends on their perceived quality and perceived accessibility. Other factors that influence information seeking are the complexity of the task and environment. A task with many interdependent elements which interact unpredictably may require broader information gathering and processing. Similarly, a volatile external environment may necessitate more information scanning.

Information use

Just as there are eight categories of information need, Brenda Dervin and Robert Taylor propose that there are eight general categories that describe how people use information: to develop a context; to understand a particular situation; to know

The Myers-Briggs personality matrix

One of the most widely used personality assessment instruments in the world is the Myers-Briggs Type Indicator (MBTI) classification, which is developed from the work of Carl Jung. MBTI analyzes personality types on the basis of four pairs of traits:

Introversion versus extroversion
Introverts draw mental energy from themselves whereas extroverts draw energy from others.

Sensing versus "intuiting"
Sensing types rely on information perceived through their five senses. Intuitive types rely more on patterns, relationships and hunches.

Thinking versus feeling
Thinking types use information to make logical decisions based on objective criteria. Feeling types depend on personal values to decide between right and wrong.

Judging versus perceiving
Judging types move quickly to closure by making use of the available information. Perceiving types keep their options open by taking their time to gather sufficient information.

These four pairs of attributes are combined to create a matrix of 16 personality types. As indicated above, each personality type is expected to have a distinctive way of processing and using information.

what to do and how to do it; to get the facts about something; to confirm another item of information; to project future events; to motivate or sustain personal involvement; and to develop relationships and enhance status or personal fulfilment.

An individual's cognitive style and preferences affect the way he or she processes information. A number of classifications have been developed to differentiate personality types and cognitive preferences. A widely used method is the Myers-Briggs Type Indicator.

Another common cognitive style variable is "field dependence". Field-dependent individuals respond uncritically to environmental cues, whereas field-independent people orientate themselves correctly in spite of environmental cues. Daniel Kahneman (Princeton University) and Amos Tversky (Stanford University, California) have discovered that when people use information to make judgments they take cognitive shortcuts to make the information easier to process. Unfortunately, these simplifications are fallible.

For example, to judge whether an event belongs to a given category, people rely on mental stereotypes, but they often ignore other relevant information, such as the distribution of categories in the general population. To judge the frequency or likelihood of an event, people over-rely on recent, vivid, easy-to-recall information. To estimate a quantity they make adjustments from an amount initially measured or suggested, but these adjustments are often inadequate.

At the affective level, people avoid using information that will arouse strong, negative emotions in others or in themselves. People use information selectively to avoid embarrassment, conflict or regret; to maintain self-image; and to enhance personal status or reputation.

For example, decision makers will positively evaluate and continue a course of action even when the available information indicates that they should withdraw to cut their losses. One psychological factor behind such "escalation of commitment" is

Quality versus accessibility: how chief executives keep up to date

Most studies of how people use information sources have found that a source's perceived accessibility is a major determinant of whether it is used or not. For example, scientists, engineers and managers are often sensitive to source accessibility, so that a library or information center on the next floor or even a few offices away may be infrequently visited, even though people recognize that it contains more complete and up-to-date information than their close-at-hand sources.

However, a recent study of how chief executives in the Canadian telecommunications industry scan their business environments for information about trends and developments found a different pattern. For these chief executives, the perceived quality of a source (in terms of reliablity and relevance) was a more important predictor of whether it was used or not than its perceived accessibility.

The study (by the author) observed that chief executives invested time and effort in contacting and interacting with less accessible sources such as customers, competitors and business associates. The chief executives rated these personal sources highly for their ability to provide accurate and usable information. The study suggested that the switch of emphasis from accessibility to quality was because the executives were trying to make sense of a complex and ambiguous business environment, and were personally interested in learning about external trends and developments.

the desire to save face. Decision makers persist because they do not want to admit to themselves (let alone others) that they have made an error. In organizations where error-free decision making is valued, managers may attempt to hide their mistakes or postpone their discovery.

Another example of using information selectively to minimize unpleasant feelings is the "not-invented-here" syndrome: the tendency of a long-standing group to reject new information from outside. Over time, people increase the amount of order and stability in their work environments to reduce stress and uncertainty. As a result, the longer individuals have belonged to a group, the stronger their emotional attachment to group beliefs and decisions that they helped create, and the more resistant they are to new ideas and information from outside.

As far as situations are concerned, the norms and rules of the group, profession or organization can influence the way information is processed and used. For example, Irving Janis of Yale University has observed how highly cohesive groups are susceptible to "groupthink". This happens when group members seek concurrence to such an extent that they choose to ignore or undervalue information that threatens group beliefs and solidarity.

Donald Schon of the Massachusetts Institute of Technology has investigated how professions develop their own languages, values, overarching theories, and role definitions. Members adopt these as frames of reference through which information is processed to describe and explain reality, and to reaffirm professional identity.

Edgar Schein of the Sloan School of Management defines organizational culture as a pattern of assumptions developed by an organization as it learns to cope with problems of external adaptation and internal integration. Because these assumptions have worked in the past, they are taught to new members as the correct way to approach those problems. As a result, the organization develops a shared framework which its members can use to make sense of information collectively.

Figure 2: An integrated model of information seeking

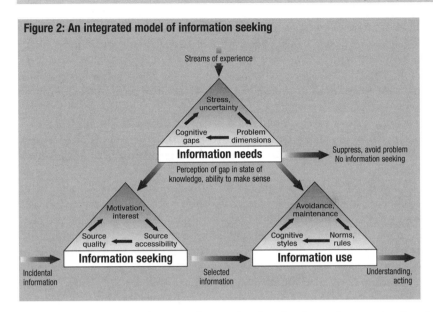

Another important feature of organizational culture is organizational politics. In contests for influence and power, information may be used as a resource to protect vested interests or to justify certain courses of action.

An integrated model

The three processes described so far can be integrated into a general model of how humans seek information. As shown in Figure 2, individuals experience information needs when they perceive gaps in their knowledge or their ability to make sense. This experience is shaped by cognitive, affective and situational factors. People may choose to suppress the need by, say, avoiding the problem situation or they may decide to bridge the gap through purposive information seeking.

During information seeking, sources and information are selected according to their perceived accessibility and quality, the complexity of the task and the personal interest of the seeker. Information may also be received "incidentally" – through a casual conversation, say, or when idly channnel-hopping – rather than through deliberate efforts.

The outcome of information seeking is a set of information that is a very small proportion of the total considered. How this information is then put to use depends on the individual's habits of thought, his or her emotional responses, and the social and cultural context around information use. The final outcome of information use is a change in someone's knowledge, allowing that person to make sense of a situation or to take action. This in turn gives rise to new experiences and new information needs, so that the cycle is continuous.

Implications for practice

The discussion here suggests several ways to improve information management:

1. **Design information systems not just to answer queries but to provide useful information that will help people solve work-related problems and deal with the specific requirements of problem situations.**
   System designers need to move beyond analyzing flows of data to understanding

251

how people construct the meaning of information and how they negotiate the context of organizational work. For example, users should be able to query systems not just with account numbers or key words but also with task descriptions ("I am writing a project plan on x – get me information that will help me") and sense-making questions ("What are the assumptions guiding our interpretation?").

2. **Increase awareness of the nature of human information seeking and processing; this involves understanding cognitive styles and limitations, and the ways that routines and emotional defenses can block learning.**

   Cognitive diversity invigorates an organization, so the intention should be not to pigeonhole people according to their presumed strengths and weaknesses. Instead, the goal should be a lively mix of styles, skills and sensitivities in a group so as to heighten vigilance in information processing.

3. **Educate everyone to manage information quality and information quantity.**

   System designers need to understand how people assign value to information. Users need to know how to evaluate the quality of sources and how to trade this off with their accessibility. In restricting the quantity of information to prevent overload, users should also guard against premature closure: divergent information gathering (which consults many sources) is necessary to prepare the ground for convergent action.

4. **Develop an organizational culture that values and encourages information sharing.**

   Some of the best information sources are one's colleagues. Yet paradoxically, as organizations become more information-intensive, the less likely it is that members will share their information freely. Organizations must now work at creating and sustaining cultures that promote the sharing of information and knowledge.

Summary

Information can be seen in two ways: as an object that can be manipulated by technology; and as the outcome of social interactions that create meaning in the minds of human beings. In this article, **Chun Wei Choo** outlines a model of how people acquire and process information. The three basic steps are determination of information needs, information seeking and information use, each of which can be considered in terms of cognitive, emotional and situational factors. Information needs arise when people experience "cognitive gaps" that hinder their progress and induce uncertainty; to bridge these, they must seek good, accessible information sources. The way they use the information acquired depends upon their personality, organizational culture, and emotional factors such as the desire to preserve group identity (hence resistance to information "not invented here"). Ultimately, if we can understand the social aspects of information we will be able to design better information systems.

Suggested further reading

Choo, C.W. (1998) *The Knowing Organization: How Organizations Use Information to Construct Meaning, Create Knowledge, and Make Decisions*, New York: Oxford University Press.

Dervin, B. (1992) "From the mind's eye of the 'user': the sense-making qualitative–quantitative methodology", in Glazier, J.D. and Powell, R.R. (eds) *Qualitative Research in Information Management*, Englewood, CO: Libraries Unlimited.

Kuhlthau, C. (1993) *Seeking Meaning: A Process Approach to Library and Information Services*, Norwood, NJ: Ablex.

Taylor, R.S. (1991) "Information use environments", in Dervin, B. and Voigt, M.J. (eds) *Progress in Communication Science*, Norwood, NJ: Ablex.

Wilson, T.D. (1997) "Information behavior: an interdisciplinary perspective", *Information Processing and Management* 33 (4): 551–72.

Managing use not technology: a view from the trenches

by Wanda J. Orlikowski

Every year billions of dollars are spent on information technologies in companies worldwide. I study what people actually do with all those technologies once they have been installed. And from my view in the trenches, recent talk about the "IT productivity paradox" (that the increased investment in IT is not producing increased productivity) is missing a central and simple point – that expecting any return on IT may be part of the problem. What we should look for instead is a return on the *use* of IT; IT in itself cannot increase or decrease productivity, only use of it can.

This may sound like semantic hair-splitting but how we talk has deep implications for how we think and act. By emphasizing technology in our talk, we have tended to emphasize it in our allocation of attention, resources and measures. Such a focus has come at the expense of understanding what happens in the trenches – what people actually do with technology in their day-to-day activities.

Vision and reality

Over the past few years, I have had the opportunity of studying a pioneering technology – Notes, from Lotus Development Corporation – as it has been adopted and used in many organizations. Notes was designed to facilitate collaboration among people, in contrast to more common software tools that emphasize transaction processing or individual productivity.

Interest in Notes has been high, as has the motivation to enable people to work together across time, space and fields of expertise. In the companies I studied in Europe and the US, managers painted compelling visions of how the technology would bring profound transformations in how, when and where work would be done.

Yet with a few exceptions, many of these companies have so far failed to realize their visions – not because their visions are inappropriate (they are not), not because the technology is immature (it is not), and not because implementation strategies have been inadequate (they have not been), but because they have failed to manage the most critical determinant of technology effectiveness in organizations: how people use it to get work done.

By neglecting technology use, we forget that technology is not valuable, meaningful or consequential by itself; it only becomes so when people engage with it in practice. Such neglect encourages us to make simplistic assumptions – that if people have technology they will use it, that they will use it as designed, and that such use will produce the expected outcomes.

On reflection, most of us would agree that such assumptions are naive or faulty. Indeed, our own experiences with technology reveal that we do not passively follow the dictates of machines or of their designers' specifications. Rather, we constantly make choices about whether, how, when, where and for what purposes to use technology. When the order entry system slows to a crawl at peak times, we bypass it. When our car exhaust breaks, we improvise a repair with a bent coathanger. When we want to use a spreadsheet, we learn the basic functions we need and ignore the rest.

We are purposeful, knowledgeable, adaptive and inventive agents who engage with technology to accomplish various and changing ends. Where technology does not help us to achieve those ends, we abandon it, or work around it, or change it, or think about changing our ends.

As users, we know this about our use of technology. But as managers, we believe that if we can just get the right set of tools, more user-friendly interfaces, better training and support, and closer alignment with business processes, then use (as anticipated) will surely follow, along with the expected outcomes. Because of such beliefs, we concentrate resources, attention and effort on getting the right technologies in the right place at the right time. Unfortunately this effectively ignores "right use".

For example, look at the budget for new systems development and see what percentage of resources is allocated to the initial analysis, design, installation and training activities, and what percentage is earmarked for supporting continuing use. Where the "up-front" budget exceeds the "day-to-day" budget, there are insufficient means – both initially and over time – for users to incorporate the technologies effectively into their work practices.

Two types of technology

In how we manage and measure, we have tended to focus on the "hard" stuff – technology, with its tangibility, relative stability and predictability of performance – and to downplay the "soft" stuff – the everyday use of technology, with its more open-ended, more variable, and less tangible outcomes.

This tendency to favor the more tangible and stable over the less tangible and more variable is a common error. In the area of learning, social scientists Chris Argyris (of Harvard University) and Donald Schon (of the Massachusetts Institute of Technology), have referred to this tendency by distinguishing between "espoused theories" (what we say about how we act) and "theories-in-use" (what our actions reveal about how we act). They note that people are usually unaware of the discrepancy between these, and a fundamental aspect of learning is recognizing and dealing with it.

I suggest that we can similarly differentiate between "espoused technologies" (the technologies we buy and install in our offices, factories and homes) and "technologies-in-use" (the technologies we actually use). Espoused technologies are the bundles of hardware and software that consistently provide a given set of predefined features. Technologies-in-use are the specific features we engage with in particular ways depending on our skills, tasks, attention and purposes.

What we buy is given and predefined (espoused technology); what we use is contingent and local (technology-in-use). The two are not the same, and managing and measuring the former as if it were the latter can lead to difficulties.

Some examples may help. One of the companies I studied in my Lotus Notes research was a multinational consultancy which had adopted the technology to facilitate knowledge sharing among its consultants. The managers implementing Notes were very impressed with its technical sophistication, believing it to be what we might now call "a killer app". They concentrated their energies and resources on installing Notes within the firm's infrastructure and on every consultant's PC. And their measurements – number of user accounts established, number of servers installed, number of databases created – indicated that the technology was implemented successfully.

Managing and measuring espoused technology, these managers did not attend much to the technologies-in-use – to what consultants were actually doing with Notes in their everyday practice. If they had, they would have found that consultants were not using Notes to share knowledge; either they did not use it at all or they used it only to transfer files, send memos or access news bulletins.

In the context of this firm, with its competitive "up or out" career path and individualistic work norms, to share knowledge was counter-cultural. Considered as an espoused technology, Notes certainly had the potential to facilitate knowledge sharing. However, what matters in assessing the effectiveness of technology is not espoused technology but technology-in-use.

A similar tale may be told of the research and development division of a large pharmaceutical company. Envisioning seamless, cross-functional project integration through Notes, managers rolled it out to hundreds of scientists across a number of laboratories.

However, this company, like many others, had a hierarchical structure in which scientists were rewarded for distinct functional contributions and individual patent applications. Not surprisingly, they chose to maximize their personal initiatives and to minimize their participation in cross-functional work. As a result, their use of Notes was limited and the company (like many others I continue to encounter today) failed to realize the potential of its investment in groupware.

Focusing on espoused technologies rather than technologies-in-use is not just an issue for corporations; it is also one for research. Another "technology paradox" was recently generated by a report from the HomeNet project, a multi-year research study at Carnegie Mellon University. The study is examining the internet usage of about 100 families in Pittsburgh during their first few years online.

Its current, surprising, findings are that "using the internet at home causes small but reliable declines in social and psychological well-being". As this project is being conducted with considerable care by leading social researchers of computing, we have no reason to disbelieve the results. Yet many find them disquieting because they are at odds with popular beliefs and personal experiences.

Users of The Well, for example, a virtual community on the internet, report quite different experiences. As chronicled by Howard Rheingold, the American social commentator, members of The Well offer each other social ties, friendship and emotional support.

Similarly, American journalist Andrew Lam reports that the internet is being used to create a global community among the 2.5m Vietnamese displaced by the Vietnam war and now living on five different continents. Through websites devoted to Vietnamese history, culture and news, many Vietnamese immigrants have created a "Virtual Vietnam", establishing social links and reconnecting with their cultural heritage.

How can we explain these different experiences of the same technology? The answer lies in the difference between espoused technologies and technologies-in-use. Stories of The Well and Virtual Vietnam are descriptions of technologies-in-use. The HomeNet project's measures of "internet use" – number of hours connected to the internet – are measures of espoused technology. They do not tell us how people actually use the internet – whether they "surf" aimlessly, shop for books, interact with friends, participate in support groups and so on.

HomeNet's results would perhaps be less puzzling if presented in terms of technologies-in-use. The decline in social and psychological well-being reported by the project may be associated with the specific technologies-in-use (not yet described in the research) of the Pittsburgh families; they may not be result of some general "internet use".

Other internet technologies-in-use may produce different social and psychological outcomes, as suggested by the experiences of The Well users and immigrant Vietnamese. The same distinction between espoused technologies and technologies-in-use may also help us make sense of and deal with the broader "IT productivity paradox".

Practical consequences

What does this all mean for practice? It suggests that we need to transfer our energies from primarily managing technology to also managing the use of technology. It requires us to take seriously the difference between the technologies we buy and the actual use that is made of them. While acquiring and implementing appropriate technology is clearly necessary, that is insufficient to ensure effective – or indeed any – use. Taking use seriously requires managers to dedicate resources to help users build effective use habits.

For example, my colleagues and I studied the implementation and use of a new computer conferencing technology in a Japanese company's product development group. The introduction of the technology was managed by nine of the group's 150 members. They not only had the requisite technical knowhow but also more importantly, because they were already accustomed to using the technology, they had the skills needed to make recommendations for effective use. The conferencing tool was thus not presented to users as a new technology, but as a solution to a particular problem in their work – in this case, the co-ordination of product development activities across six subgroups, two buildings and 17 months.

Taking use seriously requires resources to be available over time to support not just the evolving technology but also people's evolving use. It suggests expecting variation in use over time and as conditions change. Static use in dynamic circumstances is ineffective. Shifts in use over time are not deviations to be corrected but improvisations to be rewarded; managers need to encourage those innovations that improve practice, yet not punish those that do not. Taking use seriously assumes that learning happens through experimentation in, and reflection on, use.

For example, a software company that successfully implemented Notes to assist customer support, permanently assigned two technical experts to the customer support department. Their task was to facilitate users' initial adoption and their continuing use of Notes. The department's managers understood that in practice and over time, technologies break down, requirements change, use evolves and

Steps towards managing use of technology

- recognize that the technologies installed in your organization are not synonymous with the use of those technologies in practice
- understand that only use of technology can produce organizational results, and that such use will be both anticipated and unanticipated
- help people understand how use of technology relates to their everyday work processes and problems
- acknowledge that effective use of technology must evolve over time
- allocate at least as much attention, effort and resources to the day-to-day use of

- technology as to its installation and maintenance
- facilitate evolving use through continuing assignment of resources – human, financial and technical
- promote evolving use through creating expectations of frequent change
- encourage evolving use through supporting innovation and improvisation in the day-to-day use of technology
- reward the effort involved in use innovations, not the outcome
- assess the use of technology, not the technology installed.

learning takes place; so to ensure continued effective use of Notes in the department, technical experts – who knew, and had credibility with, the users – would have to be on hand. Over time, these experts also became expert in the use of Notes for customer support, and were able to improve the way it was deployed to increase the quantity and quality of users' output.

More than anything, managing use rather than technology alone requires a shift in mindset. Managers must move from managing or fixing the easy "hard" stuff – the technology – to also managing the harder, more critical "soft" stuff – the way technology is used. In over a decade of studying the use of IT in the trenches, I have more often than not seen people exhausting resources and effort because organizations were managing technologies rather than use. It need not be so.

Summary

The "IT productivity paradox" arises from the fact that companies spend billions on IT with no commensurate increase in productivity. Yet according to **Wanda Orlikowski**, the paradox is misconceived: we should expect returns from the use of technology not technology itself. Drawing on the work of social scientists Chris Argyris and Donald Schon, the author distinguishes between "espoused technologies" – what companies buy and install – and "technologies-in-use" – what employees actually use. For example, a company that invests in groupware might look at the number of user accounts and judge the project to be a success; but if no-one actually uses the technology to share knowledge – because of a competitive, individualistic culture, say – then the company will not see the returns it anticipates. The problem is that we are not very good at managing technology use. Businesses must dedicate resources over time to help employees develop effective use habits; use of technology rather than technology itself should be evaluated, and innovative uses of IT should be rewarded.

Suggested further reading

Orlikowski, W.J. (1993) "Learning from Notes", *Information Society Journal* 9: 237–50.

Orlikowski, W.J. et al. (1994) "Helping CSCW applications succeed", Proceedings of the Fourth Conference on Computer-Supported Co-operative Work, Chapel Hill, NC (October): 55–65.

Orlikowski, W.J. and Hofman, J.D. (1997) "An improvisational model of change management: the case of groupware technologies", *Sloan Management Review* 38 (2, winter): 11–21.

Rheingold, H. (1993) *The Virtual Community: Homesteading on the Electronic Frontier*, Reading, MA: Addison-Wesley.

Two views of data protection

by H. Jeff Smith

When it comes to social issues surrounding information technology, few are viewed as differently around the world as privacy. In some societies personal data about individuals' financial affairs and purchasing histories are considered almost sacrosanct. But in others, those same data are considered to be commodities that can be traded at will. These different sets of values are often codified in different regulatory approaches, which can lead to frustration and confusion for companies attempting cross-cultural initiatives.

On the one hand, US executives, accustomed to a free-wheeling environment in which personal data are freely collected, used and exchanged, are shocked when they encounter more restrictive approaches in other parts of the world. One such executive, who had many years of experience in the US credit industry, was astonished when he learned that the collection and use of financial data in Sweden would require the approval of the country's Data Inspection Board (DIB).

On the other hand, some employees of Sweden's DIB have expressed disbelief regarding the data-related practices of US companies – in particular, the practices of massaging personal data, drawing psychographic inferences from those data and exchanging those inferences with other companies. They cannot identify with most US companies' unquestioning use of transaction records, demographic data and mailing lists in their direct marketing initiatives (often without securing the permission of the consumers whose purchasing habits are being scrutinized).

Approaches to privacy

Different models of privacy regulation can be roughly categorized according to the level of governmental involvement in corporate management of privacy issues. Self-help and voluntary regulation models, both observed to some degree in the US, are in many respects consistent with a market-driven approach to privacy. In these models there is no governmental "bureau of privacy" or similar agency with overall responsibility for privacy regulation.

More common in Europe are the registration model and the licensing model. Registration models, such as the UK's, provide for a government agency with largely reactive power – that is, the registrar can "de-register" a company that does not adhere to what are viewed as appropriate practices, although this has seldom happened. Licensing models, such as Sweden's, provide for a federal bureau with proactive power (until the DIB gives its approval, a company cannot legally create files containing personal data).

While the above models explain the structure of a country's privacy regulation, they do not specify the assumptions and rules regarding the collection, use and sharing of personal data. It turns out, however, that the same splits in form we observe between the US and Europe also seem to apply to substance.

In the US, there are no federal provisions for a "right to privacy" in commercial transactions, and no overall rules regarding the collection, use and sharing of personal data that transcend all sectors of the economy. There are some specific prohibitions on the collection and use of certain forms of data, but these protections are often referred to as a "patchwork quilt" that has been constructed largely of reactive legislation. For example, video rental records receive a fairly high level of federal privacy protection but medical records are virtually unprotected by federal law.

In addition, federal US law seldom requires that consumers be told about secondary uses of data. In practice, some companies in a few US industries have adopted notification procedures by, for example, placing inserts in monthly billing statements. And some US companies have also provided "opt out" capabilities for consumers: unless the consumer takes overt action to "opt out" of the secondary data use, it is assumed that the consumer assents to the use.

In contrast, one can reasonably interpret efforts within the European Union as granting consumers a "right to privacy" in their commercial exchanges. The EU countries have passed privacy legislation that provides specific privacy rights to consumers across sectors and industries. And, with very few exceptions, uses of personal data – beyond those for which the data were originally collected – are prohibited if the consumer objects to the secondary use.

This applies across industries and is not determined by the type of data or the specific use: financial data, educational data and purchase data are viewed in the same manner, even if there is extra protection for especially sensitive data (such as mental health). Some observers have remarked that the difference is a fundamental one: in Europe and many other parts of the world, privacy is seen as a human rights issue; in the US, it is seen as an issue of contractual negotiation.

Consider how this difference might manifest itself in practice. Suppose a US credit card issuer decided to massage its database of cardholder transactions and to categorize cardholders according to their purchasing propensities. Then, based on these categorizations, the cardholders would receive different cross-marketing contacts from the issuer's affiliates.

Such an approach would serve as an excellent example of "leveraging the customer base" or "using IT for competitive advantage". However, it is also clear that privacy concerns could arise on the part of cardholders, since data apparently collected for one purpose (billing) would be used for another (direct marketing). What would be the privacy-related duties of the credit card issuer?

Under federal law in the US, the card issuer has no obligation to inform the cardholders of its secondary use of the data or to provide any option for cardholders to "opt out". In practice, some of the larger US card issuers have added language to their credit card application forms (often in small print) informing applicants that they might receive certain offers of products and services. In addition, some card issuers have also placed inserts in the cardholders' monthly statements. In most cases, the focus of these notification statements has been the offers that cardholders might receive.

The methodology for selection, including the massaging of the transaction database, often goes unexplained or is given only oblique coverage in the statement. (After being threatened with legal action by a state attorney general, one card issuer did agree to give more explicit explanations about its use of transaction data.) To effect an "opt-out", applicants are sometimes given a small box to tick, and existing cardholders are often asked to write to a certain address (sometimes a toll-free phone number is provided).

The general assumption of this approach is that transaction data belong to the company and that, without overt action on the part of the consumer, such data may be used as the company wishes. Notifications and "opt out" provisions are often seen as a courtesy to consumers rather than as an obligation on the part of the company.

The European model

This approach would not be acceptable under what is sometimes called the "European model" (not all European countries' laws read in precisely the same form, but general conclusions can be drawn from the 1995 EU Data Protection Directive and practice). This model assumes that the consumer has legal interests in transaction data and that a company cannot unilaterally choose to manipulate the data for direct marketing purposes, unless it is clear that the consumer agrees.

Thus, the US card issuer's approach is inconsistent with the European model on at least one count and perhaps two. First, merely telling (potential) cardholders that offers might be received would not constitute sufficient disclosure. Of greater importance would be the specific uses of transaction data that would lead to the offers.

Consumers must be told that transaction data, which they would otherwise probably conclude were being gathered for billing purposes, will also be used for categorization and direct marketing, particularly when data is transferred to third-party affiliates. The EU directive (which can be viewed as defining minimal levels of data protection within EU countries) demands clear notification about secondary uses of data for direct marketing. Vaguely worded statements about "offers", particularly if printed in fine print or in a form that has a low probability of being absorbed by consumers, are unlikely to clear the hurdle.

Second, there may be some question about the manner in which consumers are allowed to object to secondary use of the data. The EU directive demands that member states "take the necessary measures to ensure that data subjects are

The EU privacy directive and the US conflict

In July 1995, the EU adopted its "Data Protection Directive", which required all EU member states to have legislation establishing specific privacy protections for personal data by October 1998. Member states' laws must provide clear disclosure to data subjects of the purpose of data collection and the manner in which the data are to be used, and data subjects are allowed to object to secondary uses of data. The data subjects are also given rights to inspect and correct their data. Further, each member state must establish a public authority to monitor data processing activities. By April 1997 all member states had enacted such legislation.

Also in October 1998, the directive's provisions regarding "transfer of personal data to third countries" were supposed to take effect. These required member states to prohibit the transfer of personal data to any country that did not provide an "adequate level of protection" for the data. This provision has the potential to create great difficulties for data transfers between EU companies and the US, since many observers have concluded that, by the standards of the directive,

the US does not give "adequate" protection to personal data of many types and in many contexts. One example often cited is that of an American credit card holder who attempts to charge a purchase while in Paris; read literally, the directive could prohibit the transfer of the transaction data back into the US.

Between 1995 and 1998, many discussions were held between representatives of the EU and the US, but the discussions were somewhat frustrated by the lack of a single US entity that was able to speak with authority on privacy issues.

In October 1998, when the directive was supposed to take effect, the issue had not been resolved. No overall privacy legislation had been passed, nor does it appear likely to be passed soon in the US. Other approaches have been considered. Voluntary, industry-wide codes might serve as evidence of "adequate" privacy protection; in a few cases, US companies have signed contracts with European partners in which they agree to adhere to the EU directive's principles. At the time of writing, it is unclear whether the EU will accept either of these alternatives.

aware of the existence" of their right to object to secondary data uses. Further, it requires that a company cease using a consumer's data for secondary purposes once a "justified objection" is received.

Although some countries might demand an "opt-in" approach (that is, affirmative consent being given before data can be used), the directive does not state this as a general requirement. However, a small tick-box following a notice in fine print would almost surely be unacceptable under the European model. It is also likely that any process requiring substantial effort on the consumer's part (for example, writing a separate letter) would fail to pass muster in at least some European countries.

It is also worth noting that an "opt-in" provision would be demanded in all EU countries if the profiles included special categories of data. These categories include those indicating racial or ethnic origin, political opinions, religious or philosophical beliefs, trade union membership, and data about one's health or sex life. It is certainly conceivable that credit card transaction data could provide information on these categories (for example, purchases of religious books). The credit card issuer would be prohibited from making use of data in these categories without the consumer's explicit permission. The company could not assume that a lack of notification implied consent.

This example is just one of many that transcend industries and data types – and that cause misunderstandings when executives with one set of assumptions about privacy do business in a country that embraces a different set.

Implications for commerce

For executives contemplating initiatives that involve personal data, there are three important implications.

First, know the law in all the countries where you may do business or where you may collect, store, use or transfer data. In many cases, a country's laws apply to any data that pass through the country, even if the data are never actually used in commercial transactions there.

Further, be prepared for great variance in approaches. The EU's directive has forced a certain amount of conformity in European law, but there are still distinctions in the member states' approaches. Conformity may also be lacking in other geographic regions. For example, while the US and Canada occupy the same continent, their approaches to privacy regulation are quite distinct, Canada veering more towards the European model.

Also consider that, even within one country, there can be many subdivisions of privacy law. For example, in the US many state statutes are far more restrictive than the federal law, and in Canada the five provinces have separate legislation and there are multiple privacy commissioners.

Second, know the practices. In many industries, what might be called "generally accepted privacy practices" are emerging, even though these practices are not mandated by law. Often they are codified by industry associations (for example, the Direct Marketing Associations in both the US and Canada have often taken on this role) but they sometimes go undocumented. In consumers' minds, such practices may eventually be more important than legal dictates in determining privacy expectations.

Third, know the culture. History is full of examples of marketing approaches that worked well in one country but failed miserably in another, such as the car whose name translated as "it does not go". An approach to the collection, use and sharing of data that is perfectly consistent with law and practice in one country may lead to outrage in another.

Increasingly, technology is enabling companies to watch and categorize many consumer activities and to use these techniques in new and creative ways. But, at the same time, most industrialized countries are responding with restrictions on the collection, use and sharing of personal data – restrictions that are neither consistent nor fully predictable. Indeed, in many countries, it is companies – rather than consumers – that are receiving the closest scrutiny.*

Government involvement in privacy management

The five models can be described as follows.

1. The "self-help" model depends on data subjects' challenging inappropriate record-keeping practices. Subjects have rights of access and correction but they are responsible for identifying problems and taking them to court.
2. The "voluntary control" model relies on self-regulation on the part of corporations. The law defines specific rules and requires that each company to ensure compliance.
3. The "data commissioner" model relies on the ombudsman concept. The commissioner has no powers of regulation but relies on complaints from citizens, which are investigated. The commissioner is viewed as an expert who should advise on data handling, monitor technology and make proposals, and inspect some data-processing operations.
4. The "registration" model creates a requirement that each databank containing personal data be registered (usually upon payment of a fee) by a separate governmental institution. Although the databanks must be registered, the governmental institution has no right to block the creation of a particular system. Only when complaints are received and an investigation reveals failure to adhere to data protection principles would a system be "deregistered".
5. The licensing model creates a requirement that each databank containing personal data be licensed (usually upon payment of a fee) by a separate governmental institution. This institution would stipulate specific conditions for the collection, storage and use of personal data. This model anticipates potential problems and heads them off by requiring prior approval for any use of data.

Summary

The social aspects of information become clear when one looks at the issue of data protection. Here **Jeff Smith** considers the very different approaches taken by the US and the EU. In the US companies can collect, use and share customer data with few restrictions; federal law seldom requires them to tell consumers about secondary use of data, or to offer "opt outs". In Europe, by contrast, consumers are assumed to have a legal interest in data about themselves; companies must inform them if they want to use the data for purposes other than billing, and provide clear "opt outs". Given such differences, global executives must become familiar with different countries' laws, industry practices and cultures.

Suggested further reading

American privacy laws are well documented by Paul M. Schwartz and Joel R. Reidenberg, *Data Privacy Law* (Charlottesville, VA: Michie Law Publishers, 1996). For late-breaking developments, see the *Privacy Times* newsletter, published by Evan Hendricks (PO Box 21501, Washington, DC, 20009, USA).

European privacy legislation is well covered by the *Privacy Laws and Business* newsletter, published by Stewart H. Dresner (Roxeth House, Shaftesbury Avenue, Harrow, Middlesex, HA2 0PZ, UK).

*I am grateful to Professor Joel R. Reidenberg of Fordham University School of Law for his insights.

STRATEGIC USES OF IT

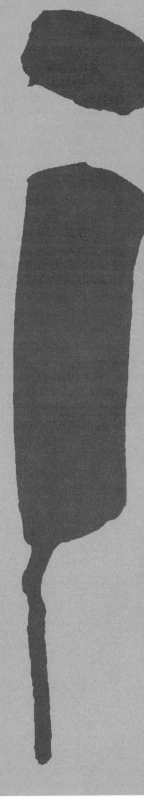

9

Contributors

Leslie P. Willcocks is fellow in the Oxford Institute of Information Management, Templeton College, University of Oxford, and visiting chair at the universities of Erasmus (Rotterdam) and Melbourne. His latest research on outsourcing, evaluation and information management appears in *Beyond The IT Productivity Paradox* (Wiley, 1999).

N. Venkatraman is visiting professor of strategy and international management, London Business School, and David J. McGrath, Jr, Professor of Management at Boston University School of Management.

Mary C. Lacity is associate professor of management information systems at the University of Missouri and a research associate of Templeton College, Oxford. Her books include *IS Outsourcing* (1993) and *Beyond The IS Outsourcing Bandwagon* (1995), both published by Wiley.

John C. Henderson is professor of management information systems and director of the Systems Research Center at Boston University School of Management.

Eric K. Clemons is professor of information strategy, systems and economics at the Wharton School, University of Pennsylvania.

Contents

Introduction

Broad strategic issues surrounding the information economy were discussed in earlier modules but here the emphasis is on strategic uses of IT. How can executives best understand the impact of networked IT on their industries, their markets and their organizations? Is outsourcing merely another means of cutting costs and improving efficiency, or is there a more strategic dimension to consider? Can IT and the clever use of information change the dynamics of whole businesses – financial services, for example – and open up opportunities for new entrants? In recent years "alignment" meant that IT strategy should support business strategy; today it means business and IT strategists working together to shape new business platforms. IT is not subordinate to business strategy – it is an integral part of it.

Strategic dimensions of IT outsourcing

by Leslie P. Willcocks and Mary C. Lacity

IT outsourcing has outlived the five-year period typical of a management fad. Global market revenues, which were $9bn in 1990, look set to grow to $121bn by 2001. The underlying compound annual growth rate was 15–20 per cent between 1992 and 1999; in the US and the UK, the leading markets, there have been more dramatic rises in years when several major deals have been signed.

From an initial focus on cost reduction, outsourcing is fast becoming a complementary, routine mode of managing IT. On our own estimates, 30–35 per cent of most large organizations' IT budgets will be managed through outsourcing arrangements by 2002. The question "why not outsource IT?" is no longer, if it ever was, an adequate base from which to make outsourcing decisions. The real question now has to be: "How do we exploit the ever maturing external IT services market to achieve significant, strategic business leverage?"

The outsourcing report card: practices and risks

It is clear that some organizations seek to address this issue through total outsourcing. Deals such as those at Xerox, McDonnell Douglas (now Boeing) and Continental Bank in the US, Commonwealth Bank, Lend Lease Corporation and the South Australia Government in Australia, and British Aerospace, BP Amoco and the Inland Revenue in the UK, are often referred to as "strategic alliances". Going by media coverage, one could be forgiven for believing this type of outsourcing to be the dominant approach. But upon investigation, a much richer picture emerges of the IT sourcing paths organizations are taking (*see* Figure 1), and many still seek tactical IT gains rather than strategic business advantage.

The dominant mode is selective sourcing, especially in the US (82 per cent of organizations) and the UK (75 per cent). A mixed portfolio, "best-source" approach typically puts 15–30 per cent of the IT budget under third-party management, with other IT needs met through buying in resources that are under in-house management ("insourcing"), and through internal IT staffing.

Many organizations (10 per cent in the US and 23 per cent in the UK) have no significant IT outsourcing contracts. These organizations perceive IT as a core strategic asset; they believe that their IT employees will strive to achieve business advantage in ways that external providers cannot match, as well as being more loyal to the business.

Total outsourcing (in which 80 per cent or more of the IT budget is under third-party management) is a minority pursuit. In the US some 8 per cent of organizations take this route, in the UK about 2 per cent; worldwide there are just over 120 such deals.

All IT sourcing arrangements have inherent risks (*see* Figure 1). A mainly in-house function needs to be continually assessed against the market if it is not to become expensive and unresponsive. Much depends on strong business/IT relationships if IT activity is to underpin strategic business direction.

Figure 1

Main approaches to IT outsourcing

	In house commitment	Selective sourcing	Total outsourcing	Total outsourcing
Attitude	Core strategic asset	Mixed portfolio	Non-core necessary cost	World-class provision
Providers	IT employees loyal to the business	"Horses for courses"	Vendor	"Strategic partner"
Emphasis	"Value focus"	"Value for money"	"Money"	"Added value"?
Risks	High cost; insular; unresponsive	Management overload	Exploitation by supplier	Unbalanced risk/reward/ innovation

Source: OXIIM

One common underestimated factor in IT outsourcing is the associated management overhead cost. This is typically around 4–8 per cent of the total outsourcing cost even before the effectiveness of the management arrangement has been assessed.

Large-scale outsourcing deals focusing primarily on cost reduction can achieve these, but often at the expense of flexibility in IT operations and business strategy. Alternatively, incomplete contracts or negligible profit margins through over-tight contracts, can (and have) led to hidden costs or opportunistic vendor behavior. Finally, as will be made clear below, underdeveloped approaches to "strategic partnerships" can be very risky. Indeed, many such deals have had to undergo significant restructuring after 18 to 24 months.

From tactical to strategic uses of outsourcing

Against this background, most organizations that have outsourced IT during the present decade have pursued one of two approaches. In incremental/tactical outsourcing the primary focus has been on cost reduction, efficiencies and improved service in the way IT is run. Our 1998/99 UK and US survey suggests that such benefits have tended to come through. Moreover, learning about outsourcing matures organizational capability, positioning organizations for larger-scale, more strategic outsourcing in future.

However, one consequence of incremental IT outsourcing has been that a large minority of organizations have encountered problems impinging on business strategy. These problems are: failure on the part of the supplier to understand the business (37 per cent); misalignment between corporate strategy and IT (35 per cent); and poor strategic IT planning (24 per cent).

Other organizations, through some combination of competitive, financial, business, technical and IT skills pressures, have taken a "hard learning" route; that is, they have outsourced to a significant degree without really developing a strategic focus on their outsourcing objectives, let alone the capabilities to achieve them. However, in our most recent research into global IT outsourcing practices, we have discerned six strategic foci, in combination or in isolation, through which organizations are increasingly attempting (sometimes with success) to achieve a business advantage.

Financial restructuring: improving the business's financial position while reducing or at least containing costs

Cost efficiency remains a key organizational goal for most selective and total outsourcers. However, organizations such as British Aerospace, Continental Bank and Sears have sought long-term, significant changes in their financial position through outsourcing.

For a company that is in financial trouble, outsourcing provides a significant cash influx from the transfer of IT assets and staff, together with tax advantages; this improves cash flow and makes it possible to restructure the balance sheet and profit and loss account. As such, outsourcing represents a long-term financial strategy, supporting a turnaround in the company's financial and competitive position over time in exchange for annual outsourcing fees representing an interest rate.

Most single-supplier total outsourcing deals in the early 1990s were of this character (*see* Figure 1); many disappointed. For British Aerospace, protected by a highly detailed contract, outsourcing bought it time to recover its financial position. By the beginning of 1999 much more was being done with the technology, and IT efficiencies were being achieved in operational areas, though the IT budget as a whole had nearly doubled from 1993.

On a wider front, companies pursuing low-cost business strategies will best reflect these by focusing on cost reduction through IT outsourcing. However, there is evidence that this creates inflexibility in both IT operations and business strategy. Companies may well experience constraints when their business strategy moves to seeking faster time to market and rapid market growth. There is also evidence that companies with objectives other than cost reduction tend to view more of their IT as a core competence and pursue relatively less outsourcing.

Core competence: redirecting the business and IT into core competences

This strategy is exemplified by British Airways' aim of focusing on transportation of passengers and cargo to achieve £1bn savings and double profits in the 1996–2000 period. To achieve this, the company needed only to own its route structure, brand and (IT-based) yield management system. Almost all other things could be outsourced, leased or bought in.

By 1990, in a worsening financial situation, BP Exploration (BPX) became much more focused on the core competence argument, according to which the company's key competence was exploration, and its key intelligence in its prospectors, not in IT or accounting (say). The accounting function, including its IT, was outsourced in 1991 in a five-year, £55m deal. According to chief executive John Browne, "failure to outsource our commodity IT will permanently impair our business competitiveness". However, this was to be achieved not by traditional outsourcing but by establishing a constellation of partners.

In 1993 BPX signed three suppliers on five-year contracts, worth $35m annually. Sema Group was selected to handle datacentre operations, SAIC for its strength in developing distributed and leading-edge systems and scientific applications, while Syncordia had the maturity, flexibility and range to manage telecommunications

269

and WANs. These were chosen to support a strategy of becoming a more diversified production company, moving into areas in which BPX often did not have the necessary in-house IT skills.

Subsequently, the in-house team focused on business processes, on information and business value-creation areas, and the vendors on more routine applications and technology. One achievement over the five years was the move to desktop computing throughout BPX, which was widely recognized as impossible without outsourcing.

Technology catalyst: strengthening resources and flexibility in technology and service to underpin the business's strategic direction

Outsourcing vendors are regularly used to "fill in" for IT skills shortages, and to provide competitively priced computing power and service. However, some organizations have used outsourcing more strategically, seeing it as a significant investment in transforming a traditional IT function, and achieving a new technology agenda to underpin business strategy.

Thus in 1994 Xerox signed a 10-year global contract with EDS for an estimated $3.2bn. It had become clear to Xerox that its business restructuring in the early 1990s had left its existing systems and skills base unable to supply the required technological support. It developed a new strategy for which a new infrastructure was required, whose hardware alone would cost $55m. Internal service was seen as ineffective, costing a lot of money without significant returns. Outsourcing allowed Xerox to refocus IT on business-critical applications, while the vendor facilitated routine operations, applications and their support, telecommunications and the move to a client/server infrastructure.

In the chemicals and speciality products sector, DuPont looked for a similar "technology catalyst" payoff from its $4bn, 10-year contracts signed with two vendors in 1997. Earlier cost cutting at DuPont had meant a lack of renewal of IT assets and skills, and an IT infrastructure requiring several hundred million dollars of investment. Outsourcing thus became a serious option.

DuPont looked to convert fixed IT costs into variable costs, and also hoped for improved service speed and flexibility, skills renewal, IT career development and further cost reductions. Currently one supplier has 2,600 staff providing global infrastructure and applications, while another has 400 supporting chemical applications. DuPont retained some 60 staff to oversee the contracts, while over 1,000 distributed business and technical people provide business IT leadership, and process control and research and development computing.

Business transition: facilitating and supporting major organizational change

Forms of transitional outsourcing have frequently been used and are generally successful. They involve temporarily outsourcing technically mature IT during a period of transition to a new technology. For example, fiberglass manufacturer Owens Corning signed a five-year contract in 1995 for a vendor to maintain legacy systems while it implemented an enterprise resource planning system at 75 sites worldwide.

However, some organizations operate even more strategically, incorporating transitional IT outsourcing into a suite of outsourcing contracts to help major organizational change. Typical areas where outsourcing has been used are during mergers and acquisitions, new business start-ups, and major devolution/restructuring of the business, including privatizations.

British Gas provides an example. Faced with privatization, deregulation and devolution in the mid-1990s, its IT director commented: "Some of the challenges have probably not been met in many other organizations in the world. We are seeing implementations in time scales thought impossible before. There is also incredible downsizing. One of the implications is you cannot do it all in-house, outsourcing is needed just to meet the challenging projects, their size, our lack of resource and the short time scales."

One effective transitional move in 1995 was to contract out all datacentres in an 18-month, £55m deal. On a larger front, in order to devolve into five autonomous businesses, British Gas needed a range of suppliers to assist in re-engineering, and in developing new billing, servicing, retail and distribution IT systems.

Business innovation: improving and innovating in processes, skills and technology, while mediating financial risk through the vendor, in order to achieve competitive advantage

Organizations looking to suppliers for IT or even business innovation through traditional outsourcing contracts have often been disappointed. BPX, for example, had to create an innovation fund for suppliers and BPX staff to bid for, such was the lack of innovation coming through. Yet business innovation can be a potent source of competitive advantage that external IT partners can assist in.

This has been recognized in various private finance initiatives in the UK public sector, in the "co-sourcing" deals arrived at by several major companies (for example, Rolls-Royce and Citibank) with suppliers, and in benefits funding mechanisms of the type used successfully by the California Franchise Tax Board in the US. The essential ingredient in all these deals is that, in its IT work, the supplier focuses on the client's business objectives – delivering re-engineered processes at Rolls-Royce, developing a travel agency commission system at Citibank, and improving the accuracy and revenues from tax returns at the CFTB.

The supplier takes the investment risk up front, and is paid according to pre-agreed performance measures as business benefits are realized. Performance-based contracts are perceived by suppliers as high risk. They may require a culture change in suppliers more used to fee-type deals, and at the moment account for a very small percentage of global outsourcing revenues.

New market: direct profit generation through joint ventures with vendor partner

Some organizations have experimented with creating a new "spin-off" supplier company from their IT function. Others have contracted with a supplier to sell jointly developed products and services to the external marketplace ("value-added outsourcing"). Another type of arrangement is "equity holding", in which a company and a supplier take share-holdings in each other; the aim is to encourage the supplier to perform well, secure the business relationship, and make investment profit.

Spin-offs are not without difficulties. The new supplier needs to build commercial and marketing skills for a competitive marketplace in which other vendors have better track records and will want to exclude the new entrant. Mellon Bank, Sears Roebuck and Boeing have had limited success with their spin-off IT companies. Like American Airlines' Sabre unit, what is needed is a core competence that will attract external customers.

Electronics multinational Philips took shares in Dutch software house BSO, and transferred its development staff, and subsequently its processing operations, into a jointly owned company, Origin. BSO had an existing reputation and customer base to build on, and Philips was a ready-made large client. Even so, it took Origin several years to build a wider outsourcing market position.

Many deals have a "value-added" element. Thus Xerox–EDS sought future shared revenues for the development of a global electronic document distribution service. Mutual Life Insurance of New York and CSC sought to market software and services to the insurance industry. But partners must truly add value by offering products and services demanded by customers in the market. In several deals this value-added element has been too marginal to the overall fee-based contract to make a difference and refocus attention on mutual business objectives. Also, when they are under pressure in other parts of the outsourcing contract, client and supplier may become less interested when they realize that commercializing and marketing a new product may require an investment nine times greater than the original development cost.

Finally, shared ownership deals such as Lend Lease–ISSC, Swiss Bank–Perot Systems, and Delta Airlines–AT&T have attractions. In principle – and in reality in the BSO–Phillips case – the mechanism of shared risks and rewards overcomes the conflicts inherent in fee-based contracts. However, the incentive of shareholder profit may operate at too high a level to influence performance on the ground. Supporting the supplier's market and profit growth can conflict with, and be at the expense of, service to the original client.

Implementing strategic uses of outsourcing

Strategic outsourcing has taken a variety of routes to success. It requires a lot of management maturity and experience of IT outsourcing. It needs complete and creative contracting; a less long-term focus in the contracting arrangements, but a more long-term one in the relationship dimension, and very active post-contract management. A cardinal insight from our research is that organizations still expect too much from vendors and not enough from themselves; put another way, vendors are still much better at selling IT services than their clients are at buying them.

Five capabilities are necessary to pursue IT outsourcing for strategic advantage:

1. **Business responsibility, and the ability to identify business models and value-drivers that will make innovation possible and create business advantage.**
   Aligning the use of the market with such analysis is fundamental. Applying supplier activity to an existing business model can at best only achieve efficiency gains.

2. **The ability to make sourcing decisions and arrive at a long-term IT sourcing strategy; this must build in learning and take into account business, technical and economic factors.**
   On this front, our research identifies two proven practices in IT outsourcing. First, selective outsourcing decisions and total in-house/insourcing decisions succeed more often than total outsourcing. Second, senior executives and IT managers who make decisions together achieve success more often than when either group acts alone.

3. **The ability to understand the IT services marketplace and suppliers' strategies and capabilities.**
   Our research shows two proven practices here. First, informed buying is a core IT capability for all organizations today. Second, organizations that

invite both internal and external bids succeed more often than organizations that merely compare a few external bids with current IT performance.

4. **The ability to contract over time in ways that provide incentives for the supplier(s) and ensure that you get what you think you agreed to.** Two things to note here are that short-term (4 years or less) contracts are successful more often than long-term contracts (7 years or more), and that detailed fee-for-service contracts are successful more often than other types of contract.

5. **The ability to manage the contract in ways that secure long-term IT objectives, and achieve the required service performance from the supplier.** This is one of the weakest areas in IT outsourcing practice. IT outsourcing requires a great deal of in-house management – to determine and deliver business requirements, to ensure technical capability, and to manage external supply and IT governance. Without these, the potential for strategic gains from outsourcing can be eroded.

Summary

While some have no significant contracts and a few put their entire budgets out to third parties, most organizations adopt a mixed approach to IT outsourcing. There are risks with both extremes – keeping everything in-house can be expensive and inflexible, while going outside can involve unanticipated overhead costs. Cost reduction, efficiency and improved service continue to drive many initiatives in the 1990s – but according to **Leslie Willcocks** and **Mary Lacity**, companies are increasingly seeking ways to gain strategic advantage from outsourcing. Examples include long-term financial restructuring, the ability to focus on core competences, the "catalyzing" effect of an external service provider, help during organizational transitions (such as mergers or restructuring), support for innovation, and joint ventures with a vendor partner. The authors conclude with a list of the capabilities required to pursue IT outsourcing for strategic advantage.

Suggested further reading

Lacity, M. and Willcocks, L. (1997) "Best practices in IT sourcing", Oxford Executive Research Briefing, Templeton College, Oxford.

Lacity, M., Willcocks, L. and Olsen, T. (1999) *IT Outsourcing: A Survey of Practices and Lessons in USA, UK and Scandinavia*, ISI/Templeton College.

Lacity, M. and Willcocks, L. (2000) *IT Outsourcing: A State-of-Art Report*, Oxford: Templeton College.

Willcocks, L., Feeny, D. and Islei, G. (eds) (1997) *Managing IT as a Strategic Resource*, Maidenhead: McGraw-Hill.

Willcocks, L. and Lacity, M. (eds) (1998) *Strategic Sourcing of Information Systems*, Chichester: Wiley.

10 Nov 1998

DIGITAL BUSINESS

Going digital can break down barriers in a business and improve communications but it is not the complete answer, Victoria Griffith discovers

Financial Times

by Victoria Griffith

In the early 1990s, some senior managers at Chemical Bank decided to put an end to the rumour mill that often created damaging uncertainty among its staff. They set up an intranet site that would chase down any rumour and get the true story. Anything was up for grabs – a threatened merger, possible closure of a division or the imminent departure of an executive at the US bank.

The first week, the site received three inquiries, which were duly answered. The second week, 200 questions were posted, and, with some difficulty, the managers addressed them all. The third week 1,000 inquiries were sent in, and the system crashed.

"There was no way they could deal with it," says Laurence Prusak, author and managing principal at IBM Consulting. "People at the bottom are desperate for information from people at the top, so if you open up the floodgates, you'd better be prepared to deal with the consequences."

One of the promises of the digital revolution is that it will increase the interaction between those at the top and those at the bottom, thus creating flatter, less hierarchical organizations.

Mr Prusak, who has been preaching the limits, as well as the possibilities of electronic connections for years, is skeptical. Digital communications, he says, are largely incapable of cutting through the cultural boundaries that created hierarchical structures in the first place.

"I have the e-mail address for the White House," Mr Prusak points out. "But that doesn't mean I influence foreign policy."

Even with the best of intentions, senior managers face time constraints that technology will not eliminate. A few years ago Bill Gates said he answered all his e-mail personally. If that is still true, it is probably all Mr Gates has time to do.

Many organizations still believe in the value of a powerful elite in the upper echelons of a corporation. Someone needs to make the decisions, they argue. Yet placing all the power at the top means putting senior managers under enormous pressure, while reducing those at the bottom to automata. Thus, corporations have been increasingly striving to function more horizontally. "There may be some value in having decision-makers at the top," says Mr Prusak. "But not if they control all strategy and access to information. It's a question of degree."

To break through the time barrier, executives need to devolve decision-making to people at lower levels. Technology plays a limited role in this. Power-sharing can, of course, be accomplished with or without electronic communications, and no amount of digital wizardry will flatten a company if senior executives are not prepared to relax their control.

So have digital communications any use in a flattening business world? Yes, says Mr Prusak. Intranets, and the internet itself, can be used to access information, and information is tied to power, since it enables people to make better decisions. In the electronic age, it is easier to achieve transparency. Simply posting corporate information to all workers – regarding a dip in sales or market shifts – makes it easier for everyone to arrive at sensible solutions to problems.

The most effective information-sharing, according to Mr Prusak, probably occurs horizontally, rather than vertically. Workers can empower themselves by organising virtual communities. At the pharmaceutical company Johnson & Johnson, for instance, workers created a forum to share information about the best software and hardware solutions for the Year 2000 problem. Many of the ideas were adopted, and the company has saved a small fortune, says Mr Prusak.

Continued

Similarly, workers at Ford Motor Company who were enthusiastic about braking systems got together to form a group. The group, involving workers from several divisions, shares scientific advances, consumer preferences and anecdotal information. "Who knows if Ford will build better brakes because of it, but I wouldn't be surprised if it did," says Mr Prusak. But such groups have limitations. The best communication still occurs face-to-face. "Ninety per cent of communications are not verbal," says Mr Prusak.

"It's difficult to read people's passion, build trust, understand the subtitles through the computer. That's why travel is up since the internet became popular. People eventually want to meet those with whom they've been communicating digitally."

Electronic communications, says Mr Prusak, cannot of themselves flatten an organization. An intranet will not increase people's capacity to absorb the information thrown at them, or allow chief executives to have a personal relationship with all their employees. But it may provide a forum for communication and so help to build a more horizontal organisation.

Sustainable competitive disadvantage in financial services

by Eric K. Clemons

In a wide range of financial service industries, recent changes in regulation, in the competitive environment and in technology have combined to erode the competitive advantage enjoyed by large, previously successful and apparently dominant institutions. New entrants are successfully challenging defenders that had considered themselves secure because of their scale, captive customers or other resources.

Markets that are newly easy to attack

Many changes make it increasingly easy for new entrants to begin to compete with established service organizations, even in markets where these companies have historically enjoyed apparently dominant market positions.

Regulatory change

Relaxation of regulatory restrictions eases entry, allowing new competitors from related industries (banking encroaching on insurance, insurance encroaching on securities trading) or from other geographic markets.

Technological change in the means of production

Contract outsourcing allows new entrants in banking and insurance to achieve necessary scale and low unit costs, even with much smaller market share than previously dominant competitors. Changes in outsourcing have largely been driven by IT.

275

Development of alternative distribution channels

Electronic trading offers lower commissions and greater speed than full-service agency brokers; on-line insurance sales offer commodity-type products such as term life insurance at lower cost, while allowing comparison shopping on price and other features. Changes in distribution, especially alternative electronic channels, are likewise largely driven by IT.

Changes in customer preferences

Younger consumers may be more comfortable with internet-based distribution and disintermediate products and services; similarly, wealthier, more up-market consumers may be the segment most likely to have personal computers and internet access at home, and may be most comfortable with alternative forms of distribution.

In financial services all these trends are occurring simultaneously.

Markets that are attractive to attack

Consumers vary greatly in the costs associated with providing service to them and in the revenues that they produce for their service providers. This is equally true among customers for credit card services or for demand deposit banking products, among customers for health insurance or life insurance, or among customers for retail brokerage services:

- some credit card customers maintain large outstanding balances and do not pay them off rapidly; rather they incur finance charges, which makes them profitable to serve. In addition, the best accounts have demonstrably low risk of default
- some banking customers maintain large balances, conduct few transactions, and seldom need assistance from tellers
- some health insurance clients have far better claims histories than their fellow employees; others have worse family medical histories and thus are far more expensive to serve.

And yet, even in the presence of costs and revenues that varied greatly from customer to customer, historically dominant established players have followed very simple pricing strategies:

- until recently, most US credit card companies charged their customers the same annual percentage rate interest (APR), often the legal maximum allowed by state banking regulations; thus, the most profitable accounts were subsidizing the banks' provision of credit card service to unprofitable accounts
- very few banks impose charges for teller usage and most banks do not carefully differentiate the prices they charge retail customers for services; indeed, almost all British and French consumers enjoy free check-writing privileges, even those who are consistently unprofitable for their banks. Once again, profitable accounts are subsidizing the provision of services to unprofitable accounts, increasing the number of consumers who have access to banking services
- in US corporations, where health insurance is commonly provided as an employee benefit, all employees who select a particular health insurance plan are charged the same rates, despite their claims history and medical conditions (excluding certain "pre-existing medical conditions"). This enables insurance providers to offer an affordable service to all employees, both those with attractive claims histories and those who have not enjoyed excellent health.

These simplistic pricing strategies have led to a significant gap between the costs that banks or financial service companies incur by providing services to most of their customers and the prices that these customers are actually charged. In the case of the most profitable customers, this gap represents the degree to which the customer is being overcharged for services, producing a surplus to subsidize less profitable accounts. Industries with extreme differences exhibit what is called a strong "customer profitability gradient".

Simplistic pricing in the presence of a strong profitability gradient represents a money transfer between customers, and the stronger the gradient the greater the transfer. Significantly, the greater the transfer the more attractive it is for a new entrant to attack. By refusing to serve unprofitable accounts, and by focusing on the most profitable segments, new entrants can free themselves of the need to transfer money from good accounts to bad accounts; instead, they can feed some of the surplus back to the good accounts to "buy" their business as low-price service providers, while transferring the rest of the money to themselves and their share-holders. New entrants without fully efficient scale can still find these industries attractive to attack via such "cream-skimming" strategies.

Simplistic pricing and the resulting customer profitability gradient can be explained in a variety of ways:

- it may be the result of simplistic historical pricing errors – until recently, it was extremely difficult for banks and credit card issuers to perform detailed customer profitability analyses. Moreover, with prior generations of IT the cost of performing these analyses frequently exceeded the profit opportunities
- it may have been encouraged by the historical near-monopoly position of the service provider – before Health Maintenance Organizations (HMOs) began to compete with Blue Cross to be the providers of employee health benefit plans in the US, there was no need for Blue Cross to perform profitability analyses on individual households
- it may be the result of deliberate regulatory policy aimed at encouraging universal access to banking, telephone services, or other entitlements. In effect, the private sector provides the entitlements through implicit transfers that result from overcharging some consumers and undercharging others.

The policy of uniform pricing works well for established players, for regulators, and for society, as long as all players in the market adhere to it. However, the attraction of the gap between costs and prices for some segments of the market, and the ease of entry described above, would suggest that these policies will have to be abandoned. As one major credit card issuer explained: "Once a competitor starts down the slippery slope of differential pricing, our only choices are to follow or to be forced out of the market."

Attackers are now able to employ a wide range of information-based strategies to target the best customers and potential new accounts. Pursuit of these strategies leaves the previously dominant players holding portfolios of less attractive and even loss-making accounts, unless they are able to respond in kind.

Restrictions on established players

It would be natural to expect an established player, under attack by new entrants, to emulate its attacker's strategy. This is more difficult, though, than it might initially appear.

277

It may be very difficult to replace old distribution systems with newer alternatives.

This is especially clear in the case of telecommunications, where existing operating companies own billions of dollars worth of copper wiring; this wiring may now be of very little value, since it is an ineffective way of providing digital data, digital telephone services, or high-quality video images. It represents an unacceptably costly sunk asset that may need to be written off to prepare for competition with new entrants. The companies' success in acquiring market share and the fixed assets to support it may have been transformed from a source of strength to a long-term weakness.

Regulators may have very little patience for an established player that wishes to shed unattractive business.

Universal service is often believed to be a social good; banking, telecommunications and other services are often seen as entitlements, albeit entitlements that are provided by the private sector, and that dominant players may be forced to provide as part of the cost of their previous success. Once again, the very success of the incumbents, and their broad coverage in all segments of the market, may be transformed from a strength to a weakness.

Regulators and consumer organizations have made it very difficult to change the pricing structure of large players.

Large banks that have enjoyed significant market share may be required by their regulators to provide banking services to the poor and the elderly. Regulations in banking make it difficult to close unprofitable branches. Consumer response, adverse publicity and extremely unflattering press coverage make it difficult to impose fees for services that were previously provided without charge, especially if those fees are imposed only on some accounts. An account that represents a "historical pricing error" to a bank will be portrayed in the press as someone's lifeline. As significantly, legislation in numerous states in the US makes it impossible for health or life insurers to inquire about genetic conditions or to use this information when pricing individual policies.

Companies may be limited by contracts that they have created with their customers.

Life insurance companies cannot unilaterally terminate the policies that they have previously written, even if historical pricing errors create opportunities for their best accounts to leave for new competitors, and even if the accounts they retain are consistently loss-making business.

Not all restrictions on the options available to incumbents are externally imposed. Success may have created a culture that relies upon strengths that are difficult to abandon, even though they have become weaknesses that now hinder future success:

- it is difficult to abandon strategies that have previously been (or appeared to be) successful, especially when the company is facing increased competitive challenges
- it is difficult to abandon assets that have previously been useful or valuable, or that have previously been seen as a measure of success
- it is difficult to abandon customers, or to abandon a time-honoured policy of treating all customers equally

- it is difficult to reduce prices, even for a select segment of customers, at a time when the company's profits are under pressure due to outside attack.

Information-based strategies for financial services companies

Strategies available to attackers

The offensive strategies available to attackers are straightforward to describe:

- scan for industries that are newly easy to attack; it is among these that untapped profitable opportunities are most likely to be found
- check to see if these industries are attractive to attack. Determine if there are considerable differences among customers and if these differences are reflected in pricing. Simplistic and uniform pricing implies a strong customer profitability gradient and untapped profit opportunities for attackers
- consider what barriers – regulatory, contractual and cultural – would constrain the behavior of the current industry participants and would delay their replication of strategies to exploit differences in customer profitability.

Difficulties encountered by successful incumbents

The defensive strategies available to incumbents are limited in newly vulnerable markets. Previously dominant companies in a range of financial services industries are likely to struggle as historical strengths are transformed into weaknesses.

Clearly, many of the advantages of new entrants are structural, and cannot be attributed solely to managerial complacency, or to slow decision processes and reaction times, or to the outdated corporate culture of incumbents. Indeed, the very factors that built the strength of dominant players may have become weaknesses that cannot easily be divested. New management teams and new strategies alone cannot begin to address these problems.

Generic strategies for incumbents

We have developed the following set of generic strategies that incumbents can use to respond to the threats posed by new entrants.

Harvester

Realize the inevitability of the company's failure due to competitive pressure from new entrants, maximize short-term profits and quit the industry. Surprisingly few companies exhibit the courage required to pursue this strategy.

Strong and silent

Take your losses as you transform your core businesses to resemble those of your challengers. This may require waiting for contracts to expire so that they can be repriced, or waiting for infrastructure to be depreciated and replaced, and it may be slow and costly. In industries such as telecommunications in the US, where customers switch rapidly and defenders have been forced to learn as quickly as attackers, all major players appear to be following similar information-based strategies.

Donner Pass

Become a new entrant in your industry, but in someone else's home territory, and in this new territory aggressively engage in new distribution, opportunistic cream-skimming, and the other activities that give new entrants competitive advantage. Capital One has effectively attacked CitiBank's credit card portfolio in the US;

279

CitiBank has responded by mastering similar strategies for use in Hong Kong. (In the Donner Pass incident of 1846, a party of American pioneers resorted to cannibalism to survive a terrible winter.)

Phoenix

Become a new entrant in your industry, and in your home territory. Create a subsidiary business that follows the new entrants' strategy and that replaces your core business; that is, become the company that causes your existing operations to fail, rather than allowing the new entrant to do so. Bell Atlantic's cell phone business in its home region in the north-eastern US is effectively competing with its own local wire telephony business. Alternatively, if it had declined to compete with itself, it would have lost much of its new wire business to other attackers.

Transformer

Take your capital, your other resources and your management team and apply them in new industries. Interestingly, the best examples of this do not come from defeated established players attempting to capture a new base of operations. Rather, they come from triumphant new entrants such as Capital One, which is replicating its credit card success in apparently unrelated industries such as cellular telephony.

Strategic responses

The following are specific suggestions that incumbents may pursue while developing an effective strategic response to cream-skimming new entrants:

- take actions to decrease costs, to improve the ability to withstand the attack of a cream-skimming competitor. Recent mega-mergers in banking, such as that of Chemical Banking and Chase Manhattan, are aimed at boosting efficiency through the consolidation of branch networks and the closing of duplicated facilities; thus, they may be seen as part of a cost-control strategy that will buy both organizations time to respond. Cost-cutting activities may also use outsourcing arrangements, or may exploit new technologies. These are classic ways of surviving market shake-out; alone, they will not be sufficient for dealing with competitors with structural advantages such as better costs due to alternative distribution, and better revenues due to better selection of customers and better pricing
- develop alternative distribution systems, including home banking or whatever products and services will be most effective and least expensive for dealing with customers
- take action to increase pricing flexibility, to facilitate emulation of the strategy of cream-skimming entrants. This means maintaining better information on customers than is done in most banks, performing better market research, and building databases to support the development and targeting of new products and new services, and to support new pricing strategies
- learn to lobby more effectively for preservation of regulatory protection. Make clear to regulators that cream-skimming strategies by new entrants are incompatible with universal service from dominant established players, and make clear the social costs of rapid and disruptive change in previously regulated industries. This may restrict or delay the ability of new entrants to attack the market, or may limit the time in which established companies are forced to compete with regulatory restrictions on their pricing strategies. On a grand

280

scale, lobbying by US insurance companies to preserve the Glass Steagal Act (which separates the functions of banks and securities companies) and protect themselves from incursion from banks illustrates the effectiveness of good lobbying as a strategy

■ learn to deal more effectively with the news media, and to present more persuasively the reasons for charging different prices and different fees to different customers, even for the same services. Thus, when the largest service providers adopt differential pricing schemes, it will be seen as an unfortunate but necessary defensive move, aimed at protecting the bank and its shareholders from the attack of opportunistic new entrants.

Large, successful organizations should seek to gain time, and should use this time to prepare for increased competition. Selecting any of the available generic strategies and successfully implementing them will be slow, difficult, and risky; failure to respond, however, will be even more dangerous.

Summary

Information technology enables new entrants to "cream skim" a market – to target a company's most profitable customers and to reprice others or shift them to less nimble competitors. According to **Eric Clemons**, this has undermined the role of scale as a source of competitive advantage in financial services. Thanks to skill-based advantage, it is not necessary to be the low-cost producer, as long as you can be the low-price provider to the most profitable accounts. Nor is it sufficient to be the low-cost producer if you cannot identify and retain your most profitable accounts. Established competitors who have previously dominated their industries are therefore increasingly vulnerable. The author here explores the strategic implications for new entrant "attackers" and established "defenders" alike.

Suggested further reading

Clemons, E. K. (1997) "Technology-driven environmental shifts and the sustainable competitive disadvantage of previously dominant service companies", in Day, G. and Reibstein, D. (eds) *Wharton on Dynamic Competitive Strategies*, 99–121.

Clemons, E.K., Croson, D.C. and Weber, B.W. (1996) "Market dominance as a precursor of companies' underperformance: emerging technologies and the advantages of new entrants", *Journal of Management Information Systems* (autumn): 59–75.

Clemons, E.K. and Weber, B.W. (1997) "Information technology and screen-based securities trading: pricing the stock and pricing the trade", *Management Science* (December): 1693–1708.

10 Nov 1998

DIGITAL BUSINESS

It's good to talk – with staff by e-mail: British Telecommunications' intranet is a key part of structural changes affecting 125,000 employees, writes Alan Cane

Financial Times

by Alan Cane

Bill Cockburn, appointed head of British Telecommunications' UK operations a year ago, recalls with relish encountering, on his second day in office, one of BT's army of field staff who put up telephone poles.

He welcomed Mr Cockburn enthusiastically to the organization, congratulating him on the sharp rise in BT's share price since his arrival.

It was, however, not Mr Cockburn's reputation that sent BT's shares soaring but WorldCom's eventually successful intervention that same day in BT's attempted merger with MCI of the US. The City, which had become increasingly unhappy about the merger's prospects, marked the share sharply higher on the news.

The story says much about BT's way of communicating with its staff these days. The BT employee had been following the progress of BT's share price on the company's intranet, a group-wide electronic communication system based on internet technology.

The system was in place before Mr Cockburn's arrival, and he has adopted it as the main vehicle through which he disseminates his plans for adapting BT's traditional structure to the new world of digital business. "We have over 100,000 computer terminals in BT," he says, "and this intranet system connects them all up. This is now the means by which a lot of our internal business is done in the UK."

Everybody in the organization has access to the system. Field staff connect to it through laptop computers or catch up with the news when they return to base.

Even after the loss of more than 100,000 jobs in the past decade, BT remains a big organization. Its 125,000 staff are located not only in the UK but in every major European country, Asia and North America. A joint venture with AT&T of the US,

announced in the summer, is in the early stages of development.

The logistics involved in running an organization of this size are complex. The company buys goods and services worth £5 billion a year and much of the business is carried out through electronic channels.

It operates one of the largest fleets of commercial vehicles in Europe while its building services department deals with 7,000 properties in the UK alone.

Given the importance of the electronic supply chain, it is no surprise that BT was one of the first UK companies to warn it would cease to do business with suppliers who could not show they were dealing with the so-called millennium bomb which threatens to disrupt computer and telecoms systems after 2000.

But communicating both the corporate vision and day-to-day operational matters is a large and costly task. Mr Cockburn, in particular, is implementing the biggest changes in BT's organization for almost a decade. He has abandoned the old demarcation lines and introduced the concept of "arenas" around marketing, products and services, and the network. This is where the communications potential of the intranet comes into its own. All BT's senior managers, including Sir Iain Vallance, the chairman, Sir Peter Bonfield, chief executive, and Mr Cockburn, have their own web sites and use them for disseminating information and collecting views from staff. "My web site has gone from zero to 200,000 hits a month," says Mr Cockburn. "When I travel round the business, we run a diary of my daily appointments on the site and we take a digital camera to record noteworthy events."

The group also uses other media to get its message across. There is a newspaper and a private

Continued

television channel, but Mr Cockburn argues for the effectiveness of the intranet. "People flock to the sites because they are interested," he says.

"There is an insatiable appetite for information about the company. Last year we saved over £140 million by using the intranet – in other words, to have used paper means of communication would have cost £140 million more. "I get vast numbers of e-mails from people at all levels in the company. These people express very strong views about what we are doing and they give me their own ideas.

"And they do not do it anonymously. I think it is good that people should feel they have the confidence to express their point of view, bypassing all their lines of command by sending their thoughts straight to my e-mail address."

Mr Cockburn gives as an illustration the introduction of profit-related pay earlier this year, a measure he strongly supported. To fulfil the government's rules, however, a certain proportion of the staff had to be in agreement.

"We were selling the benefits of this to our people. During that period I had a huge number of messages. I was using my web site to reinforce what our human resources department was telling the staff."

Robert Salvoni, Mr Cockburn's personal assistant, who works with the press office to create Mr Cockburn's web site says: "It has become our lifeline. I never go anywhere these days without the digital camera."

Business platforms for the 21st century

by N. Venkatraman and John C. Henderson

How to position IT within business operations has been a major challenge for companies over the past three decades.

In the 1970s, most companies treated IT as a utility function – largely independent and unconnected to business strategies. In the 1980s, companies began to use IT activities to support strategy: big "strategic" systems were commissioned as a means to achieve competitive advantage. Managers tried – with limited success – to reproduce the advantages gained by pioneers such as American Airlines (through its Sabre system) and American Hospital Supply (through its ASAP system).

We entered the 1990s with the realization that strategic advantage through system features is transient at best. Companies then began to position IT as driving the design of business processes, both internally and between themselves and suppliers and distributors. The prevalent view of IT's role in the 1990s has been of process-enablement.

It is time for companies to rethink the positioning logic for the 21st century. IT's role goes beyond process-enablement; it is to shape the new business platform – the strategy, organization, relationships and work methods required to capture value. Winners and losers will be differentiated by the characteristics of their business platforms and the way in which they leverage IT.

The old question was: "How to align business and IT operations?" Initially, "alignment" was a matter of ensuring that IT strategy and operations responded to and supported business strategy. Methodologies such as Critical Success Factors, Business Systems Planning and James Martin's Enterprise Modelling were developed with this end in mind. Subsequently, companies realized the need to broaden IT's role. Instead of merely ensuring that IT supported strategy, leading companies leveraged IT functionality to craft differentiated business strategies. The alignment challenge was about the two-way link between business and IT strategies.

The new question is: "How best to shape the business platform for competing in the new economy?" The term "alignment" – in its common use – connotes static equilibrium. But what we now need is an innovative, forward-looking approach to enable us to design effective new business platforms. We must move away from using IT to fine-tune business strategies that served well in the industrial economy.

As we enter the 21st century, one thing is clear: business strategy cannot and should not be designed and deployed in isolation from IT. It is no longer acceptable for business strategists to play the lead role and the IT strategists the support role; both should take the lead in designing the business platform.

By "business platform", we mean a system with the following components: the value propositions to customers; the strategies adopted to deliver the value propositions; the organizational arrangements; the core business processes; key external relationships; and the design and execution of key tasks and activities. The entire platform is shaped and supported by IT and has three vectors, a customer connection vector, an asset configuration vector and a knowledge leverage vector (see Figure 1).

The role of IT is not only to support each vector independently but also to create a common foundation that makes interdependence among the three vectors possible. We see many successful examples along individual vectors but companies create the greatest value when their strategies focus on all three vectors simultaneously. Two notable exceptions are Cisco and Amazon.com.

Continuous customer connection

A new era of customer-company connection is emerging, thanks in part to the internet. The challenge is for companies to learn about customers' preferences and to be active in their offerings without invading privacy. At the same time, customers have opportunities to be more closely connected to the product-delivery chain; they can customize offerings as well as serve themselves.

Closer relationships

The challenge is clear: to use IT to get closer to customers. There are already many examples of this. Customers who have ordered their computers from Dell, for example, can follow their computers along the various stages of the production process in real time on their personalized website. Computers can be remotely diagnosed and fixed over the network today; this may soon be true of many other appliances. Airlines now communicate special fares to preferred customers through e-mails and special websites. Cars will soon have internet protocol addresses, which will make possible a range of personal in-vehicle information services.

Customers can also be involved in the early stages of product development so that their inputs can shape product features and functionality. Pharmaceutical companies are experimenting with the possibility of analyzing patients' genes to

Figure 1: Three interdependent vectors of the new business platform

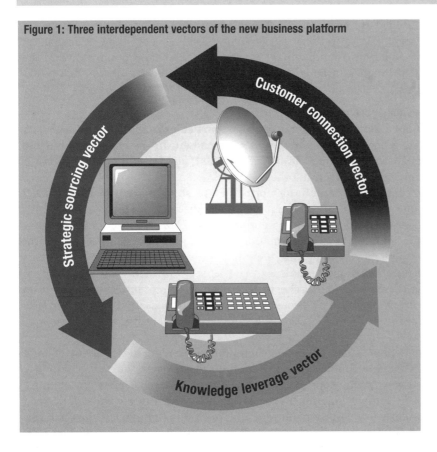

determine precisely what drugs should be administered in what dosages.

The transformation in the business platform can be seen in college textbook publishing. This industry – which has seen little innovation since the advent of the printing press – is now in the midst of major changes. Publishers are creating supplementary website links to provide additional ways for students and professors to be connected during courses (www.wiley.com; www.uol.com). The publisher's role, which traditionally was selling textbooks at the beginning of term, is becoming that of an educational consultant or value-adding partner throughout the term.

Customization
The new business platform recognizes the increased importance of customization of products and services. Increased commoditization of standard features can only be countered through customization, which is most powerful when backed up by sophisticated analysis of customer data.

Mass-marketing experts such as Nike and Levi Strauss are experimenting with ways of using digital technology to enable customization. Websites that can display three-dimensional images, for example, will certainly boost the attractiveness of custom tailoring. Such experimentation is advisable because the success of "build-to-order" models such as Dell's represents a challenge to current "build-to-stock" business platforms.

Dell is not only eliminating the non-value-added steps in its supply chains but is also leading the way in learning about patterns of product and feature selection by customers who visit its websites. Such analysis enhances its ability to price and promote different configurations aggressively. Dell is not alone. Amazon.com makes recommendations to individual customers on the basis not only of what they have browsed through and bought but by integrating data from customers with similar patterns.

Orchestrating customer communities

What makes the customer connection vector particularly challenging is the fact that in the new economy customers are interdependent. In the traditional business model customers were assumed to be independent; now the internet means that they can be connected with one another.

As online customer communities form, power shifts from manufacturers to customers. Mass advertising to communicate the distinctive features of brands is replaced by peer-level information dissemination. Information from manufacturers may be discounted in favour of information and assessments from peers and other groups. This phenomenon is nothing new but the way in which the internet can connect large numbers of individuals is.

Companies can create and orchestrate customer communities in order to get valuable feedback about their products-in-use. Companies taking this approach include Intel, Harley-Davidson, Egghead Software, Travelocity, Toyota and Apple Computers.

At the same time, some customer communities remain independent of major sellers. Areas include finance (see the Motley Fool as part of Yahoo! Finance), photography (www.photoshopper.com), cars (www.autoweb.com; www.edmunds.com), general goods (www.netmarket.com), water utilities (www.wateronline.com) and air pollution (www.pollutiononline.com). The credibility of such sites is largely due to their lack of ownership links to product and service providers. The major challenge for these communities is to maintain the trust of the consumers as they collect information about them and provide value-added services.

Asset configuration

The philosophy of vertical integration that served well in the industrial age is giving way to one of virtual integration. Virtually integrated companies assemble their required capabilities through a dynamic portfolio of relationships.

For example, Boeing developed its 777 model through a portfolio of relationships among subcontractors and lead customers, which were all supported by a powerful proprietary IT platform. This approach allowed Boeing to reduce development costs and speed up the introduction of the 777, to the discomfort of its rival, Airbus. Another example is General Electric, which is streamlining the sourcing process across its business units using a common platform (the Trading Process Network) to gain economies of scale.

Substituting bits for atoms

Physical inventory is being replaced by information about the inventory, a change which is unleashing major restructuring of activities in the supply chain. A factor in US supermarket chain Wal-Mart's success has been its ability to have precise information about inventory in the pipeline without necessarily locking excess working capital in inventory. Similarly, Dell's business model calls for the company to achieve best-in-class inventory levels, an objective which is the key to the company's competitive advantage. Dell turns over inventory 52 times a year against Compaq's 13 and IBM's 10. Companies in every industry are being forced to assess their supply chains with respect to business models that could be created by new entrants seeking to mimic Dell.

Process interdependence

IT makes it possible for companies' business processes to cut across organizational boundaries and time zones. Companies are physically locating their critical processes around the world but linking them through common technology platforms. For example, major airlines' reservation and customer service centers are distributed around the world. And pharmaceutical companies have research and development facilities scattered around the globe so that they can follow the sun and work around the clock. Such capabilities are vital in markets in which speed is of the essence – which means nearly every market nowadays.

Sourcing of business process capabilities is greatly facilitated by software and communication technologies. For example, DirecTV, a US satellite television company, has integrated its processes with Matrixx, a telephone marketing company owned by Cincinnati Bell. From a dedicated facility in Salt Lake City, Matrixx acts as an extension of DirecTV operations by providing over 2,000 customer service representatives who handle about 20m calls a year. This is the first time a major corporation has entrusted its entire customer service operation to an outside operator on such a grand scale.

New capabilities

Virtual integration is about more than efficiently sourcing standard components and processes; it is about co-operating to create capabilities. The business platform should be designed not only to optimize internal operations but to facilitate the creation of capabilities through external relationships. For example, Kraft Foods is intertwining its marketing processes with data collection and analysis by A.C. Nielsen, one of the leading information providers in the consumer packaged goods industry. Process integration between these two organizations gives Kraft access to marketing data before competitors, enabling it to respond more quickly to market trends.

Knowledge leverage

The third vector of the business platform is knowledge leverage. The signs are that we are entering a new economy where the basic resource is not land, raw materials or capital but knowledge and intellect. Unlike physical assets, knowledge assets are not subjected to laws of decreasing returns; indeed, with wider use, they increase in value.

IT plays a role in creating business platforms that will enable companies to use knowledge assets more effectively than their competitors. The focus is on expertise throughout the enterprise rather than expertise in the minds of a few isolated individuals. The creation, nurture and leverage of enterprise expertise is made possible by IT.

Expertise in action

Knowledge assets in themselves are of limited value; the challenge is to translate expertise into actions that give a company differential advantage in the marketplace. McDonald's and Wal-Mart are good examples of companies that are able to experiment selectively with prices, product mixes and promotions and to diffuse best practices rapidly to similar outlets or stores. ABN-Amro's tagline is "The Network Bank" and its competitive advantage lies in systematically leveraging the expertise in its far-flung branch networks.

And consider BP Exploration. When equipment fails in the North Sea, the drilling engineers haul the faulty hardware in front of a video camera connected to BP Amoco's virtual teamwork stations. The part can then be visually inspected by a drilling expert in Aberdeen, who can talk to the shipboard engineers at the same time.

Knowledge as an organizational asset

There is widespread frustration that accounting statements – balance sheets and income statements – do not adequately reflect the role and value of intellectual assets. Accordingly, several companies – especially Skandia in Sweden – are experimenting with new measures. Our view is that new measurements should be designed at the same time as an organizational infrastructure that creates and leverages knowledge.

The US army's Center for Army Lessons Learned (Call) provides a good illustration of the creation of organizational-level knowledge assets. After the 1994 Haiti invasion, Call had experts interview soldiers about incidents with crowds and confrontations with local authorities, observe after-action reviews and read intelligence reports. Using the information gathered, Call developed 26 training scenarios for use by replacement units getting ready for Haitian duty; in the following six months, the units encountered most of these scenarios.

The logic underlying the US army's after-action reviews is beginning to be seen in companies such as Motorola, General Electric, Analog Devices, Steelcase and BP Amoco. The availability of multimedia IT platforms is a strong enabler.

Intelligent business networks

Knowledge is not confined within an organization's boundaries. The new business platform requires the creation of a dynamic business network to gain access to and leverage different forms of intellectual asset.

The development and manufacture of Boeing's 777, which involved key airline partners (such as British Airways and United Airlines) and major subcontractors is a textbook case. About 250 cross-functional teams – which included personnel from suppliers and airlines and were distributed over several locations – created the 777. All were linked electronically through the use of common Cad/Cam software. Not only was the cost of development reduced but also the time taken to introduce the plane into the market. Indeed, the real power of the new business models lies in their recognition of the value of partnerships – not just for increasing operational efficiency but also for boosting the knowledge quotient of organizations.

Designing the business platform

The business platform of the industrial era was physical: it consisted of assets such as mines, factories and mills which could be designed and managed in an orderly fashion. The business platform of the new era is virtual: it is digital, global, interconnected, fast-changing and chaotic. We are in the midst of the transition between these two eras – and this creates major opportunities (and challenges) for companies that are adept at using information systems and technology.

Who is the architect of the business platform?

It may be a cliché, but IT is too important to be left to the technologists. IT has become so pervasive that senior managers need to understand its power and functionality if they are to translate them into business success. The ultimate responsibility for designing the IT-enabled business platform lies with the senior business management team, not with chief information officer alone.

How can investments in the new business platform be justified?

To begin with, we are not talking about IT infrastructure but about a business platform built on top of the IT functionality. We cannot build it by approaching it as a cost center where investments are justified on the basis of operating efficiency. What we are doing is akin to building the research and development platform for innovation. The required investments cannot be justified using discounted cash flow models. During the transition period, investments should reflect a "real options" perspective, of the sort espoused by Martha Amram and Nalin Kulatilaka at Boston University School of Management; this recognizes the need to manage rather than minimize uncertainty.

How to operate the business platform?

The platform is designed to be shared by other companies because, as we have seen, processes run across many organizations. So responsibility for managing it is shared among a set of alliance partners who contribute their complementary competences on the common platform. At the same time, each company should be clear about its particular value-adding role in the network and recognize that its role may change rapidly as business conditions change. The virtual model makes it necessary to design and run the platform co-operatively; no company is an island in the new economic era.

Summary

The concept of "alignment" is critical in IT strategy. In recent years it has meant ensuring that IT strategy supports business strategy. Now, say **N. Venkatraman** and **John Henderson**, it means business and IT strategists working together to shape new business platforms; IT is not subordinate to business strategy but an inextricable part of it. The best new business platforms – which essentially determine a company's value proposition to customers and its core processes – have three interdependent vectors: a customer connection vector, whereby companies sense and respond to customer's fast-changing needs; an asset configuration vector, whereby companies form close relationships with one another and outsource key processes; and a knowledge leverage vector, whereby companies identify, nurture and create knowledge assets. The role of IT is to create a common foundation for these three vectors. Companies will create the greatest value if they can incorporate all three into their strategies simultaneously; unfortunately, most companies focus only on individual vectors.

Suggested further reading

Amram, M. and Kulatilaka, N. (1999) *Real Options: Managing Strategic Investments in an Uncertain World*, Boston, MA: Harvard Business School Press.

Henderson, J.C. and Venkatraman, N. (1993) "Strategic alignment: leveraging information technology for transforming organizations", *IBM Systems Journal* 32 (1).

Kulatilaka, N. and Venkatraman, N. (1999) "Are you preparing to compete in the new economy? Use a real options navigator" Working Paper, Boston University Systems Research Center (February).

Venkatraman, N. and Henderson, J.C. (1998) "Strategies for virtual organizing", *Sloan Management Review* (autumn).

INNOVATION AND THE LEARNING ORGANIZATION

10

Contributors

Donald A. Marchand is professor of information management and strategy at IMD International, Switzerland.

George Roth is a lecturer and associate at the MIT Sloan School of Management, and director of the Ford/MIT collaboration at the MIT School of Engineering.

David F. Feeny is vice-president of Templeton College, University of Oxford, and director of the Oxford Institute of Information Management.

Soumitra Dutta is The Roland Berger Chaired Professor of E-Business and Information Technology, Professor of Information Systems and Dean of Technology and e-Learning at INSEAD.

Leslie P. Willcocks is fellow in Information Management at Templeton College, Oxford. He holds visiting chairs at the University of Melbourne and Erasmus University, Rotterdam.

Eric Clemons is professor of information strategy, systems and economics at the Wharton School, University of Pennsylvania.

Daniel Erasmus is a fellow at Rotterdam School of Management, where he teaches scenario thinking and internet strategy, and a co-founder of the Digital Thinking Network.

Contents

Introduction

Much innovation these days is IT-based, while IT itself has become a key enabler for those trying to turn their companies into "learning organizations". Both these ideas are explored in this module. Innovation is always risky but IT innovation carries particular risks – management of the culture, staffing, learning and scheduling issues are all important if expensive failure is to be avoided. As for learning, scenario planning has become a valuable tool in an increasingly unpredictable world. It can help create what one author intriguingly calls the "forgetting organization". As he puts it, "the inability to discard old skills is different from the inability to learn from new messages". This module also analyzes the "tragicomedy" of IT change programs at two financial services companies and the results of research into 35 innovative internet companies.

Hard IM choices for senior managers

by Donald A. Marchand

Hard choices are decisions for which there are no clear criteria of success or failure. Regardless of the choice made, the outcome entails risks and costs and has unclear benefits. For senior managers today, struggling to reap the benefits of digital technology and the networked economy, all their choices are hard.

In the era of re-engineering, restructuring and downsizing, the objectives seemed clearer – to improve productivity and reduce costs through delayering, redesigning processes, eliminating headcount and investing in IT. A senior manager could "count" whether the company had succeeded or failed. Had it reduced costs, increased efficiency and become leaner? Choices were not easy during this period but at least outcomes were clear.

Today, senior managers face new waves of IT and information management initiatives in their businesses as well as the disruptive effects of internet-based competition. In tackling the Y2K problem over the past five years, many companies have undertaken costly initiatives to redesign and automate their demand or supply chain processes and associated information systems.

In all too many cases, companies have been motivated by fear, uncertainty and doubt – "Fud", in sales jargon. Senior managers have made commitments with a sense of unease about the outcomes for their industry, their company or themselves. While the scope and scale of IT use in many industries have increased and lower prices have been passed on to customers, managers are left feeling that the growth in IT's price tag has been the result of competitive necessity rather than competitive advantage.

The key question for senior managers is: how should we compete with information and IT to improve business performance? I believe that senior managers struggling with this question face four key challenges: to develop the right mindset; to understand how information creates business value; to use IT to build appropriate business competences; and to balance business flexibility and standardization.

The right mindset

Over the past 15–20 years, most senior managers have considered the key levers for managing business change to be strategy, organizational structure, processes and culture. Strategy gives a company direction and vision. Structure defines people's roles and responsibilities. Processes define the business's activities, such as sales and marketing, manufacturing and distribution, and research and development. Finally, culture includes the values and behaviors that influence how people link their own performance to the company's.

In recent years many managers have begun to question this model. This is not because it has not worked in the past, but because it does not make visible three key aspects of future change programmes. Thus the emerging model adds new levers to the four traditional ones.

First, it places more emphasis on the creation and application of knowledge by people and on how companies can enhance these processes (this is often referred to as "knowledge management"). Second, there is growing recognition that the ways in which companies sense, collect, organize, process and store information are not well understood and, therefore, often not well managed. Third, IT has often been viewed as a necessity or cost center in many companies, but not as a lever for implementing business change. The traditional perception of IT continues to exist in senior managers' minds alongside the growing perception that IT is critical for future business success.

The first challenge for senior managers is to grasp the role of knowledge, information use and IT deployment in strategic change. The greatest obstacle to developing a better understanding of these new levers is the perception that the traditional levers are still adequate.

It has never been more important for senior managers to develop the appropriate mindset for managing knowledge workers, information and IT. In an earlier chapter ("Company performance and IM: the view from the top"), we called the new mindset the "information orientation" of a company and its leaders. We suggested that companies can be differentiated on the basis of how their senior managers integrate their knowledge workers, information assets and IT to improve business performance.

Information and business value

There are four fundamental ways of using information to create business value (*see* Figure 1). Not all companies are equally able to manage information along each axis, which accounts for variations in how companies use information to compete.

The first and oldest way to create business value with information is to manage risk. In the 20th century, the evolution of risk management has stimulated the growth of functions and professions such as finance, accounting, auditing and controlling. These information-intensive functions tend to be major consumers of IT resources and people's time.

The second way of using information to create business value is to reduce costs. Here the focus is on using information as efficiently as possible to achieve the outputs required from business processes and transactions. This process view of information management is closely linked with the re-engineering and continuous improvement movements of the 1990s. The common elements are a focus on eliminating unnecessary and wasteful steps and activities, especially paperwork

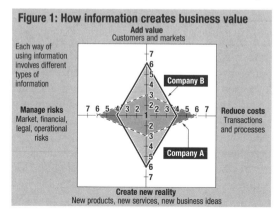

Figure 1: How information creates business value

and information movements, and then simplifying and, if possible, automating the remaining processes.

The third way of using information to create value is via the products and services offered to customers. Here the focus is on knowing one's customers and sharing information with partners and suppliers to enhance customer satisfaction. Many service and manufacturing companies have focused on building relationships with customers and on demand management as ways of using information. Such strategies have led companies to invest in point-of-sale systems, account management, customer profiling and service management systems.

Finally, companies can use information to innovate – to invent new products, provide different services and use emerging technologies. Companies such as Intel and Microsoft are learning to operate in "continuous discovery mode", inventing new products more quickly and using market intelligence to retain a competitive edge. Here information management is about mobilizing people and collaborative work processes to share information and promote discovery throughout the company.

Every company pursues some combination of the above strategies. Companies (such as Company B) that focus on using information to innovate and add value with customers on the vertical axis contrast with companies (such as Company A) that operate on the horizontal axis, where minimizing risks and reducing costs are key drivers.

I have used a scale of one to seven, where a "one" suggests that a company is doing as little as possible in a particular direction and a "seven" represents best practice. While the range of practices from one to seven will differ over time and by industry, identifying appropriate practices along each axis can help managers to consider where their company is today and where it needs to go.

IT and business competences

I have asked hundreds of executives in IMD programmes which applications they have chosen to prioritize. The vast majority name financial administration as the leading application, followed by manufacturing, inventory management, and distribution. Other executives have also listed human resource and order fulfilment applications. Invariably, these managers have claimed to be pursuing "competitive advantage" in their industries by implementing the same applications as their main competitors – and in roughly the same order.

Figure 2 provides a framework for assessing the competitive value of redesigning

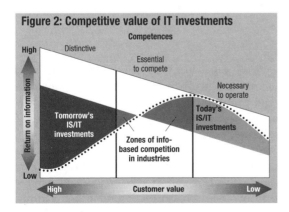

297

and implementing IT in the value chain. On the vertical access is the "return on information" that managers expect from better software and databases, in terms of three types of business competence. I define "return on information" as the business value that a company expects to receive by improving the quality, quantity and use of information in decision making.

On the right of the chart are competences such as information systems in support of the general ledger, payroll, accounting and financial reporting; applications in this category are necessary to run a business but deliver little direct customer value.

In the middle of the chart are the competences that are essential for competing, such as order fulfilment, manufacturing management, inventory management and distribution. Customers expect a company to have these capabilities if it is a major player. At best, the top five or 10 companies in the industry receive similar benefits from such applications. This is why they must execute these applications well just to stay in the running.

For example, in the bulk chemicals industry, all the leading companies have implemented SAP enterprise resource planning software for financial administration, process control and logistics. They believe such systems are essential to control costs and manage information across the supply chain to ensure punctual deliveries, and their industrial customers expect them to operate this way.

On the left of the chart are the competences that enable a company to be distinctive in providing customer value. In this category, managers mention information systems for customer profiling, product innovation, customer service and account management. They believe that these applications provide the highest return on information since it leads directly to higher perceived customer value.

On the question of how they allocate IT investments today, most managers reply that they invest in applications that are "necessary for operating" and "essential for competing". They rarely say that significant portions of their investments are focused on applications that give them distinctive competencies with customers.

Yet on the question of how they would like to allocate future IT investments, most managers reply that they would like to spend more on applications that will make their companies distinctive in creating value with customers. So although managers recognize that there are opportunities to compete with information along the value chain, most seem to believe that their IT investments provide little distinctive advantage with customers. But just because managers today tend to invest most in applications essential for operating and competing, it does not follow that they could not also in future allocate resources to applications that create distinctive customer value.

Flexibility versus standardization

Many companies are challenged to operate on a local, regional and global basis simultaneously. In these companies, managers want to attain maximum business flexibility to achieve market growth and profitability. At the same time, they also want to standardize business practices to lower costs, leverage scarce expertise and use IT to share information about customers, products and markets.

Business flexibility is required so that business unit or country managers have the freedom to tailor their operations and products and services to local market needs. On the other hand, business standardization reflects the concurrent need to reduce the working capital consumed in business operations by adopting common

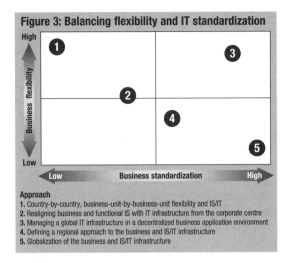

Figure 3: Balancing flexibility and IT standardization

Approach
1. Country-by-country, business-unit-by-business-unit flexibility and IS/IT
2. Realigning business and functional IS with IT infrastructure from the corporate centre
3. Managing a global IT infrastructure in a decentralized business application environment
4. Defining a regional approach to the business and IS/IT infrastructure
5. Globalization of the business and IS/IT infrastructure

processes, information systems and IT infrastructure. Balancing flexibility and standardization is a continuous challenge. The range of choice is depicted in Figure 3.

Most companies have evolved their businesses from a country-by-country, business-unit-by-business-unit model. This decentralized way of operating gives local managers the flexibility to configure their value chains to meet the needs of the local market. Typically, IT applications that support business processes and administration are also configured locally.

Decentralized operations offer maximum flexibility but they have some significant disadvantages. Many companies discover that, over time, this approach is very costly. Excessive duplication of business processes and IT support results in poor information sharing among business units.

Inevitably, senior managers are reluctant to give up the advantages of the decentralized approach, but they still wish to reduce the costs of business processes and IT across business units. Many companies move to the second approach on Figure 3 by trying to realign and standardize processes and IT from the corporate center.

A common first step is to appoint a chief information officer (CIO). The CIO is responsible for reducing the costs of IT across the company by establishing common processes and IT wherever feasible. However, CIOs can only lower costs and realize synergies among decentralized business units with the co-operation of unit managers. The political complexity often results in failure or initiatives that take many years to complete.

After several years (five to seven is typical), senior managers in some companies become frustrated with the slow progress of standardization and call for more drastic solutions. It is at this point that companies adopt approaches 3, 4 or 5. Approach 4 (regionalization) and approach 5 (globalization) require senior managers to run the business in a much more centralized manner.

Companies moving in these directions will strive over 5–10 years to regionalize their local value chains and IT systems. For example, they will seek to treat Europe as one country and to achieve similar regionalization across the world. Some companies, such as Procter & Gamble, will then go on to globalize their business processes and IT.

Approach 3 is a hybrid strategy, whereby companies operate in a decentralized business environment with a global IT infrastructure. With this approach, companies try to achieve an optimum balance between business flexibility and standardization that permits them to create significant value for customers and to lower the costs of operating globally. Hewlett-Packard has done this and has become a benchmark for companies pursuing similar strategies in many industries.

Approach 3 incorporates some important decision rules. First, senior managers must differentiate between those business processes and IT systems that create value with customers and those that permit them to lower operating costs. Second, senior managers must view IT infrastructure as an essential part of running a global business, whose value depends on how much it reduces the cost of delivering IT capabilities that meet business units' needs. Third, managers must be able to balance local needs with regional and global standardization of processes and IT.

In contrast to approaches 1 and 2, approach 3 seeks to minimize the high costs of IT in a decentralized business environment where flexibility adds no direct value for customers. This approach also speeds up IT project implementation by using a standard infrastructure that does not have to change every time the business modifies its processes and IT systems. And in contrast to approaches 4 and 5, approach 3 can provide flexibility in situations where it is critical to create value for customers, while seeking regional or even global standards for business functions where lower costs are desirable.

Meeting the challenges

Never before have IT and information management been so closely linked to business performance. Nor have they ever had such potential to destroy shareholder value, profitability and market credibility.

At the same time, senior managers are optimistic about the prospects for achieving growth, innovation and customer focus. To do so, they will have to work out how to compete with information and IT more swiftly and intelligently. And to do this, they will first have to develop and act on the right mindset – and that is a task that cannot be delegated.

Summary

Rapid developments in IT and information management have left senior managers uncertain about their strategy. They want to know how to compete with IT to improve business performance. According to **Donald Marchand**, the problem breaks down into four main challenges. First, senior managers must develop the right mindset to manage business change; they must realize that adjustments to strategy, organizational structure, processes and culture need to be supplemented with knowledge management, information management and an understanding of the critical role of IT. Second, they must also understand how information creates value – through risk management, more efficient processes, better products and services, and innovation. The third challenge is to use IT to build organizational competences that will enable a company to operate more efficiently, keep up with competitors and provide distinctive value to customers. Finally, managers need to be able to balance flexibility in local markets with cost-reducing standardization of IT infrastructure and processes.

Suggested further reading

Marchand, D.A. (1997) "Competing with information: knowing what you want", *FT Mastering Management Review* (July): 7–12.

Marchand, D.A. (1997) "Competing with information: a diagnostic for managers", *FT Mastering Management Review* (November): 18–22.

Marchand, D.A. (1998) "Balancing flexibility and global IT", in *Mastering Global Business*, London: Financial Times Pitman Publishing, 91–96.

Transforming IT-based innovation into business payoff

by David F. Feeny and Leslie P. Willcocks

The French president Georges Pompidou once observed that there were three routes to failure – gambling, sex and technology: "Of these, gambling is quickest, sex the most pleasurable, but technology the most certain." Applied to more recent information technology (IT) based innovation, this comment remains all too apt.

Consider a 1995 Standish Group study of 175,000 projects in the US. It concluded that 30 per cent of projects, representing $81bn expenditure, delivered no net benefits. Our own 1998 study of UK companies found that 26 per cent of projects produced very disappointing results, while 5 per cent were complete failures. Such studies regularly show that over 70 per cent of IT-based projects are "challenged", meaning over budget and late. Introducing new IT, even just to support the existing business model, emerges as a high-risk, hidden-cost process.

The risks are even greater when, as with many internet applications, real business innovations are also being looked for. The main reasons for disappointment cited in studies also remain stubbornly familiar: incomplete definition of business requirements, insufficiently detailed technical specifications, changing business requirements, and lack of business user input during development.

Given the catalogue of high-profile failures – such as Taurus in the London Stock Exchange (cost to the LSE and the City: £400m), California's driver license and registration system (cost: $50m) and its automated child-support system (cost: $100m), and Confirm, a US joint-venture attempt to develop a reservation system for hotel rooms and cars (cost: $200m–$300m) – it looks very doubtful whether IT-based business innovations are worth the risk. However, our own work shows a consistent picture of how business innovations based around IT occur, how the technological, organizational and project management risks can be managed, and how IT-based innovation can be translated into business advantage.

A central feature is releasing the learning potential inherent in the juxtaposition of customers and employees. Benefits also arise when users, technical specialists and outside experts work together in the same place. This enables not just the transfer but also the creation of new explicit and implicit knowledge.

What makes for success?

The first lesson is that technical innovation in itself rarely translates into business innovation. Significant payoffs arise only when IT is applied to a new business idea and model. Otherwise, no matter how advanced the IT, the most that can be expected is that some existing business idea will work more efficiently.

Consider the strategy of UK insurance company Direct Line in the early 1990s. Against traditional insurance sector models, Direct Line achieved five years of competitive advantage by identifying what customers disliked most – delays and administrative complexity in getting a policy and making claims, and high price. Its IT-supported staff were able to arrive at policies and process claims within minutes of customers phoning in. Significant reductions in operating costs were passed on to customers in much lower prices. Interestingly, the IT was not particularly new, but it was configured to support the new business model effectively.

The internet is all too often a technical solution in search of a problem. The few successes so far in business-to-consumer e-business suggest that the business-model-first logic applies. For example, the computer manufacturer Dell has used the internet as a channel to eliminate all intermediaries except a courier service. Prospective buyers visit the website, choose a PC configuration and place an order. Dell's automated assembly line and just-in-time ordering reduces costs and often allows dispatch within one working day. Its virtual store front and practice of selling directly to end users reduce the costs of sales staff, intermediaries and physical assets. Prices can be lower, with customers being assured of reliability by the brand. Dell's website regularly achieves annual revenues over $1bn.

The second lesson concerns the two main processes by which a business-led approach leads to focused, innovative IT investment. In the first, the trigger is articulation of a business issue or opportunity – for example, a breakthrough in unit costs, reduced time to market, differentiation through new services – which, if successfully addressed, would radically advance the organization's achievement of its strategy.

The business issue is owned and addressed by the organization's executive team, including the head of IT. The team accepts that "breakthough" thinking is unlikely to be achieved amid the hurly-burly of day-to-day business or in routine board meetings. It therefore adopts an "away day" culture, taking significant time out from operational activity.

The team adopts some high-level methodologies – positioning frameworks, value chain concepts and so on – that serve as a common language for debating the issues at hand. Through its own members or through external guest members it has access to knowledge about how other organizations have addressed this type of issue. The result of these deliberations is not an IT investment case, but an integrated design for a new business initiative, spelling out the requirements for IT as well as other functions. Target changes in business metrics become the driving force.

The second process leading to successful IT investment starts from being close to the customer. In practice, few IT-based business innovations have materialized from formal planning processes, routine meetings of IT investment committees, or from IT departments working alone. Even the classic cases of "competitive edge" IT, such as Sabre in airline reservation systems, Baxter in medical supplies ordering, and Merrill Lynch in account management systems, mostly developed incrementally, through a gradual process of learning and a strong external focus.

More recently, effective innovation in many sectors continues to come from close interaction between customers and those at the sharp end of the business. This provides an external view; it enables customer requirements to be identified, and indicates ways in which IT can be optimized to fulfil an updated customer value proposition. But innovation will founder at this point unless it gains a high-level project champion and obtains funding without having to go through the formal IT investment process. Continued customer involvement is also required to refine the innovation, and substantial internal marketing and political effort is needed to convert the opportunity into reality.

Implementation as innovation

Once an innovative strategy has been devised and "sold", there remains the problem of implementing it. The main features of difficult projects continue to be large size, long time scales, complex, new or untried technology, and lack of clear, detailed project staffing and management structures. Moreover, traditional "waterfall" methods of systems development seem inappropriate for implementing IT-based business innovations.

For these reasons, companies have been endeavoring to implement projects more swiftly. Since 1997, British Airways – which has 500 IT-based projects at any one time – has been adopting more rapid application development techniques and cutting typical delivery times by 30 per cent. In 1999, the Woolwich bank finished piloting the UK's most advanced and integrated suite of call-center and internet banking services, developed and built in just six months. And in 1998 Daiwa Europe, the Japanese financial securities company, achieved an IT-based innovation in eight months; the company thus met the deadline of 1 January 1999 that would allow it to trade in the euro from the beginning.

What is common to each example? The significant differentiator is not new tools for faster systems development, but innovations in staffing, culture, project disciplines and learning. Let us distil the major features of such "implementation as innovation" approaches.

Focus on users, not specialists

Projects embodying IT-based business innovation are inherently unstable. Detailed business requirements, as opposed to the overall objective, are unclear and subject to rapid change. Flexibility for further learning and innovation is required. Additionally, the technology itself may be under-developed, lacking stability and detailed technical specification.

In Figure 1 "technology maturity" refers to situations where a radically new technology is being used, or where a radically new business application of an existing technology is being attempted, or where the in-house IT department lacks the relevant technical expertise. As IT becomes increasingly pervasive in organizations, development can no longer be left primarily to in-house IT specialists or external suppliers. IT-based business innovation requires a user-focused approach involving multi-functional teamwork, personal relationships and business goals. Only when technology maturity is high, and a detailed contract and deliverable objectives can be specified in advance does it become low-risk to hand over development to internal or external specialists.

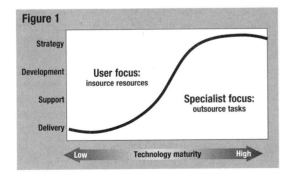

Figure 1

303

Governance and staffing

Our studies consistently show that effective IT-based business innovations require a high-level sponsor and a project champion, both usually from the business rather than the IT side. The sponsor provides no more than 5 per cent of his or her time but is involved in initiating the idea, underwriting the resources required and protecting the project until it is implemented. The project champion provides 20–60 per cent of his or her time. The role involves communicating the vision, maintaining motivation in the project team and the business, fighting political battles and remaining influential with all stakeholders, including senior management.

Effective project managers have three distinguishing characteristics: credibility with project stakeholders, a track record of success in projects of this size and type, and skill at controlling even the smallest actions needed to keep a project on track. Potential users, drawn from the best people available, need to be assigned to work full-time on the project, along with in-house IT specialists.

External IT resources may be needed to fill skills gaps, and some users and managers may need to be brought in occasionally to provide additional knowledge and opinion. The team must contain at least some people with "bridge-building" interpersonal skills, although co-locating team members also helps the key processes of team building, knowledge sharing and mutual learning.

Time-box philosophy

IT-based business innovation must be delivered within a 6- to 9-month period. Moreover the IT must be developed within the overall IT architecture of the organization, and not as a separate "portakabin"-type system. If, after examination, this cannot be achieved, the project does not start.

Good time discipline reduces the risks of a project not meeting business requirements. It transforms big projects or "whales" into a series of more manageable "dolphins", makes business benefits flow regularly rather than being delayed, and ensures that the team remains focused and fully staffed over a more realistic, limited period. Further time-boxing will place time limits on each part of the development, to reduce drift from the overall delivery target.

Development should proceed on the basis of the "80/20 rule", with the business accepting in advance that the first systems release may well provide only 80 per cent of the functionality originally demanded. Mistakes and failure should be treated as positive contributions to learning.

Iterative development by prototyping ensures close interaction between developers and users, with a workable system built quickly and constantly refined. Knowledge exchange and incessant testing and learning lead to a culture of rapid improvement, sometimes with radically new discoveries on business use of the systems. Prototyping and user involvement also ensure that the developing system is owned by the business; this eases the acceptance problems traditionally experienced when IT specialists hand technology over to users.

The role of the supplier

External perspectives and knowledge can contribute a lot to technical and business innovation. Furthermore, given the need for rapid delivery to the business and – in many companies – in-house skills shortages, suppliers can perform an important "fill-in" role.

Routine, easily defined tasks within the overall project can be outsourced. Our research suggests that with IT-based innovation, suppliers are most effectively

Imperatives for IT-based business innovation

Our research suggests six critical enabling factors for IT-supported business innovations:

- senior-level sponsorship, championship, support and participation

- business themes, new business models and re-engineering drive the choice of technology

- "dolphin" multi-functional teams, a time-box philosophy and regular delivery of business benefits

- preference given to in-house and "insourced" technical expertise

- supplier partnering – strong relationships with suppliers, who are treated as part of the team

- IT is seen not as a cost center but as a business investment in research and development and business innovation

As new generations of technology arrive, and IT penetrates closer to the core of the organization, our research is finding that these enabling factors are becoming ever more crucial.

used as resources brought in to work under in-house control. When the Woolwich bank developed its integrated banking services in 1998–99 the Visual Basic skills of the 14-strong internal development team were combined with the website and C++ programming skills of external partners. However, managers were careful to keep Woolwich people in key areas. The responsibility for innovation, and control over its precise direction, must stay with the business but "insourcing" external skill can, if properly managed, lead to valuable transfers of learning.

The alternative – of outsourcing the management and resourcing of IT-based innovation – places the external supplier in an invidious position. Consider a European insurance company that, in the mid-1990s, planned to achieve competitive advantage by transforming its policy and administration systems. A major supplier was given tough deadlines to meet detailed new requirements for the systems. However, the supplier had no great in-depth knowledge of insurance and greatly under-estimated the complexity of insurance work and information. The method it used to meet the requirements was new and relatively untried.

Project management was also made the supplier's responsibility. In effect, a business innovation was being abandoned to the supplier. After a year the insurance company invoked penalty clauses for non-delivery to cancel the project, with the supplier incurring significant costs.

Summary

Introducing new IT is a risky business. But failure is not inevitable; and according to **David Feeny** and **Leslie Willcocks**, a number of success factors can be identified. One of the most important is that technical innovations need to be applied to new business ideas to produce significant benefits. Such ideas usually come either from recognition of a business opportunity by executives, or from identification of customer requirements by those at the "sharp end". When it comes to implementation, it is important to involve users throughout the organization rather than just specialists, especially when a technology is immature. External suppliers must remain under in-house direction. A high-level sponsor and a "project champion" are also required, as is strict time management. However, companies must be prepared to accept that a system may provide just 80 per cent of desired functionality to begin with.

Suggested further reading

Feeny, D., Earl, M. and Edwards, B. (1996) "Organisational arrangements for IS: the roles of users and specialists", in Earl, M. (ed.) *Information Management – the Organisational Dimension*, Oxford: Oxford University Press.

Leonard-Barton, D. (1995) *Wellsprings of Knowledge: Building and Sustaining the Sources of Innovation*, Boston, MA: Harvard Business School Press.

Nonaka, I. and Takeuchi, H. (1995) *The Knowledge-Creating Company*, New York: Oxford University Press.

Plant, R. and Willcocks, L. (2000) "Internet-based business strategies: the search for leadership", Oxford Executive Research Briefing, Templeton College, Oxford.

Willcocks, L., Feeny, D. and Islei, G. (eds) (1997) *Managing IT as a Strategic Resource*, Maidenhead: McGraw-Hill. (See especially chapters 8, 9 and 14.)

Willcocks, L., Graeser, V. and Pisanias, N. (1998) *Developing the IT Scorecard*, London: Business Intelligence. (See chapters 4 and 5.)

A common language for strategy

by Daniel Erasmus

Organizational strategy today is inseparable from information and communication technology (ICT). Only through linking managerial and technological perspectives can we build strategies that have business value and technological relevance.

Unfortunately, most organizations are not prepared for the new technologies that have the power to transform them.

Why? Consider the following dialogue:

Q: "How will the internet change our supply chain?"
A: "Well, if we build our website on a dynamic SQL server then we can interface with our existing profile database and customize the user experience. That would change the game!"

The problem is that most managers do not have a clue what ICT professionals are talking about, and ICT people cannot explain their work to management. They are two sociological groupings that speak different languages. Consequently, conversations between the two are limited in scope and give rise to little learning. This discursive divide is responsible for many of the day-to-day ICT problems that plague the process of information management.

Scenario thinking is a powerful method for bridging the divide. It links thinking about business and technological changes into a conversational framework in which managers and ICT professionals can learn together instead of talking past each other.

Scenario thinking

From our human perspective, there is no single, determinate future; instead, there are a thousand possible futures. Building scenarios is the process of sifting, sorting and combining these possibilities into a few stories. These stories must be:

- relevant – they must matter to the future of an organization

The future of organization

Globalization and ICT are driving forces for organizational change, but to what end? In a scenario study at the Rotterdam School of Management, we arrived at two basic uncertainties over how ICT could be used to create organizations that would be effective at generating and using ideas.

First, ICT can be used to empower or to control individuals. It can enable people to work more freely and independently (as in Silicon Valley start-ups) or it can be used to monitor and control people (as in some call centers). How ICT will eventually be used will depend on our perceptions of privacy and on the distribution of encryption technology.

Second, because it can reduce transaction costs, ICT can be a force for consolidation or for fragmentation. On the one hand, we see big mergers and acquisitions in many sectors. On the other hand, organizations are being divided into business units that are encouraged to compete. Organizations seem to be consolidating and breaking up at the same time and it is unclear which force will prevail (see MIM 5 for more discussion).

Around these two uncertainties we can build four scenarios to describe the shape of organizations in the next 10 years.

"Dynamic knowledge networks" (empowerment and fragmentation)

Fast-moving knowledge workers work together in dynamic project groups. The workers are free agents, working in transient transnational networks. Though people often work together for longer periods, organizations themselves might exist only for a few days. Competition is fierce and based on rapid innovation. People are empowered, determine their own working lives and are richly rewarded for their ideas. The pace of work and the demands of being available at any time of the day lead to high levels of stress. The basic organizational assumptions are that innovative products will lead to market success, and independent networks innovate faster.

"Metropolis" (control and consolidation)

Organizations use ICT to control their employees. All activities are strictly monitored. Organizations are large and transnational. Competition is oligopolistic, fierce and based on products and price. To compete, companies innovate but the main emphasis is on efficiency. Closed-circuit television, network sniffers and other monitoring devices are used to improve efficiency. The basic organizational assumptions: controlling people leads to greater efficiency and economies of scale will benefit larger organizations.

"Modern feudalism" (control and fragmentation)

Entrepreneurs use ICT to increase spans of control to run several small, global businesses using cheap, skilled workers in developing countries. Workers are employed on a project basis and performance is controlled with ICT. Competition for these positions is fierce, and obedience and conformity are prized. The competitive environment is accelerated and based on cheap innovative products. The basic organizational assumptions are that controlling cheap skilled labor in the developing world leads to lower costs.

"Mother companies" (empowerment and consolidation)

Companies take care of their employees from cradle to grave. Companies prosper through productive, loyal and innovative employees. Organizations are large, global and have a unified culture. This shared culture enables people with diverse backgrounds to work effectively together. Competition is oligopolistic and based on quality and service. The basic organizational assumptions are that empowering employees improves work and shared values enable people to work together in large groups.

Just as there is a great variety of organizational forms today, so it is absurd to say that one type of organization will dominate in the future. Ten years from now we can expect a mix of the above organizations to coexist. The purpose of the scenarios is to indicate the directions in which organizations might evolve, to describe the associated trade-offs and to enable organizations to reflect and to plan ahead.

- plausible – they must describe futures that reasonably could happen
- consistent – they must have a coherent storyline
- surprising – they must challenge existing assumptions

A good scenario set consists of two to four stories that all meet the above criteria to the same degree. Their focus should not be on the developments that an organization can influence, but on the developments that it cannot – that is, the organization's context.

The question for an organization is not to choose which scenario to realize, because by definition it cannot, but rather to ask what to do now (what options it has or needs to create) if the scenarios materialize. Scenarios create a language for talking about the future. ICT professionals and executives share this language and can use it to discuss the link between business practice and technology.

Scenarios move the conversation from the present to the future. In creating scenarios, therefore, ICT professionals have to talk about the effects of technologies and not just about the technologies themselves.

Scenario thinking is an open, exploratory process. Building scenarios is not a matter of filling in blanks, but a process of creating new, distinct images that describe future worlds. Today's assumptions – embedded in the day-to-day conversations of managers and technicians – do not suffice to capture tomorrow's complexity. The scenario-building process thus forces participants to create a new language that is adequate to the new situation. When both technical and non-technical people take part in this process, they share the new language, which is neither technical nor managerial, but combines both types of discourse.

Scenarios are not just simple technological futures; they describe future situations in all their social, environmental, political and technological complexity. To describe these future worlds in full, managers and ICT professionals need to build on one another's strengths.

A scenario set for 1999, written in 1989, would not include the dramatic growth of the internet if it lacked technical depth. Similarly, without the business perspective the same scenario set would not discuss the effects of globalization. An organization relying on either of these one-sided perspectives back in 1989 would have focused only on the internet or on globalization and would have missed the real business opportunities arising from their combination.

The official future

Most managers never discuss the future. They are too concerned with the complexity of managing today. On the odd occasion that managers have a chance to reflect, the futures they describe tend to be set and unchanging. This is because there is a future that people in the organization implicitly ascribe to – what scenario thinkers call the "official future".

The official future embodies all the little assumptions that people in the organization share and never discuss and therefore never question. The official future for most telecommunications companies today, for example, is that the cost of communication will continue to depend on distance.

Scenarios always challenge an organization's "official future". They show that the official future is not the only one and that other possibilities are equally plausible. Managers therefore need to plan for the entire spectrum of possible futures. In the case of telecommunications, these might range from a "free global communication" future to a "pay for service not reach" future.

Best practices for scenario builders

- combine occasional face-to-face interaction (to build trust) with continuous virtual interaction (to build knowledge)
- diversity is strength – the greater the range of people involved in building scenarios (in terms of culture, education, age, role and so on), the better the scenarios will be
- archive everything – discussions from two years ago often become relevant due to changed circumstances
- condense discussions into short reports that keep people who are not continuously involved up to date
- clearly separate open, exploratory spaces
- from structured, convergent discussion areas
- use shared knowledge databases
- base virtual communities on existing real communities
- use a facilitator to link discussions, add insights and create focus
- "fluid" is better than "final" – everything needs to be thought of as a draft
- involve customers and suppliers – scenario development can be an opportunity to learn with your customers and to develop a new strategic relationship
- pull interest rather than push information.

Managers also start to discuss the future with greater sophistication. External developments are viewed as indicators of a particular scenario. These developments are debated and continuously compared with the assumptions of their effects in the different scenarios. For example, if Ericsson brings out a telephone switch that can be used for internet telephony, this might be a strong indicator that we are moving towards a world in which the internet will be the de facto public telephone network.

Not local but global

Traditionally, scenarios were developed by a small group assigned the illustrious task of strategic planning. This group would work in the same place and dutifully report back every other year with the new scenario set.

Now a new breed of scenario thinker has emerged. Their task is to facilitate the process of building scenarios rather than to present finished scenarios. The internet and intranets democratize the scenario process.

Siemens, for example, has a multidisciplinary team called FutureScape. The team is spread all over the world and its members work on FutureScape alongside their normal work. There is no rigid separation between "strategic" and "functional" thinking. The team interacts mostly on the company's intranet, although members occasionally meet in person for workshops.

At Nokia, participation in the scenario dialogue includes hundreds of people throughout the organization. Discussion spaces on the corporate intranet focus on building scenarios and matching them to business concepts. The link between business concepts and possible futures in which they will work is explicitly investigated throughout the whole organization.

Scenario planning is not restricted to individual organizations. The Global Business Network is an extra-organizational network of more than 100 multinational companies. Strategists participate in discussions on an extranet where they explore their assumptions and build global scenarios.

At Rotterdam School of Management, over the past three years, we have facilitated scenario dialogues on an extranet between people from more than 50 countries. Our online scenarios are linked to information on the research, assumptions and dialogue that created them, and to dialogues on their implications. In effect these are living scenarios, that grow and get more complex as events unfold. Thinking about the future is not an occasional activity, but a continuous conversation.

Summary

The impact of technology on organizations will be enormous. To benefit, organizations will need the skills and expertise of all their people; technical or managerial competence on its own will simply not suffice. Yet managers and IT professionals continue to talk past each other. The solution, says **Daniel Erasmus**, is scenario thinking, in which managers and technologists work together to construct plausible strategic scenarios. Because this process involves challenging old assumptions and developing new ones, the two sides together create a shared language. Internet technology will enable more employees – and suppliers and customers – to participate in a continuous process of scenario development.

Suggested further reading

Castells, M. (1996) *The Rise of the Network Society*, Oxford: Blackwell.

de Geus, A. (1999) *The Living Company*, London: Nicholas Brealey.

Turkle, S. (1996) *Life on the Screen*, London: Weidenfeld and Nicolson.

van der Heijden, K. (1996) *Scenarios: the Art of Strategic Conversation*, John Wiley & Sons.

Weick, K. (1995) *Sensemaking in Organisations*, Sage Publications.

Web sites

The Digital Thinking Network: http://www.dtn.net

FutureScape: http://www.siemens.com/

Global Business Network: http://www.gbn.org

public/uk_sys/future/sys/

Rotterdam School of Management – Future of the Information Society: http://rsmcourse.dtn.net (a summary of the "future of organisations" study is available from info-dtn@dtn.net)

sys_us.htm

IT and the challenge of organizational learning

by George Roth

In the early 1990s, I spent two years studying two financial services companies that had a vision of the office of the future. Once they had their systems running, they envisioned newly capable workers sitting at terminals and efficiently servicing policies and claims. All documents, scanned at the mailroom, would live on the network, electronically routed to the relevant department.

Freed from paper-shuffling, managers could focus on training staff and developing new information systems. They would be assisted by graphs and statistics on their computer screens, with overviews of backlogs and service levels, and of the performance of their workers.

Executives could plan new business opportunities in unprecedented ways, taking advantage of new kinds of summary reports grounded in comprehensive information systems. And the technologists who would devise and implement these capabilities would no longer be confined to the back room, but would play a key role in their companies' planning, strategy and day-to-day running.

Over the course of two years, both companies spent tens of millions of dollars implementing integrated desktop imaging systems that combined delivery of electronic images with access to customer databases and call management systems. During that period I took on the "participant-observer" role of the anthropologist as I watched them try to realize their visions. I did my best to look at them without preconceptions, as if they were exotic tribes whose strange culture I wanted to understand through their own eyes.

In "objective" terms, I had to consider their missions successful. Both companies managed to install their systems and to change the way work was done. One company reduced its staff considerably; the other found itself with new capacity, handling larger volumes of business and ultimately acquiring new businesses. At this latter company, the executive championing the new systems was featured on the cover of *CIO* magazine.

No-one can dispute the need for organizational change, particularly in this era of advancing technology for storing and disseminating knowledge. But as my co-authors and I discovered in putting together the new book *The Dance of Change*, every change initiative directed from the top bumps against challenges that cannot be overcome – not without rethinking the attitudes that led to the company's original practices in the first place.

Challenges of change initiatives

Under the surface of the triumphant technological marvels described above I found much more dispiriting stories of human interaction. In *The Dance of Change*, we describe such stories as the challenge of "believers" and "non-believers" – a challenge that occurs at nearly every company that tries to instil new behavior wholesale.

The "believers" had ample reason to consider themselves successful. Their installation had taken place on time. Statistics showed that new accounts were established effectively and customer enquiries processed more efficiently. Whenever there was any doubt or concern, they labelled it "resistance". After all, they knew their way was correct.

So the "non-believers", denied an opportunity to voice their skepticism, took it underground. These people tended to be the clerks who had endured 20 years of doing the painstakingly repetitive work of processing policy and claims documents. They had developed an incredible pride in the quality of their work. They wanted the policies or investments they had processed to be "in order" whenever customers needed them – even if that need emerged years after they had themselves retired.

Now, suddenly, the believers had labelled their concern and care as "resistance to new technology" and told them it was not important. In fact, they were told, resistance to the new system made them outdated. (However, the "non-believers" included not just the 20-year veterans of mainframe-era computing, but also some of the younger, PC-savvy generation of clerical workers.)

When managers insisted on checking the results of the new systems, validating the new entries or auditing the set-ups independently, they were deemed to be

12 Nov 1998

DIGITAL BUSINESS

An insider's guide to an online venture: Entrepreneur Tim Jackson finds that ideas are ten a penny, but that the hard part is making them happen

Financial Times

by Tim Jackson

The FT's digital business series has looked at many ways in which traditional companies can use internet technologies to improve their profitability. But these are dwarfed by a far more exciting opportunity – to start a new venture.

It was curiosity to know what this experience would be like that led me to start an internet business in London last year. Having written a column about the internet for the FT for the past two years, I had a privileged view of the opportunities – and decided that the online auction industry, which I had covered since its inception in May 1995, was the most exciting. Auctions over the internet provide a new way for buyers and sellers to meet and find market-clearing prices for products and services. But they are also local, and provide an opportunity to build a big business in Europe.

That choice was probably correct. Today, two leading US auction companies, Onsale and eBay, are both public companies; the market values them at over $3 billion (£1.9 billion). But I have learned a number of unexpected lessons and have been given an insider's view of digital business.

The first and most important lesson has been that execution matters more than ideas. In two years of interviewing founders of web startups, I had often accused them of lack of imagination, listing simple ways in which they could improve their services. Inside Quixell.com, as my company is called, matters suddenly became clear. Ideas are ten a penny; the hard bit is making them happen.

Running an internet business is less cerebral than my musings in the column on strategy had led me to expect. Particularly in Europe, where everything from finding offices to hiring people takes longer, mere analytical insights matter less than being persistent and thorough. Someone once said of socialism that it takes too many evenings. Entrepreneurship takes weekends too.

A second lesson was about risk. I did some careful financial modelling before the business began, but still underestimated how much cash it would need. By the beginning of 1998, Quixell.com had burned up more than £100,000 of my own money, and none of the venture capitalists who had appeared so keen at its launch the previous September had actually written a cheque. It was not until the spring that we were able to raise the first of three small seed rounds in the US that brought in nearly $3 million – but the company is unlikely to make money until 2001.

Finding others to share risk is a great deal harder in London than in Silicon Valley. To hire a smoothie marketing man of 28 last year, I had to match the £52,000 he claimed as his current salary. As the losses mounted, he turned down several opportunities to become a partner in the business. Once the corner had been turned, he demanded one-eighth of the company – and walked out when he failed to get it, taking at least one of the marketing deals with him. Today, the company has six talented and loyal senior managers – each of whom earns less than in previous jobs, but has stock options in the company.

A third lesson concerned technology. Robust computer systems that do what they are supposed to do are rare in the internet business. The proof of this came on New Year's Day 1998: arriving at the office at 8am to make an early start on the year, I discovered we had unwittingly sent out 50 copies of the same e-mail to our entire customer base.

Anticipating a flood of protests, I sent out a follow-up from my personal e-mail address, explaining that the multiple mailing was a mistake, and inviting customers to call me at home if they wanted to express their annoyance. Thankfully, the incident lost us only 10 customers – but it was an early

Continued

indicator of the regular need to rebuild our back-office to keep pace with the company's growth. I now understand why Jeff Bezos, chief executive of Amazon.com, holds monthly "scaling" meetings where his colleagues identify which part of the company's systems will break next – and try to replace it in time.

But the greatest lesson of all has been about speed. People often talk of "internet years", in which things happen seven times faster than normal. But experiencing the pace of change has still been surprising. In the past three months, for instance,

our company has moved offices, increased its head count from 9 to 23, rolled out a fully localized German service, tripled its product lines, and doubled its customer base. Last Friday we signed up more new customers than in our first six weeks. This week, I am in California, raising another $10 million from investors to grow the business. The pace takes its toll. At a conference a few months ago, I predicted that by mid-1999 I would be either rich or dead. On balance, the first now looks more likely than the second – but I have learned a new respect for entrepreneurs. The rewards earned by those who start companies and take them public may be impressive, but they are earned down to the last penny.

overly controlling. After all, the technologists designing and implementing the systems knew that everything would be processed faster once the electronic imaging system was fully accepted and integrated into the workflow.

Meanwhile, it gradually became clear that the organizations had not developed the human capabilities they needed to make sense of the new systems, let alone to debug their problems. This is another common issue in organizational learning and change. Managers struggled with the projections for the gains they were to get from the new systems; their staff struggled to keep up with expanding workloads because their managers insisted on "controls" (such as validating entries and having independent audits of new policy and investment set-ups).

As it happens, the study I am describing here was part of my transition into a career as an academic researcher on business and management issues. Previously, I had worked at a large IT supplier, developing, implementing and marketing IT solutions. Even then, I had always been fascinated with "backstage" stories of things not going well, and had wondered about the deficiencies that people blamed on computers and networks.

Now I was seeing such events from the more comprehensive perspective of the researcher. I sat in technologists' planning sessions, helped to train workers and interviewed executives about the capabilities they needed from their technology. Most importantly, I sat in the front line with workers, talking with them at length and timing, with a stopwatch, how long it took them to accomplish their tasks using both the old traditional approach and the new "paperless" system.

The results were not what one might expect. I found that while individual records handled by multiple workers took less time to process, the total time that workers spent on items increased by between 41 and 228 per cent.

As the two years went on, I watched the work ethic and customer care drain out of workers. I sat with managers who broke down in private conversations, telling me how they felt crushed between caring for people and having to make quotas. I took photographs of offices stacked high with paper, where people no longer had time to process important documents – and I noticed that these misplaced documents, because they did not get scanned, no longer appeared in the statistics kept to monitor peoples' work. I saw technologists falter in their efforts to explain why the efficiency of the system broke down; ultimately they blamed the workers for their "resistance", while reducing their own staff as the funds for developing software and systems were used up.

Meanwhile, the system still looked good on paper; more than one executive gave me a curious look when I described the symptoms I had seen and asked how he or she would respond when the effects emerged into the light. I now realize that the issue I had stumbled across – the challenge of measurement and assessment – is not uncommon. In a nutshell, the ways in which organizations measure their operations tend to misrepresent the success and results of any new approach.

Technological tragicomedy

All of this added up not so much to a tragedy as to a tragicomedy. Even as people suffered grievously, they recognized the ludicrousness of their situation. Tragicomedy balances loss and farce, and the losses were very real; in fact, three key gaps came up again and again as the driving forces behind the failure.

Like the challenges of profound change, these three key gaps are universal, although they are particularly pronounced and predictable in offices undergoing the development of new information technologies. In my own experience, and from the comments of every information systems professional that I have talked with, these elements are present in all cross-department IT projects. This universality suggests that there is a fundamental disjunction between the way most corporate people conceptualize technology and the learning and change processes through which it is put into use.

What are the three gaps? The first is the perspective gap. The various occupations that make up an organization are affected by new technology in different ways; people in different professions and roles bring different orientations to the idea of new technology. Thus, in the organizations I studied, the drama differed according to where people sat.

For IT professionals, the imaging system represented an opportunity to work with the latest technology, to enhance their skills and knowledge, and to become a more important part of core business processes. For clerical workers, the system mediated all their work, left them less able to judge the quality of their efforts, and ultimately required them to work harder and less effectively. For line managers, the system presented a new managerial challenge and opportunity. It would make it easier to balance and monitor production. However, as they later learned, it required additional work, and many steps in the flow of tasks took more time; at the same time, they were under an imperative to reduce staff or take on greater workloads.

Senior executives saw the technology as a spur to productivity, but their enthusiasm went much deeper; the new technology was a statement of their strategic intent to invest in customer service. They saw it as a way to leverage their organization's customer-service ability in the struggle against competitors.

The second gap exists between aspirations and results. In the cases we are looking at here, no one got what they wanted. The companies expended limited investment funds, and huge amounts of individual and collective energy were misapplied. Individuals remained dissociated from one another in carrying out development tasks that affected others' activities.

This problem is part of the legacy of Frederick Taylor and his stopwatch. IT design is often carried out in accordance with the same assumption that Taylor

314

used in his time-and-motion studies of factory workers early in the 20th century. To be sure, new forms of information-gathering – such as user interviews, flow charting and work flow analysis – give the impression that the entire organization is participating in its own redesign, but in fact everything is based on the implicit idea that the people doing the work are not capable of judging the most effective ways to carry it out.

This assumption explains why companies do not invest in the education of office workers, to help them understand their work as part of a process. Yet the lesson from "total quality" methods, particularly the *kaizan* approach to factory floor improvement, is that teaching workers new skills and techniques, and allowing them to act autonomously, can boost not only their effectiveness, but also their motivation and commitment.

Perhaps the worst gap is that between experience and learning. In the organizations I looked at, there was little or no feedback, and certainly no collective reflection, on what was and was not being accomplished. Thus there was nothing that could be a basis for organizational learning. It was as if organizational practices were designed so that people would collectively be unable to address the challenges facing them.

As individuals we deal with the stress of change through our natural tendencies for fight or flight (or by pinning our hopes on a leader). We are generally unable to tolerate an inquiry or engagement among protagonists, opponents and bystanders that leads to outright conflict or to underground conflict in the form of covert subversion. In organizations, we deal with mistakes that were made and capabilities that were not achieved by covering them up. We tell lies to others or ourselves and make the mistakes undiscussable.

The technological elements of competitive, knowledge-driven organizations are squandered in such cases because the human considerations have not kept pace. Organizational longevity in Western countries requires your company to learn faster than your competitors. If you do not innovate faster than others, to stay competitive you will have to cut costs. A cost-cutting strategy risks triggering a continual cycle of cuts, draining people of energy while depleting organizational resources.

Investment in IT is like many other capital choices – it is most effective when it is designed and implemented so as to leverage the human element. The office-of-the-future scenarios failed to engage the organization as a whole in designing its future, leaving that task to the technical professionals who were also responsible for IT implementation and work process redesign. The insights that were achieved as both organizations implemented new workflow designs and imaging systems were lost. There was no collective energy or motivation left to reflect upon and learn from experience.

An alternative approach would have been more effective – to embody learning in all phases of the IT projects. This approach would have rested on the simple and natural universal premise that humans are fundamentally "wired" to learn. People do not need to be motivated; they intrinsically aspire to do better. If they genuinely believe a new technology will help them work more effectively, and especially if it will involve them in making their work more effective, they will accept it. Some will embrace it.

In the end, individual people, working informally and unobtrusively together beyond the specific mandate of new technology implementation, saved both these

315

companies. The companies did not collapse under the burden imposed by the new work designs and IT systems because people, sharing knowledge informally amid the resentment and turmoil, kept the operations going. Senior managers often do not realize how much they depend upon existing, unseen communities of practice to run their organizations after they impose change upon them.

IT and knowledge

I have spent much of the past five years in experiments with colleagues to change corporations through learning initiatives instead of through top-down planned or technology-based change. These learning initiatives may be instigated at the top of a hierarchy or elsewhere, but they allow people to experiment with their work, train them to talk effectively about results, and encourage them to build on each others' experiments.

These approaches diffuse power and credit to various organizational levels, and thus challenge corporations' traditional managerial and control processes. They help teams to make their own case for which "numbers" should be gathered and assessed. They assume that people throughout an organization already know the answers that the organization as a whole is seeking to find. They also recognize the value of internal change agents – helpers who "walk the talk" can have a profound effect on the capabilities of people around them.

As learning becomes the core process for organizational change, the role of IT is shifting. Information systems have been widely used for reporting, measuring and controlling processes. Now IT is becoming more of an enabling and supporting tool for learning. There is growing interest in knowledge management as a vehicle for learning, together with recognition that new types of IT capabilities are needed.

Most of the knowledge management efforts of the past have focused on the easiest element of a learning system – codifying, archiving and retrieving the information needed for effective action. This is unfortunate because it misdirects IT design efforts. If organizations thought of the creation, articulation, development, codification, archiving and application of knowledge as a supply chain, they would recognize that their efforts are focused on only a small part of the chain, and perhaps the part that has the lowest leverage for organizational knowledge.

Thinking of knowledge as something that can be stored and retrieved confuses it with information. Knowledge is the capacity that an organization and its people have to act effectively. It is part of how people do things, and is related to their capabilities. Learning is the process by which people and organizations enhance these capabilities; and information is simply the data that people need to direct their action appropriately. IT is important in getting the right information to the right place at the right time. Claims for IT systems that support "knowledge" in organizations are only valid when all these factors come together and there is evidence that the right information was available in time to be used to produce desired results.

As organizations and their leaders recognize the importance of learning, they will look for IT that can help them develop and apply the knowledge assets of their workforce. They will move beyond the concept of "knowledge" as material archived in information systems, to recognizing "knowledge" as the full measure of human capability, the capacity for action embodied in us. They will understand that this critical element of organizational competitiveness can only be tapped by treating people not as stages in a process, but as people.

Summary

Major IT change programmes often run into major difficulties. Yet even as things fall apart on the ground, the view from the top remains rosy. A technology's advocates may characterize "non-believers" as simply resistant to technology, and use measurement systems with too narrow a focus. Here **George Roth** discusses this and other ways in which IT projects, like other organizational improvement initiatives, overlook opportunities for building an organization's learning capabilities. We usually think of introducing new IT as a one-time opportunity for change. But if we consider the use of the technology as an opportunity for learning, we can continually improve the organization's functioning. Learning implies engaging people at all levels in the change process, not just requiring new behaviors in the traditional "top-down" way. Organizations that can overcome the challenges of continuous learning-driven change will escape the "gaps" – between different perspectives at different corporate levels, between aspirations and results, and between experience and learning – that mar all too many IT initiatives.

Suggested further reading

Kleiner, A. and Roth, G. (1997) "How to make experience your company's best teacher", *Harvard Business Review* (Sept.–Oct.). (For more information see www.fieldbook.com/rla-what.htm)

Roth, G. (1998) "Crossing theory and practice boundaries to create new knowledge", Academy of Management Conference Proceedings, San Diego, California (August).

Roth, G. (1998) "Paper documents: implications of changing media for business process redesign", in Wakayama, T. et al. (eds) *Information and Process Integration In Enterprises: Rethinking Documents*, Boston, MA: Kluwer Academic.

Roth, G. and Kleiner, A. (1998) "Developing organisational memory through learning histories", *Organisational Dynamics* (winter). (For more information see http://ccs.mit.edu/lh and http://www.solne.org/res/wp/18001.html)

Senge, P., Kleiner, A., Roberts, C., Roth, G., Ross, R. and Smith, B. (1999) *The Dance of Change: the Challenges to Sustaining Momentum in a Learning Organization*, New York: Doubleday Currency. (For more information see http://www.fieldbook.com)

Lessons from the internet leaders

by Soumitra Dutta

In the last quarter of 1998, INSEAD, in conjunction with British Telecom, conducted research into how leading internet companies were innovating for success in cyberspace. ("Internet companies" are here defined as companies making substantial use of internet technologies.) Drawing on extensive interviews and detailed library research on more than 35 companies, the following critical success factors for organizational innovation were identified:

- clear leadership from top management
- strategic thinking and action in extremely short cycles
- using technology as a catalyst for change

317

- leveraging the intrinsic value of internal and external networks
- building a real-time organization
- integrating the customer into the organization
- encouraging experimentation to push the boundaries of what is possible
- investing in talented people.

In the rest of this article, we will see just how these factors enable internet leaders to succeed.

A clear push from the top

Senior management makes an important difference: this was repeated time and again by executives from different organizations. The organizations most successful at exploiting new internet technologies were the ones whose top management made it a priority.

For example, Guido Jouret, Cisco's IS manager for Europe, the Middle East and Africa, described how John Chambers, the company's chief executive, sees the internet "not just as Cisco's business but also as its way of doing business".

Michael Dell's role within Dell is also exemplary. According to Aine O'Dwyer of Dell Europe, Dell's evangelistic commitment to the internet has been critical to his company's online success. All senior managers have had to buy into the web. Dell's goal is to generate 50 per cent of sales online by 2001.

Strategy on the edge

On the web, companies live in the fast lane. Things change swiftly and often in an uncontrolled manner. Notions of strategic thinking and planning must therefore change. Organizations can no longer rest content with yearly forecasts and three-year planning horizons; strategic thinking needs to happen in internet time.

Jenna Marshall, one of the founders of HomeShark, a leading on-line mortgage lender notes: "Our strategic horizon is six months, perhaps nine months at most. We never plan for more than a year. We know that our business will look very different in two years as compared to now. And we don't exactly know what these differences will be."

Real-time organizations

The first step is the desire to move quickly. The second, more critical step, is having an organization that is capable of reacting in real-time to your strategic changes. Central to this capability is tight integration across different functions. The level of cross-functional integration required in the high-speed environment of the web is an order of magnitude greater than was necessary in the past.

David Cooperstein, a senior analyst with Forrester Research, which was one of the companies examined in the survey, described the situation using an analogy with cars: "In the past, different functions were in their own cars driving at different speeds. Today, they are not only being asked to drive at the same speed, but they all have to be driving together in the same car." Companies that cannot break free of their legacy processes fail to build real-time organizations.

Technology as a catalyst for change

Going online must be a tremendous catalyst for change. To manage such change, there needs to be close integration between IT and the business. Fred Matteson, a manager of IT for Charles Schwab, put this as follows: "In most IT projects, IT and business people sit down together to define the specifications. As far as business is concerned, it is 'fire and forget'. They almost don't see the system until it is time for testing. That is patently different in the web environment, where the collaboration between the business and IT has to be much stronger. We do almost three [software] releases for our website each month. This is much faster than anything that we did before. This would not be possible without constant collaboration with the business."

Management boards need more technology skills than before to lead such change. It is no longer adequate to have business skills or IT skills alone – both must be combined.

Network leverage = value

The internet is a network, and its success lies not in any one node but in the interconnectivity across the nodes. This simple insight into the power of networks is shared by all the surveyed organizations.

The network begins at home. Organizations are rich in bright, creative individuals. Intranets can enable them to talk to each other, share ideas, challenge each other and create new knowledge. The intranet can become a fertile ground for experimenting with new ideas, products and services before they are moved out to customers. Not only does this bring better products to market, but it also encourages the whole organization to participate in the success of the company.

Networks extend into partners and customers. Cisco, for example, has made substantial use of extranets to enhance customer relationships and manage its supply chain. About 45 per cent of Cisco's unit volume is shipped to the customer without Cisco touching the product. The on-line order is transmitted directly to partners who manufacture, assemble and ship the product straight to the customer. Sixty-nine per cent of total company revenues are generated on-line. The percentage is even higher in Europe, where 77 per cent of revenues are due to internet commerce.

The customer as driver

A critical aspect of building a successful e-strategy is the ability to integrate the customer into each and every key process.

Both Yahoo! and Netscape draw upon tens of thousands of volunteer beta testers who play a critical role in evaluating prototype versions of products. Newsgroups bring customers together to discuss product features; their continuous feedback helps Netscape and Yahoo! change product designs swiftly.

Putting the customer in the driving seat makes business sense, especially given the one-to-one marketing focus that is becoming the hallmark of e-commerce. Amazon.com not only welcomes you by name (if you have previously purchased a book) but remembers your preferences and uses data-mining software to suggest related books and relevant subject areas. Amazon.com hopes to make customers feel so at home that they do work for it – such as entering book reviews (which help the company sell books to other customers) and doing the order entry.

Customer feedback is a great direction-setting force in the uncertain world of the internet. In fact, listening to customers may be the best way to arrive at a strategic vision for internet activities.

Experimentation to push boundaries

New ways of working are essential because the internet is a new medium. "It is a new space," says Kathleen Earley, vice-president of AT&T's EasyCommerce Services.

319

"There are no business processes to support you. There are no ground rules to tell you how to do things. You cannot look back at anything that has been done before that will tell you how to do this now."

Successful internet companies are continually experimenting. Yahoo!, for example, is desperately trying to do it all – finance, travel, real estate, health, shopping, news and more. As its chief executive Timothy Koogle stated in an interview with *Business Week* (7 September 1998): "We've taken the lid off." Amazon.com is moving from books into CDs, medicines and other products.

While the market will judge the validity of their strategies, the important lesson is that these companies are taking risks – they are trying to become all that they can be. Large, successful companies frequently resist taking such risks. Bertelsmann, the German publishing company, has taken four years to muster a response to Amazon.com.

Embracing risk often leads to failure: companies therefore need to be able to tolerate failure. Yahoo!'s motto is: "Do what's crazy, but not stupid." A manager from one internet start-up summed up its attitude as follows: "In our organization, failing is acceptable, but failing to learn from failures is not acceptable."

Talent premium

Companies are built on people. Brains are more important than computers. Thus it is not a surprise to see successful companies going the extra mile to get the best people. However, you not only need the best people, but also people of a special kind.

According to Kevin Brown, director of marketing at Inktomi (which provides software for internet infrastructure and media companies such as AOL), "a special breed of people" is required: "These are people who accept an environment of rapid change, aggressive growth, are optimistic and like to have fun while working hard."

Finding such people is not easy, especially when business schools are not producing such graduates en masse. Tapan Bhat, the manager of Quicken.com at Intuit, says the problem is that business schools teach "linear thinking". Yet "the internet is fundamentally a non-linear environment. We need people who can think and act in a non-linear fashion."

Summary

Much has been written about the "front end" of electronic commerce – what actually happens on a website. Yet little attention has been directed to "back end" issues – in particular, to the organizational redesign and innovation that is so critical for success on the internet. As **Soumitra Dutta** explains here, new models of strategic thinking and new business processes are required, while corporate hierarchies need to learn flexibility and to open up departmental boundaries to speed up information flow and decision-making. Drawing on the findings of a recent study of successful internet companies, the author offers advice on how to promote organizational learning.

This article is based on research sponsored by British Telecom's Global Information Exchange (www.infoexchange.bt.com) a free cyber-community of telecoms and IT managers worldwide. More details of the methodology, and a sample survey, are available on the website.

Suggested further reading

Dutta, S. and Srivastava, S. (2000) *Embracing the Net*, London, FT.com

De Mayer, A., Dutta, S. and Srivastava, S. (2001) *The Bright Stuff*, London, Financial Times Prentice Hall.

Strategy and the forgetting organization

by Eric Clemons

During times of environmental turbulence and strategic uncertainty, many previously successful companies decline; some even fail outright. Today's rapid progress in the design and use of information technology has accelerated the speed of market change, and thus the rise of new winners and the decline of previously successful innovators.

These trends are particularly clear in technology-related industries. IBM owned the mainframe business but was slow to see the development of the minicomputer business, which was controlled for years by Digital Equipment; Digital failed to see the transition to smaller and cheaper PCs and rapidly declined, along with Data General, Prime and other players in the minicomputer industry. Wang took the word processing market away from IBM, which had long dominated it with its Selectric Typewriters; Wang's stand-alone word processors, however, were soon overrun by word-processing software systems such as WordPerfect and Word.

Similar trends, only slightly less extreme, are observed in industries that use rather than create IT. We see IT as creating a high degree of strategic uncertainty, which speeds the rise and fall of corporate giants. This has produced a corresponding interest in explaining why some companies innovate and others do not, and why some successful companies adapt and others fail to do so.

Experience suggests that core competences of the past can become codified and inflexible. In times of rapid change they become core rigidities and, ultimately, core incompetences. But while past success can often be a precursor of market failure, there is no single, generally accepted explanation.

Difficulties in changing successful organizations

Two promising explanations have been offered for the difficulties experienced by previously successful companies when confronted with the need to innovate: resistance to competence-destroying change, and listening to the wrong customers.

Competence-destroying change

The difference between continuous or competence-enhancing change and frame-breaking or competence-destroying change has been examined by Michael Tushman and his colleagues at Harvard. According to their framework, competence-enhancing change, while requiring adaptation, does not require a change in skill sets; in contrast, competence-destroying change requires not only a change in strategy and operations, and in the resources to support them, but also the fundamental skills possessed by key executives.

The shift from scale-based marketing in retail banking services to profitability-based, information-intensive, skill-based marketing is an example of competence-destroying change. It reduces the value of the core skill sets of many key employees, especially in marketing and operations, and, theory predicts, will be resisted by them.

12 Nov 1998

DIGITAL BUSINESS

Time for new trade-offs: Peter Martin concludes this series by examining some of the profound changes that will determine whether enterprises flourish or wither in the new digital era

Financial Times

by Peter Martin

It is easy to overstate the importance of the coming of digital business. Although it is powerful and pervasive, affecting most industries and areas of economic activity, it is not the first such "horizontal" change. The coming of the railway, the arrival of fractional-horsepower electric motors, the universal adoption of motor cars and trucks, the emergence of a mass consumer market – all these have had similarly pervasive effects.

But, paradoxically, it is also easy to understate the importance of all such sweeping technological changes, by assuming that they apply only to the companies most directly affected. As the articles in this series have revealed, the real importance of "horizontal" technological change lies in the way it rewrites the trade-offs that underpin established business in all sectors.

These trade-offs – between scale and inflexibility, between service and price, between choice and stocking costs, and so on – are so embedded in the way business works that we scarcely think about them.

In any industry, established businesses gravitate towards the same set of trade-offs, adopted more or less unthinkingly by all participants. Sometimes an innovative company manages to come up with a slightly different set of trade-offs that works. A famous example is General Motors' introduction of model variations and frequent styling changes, to compete with Henry Ford's "any colour you like as long as it's black" Model T.

When this happens, either the industry shifts to a general adoption of the new approach – as happened in the GM/Ford case – or the innovator's discovery turns out to be relevant only to a niche market, and the mainstream approach survives for most customers. Either way, the established set of trade-offs survives, adjusted slightly at the margin. This is the very definition of "business as usual".

The importance of sweeping technological change is that it requires a renegotiation of many of those trade-offs. Just as important, it is hard to tell in advance which trade-offs will survive and which will be completely replaced. A period of intense experimentation and uncertainty begins.

Innovators who guess right about the new pattern of trade-offs – whether they are new entrants or fast-moving established firms – are lavishly rewarded. Companies that guess wrong go out of business. For everyone, the stakes rise immeasurably. That is now happening in the era of digital business.

To conclude this series, let us stand back from the early, currently visible efforts to profit from digital business, and attempt to chart the deeper trade-offs that will change in the new era. Some of these shifts are already being exploited; others await their innovators. Here are three trade-offs that are changing:

■ **Customization versus price.** Giving individual customers exactly what they want is usually too expensive to contemplate. So customers have to choose between a product or service that is approximately right and relatively cheap, or one that is exactly right, but extremely expensive. The coming of digital business changes the trade-off significantly.

In some industries, what prevents the delivery of cheap customized products is ineluctable economies of scale, such as those which make individual computer chips so astonishingly cheap. But in many industries, the real barrier is the cost of information: if you could economically capture the details of the customer's needs and transmit them to the shop floor, you could deliver a customized product but still benefit from the factory's economy of scale. This is particularly true in service industries, or where delivery takes electronic form.

322

The era of mass customization has been promised for at least a decade, but it took the arrival of digital business to make it possible. The secret lies in the creation of a global, standardized communications infrastructure, the internet, and a powerful, universally accessible user interface, the web browser.

As yet, relatively few companies are attempting to make use of the mass customization potential of digital business, and these are mainly companies that had already ventured down this road before migrating to the internet. Online computer vendors, such as Dell and Gateway, were already providing semi-customized products. They are able to do more of this, more cheaply, over the web. And, in Dell's case, they are also able to provide a customized service to corporate purchasers, who have their own dedicated web pages on Dell's site.

Other tentative steps towards mass customization are under way on the web: tailored clothes, customized CDs, personalized information services. Some will turn out to be successful; others will not offer customers enough benefits to overcome the inconvenience of making choices. But either way, the historic trade-off is changing.

■ **Bundled products versus focused ones.** Few products and services are "pure". Most are bundled together with something else. Garages bundle together in one physical location the sale of new cars, the purchase of second-hand ones, the provision of customer finance, the delivery of repairs. Banks bundle together payment services, security of savings, the provision of account information, and so on. Newspapers bundle together news, opinion, classified advertising, entertainment, listings. The trade-offs that produce these bundlings are heavily influenced by information costs: the costs of establishing what particular mix of benefits a customer needs, and then ensuring that it is delivered precisely.

These bundlings involve powerful but implicit cross-subsidies. They survive because they deliver the best mix of benefits at the lowest price. But one customer's cross subsidy is another's mis-pricing. Digital business allows new, focused entrants to expose those cross subsidies and mis-pricings. Electronic classified advertising boards eliminate the cross-subsidy to news (though they also have to survive without a cross-subsidy from display advertising). Electronic new car sales

agencies, such as Microsoft's Carpoint, unbundle a garage's offerings. A flood of financial services products exploit and compete away the cross-subsidies inherent in retail banking.

But remember: bundling exists because it solves problems, either for consumers or producers. Ultimately, the choice will not lie between bundled products and focused ones, but between an old pattern of bundling and a new one. In the meantime, however, any company offering a bundled product or service – which means most companies – must reassess the way the combination works, and ask itself if a different configuration is now more appropriate.

■ **Vertical integration versus "share of customer".** Growth-minded companies have come to an implicit understanding of whether their best opportunities lie in offering a wider range of products to the same customers, or seizing more of the value-added inherent in their existing range of products. Each has drawbacks. One of the principal difficulties in offering more to existing customers lies in getting the sales channel to handle a wider, more complex product range. One of the principal advantages of vertical integration has been the elimination of the information costs of dealing with supply chains.

Digital business changes both of these. Dealing with customers directly, electronically, eases the complexity overload on sales channels. Dealing with suppliers directly lowers the costs of vertical dis-integration. Companies will need to revisit the trade-off between seeking a larger share of the value added they provide the customer and seeking a larger share of each customer's purchasing. Industry value chains will be redrawn.

In resolving this trade-off, much will depend on the company's brand. Is it one which can be effectively extended to cover a wider range of products? If not, the old trade-off may still apply. But in many companies, and in many industries, digital business has changed this trade-off profoundly.

The purpose of this series has been to illustrate the way in which such issues apply to all companies, not just those involved in online retailing or computers. Digital business is not an unprecedented change in the nature of economic activity. But, like other pervasive changes, it will affect every aspect of the business world. And those impacts are already being felt.

Two very different explanations are offered for this behavior. One suggests that key executives will rationally, selfishly and consciously resist acknowledging changes that devalue their skills and lead to their replacement by employees with newer, more appropriate, skill sets. The other, more charitable, explanation suggests that employees have been programmed by previous success. They have been rewarded with promotions, salaries, perks and publicity. Much as American psychologist B.F. Skinner trained pigeons to peck at different shapes and figures in his "Skinner Box", executives have been trained to repeat the strategies and actions that they believe have been rewarded in the past. This unconscious repetition of previously successful actions, when amalgamated over the pool of senior managers and executives, results in an organization's inability to learn new skills.

Listening to the wrong customers

According to Harvard academic Clayton Christensen, in his book *The Innovator's Dilemma* (1997), the greatest problems for successful companies occur when the next innovation is required by a new set of customers. He provides several examples, but the most striking is the introduction of 8-inch and 5-inch disk drives. Existing customers of disk drive manufacturers continued to want larger-capacity, faster disk drives; 14-inch drives remained the norm for their mainframe installations and corporate databases. New customers, who were not yet the customers of disk manufacturers, wanted smaller disk drives for PCs. Since they were not yet customers, manufacturers did not hear them clearly. This is a general phenomenon, the inability to perceive weak new signals ("We will want small and cheap drives for PCs soon") in the presence of stronger, older signals ("We want big and fast drives for mainframes now!").

The most popular prescription for facilitating successful innovation has been to create a learning organization. However, the inability to discard old skills is different from the inability to learn from new messages. Failure to differentiate between them mis-states the problem and thus mis-states the appropriate solution. Organizations do continue to learn during times of stress caused by environmental shifts; unfortunately, they often continue to learn the wrong lessons. Before effective learning can occur it is necessary to forget the well-learned, previously useful and now inappropriate lessons of the past. That is, it is necessary to create a forgetting organization.

The remainder of this chapter explains the need for the forgetting organization and describes some mechanisms for achieving it.

The role of doctrine

Doctrine, in the sense that it is used in military circles, comes before strategy and both guides and constrains it. "Tanks can seize territory, but only infantry can hold it", or "the principal threat to established states comes from other states, with armies and navies and modern weapons" are two examples.

In a commercial setting we can think of doctrine as codified expertise:

- software costs are critical and are largely independent of the size of an organization; thus profitability is inescapably tied to scale and market share in our industry
- retaining an existing customer is much less expensive than acquiring a new customer; thus the satisfaction of every customer, leading to customer loyalty and the retention of every customer, will be critical to our success.

Doctrine is often useful, in that it enables employees to exploit prior learning and to focus on relevant issues. This supports rapid development of strategies and operational plans. Unfortunately, over time, doctrine becomes both inflexible and unconscious; thus it becomes unquestioned and unquestionable. It also loses its applicability over time, changing from the foundation for a core competence to a core rigidity and, ultimately, to a core incompetence. Inappropriate guidelines, like outdated maps, lead to disaster. The problem is that experts want to be guides, and expertise wants to be used and followed, even when the guidance is inapplicable and dangerous.

A group of insurance executives I advised were attempting a radical redesign of their entire company in response to changes in technology and regulation. The redesign was intended to result in changes to their product design, sales and service and the executives assured me that they had "been bold". When I asked what their unstated assumptions had been, they reiterated that they had been bold and that no assumptions had gone unchallenged. I finally shifted my line of inquiry and asked them what facts were so basic that they were known by everyone else but me; they responded by saying they had only two:

- all consumer products would continue to be sold and serviced through agents
- all products would have to be simple enough to be explained by agents and understood by consumers.

The second assumption also implied that they would continue to sell primarily traditional property and casualty products (for example, car insurance) and death benefit products (for example, life insurance). Together these imply that anything can change except the product and its distribution channel. This is, to say the least, not bold. Worse, these assumptions ignore the following trends in the insurance industry:

- improved technology enables agentless alternatives to the current sales and distribution system; agent-based distribution costs are so high that the surrender value of life insurance products is actually negative for the first few years after a policy is purchased
- the increased information endowment of consumers will require fundamental changes to the pricing structure used by most insurance companies. If consumers know whether they are high-risk or low-risk individuals and insurance companies do not, then the highest-risk consumers will purchase the largest policies, increasing company payouts and leading to losses. If an insurance company were to decide to raise premiums to cover the losses, it would simply drive off more of the low-risk individuals
- changes in consumer attitudes towards insurance mean that consumers are less interested in purchasing policies that assure an estate for their heirs, and more interested in policies assuring them income security as they age; income-shifting products demanded by consumers will look more like high-yield investments and less like traditional life insurance products.

In brief, the accumulated wisdom and knowledge of the insurance company's officers were preventing them from perceiving, understanding or adapting to the environment in which they would have to compete. Although the company was ultimately able to understand the implications of these profound changes, they were only able to do so after they had accepted the need to unlearn much of the previously valuable wisdom of the previous decades.

Scenario analysis

To help my insurance colleagues I constructed a brief story, based upon a hypothetical video game called Beat the Reaper. In this game, the objective is to live as long as possible, avoiding disease, car accidents and the like. When Level 1 is mastered, the player is outliving his savings, relying principally upon a limited pension and the generosity of his children. When this becomes embarrassing the player shifts to Level 2, which focuses on developing strategies for personal investment, risk management and income shifting, so that an acceptable quality of life is maintained throughout the course of the game and well into retirement and old age.

When Level 2 is mastered an investment advisor appears on screen, asking if you are satisfied with the financial package you have designed for yourself, if you have any questions, and if you would like quotes on any of the services you have indicated might be appropriate for you. The executives considered this story at least plausible, although it represents a fundamental repudiation of the concept that the insurance industry will continue to offer the same set of products via the same distribution channel. They asked for a process to institutionalize the development of such stories and I introduced them to scenario planning.

Scenario analysis is a tool for strategic planning during times of rapid strategic change, when discontinuities in the business environment make extrapolation from available historical data misleading or meaningless. Rather than deal with the resulting uncertainty by considering best-, worst- and average-case performance, scenario analysis attempts to delimit the environment in which the company may have to operate and to provide a spanning set of alternative futures that cover any eventuality. Again, these scenarios are not intended to represent good, bad and average cases; rather, they are based upon the fundamental driving forces that will determine the business environment, and are intended to enable the company to develop an appropriate strategy.

Scenario planning can be considered as uncertainty-driven rather than data-driven planning, since it begins with questions rather than answers. The basis of scenario planning is to identify the things you cannot know, such that if you could know them, you then would know precisely what you needed to know.

Imagine that an infallible advisor could reliably assure you that after 2005 no consumer will ever go back to a store for shelf-stable packaged goods such as detergent or paper towels. If you were a senior officer at Sainsbury's or Carrefour or Wal-Mart this information would profoundly alter your investment strategy, your acquisition of real estate, and indeed all aspects of your long-term competitive strategy.

Scenario planning does not rely on data; it relies instead on identifying key uncertainties – areas where data would be very useful – and then exploring the implications that would emerge if the data were to assume its most extreme possible values.

One executive I worked with was concerned about the future of electronic securities trading, and wanted to know what data to provide to other members of his company's executive committee to help prepare for a strategic planning session. I suggested that the committee members be provided with no data, and that they attend the meeting armed with their intuitions. I was told that this was irrational, unprofessional and unlikely to lead to a successful planning session. I then asked the following questions, and received the following answers:

"What percentage of equities have been traded purely electronically, off-exchange in this country in the previous six months?"

"Essentially none."

"What percentage of equities have been traded purely electronically, off-exchange in this country in the previous year?"

"Essentially none."

"What percentage of equities have been traded purely electronically, off-exchange in this country, in the previous two, three and five years?"

"None, none and none."

"What percentage of equities have been traded purely electronically, off-exchange in this country, in the previous 25 years?"

"None, of course."

Our discussion continued as follows:

"That's great! We have 25 years of data, and a clear trend-line. Electronic equities trading does not matter. You can cancel the meeting."

"That's ridiculous!"

"How do you know?"

"I just know!"

"That's great! Bring that intuition and ask your colleagues to bring theirs!"

Although the scenario process does not require data, it is still highly structured. Different practitioners follow slightly different procedures, but the following steps are generally performed, in the following order:

Bring the most important uncertainties to the surface
Identify questions that cannot be answered but that appear to matter greatly.

Rank key uncertainties to provide the key drivers
These are the two or three most important unanswerable questions, the things that we cannot know. Yet if we could know them, we then would know precisely what we needed to know.

Combine key uncertainties to yield concrete scenarios
That is, define alternative futures in which each uncertainty is assumed to take one or the other of its extreme values.

Provide details
Turn each scenario into a plausible story, with information on how it might come about and how it would feel to be a consumer, an executive in the company and an executive in a competing company.

This makes it possible to develop an alternative doctrine, or at least to accept the fact that a lot of previous learning and many previous assumptions have now become outdated and inappropriate. This can be determined leisurely, in the relative comfort and safety of an off-site meeting, rather than in an emergency meeting called in response to a collapse of earnings forecasts.

The scenarios tell stories, and these stories have a powerful logic. They are based on the key uncertainties brought up by the executives themselves; they cannot be denied, they cannot be called certain and they cannot be called anything less than critical. The stories are outside current doctrine and sweep it away, together with outdated core rigidities and core incompetences.

Maintaining a learning organization will always be a challenge. It will always be difficult to listen to the weak signals of future change and respond to them rapidly and effectively. This difficulty is only increased when the necessary responses involve competence-destroying rather than competence-enhancing changes. Such changes require the difficult decision to discard under-performing assets that are owned by us, and the even more difficult decision to discard under-performing assets that *are* us. In an environment of rapid, technology-driven change, organizations must be perpetually willing to forget, so that they can continue to learn.

Summary

The corporate scene – notably but by no means exclusively in technology-centered industries – is littered with examples of new players that have overtaken previously successful innovators. There are several explanations for this, including vested employee interests and the common tendency to focus too narrowly on the needs of existing customers. Learning organizations are all very well, explains **Eric Clemons**, but until companies have discarded their old skills the danger is that they will continue to learn the wrong lessons as they go forward. Hence companies must embrace the ideal of the "forgetting organization". This article illustrates how corporate doctrine, often unconsciously, encourages core rigidities; the author urges executives to employ scenario analysis to identify and rank key uncertainties, to create alternative futures, and to turn them into plausible stories to sweep away outdated and inappropriate assumptions.

Suggested further reading

Christensen, C.M. (1997) *The Innovator's Dilemma*, Boston, MA: Harvard Business School Press.

Clemons, E.K. (1995) "Using scenario analysis to manage the strategic risks of reengineering", *Sloan Management Review* (summer): 61–71.

Clemons, E.K. (1997) "Creating the forgetting organization: using the scenario process to facilitate learning during rapid technology-driven environmental change", in Kemerer, C. (ed.) *Information Technology and Industrial Competitiveness: how IT Shapes Competition*, Kluwer, 197–214.

Schwartz, P. (1991) *The Art of the Long View*, New York: Doubleday.

Tushman, M.L. and Anderson, P. (eds) (1997) *Managing Strategic Innovation and Change*, New York: Oxford University Press.

GURU AND PRACTITIONER PERSPECTIVES

11

Contributors

Peter F. Drucker is probably the best-known and most highly-respected management writer. His interest in the topic dates back to the early years of the second world war. He has been Clarke Professor of Social Science and Management at Claremont Graduate University in California since 1971. He has written 30 books on politics and economics.

Brian Davis is chief executive (and former general manager, technology) of the Nationwide Building Society.

Donald A. Norman is professor emeritus at the University of California, San Diego, and a former executive of Apple Computer and Hewlett-Packard. He now has his own company, the Nielsen Norman Group.

Sue Sentell is president, marketing and operations, of Sprint Business, a US telecommunications company.

Louis J. Burns is vice-president and director of information technology at microchip manufacturer Intel.

Contents

Introduction

Earlier modules of *Mastering Information Management* have been peppered with case studies of how real companies cope with the challenges of the information society – but so far the executive voice has not been directly heard. Here we present three very different perspectives from the front line, that of: the director of IT at Intel; the chief executive of the UK's Nationwide Building Society; and the president of marketing and operations at Sprint Business.

History lessons for today's revolutionaries

by Peter F. Drucker

Half a century ago, around 1950, prevailing opinion overwhelmingly held that the market for that new "miracle", the computer, would be in the military and in scientific research. A few of us, however – a very few indeed – argued even then that the computer would find major applications in business and would have an impact on it. These few also foresaw – again very much at odds with the prevailing opinion (even of practically everyone at IBM, just then beginning its ascent) – that in business the computer would be more than a very fast adding machine doing clerical chores such as payroll or telephone bills.

On specifics, we dissenters disagreed, of course, as "experts" always do. But all of us nonconformists agreed on one thing: the computer would, in short order, revolutionize the work of senior management. It would, we all agreed, have its greatest and earliest impacts on business policy, business strategy and business decisions.

We could not have been more wrong. The revolutionary impacts so far have been where none of us then anticipated them: on operations.

Not one of us, for instance, could have imagined the truly revolutionary software now available to architects. At a fraction of traditional cost and time, it designs the "innards" of large buildings. Not one of us could then have imagined the equally revolutionary software available to today's medical students. It enables them to do "virtual operations" whose outcomes include "virtually killing" patients if the surgeon makes the wrong surgical move.

Half a century ago no one could have imagined the software that enables a major equipment maker such as Caterpillar to organize its operations, including manufacturing worldwide, around the anticipated service and replacement needs of its customers. And the computer has had a similar impact on bank operations, with banking probably the most computerized industry today.

But the computer and the IT arising from it have so far had practically no impact on the decision whether or not to build a new office building, a school, a hospital or a prison, or on what its function should or could be. They have had practically no impact on the decision to perform surgery on a critically ill patient or on what surgery to perform. They have had no impact on the decision of the equipment manufacturer concerning which markets to enter and with which products, or on the decision of a major bank to acquire another major bank. For senior management tasks, information technology so far has been a producer of data rather than a producer of information – let alone a producer of new and different questions and new and different strategies.

The people in management information systems (MIS) and in IT tend to blame this failure on what they call the "reactionary" executives of the "old school". It is the wrong explanation. Senior executives have not used the new technology because it has not provided the information they need for their own tasks. The data available in business enterprise are, for instance, still largely based on the early 19th-century theorem that lower costs differentiate businesses and make them

333

compete successfully. MIS has taken the data based on this theorem and computerized them. They are the data of the traditional accounting system.

Accounting was originally created, at least 500 years ago, to provide the data a company needed for the preservation of its assets and for their distribution if the venture were liquidated. And the one major addition to accounting since the 15th century – cost accounting, a child of the 1920s – aimed only at bringing the accounting system up to 19th-century economics, namely, to provide information about, and to control, costs.

But, as we began to realize around the time of the second world war, neither preservation of assets nor cost control are senior management tasks. They are operational tasks. A serious cost disadvantage may indeed destroy a business. But business success is based on something totally different, the creation of value and wealth. This requires risk-taking decisions: on the theory of the business, on business strategy, on abandoning the old and devising the new, on the balance between immediate profitability and market share. These decisions are the true senior management tasks.

It was this recognition that underlay, after the second world war, the emergence of management as a discipline, separate and distinct from what was then called business economics and is now called microeconomics. But for none of these top management tasks does the traditional accounting system provide information. Indeed, none of these tasks is even compatible with the assumptions of the traditional accounting model.

The new IT, based on the computer, had no choice but to depend on the accounting system's data. No others were available. It collected these data, systematized them, manipulated them, analyzed them and presented them. On this rested, in large measure, the tremendous impact the new technology had on what cost accounting data were designed for: operations. But it also explains information technology's near-zero impact on the management of business itself.

Senior management's frustration with the data that information technology has so far provided has triggered the new, the next, information revolution. Information technologists, especially chief information officers in businesses, soon realized that the accounting data are not what their associates need – which largely explains why MIS and IT people tend to be contemptuous of accounting and accountants. But they did not, as a rule, realize that what was needed was not more data, more technology, more speed. What was needed was to define information; what was needed were new concepts. And in one enterprise after another, senior management people during the past few years have begun to ask, "What information concepts do we need for our tasks?" And they have now begun to demand them of their traditional information providers, the accounting people.

A little humility

The current information revolution is actually the fourth information revolution in human history. The first was the invention of writing 5,000 to 6,000 years ago in Mesopotamia; then – independently but several thousand years later – in China; and some 1,500 years later still, by the Maya in Central America. The second information revolution was brought on by the invention of the written book, first in China, perhaps as early as 1300 BC, and then, independently, 800 years later in Greece, when Pisistratus, the tyrant of Athens, had Homer's epics – only recited until then – copied into books.

The third information revolution was set off by Gutenberg's invention of the printing press and of movable type between 1450 and 1455, and by the contemporaneous invention of engraving. We have almost no documents on the first two of these revolutions, although we know that the impact of the written book was enormous in Greece and Rome as well as in China. But on the third information revolution, printing and engraving, we have abundant material. Is there anything we can learn today from what happened 500 years ago?

The first thing to learn is a little humility.

Everybody today believes that the present information revolution is unprecedented in reducing the cost of, and in the spreading of, information – whether measured by the cost of a "byte" or by computer ownership – and in the speed and sweep of its impact. These beliefs are simply nonsense.

At the time Gutenberg invented the press, there was a substantial information industry in Europe. It was probably Europe's biggest employer. It consisted of hundreds of monasteries, many of which housed large numbers of highly skilled monks. Each monk labored from dawn to dusk, six days a week, copying books by hand. An industrious, well-trained monk could do four pages a day, or 25 pages during a six-day week, for an annual output of 1,200 to 1,300 handwritten pages.

Fifty years later, by 1500, the monks had become unemployed. These monks (some estimates go well above 10,000 for all of Europe) had been replaced by a very small number of lay craftsmen, the new "printers", totalling perhaps 1,000, but spread over all of Europe (though only beginning to establish themselves in Scandinavia). To produce a printed book required co-ordinated teamwork by up to 20 such craftsmen, beginning with one highly skilled cutter of type and going up to a much larger number, maybe 10 or more, of much less skilled bookbinders.

Such a team produced each year about 25 titles, with an average of 200 pages per title, or 5,000 pages ready to be printed. By 1505, print runs of 1,000 copies were becoming common. This meant that a printing team could produce annually at least 5m printed pages, bound into 25,000 books ready to be sold – or 250,000 pages per team member as against the 1,200 or 1,300 the individual monk had produced only 50 years earlier.

Prices fell dramatically. As late as the mid-1400s – just before Gutenberg's invention – books were such a luxury that only the wealthy and educated could afford them. But when Martin Luther's German Bible came out in 1522 (a book of well over 1,000 pages), its price was so low that even the poorest peasant family could buy one.

The cost and price reductions of the third information revolution were at least as great as those of the present, the fourth information revolution. And so were the speed and the extent of its spread.

Implications for the technologists

The last information revolution, the printed book, may also have a lesson for today's information technologists, the IT and MIS people and the chief information officers: they will not disappear – but they may be about to become "supporting cast" rather than the "superstars" they have been during the past 40 years.

The printing revolution immediately created a new class of information technologists, just as the most recent information revolution has created any number of information businesses, MIS and IT specialists, software designers and CIOs. The IT people of the printing revolution were the early printers. Nonexistent – and

335

indeed not even imaginable – in 1455, they had become stars 25 years later. These virtuosi of the printing press were known and revered all over Europe, just as the names of the leading computer and software firms are recognized and admired worldwide today. Printers such as was the famous Venetian Aldus Manutius (1449–1515) and Christophe Plantin of Antwerp (1514–89) were courted by kings, princes, the Pope and rich merchant cities and were showered with money and honors.

By 1580 or so the printers, with their focus on technology, had become ordinary craftsmen, respectable tradesmen to be sure, but definitely no longer of the upper class. And they had also ceased to be more profitable than other trades and to attract investment capital. Their place was soon taken by what we now call publishers (though the term wasn't coined until much later), people and firms whose focus was no longer on the "T" in IT but on the "I".

This shift got under way the moment the new technology began to have an impact on the meaning of information, and with it, on the meaning and function of the 15th century's key institutions, such as the church and the universities. It thus began at the same juncture at which we now find ourselves in the present information revolution. Is this where information technology and information technologists are now?

The new print revolution

There is actually no reason to believe that the new information revolution has to be "high-tech" at all. For we have had a real "information revolution" during the past fifty years, from 1950 on. But it is not based on computers and electronics. The real boom – and it has been a veritable boom – has been in that old "no-tech" medium, print.

In 1950, when television first swept the country, it was widely believed that it would be the end of the printed book. The US population since then has grown by two-thirds. The number of college and university students – the most concentrated group of users and buyers of books – has increased fivefold. But the number of printed books published and bought in the US has grown at least 15-fold, and probably close to 20-fold.

Even faster than the growth of the book publishers has been the growth of another print medium: the "speciality mass magazine". A good many of the huge-circulation "general magazines" that dominated 1920s and 1930s America – *Life*, for instance, or *The Saturday Evening Post* – have disappeared. They did indeed fall victim to television. But there are in the US now several thousands – one estimate is more than 3,000 – speciality mass magazines, each with a circulation between 50,000 and 1m, and most highly profitable.

The most visible examples are magazines that cover business or the economy. The three leading US magazines of this type – *Business Week* (a weekly), *Fortune* (a biweekly) and *Forbes* (a monthly) – each have a circulation approaching 1m. Before the second world war the London-based *Economist* – the world's only magazine that systematically reports every week on economics, politics and business all the world over – was practically unknown outside the UK; and even there its circulation was quite small, well below 100,000 copies. Now its US circulation alone exceeds 300,000 copies a week.

And there are similar speciality mass-circulation magazines in every field and for every interest. So what explains the success of the print media?

College students probably account for the largest single share of the growth of printed books in the US. It is growth in college texts and in books assigned by college teachers. But the second-largest group are books that did not exist before the 1950s, at least not in any quantity. There is no English word for them. But the German publisher who first saw their potential and first founded a publishing house expressly to publish such books, the late E.B. von Wehrenalp (who founded Econ Verlag in Düsseldorf – still my German publisher), called it the *Sachbuch*, a book written by an expert for nonexperts. And when asked to explain the *Sachbuch*, Wehrenalp said: "It has to be enjoyable reading. It has to be educational. But its purpose is neither entertainment nor education. Its purpose is information."

This is just as true of the speciality mass magazines – whether written for the layman who wants to know about medicine or for the plumber who wants to know what goes on in the plumbing business. They inform. And above all, they inform people about the outside. The speciality mass magazine tells the reader in a profession, a trade, an industry what goes on outside his or her own business, shop or office – about the competition; about new products and new technology; about developments in other countries; and, above all, about people in the profession, the trade, the industry (and gossip has always had the highest information – or misinformation – quotient of all communication).

And now the printed media are taking over the electronic channels. The fastest-growing bookseller since Aldus Manutius, 500 years ago, has been Amazon.com, which sells printed books over the internet. In a few, very short years it may have become the internet's largest retail merchant. And Bertelsmann, in the autumn of 1998, bought a controlling 50 per cent in Barnes & Noble, Amazon.com's main competitor. More and more speciality mass magazines now publish an "online" edition – delivered over the internet to be printed out by the subscriber. Instead of IT replacing print, print is taking over the electronic technology as a distribution channel for printed information.

The new distribution channel will surely change the printed book. New distribution channels always do change what they distribute. But however delivered or stored, it will remain a printed product. And it will still provide information.

The market for information exists, in other words. And, though still disorganized, so is the supply. In the next few years – surely not much more than a decade or two – the two will converge. And that will be the real new information revolution – led not by IT people, but by accountants and publishers. And then both enterprises and individuals will have to learn what information they need and how to get it. They will have to learn to organize information as their key resource.

Summary

The "unprecedented" information revolution that we are now witnessing is nothing of the sort. The invention of the printed book over 500 years ago had an impact that was every bit as great and immediate. And today's most significant changes may be less "high-tech" than we suppose.

337

The invisible computer

by Donald A. Norman

Today we are at a critical point in the deployment of information technology. Businesses and other organizations have come to rely heavily on the personal computer and its attendant communication and network structures. The PC has evolved to become the standard way of doing many things, despite its many flaws, despite its complexity, despite the fact that it is amazingly ill-suited for many of the tasks that it performs.

Once an infrastructure gets established, it is very difficult to change. Even when it is clear that new methods would provide superior results, the old ways linger on, for they are so deeply embedded in the culture of a society, so deeply ingrained in the ways that people have learned to live, work and play, that change can take place only very slowly, sometimes taking decades.

Why you don't really want to use a computer (even though you think you do)

Do you really want to use a computer? Do you want to use a word processor? Of course not. The fact that you think you do is the triumph of marketing and advertising over common sense. Now, maybe if you are a confirmed technology addict, or a computer programmer, you love using computers – but that's not true of the rest of us. We want to get on with our lives.

I don't want to use a computer. I don't want to do word processing. I want to write a letter, or find out what the weather will be, or pay a bill, or play a game. I don't want to use a computer, I want to accomplish something. I want to do some activity, something meaningful to me. Not "applications", not some bizarre, complex computer program that does more than I ever want to know about and yet doesn't really do exactly what I need. I want computing that fits my activities. I want the technology hidden away, out of sight. Like electric motors. Like the computers that control my car.

Once upon a time, cars were difficult to use. They had controls, meters and gauges. Drivers needed to understand spark adjustment, fuel priming, choke and throttle. There was little standardization, so every car worked differently. Some were steered with wheels, some with tillers, some with levers. The speed of the engine was adjusted by foot or by hand, by pedals, levers or knobs.

In the earliest days of motoring you had to take your mechanic along with you when you went for a drive. To start your car you had to prime the fuel, adjust the spark setting, set the choke, open the throttle, and then stand outside the car beside the engine and crank it by hand, being careful that it didn't start at the wrong time and break your arm.

Today, now that cars are extremely reliable, all you really need is a speedometer to tell you how fast you are moving and a fuel gauge to tell you when you are running low, and that's about it. Anything else can be done with warning lights or messages that only come on when they are needed, ideally to warn you before problems arise, when there is still enough time to take corrective action or get help before there is trouble.

But there is still room for improvement. Manufacturers should get rid of the current fuel gauge that says what fraction of the tank still has fuel in it and replace it with one that says how far or how long we can go with the remaining petrol. Start driving more efficiently and the remaining distance goes up. Start driving less efficiently and the distance goes down. It wouldn't be difficult to add a time estimate: "Twenty minutes to empty."

Notice that this computer is very limited in its functionality: it tells the range of driving with the remaining fuel. Nothing more, nothing less.

This is the way computers ought to be – invisible, automatic and useful – not just in the car, but in the home, at schools and in the office. Useful for doing things, for getting answers, for having fun, for presenting us with the information we need to know, information we can use directly without further thought. This is what information appliances are all about.

Information appliances are designed specifically to fit the task, to fit the needs of their users. This makes them far better suited to do the job well, simply and in a manner appropriate to people.

Now, the concept worries people, for the specialized nature of the information appliance means that we are apt to need a lot of them. No problem, because they will be like all our other appliances: we will buy just the ones we want, just the versions that fit our lives. Their simplicity and utility make up for their specialization.

Why the PC is so complex

The major problem with today's PC is complexity. The complexity of the PC is fundamental to it, and there are three major reasons for this: the attempt to make a single device do too many things; the need to have a single machine suffice for every person in the world; and the business model of the computer industry.

Make a single device do everything and each task will be done in a manner that is adequate but not superior. A multi-purpose device cannot be optimized for any single task; it has to be a compromise. Its physical shape, the nature of its controls and displays, are all compromises.

Imagine a musical instrument that combines the violin, guitar, flute and piano keyboard. Can it be done? Of course: a good PC's music synthesizer program will produce the sounds of all these instruments from a typewriter keyboard. But will it produce inspired music? Will a real musician use it? Of course not.

The second cause of the computer's inherent complexity is that computer companies make products intended to be used by hundreds of millions of people all around the world. "Know your customer" is the mantra of good design, but how can you possibly know your customers when there could be millions of them, of every age, every educational level and every social and cultural group. How could you hope to satisfy every conceivable need and style of work?

Because each country, each culture and, for that matter, each individual, has different interests and needs, the product has to have a large set of features and operations in order to satisfy everyone who might use it. No matter that any individual is apt to use only a very small number of features or commands: to satisfy the world market, the product must have everything. Trying to make one device to fit everyone in the world is a sure path towards an unsatisfactory product: either it will fail to accommodate the critical needs of some of its intended users, or it will provide unnecessary complexity for everyone.

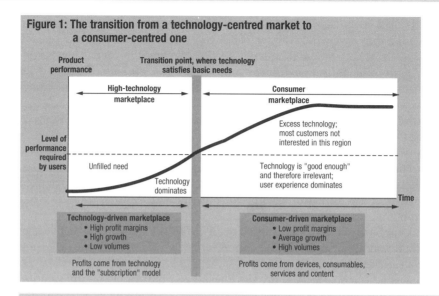

Figure 1: The transition from a technology-centred market to a consumer-centred one

When technology reaches the point at which it satisfies user needs, consumers no longer seek the best technology; they seek the most convenient, the one with the most satisfactory user experience, lowest cost and high reliability. In some cases, they seek prestige.

Brand name and reputation become major selling factors. Profit margins drop but sales volumes rise; the entire business structure changes. As a result, the company itself must change if it is to survive the transition.

Finally, there is the business model, the strategy that the computer industry follows in order to ensure that it can make money year after year. There is nothing wrong with this: a company that fails to make money soon goes out of business and then it cannot be of use to anyone, even if its products are loved and respected. But the strategy adopted by the computer industry is also one that dooms it to build an ever-increasing level of complexity into its products.

The business model of information appliances

The business model of the information appliance is very different from that of the PC. The information appliance industry is disruptive to the PC industry; it changes everything: design principles, marketing, the role the product plays in business, family and education. And the manner in which companies make their money also changes.

Appliances are consumer products, whereas computers are technology products: therein lies the major difference in the market. Computers emphasize technology, appliances emphasize convenience and ease of use; they downplay or even hide the technology. Computers are really targeted at technology enthusiasts, even if they are bought by a larger segment of buyers. Computer companies stand in strong contrast to consumer electronics and consumer appliance companies.

The differences in these two markets reveals itself in another way, as shown in Figure 1. In the world of high technology, profits come from the technology itself, from the sale of hardware and software. The continued revenue stream is generated by the "subscription" model of marketing, in which a planned obsolescence – and complementary upgrade – of both software and hardware occurs yearly. Most users try to resist the yearly upgrades, but they soon discover that a two-year-old computer is incapable of running the most modern software, and unless they use the most recent versions of software they can no longer share files and data with their colleagues. In the high-technology industry, goods have high profit margins and there is a high rate of growth, but the sales volumes are low, at least compared to the potential marketplace of all the households in the world.

The information appliance business is very different from the computer business. Here, the model is much more like that of consumer products in general, especially household appliances, hardware and consumer electronics. In the consumer electronics market, companies sell relatively inexpensive devices that last for years with no maintenance. In this market, competition is fierce and, as a result, profit margins are low. Growth is reasonable, but not at the rate that high-technology companies are accustomed to. But sales volumes can be huge.

Putting humans first

Now comes the fun. The time has come to move to the third generation of PC or, if you will, personal technologies. This will be the generation where the technology disappears into the tool, serving valuable functions but keeping out of the way – the generation of the invisible computer.

The first steps have already occurred. We already use a variety of information appliances, usually without even being aware of the fact – which is the way it ought to be. The list of existing information appliances is surprisingly long: electronic reference books, address books, calendars and diaries; dual- and multiple-language dictionaries and encyclopedias; physician's guides and travel guides; navigation systems for cars that provide specific driving instructions and sometimes relevant restaurant, hotel and entertainment information; digital cameras; the stand-alone printer that prints anything beamed to it by a standardized infrared protocol (which is used only for digital cameras today but will soon encompass many other devices); electronic test equipment, such as oscilloscopes, voltmeters and circuit checkers; a wide variety of calculators – some simple, some specialized for business, for real estate, for statistics or for algebra and calculus, some that contain communication protocols, some that don't; the pocket-size stock quote machine that can be customized to reveal just those statistics and quotes of interest to the owner; the cellular telephone; the fax; the pager; the variety of game machines for the home; and the ever-increasing number of internet appliances for browsing, for e-mail, and for a variety of services and catalogue purchases.

Most of these appliances have taken only the first step. They perform sophisticated information processing without requiring guidance from their users in ways appropriate to the task and the environment. They have been designed with the specific needs of the consumer in mind: they provide value, ease of use and simplicity. But they are isolated from one another. They seldom communicate, except perhaps through proprietary protocols; the devices of one manufacturer can interact with other devices of the same manufacturer, but not with others. As a result, these information appliances have only partially fulfilled their potential.

I imagine a thriving appliance industry offering a large choice to the consumer. Different manufacturers will have different philosophies of what their customers need, thereby providing consumers with a wide array of choices: whatever their preferences, whatever tasks and activities they want to go together, they will be able to get devices to suit. Couple this with a standardized, international protocol for sharing information so that any manufacturer's device can share information with any other manufacturer's device, and the result will be whole systems of powerful, interconnected appliances, offering benefits not even contemplated today.

We already see this working in the music industry, with its array of instruments intended for a range of musical tastes, abilities and budgets. We see it working in the consumer electronics industry, with its huge variety of kitchen, entertainment and business appliances. The result is a healthy market for all concerned, whether consumer, retailer or manufacturer.

Although industry may question the change, consumers do not: for the consumer, there are only benefits. From the consumer's point of view, the change is highly desirable: it will reduce cost, increase functionality, and provide new services and useful, informative, enjoyable content.

Information appliances will mean less fuss and bother, and simpler, more convenient devices. Flexibility and versatility will increase; people will discover new modes of interaction, of learning, of conducting business and recreation. Products will be more reliable and offer greater pleasure. It is a magnificent win.

The successful family of information appliances will be built around the people who use them and the tasks to be performed. Products in the world of IT have suffered far too long under existing technology-centred designs. It is time for a change, time for a human-centred design philosophy. People are not machines; they have very different requirements.

Today, it is the person who must conform to the needs of technology. It is time to make a technology that conforms to the needs of the person.

Summary

The personal computer has become central to today's business infrastructure, yet it is poorly suited to many of the tasks that it has to perform. Perhaps its worst fault is excessive complexity, which stems from the fact that it is designed to suit multiple tasks and customers. Another factor is the PC industry's business model, in which a revenue stream is generated by continuous upgrades of "obsolete" hardware and software. This produces high profit margins and growth but sales volumes – relative to the potential market – are low. The time has come, says **Donald Norman**, for a new generation of technology – the information appliance. The information appliance is specialized for a particular task and matches the needs of the user; unlike the PC, the technology it contains is invisible and is subordinated to function. Information appliance markets will be characterized by massive sales volumes but relatively low growth and profit margins. Information appliances exist today – examples are mobile phones and electronic reference books – but only when there are universal protocols for sharing data will their full potential be realized.

This article is taken from *The Invisible Computer: Why Good Products Fail, the Personal Computer is so Complex and Information Appliances are the Solution* by Donald A. Norman (MIT Press, 1998).

The view from the top

by Louis J. Burns, Brian Davis and Sue Sentell

Adding value, not cost

by Louis J. Burns

In the past, most IT organizations have focused more on managing technology – by deploying cost-effective servers, systems and networks – than on managing information. And today, many organizations still view IT as a service provider and cost center rather than a strategic business partner. In this model, the focus is on driving down the cost of IT products and services with little consideration for the competitive advantage they provide.

Cost reduction and other goals

Total cost of ownership (TCO) is an industry indicator used by IT consulting and analyst firms to measure IT efficiency. In addition to system depreciation and support costs, TCO metrics include the lost end-user productivity due to system downtime.

While reducing TCO continues to be a key objective for IT groups, we need to ask ourselves, "What do we get in return for our investment?" One of the key drivers for IT at Intel is the need to provide a computing environment that operates at near perfect uptime. Reduced cost of ownership is not in itself viewed as our main strategic goal but is a result of enabling employees to perform their business tasks more effectively and efficiently. Our charter is to provide an IT capability that enables Intel to run continuously by reducing downtime and delivering an excellent service. We look at TCO as a measure of how effective we are at making the corporation more competitive, making our employees more productive, and creating business opportunities.

Problems and solutions

In terms of shifting the focus from cost to IT value and competitive advantage, there are many examples of how IT organizations can produce a staggering return on investment by providing constant computing capabilities.

Several years ago, Intel's IT was faced with three serious problems that plague most IT organizations. Our customers were not satisfied with the quality of our services, the number of employees we were supporting was growing rapidly and the finance department was looking for budget reductions. We knew that if we focused solely on reducing cost of ownership, we would not be able to guarantee the reliable and powerful computing environment Intel requires. However, as we explored our options, we realized that a comprehensive approach would allow us to relieve all three pressures.

Over the past three years, we have worked to build a network which not only brings us reduced cost of ownership, but also provides the computing flexibility the company needs for the future. We use PC processing power to compress and encrypt files before they are sent over the network, and to monitor systems to detect viruses before they affect our enterprise environment.

A single roadmap for information management

Intel's IT function is responsible for delivering the critical business applications that run the company – from general ledgers and employee records to e-mail and supply chain management. In the past, critical business applications inside Intel were distributed among business groups, each with its own development roadmap. This affected our ability to give customers the service and support they required. Customers were experiencing long lead times and delays in order fulfilment.

To address these problems, Intel rallied the key business groups within the company to develop integrated business processes worldwide. The IT function facilitated the transformation by designing, building and supporting a three-tier computing infrastructure, consisting of a database engine, application servers and a client interface. The greater integration gives Intel world-class capabilities in the areas of order management, production planning, factory execution and worldwide direct shipping; this delivers real business benefits for Intel customers and a competitive advantage for the company.

Today, Intel's order management system allows business groups to provide instant price and product availability quotes, reserve materials for future orders, take orders for material, and bill the customer when delivery is made. Customer service representatives can place orders, monitor deliveries, look at real-time supply information from factories, and book against worldwide availability. Over time, the system and the information it provides has also helped the factories to achieve optimum production levels. Delivery performance today is at an all-time high and missed delivery dates have been halved since 1995.

A major productivity issue facing Intel and other large organizations is the difficulty employees face when they attempt to access the information they need, when they need it. While corporations have enormous amounts of intellectual property, company information, documents and presentations, most employees are unaware of this information and many are unable to find it even if they know what they are looking for. Therefore we are developing decision support tools that will deliver a consistent, easy-to-use interface for viewing, analyzing and modelling business information.

Another challenge is the complex task of managing the chain of events from a customer's order, to manufacture, to distribution and support. Intel's solution has been to integrate the information required to manage these events into a single supply-chain business application. In addition to increased supply chain synergy, this system is the foundation for our electronic business capability that enables OEM customers to order products directly from our supply chain systems via a secure web interface.

In 1998, we invested a lot of time, money and effort in creating a new electronic business capability for the corporation. The business case was based on the goal of capturing $1bn in revenues through the e-business system by the end of 1998; we surpassed that goal by more than three times. E-business now accounts for a significant portion of Intel's worldwide revenues because it gives customers more timely, accurate information and responsiveness. That is truly a strategic business advantage. That is the business value of IT.

From cost center to value center

Business and IT executives need to work together as strategic partners to maximize the value of corporate information. For many, this may involve a transition from viewing IT as a "cost center" that provides basic services to viewing, and investing in, IT as a "value center" that meets strategic business objectives.

Air time for technologists

by Brian Davis

I am a scientist by training and inclination and it never ceases to amaze me how people are surprised to discover that I am a chief executive. It is almost as if I have succeeded despite the hefty handicap of being a scientist.

Yet people are eager enough to apply the term "rocket scientist" to whizz kids in financial markets. The implication is that, because of the leading-edge activities and mega-deals that comprise their working lives, these people are operating beyond the realm of mere mortals. It is as if there is a point at which day-to-day science, knowledge of which puts people into the "oddball" category, becomes super-science, knowledge of which is slightly awe-inspiring. This amuses me because I am a rocket scientist; my PhD thesis looked at why solid-fuel rockets sometimes explode unexpectedly.

Why is there this strange reaction to scientists operating in a commercial world? After all, running a business – any business – involves a lot of interaction with numbers and an increasing use of computers. The one thing most scientists have in common is a pretty good understanding of mathematics and, because computers have been used since their invention to monitor experiments and analyze results, we also have pretty good knowledge of how they can best be used.

My conclusion is that the reaction is due to another skill requirement which, sadly, is not commonly associated with technically minded individuals – communication. And to avoid any confusion I am, of course, referring to speaking and presenting rather than the bits of wire and fiber-optic cables that make modern communications possible. Anyone reading this is probably already tut-tutting about my command of the written word.

For me I think the communication issue was brought home most acutely during the merger between the Anglia and Nationwide Building Societies. At the time, in 1986/7, this was the largest building societies' merger and was characterized by the fact that it really was a merger. This meant that a great deal of give and take was required to ensure that not only were the best solutions adopted from the two organizations, but that balance was maintained in the allocation of jobs, the retention of branches and the use of technology.

I was in charge of the technology division and it was fascinating to sit in meetings between the technical and marketing task forces who were grappling with the merger issues. The marketers, not surprisingly, wanted members of the new building society to be able to carry out transactions on the premises of either of the precursor organizations, regardless of which society they had originally belonged to. The technologists had to explain that, since both organizations had entirely different computer systems, a common member interface was, to put it mildly, tricky.

However, because the marketers were so good at making their case (and the technologists were not so experienced at the gentle art of persuasion) there was a clear danger that the technical experts would find themselves agreeing helplessly to all sorts of things that they could not realistically deliver. It was crucial to allow the technical teams about four times as much "air time" to get their messages across, in order to counteract the marketers' superior presentation skills.

Everyone was, of course, on the same side; but an interesting observation – and one that is still true of many senior management meetings in other organizations today – is that, because of the nature of the debate, the technical people were thought by many to be (a) on the defensive, (b) constantly saying "no", and (c) always wanting to spend more money.

I genuinely think that there are many organizations that still see technology as a cost to be constantly managed down instead of an investment in the future. It is particularly frustrating to realize that in the UK we could solve some of the most serious problems we face today by investing in technology.

Take road and rail congestion. Weekday travel is characterized by millions of people moving from the community in which they live to a workplace many miles away. Multitudinous off-site meetings make even more journeys – and pollution – necessary. An investment in building electronic motorways instead of the asphalt variety would enable greater use of home- or community-based workers and dramatically reduce the need for travelling. Could this happen? A crude example was once said to be alright for social purposes but highly unlikely to catch on for business use – yet where would we be today without the telephone?

Investment in electronic motorways could also benefit public health. At present, anyone who thinks they are ill has to travel to a surgery, wait with people who probably are ill, see a doctor who gets called away on an emergency just when it is their turn, and finally travel home. Online diagnosis over a video link, initially with an electronic doctor, would speed everything up and reduce the risk of infection (not to mention traffic and pollution).

I'll stop at education. It is pleasing to see the UK government investing in computers for schools and teachers. Computer-based training is well established in industry; computer-based education – incorporating sound, video, regular updates, educational games, tests with built-in feedback and coaching – could bring tremendous benefits.

To achieve progress we need people who are able to see the benefits that investing in technology can bring. I hope to see more technologists in boardrooms – and in national and local government too.

And as a final comment I would also commend any young technologists with managerial aspirations to hone their communications skills. Try joining an amateur dramatics group – I did. At the very least you will be surprised how much your technical skills are appreciated.

A 'decision warehouse' for all

by Sue Sentell

One of the most common challenges for businesses is developing a mechanism for gaining comprehensive, useful and accessible enterprise-wide knowledge about customers. Some 12 years ago, Sprint faced this very problem. The telephone industry was rapidly becoming an integrated telecommunications industry, our customer base was briskly expanding, and new technologies such as the internet were taking off. It became clear that the ability to compete in the future would depend upon a level of customer information and technical sophistication that we simply did not have.

With this in mind, Decision Warehousing, a division of Sprint's IT department, was developed in 1988. Its purpose was simply to improve customer interaction through data collection and reporting. Decision Warehouse is a roughly 10-terabyte database that integrates data from customer service representatives, automated use data, internal research and other sources. It contains information on some 24m customer accounts, including, among other things, use, demographics and billing.

By 1998, when the system came fully online, it had expanded into every sector of Sprint, from financials to product testing. During the previous decade, it had moved through five sometimes stressful stages of development and integration:

Phase I (1988–90): "Infrastructure"
We began to look at large database concepts with the single goal of improving interaction with customers.

Phase II (1991–93): "Experiment, learn, grow"
Initial concepts and services were rolled out to the consumer services department so that it could experiment with marketing opportunities and product development.

Phase III (1994–95): "Field of dreams"
With what we learned in Phase II, information from the small and large business divisions was integrated into the Warehouse. The primary internal client was no longer just marketing but also financials.

Phase IV (1996–97): "Rethink, redesign"
The entire system was redesigned with the goal of integrating all the company's data needs, from customer service to sales, finance and operations.

Phase V (1998): "Franchise management"
With Decision Warehousing fully integrated across Sprint, the system began to affect the entire company, from the products and services level to the corporate division level.

The transition to company-wide acceptance and use of the system has not been easy. Since the first internal clients for Decision Warehousing were consumer services and marketing, as the rest of the company was brought online people tended to view it as just a customer service device. It has taken a lot of time to get people to view Decision Warehousing as a fundamental change in the way Sprint gathers and leverages information – to see it as a means of continually increasing speed-to-market and creating operational efficiencies.

The "rethink, redesign" phase of 1996–97 was required to establish an enterprise-wide protocol for capturing data at each touchpoint (whether customer service, accounting or use), analyzing that information, and redistributing it as value-added intelligence. We had to convince ourselves that collecting and using intelligence would indeed bring benefits for people in all parts of the organization. People are naturally protective of the information they possess, so getting them to share it has been a constant challenge.

Since it has been established, however, Decision Warehousing has had some dramatic business effects, including a surprising reduction in the cost of product testing. The system has enabled us to double the number of product tests that can be performed on a given number of products and services; the speed to market of many products has effectively halved. Electronic product testing uses customer information in the Decision Warehouse to analyze the propensity of a given set of customers to buy a product or discount. No market study needs to be done, and market tests are all run against the existing database.

Another consequence of Decision Warehousing has been increased customer relationship management. Since we know exponentially more about customers and their needs, we can identify products and services that best fit a customer's lifestyle and thereby extend Sprint's relationship with that customer. The system looks at the products and services a customer signs up for and determines their costs both to Sprint and to the customer. Since Decision Warehousing automatically tracks customers' behavior patterns, Sprint can actively and very quickly identify targeted products for specific customers that will yield maximum profits for Sprint and cost the customer less.

Decision Warehousing is constantly evolving. The database gets larger every day and it is a constant challenge to keep the information up to date. And it has not come cheap – 10 years of design and redesign by 3,000 software developers never does. But the savings in terms of product testing, speed-to-market, customized marketing management, customer profiling, risk management and other activities have had a direct and positive effect on our operating margin.

Glossary

application: A piece of software designed to meet a specific purpose.

chief information officer (CIO): The senior executive in a company responsible for information management and for delivering IT services.

client/server architecture: A type of network in which computer processing is distributed among many individual PCs (clients) and a more powerful, central computer (server). Clients can share files and retrieve data stored on the server.

collaborative software: Groupware, such as Lotus Notes or Microsoft Exchange.

computer-aided design (CAD): Refers to any computer-enabled method of design; also called computer-assisted design.

database: A computer software package for storing data.

data-mining: The process of discovering previously unknown information from the data in data warehouses.

data warehouse: A place – virtual or physical – in which business knowledge and information is stored.

e-commerce: business transactions conducted over extranets or the internet.

enterprise resource planning: An integrated system of operation applications combining logistics, production, distribution, contract and order management, sales forecasting, and financial and HR management.

electronic data interchange (EDI): Electronic transmission of documents through point-to-point connections using a set of standard forms, messages and data elements; this can be via leased lines, private networks or the internet.

e-mail: A system that enables computer users to send messages to one another's machines; ideally it should allow them to attach files and find other users' mail addresses.

extranet: An extended intranet, based on internet-standard protocols which allows access via the internet by people outside the enterprise.

hardware: The magnetic, mechanical and electrical components of a computer and its peripheral devices.

infopreneur: An ugly word used to denote the entrepreneur of the information society.

infotainment: An even uglier word used to describe the products that result from the convergence of information and entertainment.

information highway or superhighway: The internet and other digital technolgies.

information mapping: The process of locating important information and knowledge in an organization, then publishing a list or diagram showing where to find it.

internet: The global computer network.

intranet: A private network within an organization, often protected from internet traffic by a "firewall" (software that controls access from the outside).

intangible asset: A non-physical asset, such as a patent, a brand name or goodwill; it also encompasses the knowhow embodied in employees or working practices.

information systems (IS) strategy: The identification and prioritization of systems of applications for development.

information technology (IT): The hardware and software that is used to process information.

IT productivity paradox: A term used at both the macro- and micro-level to describe the apparent gap between what companies spend on technology and the increase – or not – in their business performance.

knowledge management (KM): A term with many meanings; it includes deliberate efforts to maximize an organization's performance through

349

creating, sharing and leveraging knowledge and experience from internal and external sources.

Lotus Notes: A proprietary software that allows users to share many different types of unstructured and semi-structured information. Lotus is owned by IBM.

mainframe: The central processing unit of a large computer, usually receiving input from a number of terminals.

marketspace: The "marketplace" in e-commerce.

microprocessors: Complex electronic circuits that comprise a computer's central information processing unit.

paradigm shift: Term used to describe a complete re-think of the business or economic outlook, caused by a startling intellectual or technological discontinuity.

PC: It once meant "not IBM", then "not Macintosh" – now it refers to any personal computer.

program: A set of digitally coded definitions and instructions that enables a computer to perform a particular task.

protocol: The language that one computer uses to communicate with another.

software: The programs that are run on a computer system.

supercomputer: An extremely powerful computer; designed to deal with very large amounts of data at very high speed, and often used for military or scientific tasks.

value chain: Concept widely associated with the management thinker Michael Porter which focuses on a company's internal processes and the interactions between different elements of the organization. Analysis of it shows how and where value is added.

virtual organization: An elusive combination of technology, expertise and networks with little or no physical infrastructure.

virtual reality: Term which describes computer-generated but almost lifelike simulated environments.

worldwide web: An application which runs on the internet; it provides a standard way of publishing and accessing information.

Subject index

354

technology expenditure 5, 9, 10
virtual value chain 18–20
see also value realization
personal computers *see* computers
personality matrix 249
personalization 204
postwar reconstruction 54
pricing 59
printed media 336–7
privacy 198, 258–9
problem solving 247
processes 112, 155
    process independence 287
    value realization 155
processing information 245–52
    information needs 246–7
    information seeking 248
    information use 248–50
    integrated model 251
    Myers-Briggs Type Indicator 249
    sensemaking model 246
procurement 151, 212–13
    see also outsourcing
productivity paradox 10
products 153, 155, 297
    bundled products 214, 215–16, 323
    development 184
        see also distributed product
          development
    differentiation 105
    electronic commerce and types of
        214–16
professionals in IT 83–6
project success factors 148–50
promotion of IT professionals 83, 84, 85
punch cards 27–8
purchasing 151, 212–13
    see also outsourcing
pyramid schemes 199

re-engineering 110–13
reality checks 55
recording information 202
regionalization 107–8
regulation 17
reputation building 200–1
responsibility sharing 98–9
results-driven knowledge management
    187–9
richness/reach trade-off 37–9

salaries 83
scenario analysis 326–8

scenario thinking 306, 308–9
scientific management 27
screening 60–3
security in electronic commerce 198
selective sourcing 156–7, 267
    see also outsourcing
senior managers 295–6
    see also professionals in IT
sensemaking model 246
services, digital services 214–15
share option schemes 83
shared vision 69
sharing information 12
signalling 60–3
skills 234–5, 235–7
    see also competences
Skinner Box 324
software 28, 29, 80–2, 150
    agentware 186
    bespoke 236
    collaborative 11
    open sourcing 137
    packaged 236–7
    standards 123–5
sourcing 73–6
    selective sourcing 156–7, 267
    see also outsourcing
spreadsheets 234
staff *see* employees
standardization 39, 122–3, 148–52,
    298–300
strategic alignment 158
strategic alliances *see* joint
    ventures/alliances
strategy 37–42, 306–10, 321–8
    branding 219
    breakout strategies 225–6
    for global businesses 86–91
    and information 17–18
    information resource (IR) strategy
        20–1
    information systems (IS) strategy
        20
    reach/richness trade-off 37–9
    scenario analysis 326–8
    scenario thinking 306, 308–9
stress 85
success factors 148–50
supermarkets 202
    banking services 56–7
suppliers 212–13, 304–5
    customer-supplier life cycle 224–7
    see also outsourcing

Organization index

Oxford Institute of Information Management 73

Pacific Bell 240
Passport Agency 74
Peapod.com 202
PeopleSoft 111, 123
Perot Systems 272
Pfizer 240
Philips 107, 271–2
Pinnacle Alliance 157
Pratt & Whitney 218
PriceWaterhouseCoopers 83
Procter & Gamble 109, 125, 127, 241, 299
Prudential 56

QED 123

Range Rover 22–3
Ritz-Carlton 155
Rolls Royce 271
ROLM 145
Rotterdam School of Management 309–10
Royal Bank of Scotland 56, 57
Royal Caribbean Cruises 220

Sabre 302
Safeway 20, 73
SAIC 69
Sainsbury 105, 128, 158
SAP 52, 106, 111, 112, 113, 123, 148, 298
S.C. Johnson 107
Schlumberger 158
Schwab 124, 221
Seagram's 223
Sears 269
Sears Roebuck 271
Seven-Eleven Japan 19
Sharp 167
Shell 148, 157
Siemens 57, 309
Siemens Business Services 74
Skandia 107, 145, 288
Sky 17
SmithKline Beecham 17
Soccernet 50
Sony 25, 145, 184

Southwest Airlines 44
Sprint 346–7
Standish Group 301
Super-Quinn 357
Swiss Bank 143, 144, 146, 272
Swiss Life 143
Swiss Reinsurance 143, 144
Syncordia 269–70

Tabulating Machine Company 28
TC Team Consult 52
Tesco 105, 128, 223
Tesco Personal Finance 56–7
Thames Water 76
Thomas Miller 148
Thomson 128
3M 184
Topsy Tail 139
Toyota 37, 48, 226, 286
Travelocity 286

Unilever 54, 107, 127, 244–5
Union Bank of Switzerland 143, 144, 146
United Airlines 128

Verifone 8, 242
Verity 186
Victoria's Secret 217
Volvo 157

Wal-Mart 37, 109, 128, 155, 223, 286
Wegman's Food Markets 114
Winterthur 143, 144, 146
W.L. Gore 168
Woolwich 303, 305
World Bank 183
Worldspan 128
W.R. Grace 218

Xerox 156, 157, 240, 241, 267, 270

Yahoo 216, 319, 320

Zeneca 148, 189, 190
Zurich Insurance 143, 144

Name index